GUITAR EFFECTS
PEDALS the practical handbook

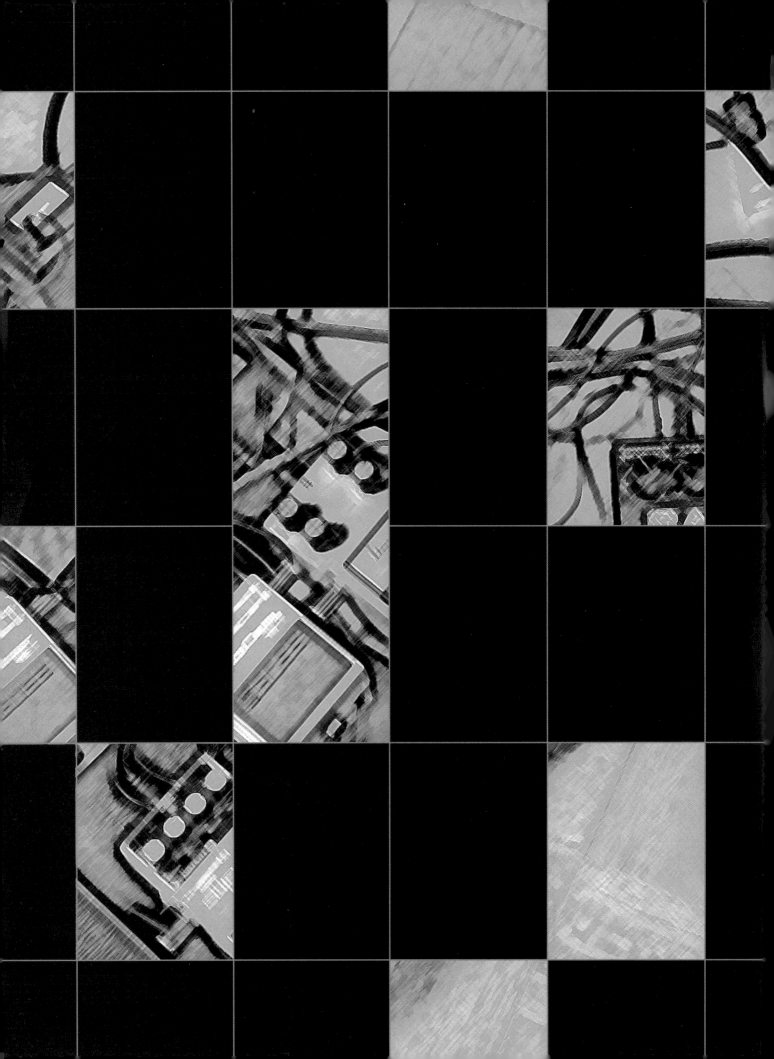

GUITAR EFFECTS
PEDALS the practical handbook

Dave Hunter

GUITAR EFFECTS PEDALS
the practical handbook
Dave Hunter

A BACKBEAT BOOK
First edition 2004
Published by Backbeat Books
600 Harrison Street,
San Francisco, CA94107, US
www.backbeatbooks.com

An imprint of The Music Player Network United
Entertainment Media Inc.

Published for Backbeat Books by Outline Press Ltd,
Unit 2a Union Court, 20-22 Union Road, London, SW4 6JP, England.
www.backbeatuk.com

ISBN 0-87930-806-0

ART DIRECTOR: Nigel Osborne
EDITOR: Paul Quinn
DESIGN: Paul Cooper Design
EDITORIAL DIRECTOR: Tony Bacon

Origination and Print by Colorprint Offset (Hong Kong)

03 04 05 06 07 5 4 3 2 1

CONTENTS

Introduction

Guitarists playing today are fortunate to find themselves in the middle of an effects pedal renaissance. More is understood than ever before about the sounds and workings of the hundreds of great vintage pedals from the 1960s, 1970s, and early 1980s that are still afloat on the market, while dozens of creative contemporary makers are seeking to improve on old designs to bring us even better models – along with a few new noises too. It wasn't always like this. Any guitarist who has been playing since the early 1980s will have weathered a time when the humble pedal was on the verge of dying out completely.

By around 1984, digital was looking to be the only way to go for all things sonic. Delay, chorus and reverb effects were rapidly moving to 'more powerful' rack-mounted formats, the rack-mounted preamp was fast becoming the distortion choice of the day (if you didn't already play a Mesa/Boogie with all effects injected through the loop), and pedals were largely consigned to garage bands and amateurs. A shameful number of us were gripped by the notion that 'toneful' distortion had to be amp-generated – which in those days mainly meant tube preamp generated – and that analog effects were weak, noisy, and just generally inferior beasts. The big manufacturers started grouping devices together as 'multi-FX' units to be either triggered from a rack or positioned on the floor for direct stompability, and the individual effects pedal looked ever more redundant. The mania lasted a good ten years or so, but slowly something started to shift…

In the early 1990s a number of factors seemed to introduce a tonal rethink among many guitarists. It's impossible to document them all accurately, but coincidence or not, you see certain waves converging: the mammoth rise of grunge (and with it, the reintroduction of loud guitars to the pop charts); the 'cultification' of Stevie Ray Vaughan and his raw, hot blues ethos; the wider rediscovery of the virtue of vintage-style, non-master-volume amps; and a resurgence in the popularity of vintage effects pedals. A booming pedal market naturally led to a wave of makers keen to make low-noise, reliable and good-sounding new models available; the greater availability spawned a greater interest among guitarists who ran across the things – and the whole party just snowballed… till here we are today.

This book is intended far more as a players' guide to pedal sounds and functions than as any sort of collectors' compendium. I'm not a collector myself in the truest sense of the word (despite having owned close to 50 pedals in my lifetime, and played hundreds more), but being a player for nearly 30 years and a guitar journalist for ten, I've approached the subject first from a guitarist's perspective, and second from a writer's – nearly equal parts dabbling and hard-graft research. What you'll find here are objective facts about the majority of the most important vintage and contemporary pedals, along with subjective opinions on a few, and a wealth of information on how to approach your own hunt for sonic perfection.

It should be said at this stage that, like many guitarists today, I consider 'effects pedals' and 'multi-FX units' to be devices from entirely different galaxies, with largely different uses and design parameters – and given the number of pages required to adequately cover the former here, there just isn't room to deal with the latter. No disrespect intended to rack-mounted or floorboard multi-FX, and they suit many players' needs extremely well, but they don't tend to be of as much interest to players who are enthusiastic about individual effects pedals. On top of that, there is often less to distinguish between different models of multi-FX than there is between different models of standalone footpedals – and they just don't have nearly the same cult following that has grown up around pedals, both old and new. Similarly, modern 'digital modelling' effects units, which claim to emulate numerous classic pedal and amp sounds, are not covered here, for much the same reasons.

What this book doesn't set out to do is tell you which effects pedals you should buy. The aim here is to give some basic specs of functions and brief 'sonic sketches' of a broad range of cool units. (Over 200 individual models are given a brief write-up, and 92 audio examples can be heard on the attached CD.) It should at least help you narrow down a list of those that might be of interest to you, as well as helping you make the most of the pedals you already own – and, in fact, get the best from your entire sound chain.

If you are on the market to buy some new effects, visit a reputable dealer who carries a wide range of stock from different makers, and test as many pedals as you can get your hands on. Try to use your own guitar, and ideally your own amp – or at least a guitar and amp combination of the same models that you play most. In the end, the pedals that sound and feel the best to you are the ones you want, no matter what I or anyone else will tell you about what's cool, hip or otherwise.

Dive into the wonderful world of effects pedals: with just a few good combinations, the variety of sounds available is pretty near infinite.

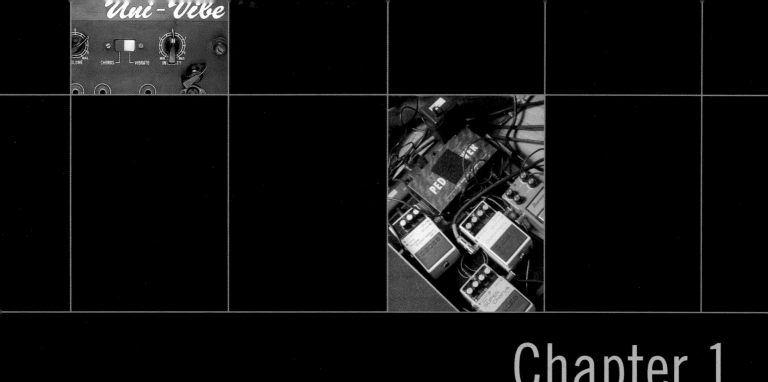

Chapter 1
EVOLUTION

Hard to believe it nowadays – when faced with the sight of a leather-clad, Les Paul-toting Zakk Wylde wailing straddle-legged in front of a blaring pair of Marshall double-stacks – but guitarists in bands once had a serious inferiority complex. Back in the 1930s and 1940s when the guitar finally ousted the banjo to become a regular member of the jazz or big-band, the sax and trumpet men got all the solos, the singers got all the girls (or guys), and even the drummers got the fireworks in the occasional flailing-limbed jungle-beat break. The guitarists, meanwhile, sat off toward the side of the stage, chopping away four to the bar, wondering if anyone could hear them.

When the rare guitar solo rolled along, it was – no matter how skillfully executed – a dry, straight, and thin-sounding affair. No roaring, frequency-soaked cascade of trills, no breathtaking climactic bends. You played your piece, hoped a few people stopped talking and clinking glasses long enough to listen up, then you went back to hacking out the rhythm. Hell, the guitarist wanted to be the horn player. Or, more accurately, still wanted to play the guitar (addicted, you see, to that vibration in the gut, the tremor of fingertip pressed to wire and wood), but wanted to *sound* like a sax, like a trumpet, maybe even like a voice or a violin. Those were the instruments that could roar, wail, cry and sing. Guitarists wanted to get themselves some of that tone.

And pretty soon, in an ingenious array of ways, that's what they did...

We tend to think of guitar effects as a phenomenon that began in the rock'n'roll era, and exploded in the 1960s and 1970s. But thanks to the first amplified guitarists' search for something to have an 'effect' on their guitar sound – any kind of effect – devices designed to enhance the straight sound of an electric guitar were born virtually alongside the notion of amplified guitar itself. The whole deal just got a lot easier when transistors became more widely available and entered into common use in the early 1960s. Before that, if you wanted reverb, you played in a big empty room, or put your amp in an old water tank; if you wanted echo, you looped together two big tape recorders, running slightly out of sync; if you wanted vibrato, you rigged up a motor to literally vibrate the guitar's bridge; if you wanted a whirling chorus, you spun a pair of speakers in an enormous wood cabinet. Be glad you're a guitarist today: back when it all got started, effects were big, heavy, cumbersome, and very prone to breakdown.

Early thinking concluded that if an amplified guitar was going to sound like anything other than a louder version of an ordinary guitar, some tangible, physical force was going to have to be imposed upon it. Rickenbacker's short-lived Vibrola Spanish electric guitar of the 1930s followed this theory. It was constructed with a system of motorized pulleys built into the guitar's body that would rhythmically jiggle

Session guitarist Perry Botkin cradles a Rickenbacker Vibrola Spanish model guitar in this 1930s catalog photo. The instrument carried motorized pullies that moved the bridge to create an automated vibrato effect.

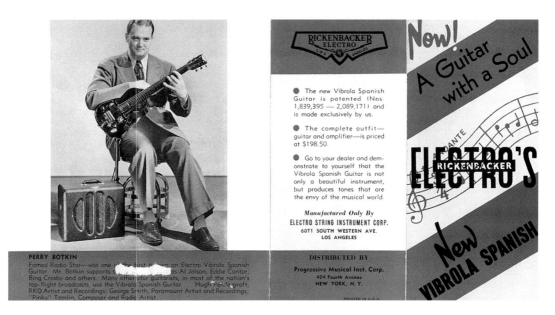

the bridge to create an automated vibrato effect. Paul Bigsby's vibrato tailpiece that appeared in the 1940s achieved similar results more simply, but required the player to adapt, and often compromise, his pick-hand technique. Clearly these early efforts – and many others that followed – revolved around forms of vibrato or tremolo (Chapter 2 will spell out the exact differences between vibrato and tremolo). After all, what could you do to a note plucked on a guitar string other than shake it a little? Ah... those simpler times.

The first commercial standalone effect ever manufactured appears to have been a tremolo unit offered by DeArmond in the late 1940s, which used a spinning motor to trigger a mercury switch to stutter the signal passing through it. By the late 1950s, tremolo, vibrato and reverb were offered as built-in effects on many guitar amplifiers: makers like Premier, Danelectro and, most prominently, Gibson were putting tube-based tremolo and sometimes vibrato circuits into combo amps from the late 1940s onward. Gibson included tremolo circuits in amps throughout its range, culminating in the GA-79RVT of the early 1960s, which had stereo reverb and tremolo. Also in the Fifties and Sixties, Magnatone created some amazing true vibrato sounds in stereo with its complex model 280 and 480 tube amps – as used by a Flying-V toting Lonnie Mack for his characteristic swamp-blues sound.

Fender's vintage tremolo amps are among the best known today, but the company didn't offer the option until 1955, when the Tremolux appeared, followed by the Vibrolux in 1956. These were medium and small amps (an 18W 1x12" and a 10W 1x10" respectively), and the effect didn't feature on examples from across the Fender range until 1960 and after. Fender was often guilty of mislabeling an amp 'vibrato' when the effect it carried was actually tremolo (conversely, Leo Fender also named his Strat's vibrato unit a 'tremolo' arm). But the company also built a few of the first front-control-mounted, brown Tolex-covered amps with a subtle form of true vibrato. Despite its name, the earlier tweed Vibrolux carried tremolo, produced by a circuit similar to that used in the Tremolux, and the mislabeling continued right up into the 1960s and 1970s.

Being mostly tube-powered effects that required bulky transformers and high voltages, tremolo and vibrato didn't crop up in very many separate 'add-on' units in the early days, and were expensive when they did appear. Gibson's pioneering GA-V1 Vibrato unit, introduced in 1956, cost a whopping $75 – more than half the price of an entire Fender Vibrolux combo. Others followed through the years, both tube and later solid state, but tremolo wasn't much in demand as a separate item in the days when it was included onboard with so many great amplifiers.

The Bigsby vibrato tailpiece, as seen on this Gretsch Round Up guitar from the mid 1950s, has become one of the more enduring means of creating a manual vibrato effect for electric guitar.

...don't bug me baby...

...I've switched to **MAGNATONE**

Hair loss? No problem. Magnatone promotes the sheer babe-magnetism of its 'stereo vibrato'-equipped amps in an early 1960s ad, seen left.

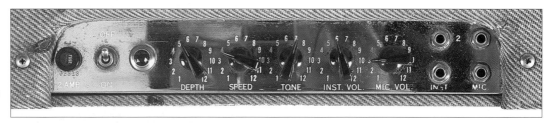

Fender first offered what they called 'vibrato' on its Tremolux amp in 1955 (the picture at the top shows the control panel on the 1960 model), although the effect was actually tremolo, as the model name implied. At this stage, makes like Gibson and Maestro (whose RVT amp is seen in the other photo here) were somewhat ahead of the game.

Any early electric guitarist who soundchecked in a large, empty hall before the audience filled the seats knew the pleasing effect of echo and reverberation. The earliest studio reproductions of reverb and echo were simply recreations of the real thing on a smaller scale, achieved by miking a speaker positioned in a purpose-built sonically reflective room (literally a reverberation chamber), or an empty corridor, or bathroom – anywhere that natural ambient echoes and reverberation would be present. For his early studio work, Duane Eddy used a 500-gallon metal water tank with a speaker at one end and a microphone at the other. "We used to have to go and chase the birds off it in the morning," he once said, "but running things through it made it a great echo chamber." Of course he wasn't about to carry that tank around on stage with him...

By this time Les Paul had already advanced the notion of echo in the studio with an electromechanical solution based around a modified reel-to-reel tape recorder (Paul was also pioneering multi-track recording at this time). But this remained a personal gizmo of his own for years – occasionally practiced by other guitarists and engineers – until more compact looped-tape echo units became commercially available.

In the early 1950s, amplifier builder Ray Butts pioneered a loop-based echo system – first based on recording wire, then tape when it was available – which was small enough to be built into a combo amp. By the mid to late 1950s his shortlived EchoSonic amp had been a major player in establishing the archetypal rock'n'roll slapback echo sound, and was the choice of Elvis sideman Scotty Moore, Carl Perkins, Chet Atkins, Johnny Cash sideman Luther Perkins, Roy Orbison and a few others. Standalone tube-powered tape units soon followed, including models like the Fender-distributed EccoFonic, Maestro Echoplex, Watkins/WEM Copicat, Binson Echorec (which used magnetic recording discs rather than tape loops), and Meazzi Echomatic.

Europe's first portable tape echo, the Watkins Copicat, was a major part of the British 'beat' sound of the early 1960s. It was impressive for the way it condensed the notion of looping two large recording consoles into a small, shoebox-sized cabinet, though other aspects of its engineering were nothing to write home about, as Charlie Watkins himself is the first to admit. "The mystique of the Copicat really comes from a piece of bad engineering that went into it – but I won't tell you what," says Watkins. "Whenever a company tried to make their own version of our Copicat, they would copy it faithfully until they came to that part, then couldn't bring themselves to do it so badly." Nevertheless, the early tube Copicat and even the solid state models that followed remain much sought-after echo units... and exemplify how minor imperfections in engineering can lead to many a guitarist's notion of perfection in tone. It's a principle that has helped to lay the foundations of great rock sound time and time again. After all, where else does distortion = good, and accurate sound reproduction = bad?

Like natural echo, reverberation is a 'large' sound effect in terms of the physical dimensions required to create it pleasingly in the natural world. When engineers finally squashed it down to a compact and reliable electromechanical interpretation of the wash of repeated echoes heard in a large hall, it came to us as an onboard effect built into combo amps, hot on the heels of tremolo. The reverb with which guitarists are most familiar achieves its atmospheric sound by driving a signal down a set of springs and then tapping the resultant shimmering effect with a small transducer and blending it back with the 'dry' guitar signal. Tube-powered spring reverb circuits are really just small amplifiers within themselves, with little output transformers (OTs) that drive a signal through a set of long springs much the way any tube amp's larger OT does through a speaker. The most common professional studio reverbs of the pre-digital days, called 'plate' reverbs, worked in roughly the same way, driving the signal through thin metal plates suspended in a large cabinet, instead of through springs. Despite the apparent wonders of more recent digital reverb, both of these early analog varieties remain much-loved by guitarists and recording engineers alike.

Tube-driven spring reverb first arrived in amps by Premier and Gibson in the late 1950s, and relatively late in Fenders – again, one of our archetypes for classic tube-amp spring reverb sounds today – first in the Vibroverb of 1963, then in a range of others from 1964. These and other makers also offered separate reverb boxes from the late 1950s, but the long spring can, tube-based circuitry and large transformers necessary to produce the effect meant the units were about the size of an amp head cabinet, and bulky to carry around. With all the juicy, crunchy roar of a cranked blackface Fender Super Reverb, with its hypnotic, multidimensional tremolo and reverb – or a Twin Reverb if you needed it loud'n'clean – who wanted to fuss with bulky external effects units? Unless, of course, you might want your sound to twirl around in the air…

Elvis Presley's guitarist Scotty Moore sent this photo to amp-maker Ray Butts – he's written on it, "Ray – Here's the amp," to show his use of Butts' EchoSonic amplifier onstage.

Fender persisted in its use of the term vibrato well into the silverface era of the 1970s, although some of the tan-Tolex amps of the early 1960s – such as the example here on the far left – did carry something close to true vibrato. Near left, Europe's first portable tape echo arrived in the form of the Watkins/WEM copicat.

For many years after Don Leslie introduced his rotating speaker cabinet for Hammond organs in the early 1940s, guitarists lusted after its luscious, three-dimensional choral tones. The most popular Leslie models for organ create their sound by splitting the signal to a low-end 15″ speaker mounted within a rotating drum at the bottom of the cabinet, and a high-end horn mounted at the top. Not only do the horn and drum spin in opposite directions, they spin at slightly different speeds, creating a dense and constantly shifting warbling sensation, aided by the application of the Doppler effect on two different planes. What's more, the shift between the cab's two speeds – slow (originally called 'chorale') and fast, or 'tremelo' (sic) – doesn't happen instantaneously. There's a lag while each rotor accelerates – at a different rate, naturally – and a stunning, shimmering, phasing effect as they finally catch up to each other and fall closer into synch. To be in the same room with a Leslie used right can be breathtaking.

You might think this would have limited applications for guitarists: a large, heavy, expensive effect developed for electric organ that is very rarely encountered in the real world of guitar. But the warm, enveloping sonic splendor of a guitar played well through a Leslie cab (or similar) can be instantly addictive, and has driven designers to attempt to reproduce it on a smaller scale for guitar in many, many more instances than you might at first realize. Attempts to reproduce that hypnotic, moving, slightly out-of-phase Leslie sound ranged from early complex tube vibrato circuits (meaning true vibrato), the first solid state chorus and phaser pedals such as the Univox Uni-Vibe and, a little later, the Maestro Phase Shifter, to – perhaps less consciously by this time – the brigade of chorus and phaser pedals that followed in the 1970s as the sound reached its peak of popularity in pedal form.

Check the 'special effects' buttons on many an old console organ and you can trace the roots of this sound. Most carry a switch or pushbutton labeled 'chorus.' The original Leslie itself was intended to produce a spacious, warbling choral effect – to bring some of those cavernous cathedral pipe organ acoustics into the small chapel or living room – and in turn the solid state chorus pedals of the 1970s were following on from units intended to mimic the sound of a Leslie cabinet. What goes around comes around – quite literally, in the world of the rotating speaker.

It's another sound that devotees of the original will claim simply cannot be done right in a stationary, non-mechanical, circuit-based device. And yet attempts to do so have yielded some of the best-loved effects pedals of all time, so it was obviously worth trying. Fender released its own relatively more compact and guitar-friendly rotating speaker cab, the Vibratone, in 1967. Since CBS owned both Fender and Leslie at the time, it was freely able to use the Leslie patents and apply them to a cab aimed at the guitarist. The design employed a single 10″ speaker housed within a drum that rotated on the vertical plane rather than the horizontal, as the rotors did in the larger Leslie cabs, and the Vibratone also functioned purely as an extension cab, without the Leslie's onboard power amp, intended for organists and redundant for most guitarists anyway. With just one speaker, the unit was a little lighter and less cumbersome to carry around (though still a little bigger and heavier than, say, a Super Reverb amp), and was easier to mike up on stage and in the studio. (Leslie's model 16 is identical to the Vibratone aside from the name and cosmetics, and the model 18 is the same thing again but with a 12″ speaker).

The Univox Uni-Vibe of the late 1960s (pictured here) was a cumbersome and often noisy device, but has inspired an army of imitators.

The Vibratone's bubbly, lush sound was rediscovered thanks largely to Stevie Ray Vaughan's use of the cab on the track 'Cold Shot' from his album *Couldn't Stand The Weather* (although it is put to equal or better use on 'Things That I Used To Do' and other tracks from the same album). But great examples of the Vibratone were recorded in the early days of its release, as heard on The Beatles' 'Lucy In The Sky With Diamonds' and 'You Never Give Me Your Money' (along with plenty others), Hendrix's 'Little Wing,' Jimmy Page's guitar solo on Led Zeppelin's 'Black Dog,' and a whole range of tracks from Pink Floyd's *Dark Side Of The Moon*.

Pink Floyd pictured in the studio in the late 1960s. They were pioneers of the extreme psychedelic use of tape flanging.

By the time guitarists had heard how good the transistorized emulations like the Uni-Vibe could sound in the hands of a Jimi Hendrix ('Star Spangled Banner' or 'Machine Gun') or a Robin Trower ('Bridge Of Sighs'), it hardly seemed worth the trouble of hauling around a Vibratone, much less a Leslie. Fender discontinued the Vibratone in 1973, though Leslie continues to make its rotating speaker cabinets to this day. Maestro offered its somewhat different, cylindrical Rover rotating speaker system in the mid 1970s; Farfisa made a clone of the Vibratone/Leslie 16, and contemporary makers like Mesa/Boogie and Songworks still offer variations on the theme (the Revolver MkII and Little Lanelei Rotary Wave respectively). Clearly the Doppler effect created by actual moving sound from a rotating speaker – cumbersome as any such unit inevitably is – holds a firm grip on many players as the epitome of the chorus sound.

The swooshing, spacey extreme of the softer swirling chorus or phaser sound – commonly known as flanging – was in use for more than 20 years before the first portable stompbox to produce the effect was offered to guitarists. Anyone with an ear cocked to a rock radio station over the last 30 years will recognize the sound of tape flange from songs like The Small Faces' 'Itchycoo Park' and The Eagles' 'Life In The Fast Lane,' and from plenty of songs by The Beatles, Pink Floyd, and others, where the manual studio effect was artfully applied to portions of the entire band mix. It's a moving, trippy effect when used subtly, as in these instances. Applied with a heavy hand – I'm thinking, say, 'Sky Pilot' by The Animals – flanging's incessant sonic smearing overwhelms the music with its predictable to-and-fro, and induces a kind of seasickness in the listener.

Put very simply, flanging of whatever variety is accomplished by splitting a signal and alternately slowing and speeding one path, then blending it back with the unaffected path. It was achieved on these songs by running identical recordings in sync on two separate reel-to-reel recording machines, and placing a finger against the flange of one to slow it slightly, then releasing it again to let the reel speed up again and chase the unadulterated machine. As far back as 1945, though, Les Paul was yet again proving himself a pioneer of studio sound trickery by achieving the same effect with two disk recorders.

Obviously either technique was too bulky and too labor-intensive for musicians to use on stage mid-flow during performance. Again, transistorization worked the magic on a pair of reel-to-reel tape decks that it had on the Leslie cab before them, and put the dramatic flanging sound into a box that could be triggered instantaneously by the player and used in real time, rather than applied only to recorded tracks. The flangers from companies like A/DA, MXR and Electro-Harmonix (E-H) seemed to usher in a whole new era of psychedelic experimentation when they arrived in the mid 1970s, and guitarists sold their old phase pedals in droves. But many soon discovered that flanging's imposing, synthesized sound stamped too much of its own signature on their playing, and ultimately the softer, less imposing 'swoosh' of the great early phasers made them far more revered as classic pedals than the more expensive flangers that were their contemporaries.

From the mid 1960s the same transistor revolution that left most players cold when applied to guitar amplification set the rock world alight when used to design and build compact, portable and versatile effects units. The new technology sparked an effects pedals boom in the late 1960s and early 1970s that settled into a major new gear market later in that decade. Transistorized circuits took what I would, in technical parlance, call the 'weirdness potential' of sound effects way beyond the capabilities of electromechanical or tube-powered devices. More to the point, for most purposes, it made them small and manageable. (Interestingly, many guitarists still consider the sonic qualities of vintage electro-mechanical sound effects devices like the Leslie cab or the tape echo to be unsurpassed; most would also agree that many such units are impractical for constant day-to-day use in all applications, especially carrying on tour.)

When the guitar industry as a whole suffered at the hands of the synth insurgence in the early 1980s, effects were seen as a way for the electric guitar to compete. Wackier analog pedals and the early digital units helped the guitarist at least tread water in the boom days of electronic music, while waiting for that day – surely not far off, we felt – when our ears would tire of the mechanized sounds of the drum machine and the sampler.

The humble 'one sound' pedal nearly went the way of the dinosaurs during the synth and rack-effects boom of the 1980s and 1990s, but keen-eared guitarists have brought them back with a vengeance.

Guitar music held its grip through the hair bands at one extreme and the underground, garage groups at the other, with only a sprinkling of U2s and REMs in the middle ground. But somehow the notion evolved that any real player needed to go through a rack of digital stereo delays and flangers and reverbs if he wanted to be taken seriously – partly, I suppose, a legacy of inferiority at the hands of the synth brigade, and partly just because the technology drove the demand – and the humble pedal remained on the floors of garages and the stages of dark, cramped 'indie' clubs. But while producers and engineers in studios from LA to London were convincing guitarists to record dry and let them ladle on their 'superior' digital sound effects in the mix, analog pedals were still clicking away under the feet of a surprising number of players who proved to be the innovators of the era.

Come the late 1980s and early 1990s, and a lot of the rest of us realized (or just remembered) that many of those old pedals sounded pretty damn luscious. Patch a Quadraverb and an early 8-bit Ibanez digital delay line into your top-of-the-range Mesa/Boogie's effects loop and just feel your tone get sucked into a black hole. Stick a Rat distortion and a Memory Man into the front end of a blackface Fender Pro Reverb and, ooh la la…

Slowly but surely these little stompboxes started clawing their way back onto the stage and into the studio. Then late in 1991 Nirvana's *Nevermind* slung 'Smells Like Teen Spirit' onto the radio airwaves worldwide – with its fuzz-box dynamics and swirling Small Clone chorus sounds – and suddenly grunge hurled loud guitars back to the top of everyone's hit list. Faster than you could say 'digital distortion,' pedals were the rage all over again. 'Discrete' and 'transistorized' are no longer dirty words, when they occur together in a series of chipped and scuffed little metal boxes linked between guitar and amp, and despite all the convenience and options offered by multi-FX floorboards few players question the sonic superiority of the individual, external effects pedal.

Other than the near-audible sighs of relief from guitarists – gleeful at being allowed again to mix'n'match their way to sonic ecstasy with a series of affordable boxes from music exchange centers and pawn shops – the most notable result of this rediscovery of classic pedals was the burgeoning collector's market that followed it. Suddenly you were glad you stuck your MXR Distortion+ under the bed rather than part-exchanging it for $10 toward an ART ProVerb the way your pal did, and you'd start combing the classified ads on a daily basis for original Small Stone phase shifters offered for sale by musicians who still had their heads stuck in the Alesis showroom. Ibanez TS-808 and even TS9 Tube Screamers suddenly started fetching $100, then $200, and even Hawk-Shop Tony chomping a stogy below the flickering neon of a 'Guns-Jewels-Guitars' sign seemed to know he could slap a $400 sticker on a battered old Uni-Vibe.

It looked like we'd need to remortgage the house and hitchhike to work in order to scrounge the cash to purchase half a dozen little bundles of outdated solid state technology that crackled when you nudged them, sizzled under fluorescent lights, and picked up Radio Moscow on a clear day. But once again the solder-sniffing boffins came to the rescue. Even though there probably wasn't big money in it yet, a handful of guys and gals who knew their metal film from their carbon comp got the notion they could reanimate most any vintage circuit a guitarist had a taste for, and in many cases could build it better. Voila! The boutique pedal was born.

The growth of the small-run, independent pedal manufacturer didn't undercut the spiraling collector's market entirely, but it did mean the average Joe could lay hands on a box that would do much the same trick as almost any venerable vintage device, usually for less money than the 'real thing,' and often with quieter, more transparent operation and and a circuit guilty of less 'tone sucking.' Makers like Fulltone, Way Huge, Prescription Electronics, and a little later Z.Vex, Lovetone, Frantone and others brought back many of the juicy, tactile sounds of the Sixties and Seventies in reliable, consistently available packages.

Meanwhile, some great names from the past returned: Roger Mayer, who had actually been building production pedals again since the early 1980s, gained newfound respect and flourished amid this renaissance; Electro-Harmonix progressed from budget-grade, Russian-made versions of some old classics to full-blown, New York-built reissues; and Colorsound has even reissued many of its great designs. Big names like Boss, Ibanez and DOD, who had always made some popular pedals, benefited from the whole big stompbox love-in and, in some cases, brought back a few of their own classics, while a number of others like MXR, Cry Baby and Uni-Vox popped up under the broad Dunlop banner. And on and on...

There is indisputably more choice in effects pedals now than ever before. Hands-on (and, more importantly, ears-open) experience with many of them has convinced this author that better and more interesting units are being made today than in any previous era. Sure, the supplies of good germanium transistors are close to drying up, and maybe the original JRC4558 chips are no longer made. But great designers of the new millennium are working their way around the problems, by and large using far superior components anyway, and constructing pedals with very conscious and elevated sonic goals in mind, rather than hit-and-miss mad-scientist flash fires that sometimes work, but often don't. Conversely, in my opinion, many of the actual reissue pedals re-offered under their original names don't sound quite as good as the classics that inspired their return. Many are good pedals in their own right – some are even excellent – but only a few get full marks for accuracy of circuit and sonic results.

Now that the boutique 'cloners' have taken care of availability and reliability issues surrounding vintage pedals, they have moved on to develop new units that push the boundaries of sound shaping. Consequently, players have access to a plethora of new products with vintage analog esthetics but entirely avant-garde tones. On top of this, ever-improving digital pedals are making certain sounds possible – and particularly multiple options or combinations – which were only achievable in the past with expensive studio gear.

Some players complain that a lot of these new pedals that are hand-built by smaller, independent makers – and even many of the current high-end mass-production models – are too expensive for what they offer. Certainly a good number do carry weighty price tags. But remember, the E-H Memory Man would have cost you $150 when it was introduced, and the Electric Mistress was more expensive than that. You also paid around $50 for a Big Muff fuzz box, or even more for the purportedly 'upmarket' MXR Distortion+ or MXR's sleek phasers and flangers. That was a lot of money in the 1970s. Paying $280 for a Frantone Vibutron or $200 for a Fulltone Full-Drive 2 overdrive pedal 25 years later – taking inflation into account – seems a bargain.

Today's guitarists have fewer fears about being kicked to the back of the stage than they did in 1937. But to a great extent the feeling has stuck with us that the unadulterated guitar sound is a bland and uninspiring thing. For all that we obsess about 'tone,' the straight, pure sound of the naked electric guitar still doesn't get the pulse racing... (If you doubt this, restrict yourself to playing your treasured '61 Strat, '58 Les Paul Jr, Paul Reed Smith McCarty or Tom Anderson Drop-Top DI'd into a mixing desk for a while. You rocking yet?) The solution, for most of us, is still to do something to seriously screw up the natural sound of the instrument. And here at the dawn of the 21st century, there is no shortage of ways to do so.

Guitar effects have evolved from cumbersome, fiddly, temperamental gizmos with multiple moving parts that were noisy and prone to breakdown, into compact, versatile, reliable tools. With just three or four good pedals in your chain, the sonic variables offered by contemporary makers can be virtually inexhaustable. And if you really thirst for an authentic taste of yesteryear, you can still track down a beautifully archaic box of outdated discrete circuitry that was hand-soldered in the late 1960s... and, with any luck, might still sound like God on a good day.

These are indeed high times for the creative guitarist.

Chapter 2
EFFECTS EXPLAINED

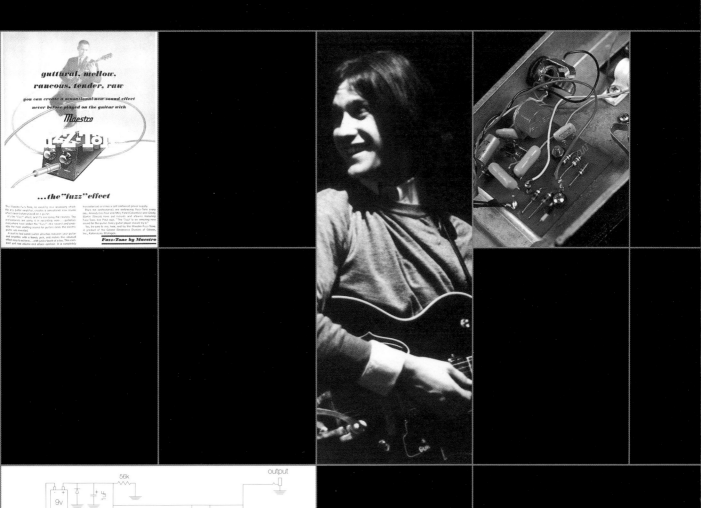

Effects pedals can be separated into several categories, but there are undeniably some gray areas between these. The distinctions get blurrier when we throw digital technology into the brew. An analog and a digital chorus, for example, are very different circuits, approached from very different design standpoints, although the sonic results may sound roughly similar – except in the really good ones, where the subtleties are usually quite distinctive.

For our purposes, we'll split them into four broad headings: 1) Boost, Compression, Distortion & Fuzz; 2) Modulation (including phase, flange, chorus, tremolo); 3) Echo & Delay; and 4) Filtering & EQ-based effects. Some manufacturers, or other writers, might categorize things differently, and certainly a few models we'll mention could be safely lifted out of one group and placed in another. It doesn't matter all that much. These groupings are mainly a means of breaking down the sonic results of the enormously varied range of pedals out there, so we can take a brief look at what makes them tick.

BOOST, COMPRESSION, DISTORTION & FUZZ

This is easily the most popular category of effect, and sonically is the natural first step away from the thin sound of a straight, clean amplified guitar. If a player only owns one pedal, chances are it's a distortion, fuzz or booster box, and plenty of players have collections of several or even dozens of units from this genre, and use two or three at a time on their pedalboards for different colors and textures and levels of sonic sizzle. Yep, of the players who want to change their guitar's pure sound in the first place, more probably want to filth it up than all of the other options combined.

Who created the first distorted electric guitar sound in history? I'll tell you. It was the first adventurous player to plug an electro-Spanish guitar into a tube amplifier way back in the 1930s, that's who. We might have forgotten his name, or maybe there was no one there to witness the event, but you can bet he lifted up that guitar, checked out his new amp, saw that the loudness control went to 10, and cranked it up to hear just what it could do.

Players and rock historians alike will talk endlessly about who either created or discovered or

After getting bored with his guitar sound while recording in the summer of 1964, Dave Davies of The Kinks shredded the speaker of a small Elpico amp and created one of the most famous early examples of distorted guitar on the hit single 'You Really Got Me.'

recorded the first distorted guitar tone. They argue, pontificate, debate, and even break it down into categories of type and of geographical location. "So, do we mean distortion, overdrive or fuzz tone?" or "Do you distinguish between North American and European 'firsts'?" Dave Davies of The Kinks is often credited with the first appearance of a heavily distorted electric guitar sound in the British charts on 'You Really Got Me' in August 1964.

As Davies recalled to the author in the late 1990s: "I was getting really bored with my guitar sound – or lack of an interesting sound – and there was this little radio spares shop up the road that had a little green amplifier in there next to the radios. An Elpico. I twiddled around with it and didn't know what to do. I tried taking the wires going to the speaker and putting a jack plug on there and plugging it straight into my [Vox] AC30. It kind of made a weird noise, but it wasn't what I was looking for.

"I started to get really frustrated, and I said, 'I know – I'll fix *you*...' I got a single-sided Gillette razor blade and cut round the cone like this [demonstrates slitting from the center to the edge of the cone], so it was all shredded but still on there. I played and I thought it was amazing, really freaky. I felt like an inventor... We just close-miked that in the studio, and also fed the same speaker output into the AC30, which was kind of noisy but sounded good."

Others might look to Jimmy Page, Pete Townshend or The Beatles, or credit the first recorded use of a fuzz box in Britain to Big Jim Sullivan's performance with a custom-built Roger Mayer fuzz on P.J. Proby's 1964 Number One hit single 'Hold Me' (according to Mayer himself) – or, supposedly, Bernie Watson's solo on Screaming Lord Sutch's 'Jack The Ripper' in 1960. Or, a little later, the one more of us remember, Keith Richards' worldwide smash-hit fuzz riff for the Stones' '(I Can't Get No) Satisfaction,' courtesy of a Maestro Fuzz-Tone.

The Fuzz-Tone connection hints that we need to look further back, and across the pond, for even earlier examples of recorded guitar distortion. Gibson, and hence their subsidiary brand Maestro, was given the circuit that became the Fuzz-Tone by studio engineer Glen Snotty. Snotty, in turn, had devised the transistorized fuzz-generating design to replicate a sound he'd heard while recording Marty Robbins 1961 hit record 'Don't Worry,' when a tube preamp in one of the mixer channels had started to fail and yield a distorted tone on Grady Martin's bass solo. Whoever decided to stick with the track, rather than re-record it through a properly functional channel, was on to something; the result was Nashville's first recorded fuzz guitar (a short-scale Danelectro bass, in fact). Courtesy of Maestro, Snotty's fuzz circuit soon made the trendy new sound available to the world.

But if Nashville was recording it in 1961, you gotta' believe some hipper cats were doing it somewhere a little southwest of there a good few years before.

It's 1951, a dark, rainy night on the backstreets of Memphis, Tennessee. Ike Turner & His Kings Of Rhythm are packing the gear into the station wagon, getting ready to head off to the studio to record a track for producer Sam Phillips – a track that the Rock'n'Roll Hall Of Fame will one day honor as the first rock'n'roll song of all time, 'Rocket 88' (although, distinctly unfairly, the song will be credited to singer Jackie Brenston and the imaginary band 'His Delta Cats'). "The Fender Bassman was in the trunk of the car and it fell out, right on the road," Ike Turner told Rick Batey of the UK's *Guitar Magazine* in 1998. "And it was raining, so the amp got wet. When we got to the studio and plugged it in, one of the tubes went 'pop.' We didn't have no more tubes – so that's where the fuzz came from.'

This recording, by Rhythm Kings' guitarist Willie Kizert through a failing tweed Fender, predates the more talked-about 'fuzz firsts' by a good ten years (although he probably actually did it through a TV-

Maestro's Fuzz-Tone launched a rock revolution, but the effect was originally aimed mainly at helping session players and jazz guitarists mimic trumpet and saxophone sounds.

front Pro – a 1x15 like the first Bassmans – or a Super, since the Bassman model itself didn't hit the market until 1952). So, is that where fuzz began?

Kink Dave Davies believes the concept goes back even further: "The blues players were the first to crank it up, and the music had that spirit, that anguish. We used to listen to all those guys. Like John Lee Hooker – he had that buzz, that drive. I used to listen to him and think, 'What the hell's he doing there? That's amazing – how do you get that sound?' I think all those elements led to me messing around with amplifiers, because all the amplifiers were clean, soulless."

T-Bone Walker, seen here, was one of the most flamboyant early showmen to brandish an electric guitar. What are the chances that he never cranked up his volume and drove that amp into distortion?

Whoever first got the sound down on tape, vinyl, acetate or whatever, it's hard to imagine that adventurous, pioneering electric guitarists like Charlie Christian, Lonnie Johnson, T-Bone Walker and others didn't crank up that brown electric suitcase to see just what it could do. Even if they were banned from such sonic mayhem on the bandstand or in the recording studio, you can bet a few juke joints and basement jams rang with the sound of distorted guitar right back into the 1940s and even the 1930s. Do you doubt it? Just plug a fat-sounding Gibson ES-150 – with its beefy 'blade' pickup – into an EH-150 or BR-1 amp wound up to max. Dirty? Damn right. There are no more 'firsts' to be claimed for distortion – although for sheer variety of sounds, modern guitarist are far better off than their predecessors.

Few dispute that, for tonal purity, the best distortion sounds come from cranking up a good tube amp. In particular, those with ears for tonal nuances buried even within a heap of distortion agree that a vintage-style, non-master-volume amp (or good boutique amp with the master up full to effectively take it out of the circuit) driven to the point where the output tubes are beginning to distort offers most players' dream visions of the perfect overdrive tone.

Not to say that other sounds don't have their place: the total freakout – sometimes very, very cool in itself – of a second-rate tube amp pushed way past its normal operational capabilities; the smooth, pliable, ultra-saturated sound of a cascading gain preamp; the cheesy, buzzy fizz of a cheap tranny amp slammed with too much gain and clipping to beat the band… Any of these can yield the godlike tone of the day in the right application, with the right player. But think Page, Hendrix, SRV, Blackmore, Eric Johnson, Clapton, Van Halen, Gary Moore, and it's cranked vintage amps and touch that are producing the tone. They were often aided by some type of distortion pedal, sure, because that was the only way to switch textures between verses, choruses and solos, or to push the big amps into distortion at less than full volume. But who wouldn't choose to get their rock overdrive sound from a 50W 1968 Marshall Plexi on 10, or their blues lead sound from a tweed Bassman on 12, if the ears and the noise police would stand for it?

For most players in the broad spectrum of rock – even those usually chained to the back of the stage hacking away at a clean rhythm part – these yield the sweetest, most tactile, touch-sensitive and playable tones available. Get that amp cooking to where the riffs get juicy and fluid and effortless, where sustain and harmonic feedback hover into view at the tap of a fret, and the racing of the preamp and power amp tubes, as they try to keep up with the pick attack, lends a comforting softness and compression to the feel – a sensation enhanced by the natural sag of any tube rectification... Mmmm. You can almost feel it now. If we could only get that play-it-all-day vibe at tolerable volume levels, any time we liked.

With this in mind, rather than taking the category chronologically, let's accept our good fortune today in having all of history's distortion sounds at our fingertips, and look first at those which transform the guitar and amp's natural tone least, working toward those which distort it most. In other words, from the cleanest to the dirtiest of the genre.

> **NOTE:** the schematic diagrams used in this chapter are for illustrative purposes only, and not intended as a basis for actual construction of the effects in question.

Boosters [CD tracks 27-30]

Transistor booster preamp stages are often billed as 'linear,' 'clean,' or 'distortion-free' boosters, and are intended to boost the guitar signal before it reaches the amplifier, without adding any artifacts like fuzz or distortion. The 'linear' bandied about in the names or literature for such units means, in basic terms, that the guitar's frequency range – and therefore its tone – should be unchanged as it passes through them. Only the signal level should be increased.

In fact, the resultant sound of the majority of boosters is anything but an entirely clean, transparent level increase – many do fatten the guitar sound slightly or enhance the treble. More significantly, most players use boosters to drive their amps (mainly tube amps) harder in order to produce some distortion. Plenty certainly use them for a supposedly 'clean' volume lift for undistorted lead lines, but this perceived clean tone is always thickened by a degree of distortion anyway. And the best way to get purely an unadulterated volume lift would be to tweak the level at the amp's output stage, not stack another gain-boosting stage in front of the amplifiers own preamp. Clean boosters they may be, but the good ones are extremely effective at coaxing a good tube amp into coughing up its luscious distortion sounds at slightly lower volume settings – say your blackface Fender Super Reverb on 4 rather than 7.

Boosters can range from the simplest of circuits to the extremely clever, verging on the complex. The fact that most other pedals in this genre – many fuzzes, overdrives, distortions and compressors – contain a booster stage in addition to their other sound-shaping circuitry hints that the booster pedal itself is a lesser engineering task than any of these. But the effort of keeping it transparent, altering the timbre and tonality of the raw guitar sound as little as possible, is an art in itself.

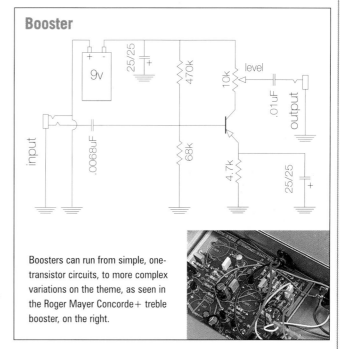

Booster

Boosters can run from simple, one-transistor circuits, to more complex variations on the theme, as seen in the Roger Mayer Concorde+ treble booster, on the right.

At about the same time fuzz pedals were becoming big stuff in the rock world, plenty of other guitarists wanted a means of boosting their attack and sustain without adding the artificiality of the fuzz sound – ostensibly retaining their natural, clean guitar tone. Perhaps surprisingly, considering its simplicity, Electro-Harmonix's LPB1 (Linear Power Booster), the first widely available commercially-produced booster, arrived a few years after fuzz boxes had already flooded the market. Where even the more basic fuzzes used a pair of transistors and a handful of other components, the LPB1 used a single transistor for its gain boost. It was an enormous success. E-H's Mike Matthews had already marketed a fuzz, and even sold a great number of them to Guild, but it was on the back of the LPB1 that he founded his now-famous company in 1968. Other boosters followed, such as MXR's popular, upmarket Micro Amp, and Dan Armstrong's Red Ranger. For plenty of early-1970s guitarists, one of these was all that need come between guitar and 100W stack for rock heaven to be attained.

The format is equally popular today, if not more so, and 21st century guitarists use boosters individually to overdrive amps or offer clean level increases for soloing; at the front of a long chain of effects to act as a buffer and line driver; or at the end of a similar chain to boost levels again after the signal drain of six or ten pedals.

There's a myriad of boost pedals available today: some relatively straightforward units – like Fulltone's dual-JFET-driven Fat Boost, Roger Mayer's Voodoo Boost or Carl Martin's Boost Kick; and some more unusual, such as Z.Vex's simple but clever Super Hard On, which uses a single BS-170 MOSFET transistor and has a unique negative-feedback control for a volume knob (labeled 'Crackle Okay' because of the crackle inherent in such controls when turned while in circuit).

Other designs add a clean-boost function to an overdrive pedal – sometimes independently switchable, sometimes not – resulting in products like Carl Martin's Hot Drive'n Boost, Fulltone's Full-Drive, or Voodoo Lab's Sparkle Drive.

Other boosters are deliberately designed to enhance certain frequencies. Vox offered a Treble Booster and Treble/Bass Booster way back in the mid 1960s, and Electro-Harmonix followed its LPB1 with the Screaming Bird and more powerful Screaming Tree treble boosters. Though these certainly emphasized high frequencies, as desired by countless guitarists at the time trying to cut through the mix as bands got louder and louder (and often, as a result, muddier), they also offered a general signal boost that had a similar overdriving effect on an amp as the more linear boosters.

Compressors [CD tracks 8-17]

These generally contain a boosting stage too, but are designed as compact versions of the large studio compressors – leveling devices that, to put it simply, smooth the attack and decay of a signal by softening the front edge of the note and amplifying its tail.

Part of the compressor's original appeal to guitarists was its ability to replicate the natural compression, or sag, of a tube amp run at medium to high levels. Whether induced by a pedal or by the amp itself, compression is often as much a 'feel' thing as a tonal element, making the guitar feel more tactile, touch-sensitive and playable. Many players favor compressors as sustainers, and some guitarists also use them as booster pedals, by turning down the compression or sustain control and winding up the gain or volume.

Beyond the intended squashing and sustaining effect, certain compressors have been attributed with magical tonal properties, especially the gray Ross Compressor, MXR's Dyna Comp, and Dan Armstrong's little Orange Squeezer. The first two in particular are frequently copied, and sometimes even improved upon, by boutique builders and hobbyists alike. In addition to softening the attack of the note and sustaining its decay, each of these adds its own characteristic thickening of the tone, often with a little appealing grit thrown in as a bonus.

Plenty of players go their entire careers without using a compressor pedal; others give one a try, and like its appealing swell and fatness so much they never switch it off from that day forward. The compressor has long been considered an essential weapon in the Nashville session-player's arsenal. It helps to smooth out snappy chicken pickin' runs or to thicken up otherwise thin, clean rhythm and lead parts. But the effect is big with players from all genres – from LA session player Jay Graydon to British Strat-picker Mark Knopfler to alt-rocker Trey Anastasio of Phish. And while even a good compressor's range of settings is far narrower than those of, say, a fuzz (which might go from mild distortion to freakish buzz) or a chorus (which can shift from gentle swirl to nauseating wobble), skilled players manage to make their own very individual sounds with the units. In fact, listeners with no first-hand experience of a compressor's sound and function may often hear a glorious part played through one and attribute the results to 'just great tone' – some magical combination of guitar and amp and touch.

While a compressor pedal's function is somewhat like that of a large studio compressor/limiter, only

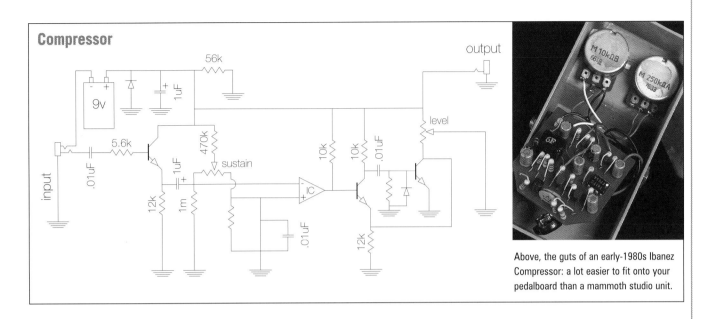

Above, the guts of an early-1980s Ibanez Compressor: a lot easier to fit onto your pedalboard than a mammoth studio unit.

in miniature, many guitarists use the effect for rather different reasons than a recording engineer would – although these do cross over in certain respects. Compression as a studio tool is usually intended to be transparent, a means of keeping sonic peaks from overloading the desk or the tape or causing digital distortion, while boosting quieter passages to give an overall impression of greater loudness and presence to a part or an entire mix. Guitarists, on the other hand, turn to compressors more for sustain, for punch, for thickening up thin sounds and, as described above, to increase the 'touch' and dynamic feel of their set-up. While compression applied too heavily in the recording environment can kill off dynamics in a song or part, guitarists, conversely, often think of a compressor pedal as a tool that increases the dynamics in their playing and tone. In reality, of course, extreme use of compression from a pedal will inevitably level out the peaks and troughs of a guitar part, too, and thus literally decrease its dynamic range.

The big rack-mounted or standalone studio compressor units were made with fairly complex tube circuits in the early days, or used equally intricate solid-state circuits based around an opto-cell, as in many classic designs of the 1960s and right up to today. Most pedals for guitar comprise far simpler circuits based around relatively basic opamps, or sometimes slightly more complex ICs, and the usual handful of transistors, resistors and capacitors that enables them to function in the desired manner. (An opamp – short for operational amplifier – is a compact form of integrated circuit (IC) that squeezes amplification duties into a small eight-pin chip. Other than the tiny resisters and capacitors that link them, these are the most common ingredients in most types of analog effects pedals.) The original models of the little Dan Armstrong Orange Squeezer used a single JRC4558D dual opamp just like that in the most revered versions of the Ibanez Tube Screamer (detailed in a moment), and a couple of JFET transistors. One of the more advanced compact compressor pedals, Demeter's Opto Compulator, is an exception to the rule, and is built around an 'opto-cell' like many revered studio units.

The more complex units often boast about their 'transparency' – meaning their ability to color the signal very little, or not at all – while other desirable but more basic models make a virtue of the way they liven up and enrich the guitar's straight sound.

Overdrives [CD tracks 41-56]

Confusion sometimes surrounds the distinction between overdrives, distortions and fuzzes, but in theory each should do roughly what it says on the box – even if some do a little of the others' jobs too.

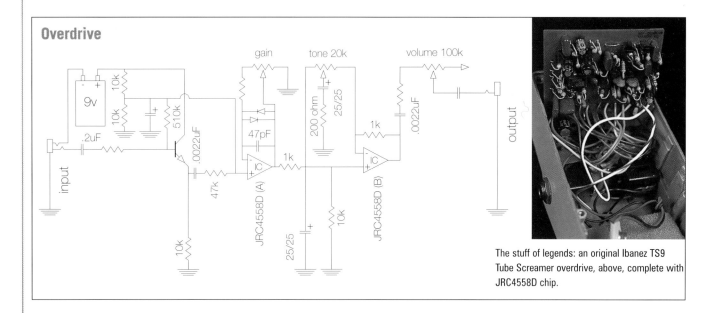

Overdrive

The stuff of legends: an original Ibanez TS9 Tube Screamer overdrive, above, complete with JRC4558D chip.

In the case of overdrive pedals, the intention is often twofold: either to provide a gain boost to drive a tube amp over into distortion, or to approximate the distortion sound of an overdriven tube amp. In practice, most do a little of both. Crank the average overdrive toward the max and it usually yields an element of self-generated distortion, which can easily be heard DI'd into a desk set to well below overload levels; generate enough distortion, and things can also sound a little fuzzy.

Despite the gray areas, there are definitely distinctions between the types. It all makes some sense if you think in terms of the degree of clipping achieved by the pedal, with overdrives generally being soft-clipping devices and distortions being hard-clipping devices. (Clipping is the term used to describe the way a signal is cut off when it runs into distortion. Drive it hard enough into distortion and eventually the top of the sound wave is entirely cut off, that part of the signal lost; most musical distortion devices don't go to such extremes, however, and seek to emphasize the affect on the sound wave as it approaches this full-clipping – either the smoothness and texture added by 'fuzzed up' peaks of the wave in soft clipping, or the harsh, jagged edginess of the peaks in hard clipping.)

Most pedalheads consider the Ibanez TS-808 Tube Screamer and, to a slightly lesser extent, the TS9 which followed it to be the grandaddies of overdrive pedals – and, yes, they certainly generate an element of distortion too. Indeed, more 'boutique' overdrives are based on the late-1970s and early-1980s Tube Screamer template than any other. But despite the claimed improvements and undeniable quality of many of these, the original units still usually fetch far higher prices on the vintage market (ain't it always the way?) than new units do in the stores.

With all of these – and other vaguely similar units – the guts of the sound comes from a clipping amp based around the first section of a dual opamp (purists swear by the JRC4558D chip in the early Ibanez units) and a pair of clipping diodes, with transistorized buffer stages at both the input and output, and a section for tone-shaping and output level control which uses the second part of the dual opamp in conjunction with a network of capacitors and resistors.

Pedals of this template offer a sound that's considered 'natural,' 'warm' and 'tubey,' partly by achieving smooth, symmetrical clipping, and partly by reining in harsher high harmonics that can result in sounds that are heard as jagged and spikey in other pedals.

Other early overdrive pedals were designed around discrete transistorized clipping and boosting circuits, though many leaned toward distortion units as properly defined, and added more artificiality to the sound – hence the Tube Screamers' near-instant popularity when it was introduced.

MXR's Distortion+ preceded the Tube Screamer and is an even simpler design – and, despite its name, is more an overdrive than a distortion. That said, its sound is considered by many to be a little more 'opaque,' or colored, than the Tube Screamer's. The box uses a 741-type IC and a pair of germanium diodes to achieve its soft-clipping sound. These are different components than the famed germanium transistors, but are made of the same material. Germanium is generally attributed a 'softness' of tone, and the same applies to the diodes used in the Distortion+ (and other units); change them for silicon diodes and you've got a hard-clipping distortion pedal – more of which later...

An overdrive is almost always at its best played through a tube amp set at medium to upper-medium volume, since the amp itself is doing a major part of the job, the pedal just being the boot that kicks its butt into juicy break-up a little quicker. Conversely, try one DI'd into a mixing desk or portastudio as described earlier, and in most cases it'll sound absolutely awful: harsh, raspy, cold and artificial. It can be a shocking look at the evil side of that $350 vintage Tube Screamer you just bagged from eBay. Now stop crying and plug it back into your AC30.

Dissatisfaction with 'vintage' units of this type usually centers around their lack of real high-gain sounds and inability to be truly fierce with Drive cranked up full. The more exemplary users of this type of pedal – such as Stevie Ray Vaughan and Eric Johnson, famous for their use of the Ibanez Tube Screamer range in the earlier years of its production – usually kept the Drive control in the lower part of its range, where the sound remains more natural and, yet again, serves as an excellent pre-boost to drive a good tube amp into distortion when the Level control is set high enough.

Some players also find older pedals built to this design have a distinct mid hump, a slightly wooly tonality, and/or a lack of low end (as ever, depending on the ears of the player you ask). Consequently a lot of newer makers have taken this into account in their 'redesigns.' Visual Sound's Route 66 pedal (which carries a JRC4558D chip like the early Tube Screamers) has a Bass Boost switch, Ibanez's own recent-era TS9DX Turbo Tube Screamer has a Mode control that takes you from classic sounds to settings with more distortion and more low end, and plenty of other makers address such issues in their variations on the circuit.

Fulltone's popular Full-Drive pedal has the bonus of a switchable booster channel, while its overdrive channel goes to a fairly high gain and, unusually, uses asymmetrical clipping for a more jaggedly textured sound that is quite different from the Tube Screamer's (although it's yet another overdrive pedal with a JRC4558D onboard). Asymmetrical clipping is also at the center of Boss's SD-1 Super Overdrive (as used by Eddie Van Halen), generated by a circuit that uses two silicon diodes in series in one direction, and only one in the other, to clip each side of the waveform differently. Some players credit asymmetrical clipping with more richness, body and character; others say it sounds clanky and harsh, like an amp with mismatched output tubes. Then again, some guitarists – those in the former camp, probably – say they prefer the sound of mismatched output tubes for these same reasons. As ever, what 'works' is up to you.

A selection of makers within today's high-end, hand-built crowd do offer variations on the opamp-based template discussed above. Blackstone Appliances bases its MOSFET Overdrive on a discrete transistorized circuit centered around, yes, MOSFETS, and Klon's Centaur pedal uses... well, who the hell knows? They cover the entire circuit board in epoxy goop to keep the cloners at bay, but this expensive overdrive certainly sounds different.

Distortions [CD tracks 71-76]

By definition, distortion pedals are designed to achieve serious adulteration of the guitar's signal. To use a rough analogy to tube amp tone, while overdrive pedals are looking to take you anywhere from pushed to cranked JTM45 or tweed Bassman sound, distortion pedals aim to do the Mesa/Boogie Triple Rectifier, Bogner Ecstasy or six-Laney-full-stacks trick, all in a 3″x5″ box.

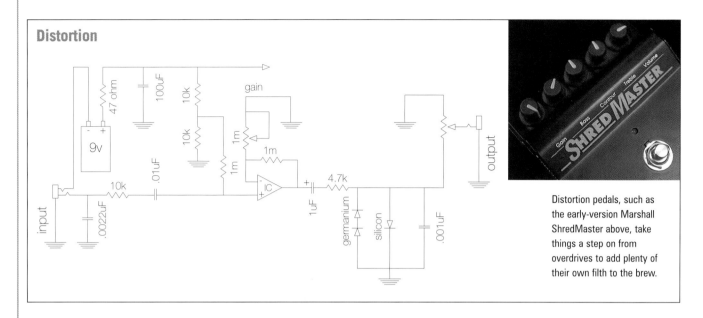

Distortion

Distortion pedals, such as the early-version Marshall ShredMaster above, take things a step on from overdrives to add plenty of their own filth to the brew.

These pedals unashamedly screw with your sound. They generally filth it up and slap their own notion of the ideal heavy rock or metal EQ all over your tone's backside. But of course they will boost the guitar signal as well (depending on the volume/output/level settings), and the sound we associate with them is still some confluence of pedal and amp, not to mention guitar. Still, a decent distortion box will usually sound a lot more like itself when DI'd into the desk or played through a mediocre tranny amp or a big but cold tube amp than even a great overdrive, since its purpose is to more drastically alter the sound in the first place.

Basic distortion boxes can be built around a simple network of transistors and clipping diodes, to both boost the signal and alter the waveform. Most units, though, very roughly resemble the standard mass-production overdrives detailed above, with the heavy work done by opamps, some tone-shaping stages, and input/output buffers.

The ProCo Rat set the standard for heavy distortion sounds above and beyond the capabilities of the MXR Distortion+ and the Ibanez Tube Screamer, although in fact its design is surprisingly similar to the aforementioned MXR, with silicon diodes in place of germanium, and an added tone control.

All mass-market brands offer at least one distortion pedal – and often several. Boss, for one, tries to cater to all possible tastes. Its DS-1 (not to be confused with the SD-1 overdrive mentioned already) is one of the workhorses of the breed, with some big-name players happy to stomp on its flat rectangular switch, including both Steve Vai and Joe Satriani. The DS-2 takes things a step further, while the MT-2 Metal Zone and MD-2 Mega Distortion get successively more evil. And Boss isn't the only one, with DOD, Ibanez, Marshall and many, many others playing the distortion game too, along with a few of the boutique makers.

The proliferation is most distinctive in many 'metal' pedals that go beyond even the standard distortion sounds. These generally offer the archetypal scooped-mid sound with thudding lows and crispy highs. Many are adjustable for anything from classic rock to metal sounds, with a tone control that acts more to reduce or accentuate mids rather than the usual high boost/cut, and often a 'resonance' control or similar to adjust the fullness of the bass.

Fuzz [CD tracks 1-7]

Fuzz is the grandaddy of distortion devices – if you don't include the old cranked amp or faulty preamp channel. Fuzz boxes were also among the first of the transistorized guitar effects being built back in the early 1960s – which is no real surprise when you discover how simply most of them are designed.

It's almost pointless trying to describe the sound of a vintage-style fuzz tone – the name says it best. They slather a slightly wooly, rounded, warm but sparkly distortion all over the guitar signal (see, you could just say "fuzzy") to give more meat, girth and sustain to the sound. More imposing units can be guilty of taking charge of the entire signal and bending it to their own synthetic demands – "brick-wall processing," as Roger Mayer puts it (meaning your signal hits that wall and cannot pass through without a total transformation of its nature and character) – while those generally considered to be the more playable devices retain elements of your dynamics, touch, feel and core tonality. In either case, the resultant sound is still, usually, more processed and artificial than any of the preceding types of pedals in this category. Turn a tube amp up to where it's starting to break up and you've got gentle overdrive; crank it to the max and you've got heavy distortion. Pull out one of the pair of output tubes, use the wrong-value bias resistor on a preamp tube, or beat it senseless with a crowbar and you might just get it to sound like fuzz. It's not a natural sound, but it can be a great one, and it's a major part of many players' signature tones.

If fuzz is the grandaddy, the Dallas-Arbiter Fuzz Face (introduced in 1966) is the grand-poobah of the grandaddies' social club. A handful of other fuzzes came first, but this distinctive, round, smiling box is the one most guitarists point to when identifying the fuzz tone of the gods. Why? Two words: Jimi Hendrix. Apparently he died and took it up there with him. Oh, and two other words: germanium transistors. When these fuzz fans point to the Fuzz Face, of course, they don't point to just any Fuzz Face. They point to a good one. The quality of these pedals varies wildly, mainly because the tolerances of germanium transistors themselves varies wildly, and sorting out the good ones was more work than the makers could afford to put in (or perhaps knew was necessary). Contemporary makers from Fulltone to Z.Vex to Roger Mayer himself now take the time and trouble to laboriously sort their germanium transistors, and it pays off in spades in terms of tone and consistency.

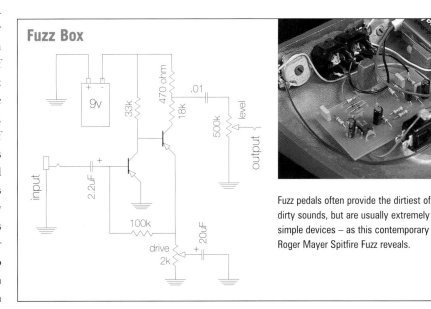

Fuzz pedals often provide the dirtiest of dirty sounds, but are usually extremely simple devices – as this contemporary Roger Mayer Spitfire Fuzz reveals.

Germanium has been very much the effects buzzword of the past many years. Germanium transistors were made from the semi-metalic element of the same name, and were a common component of many solid-state audio devices until more consistent and reliable silicon transistors became widely available in the late 1960s. The germanium transistors of the mid 1960s were relatively noisy and unstable, and their specification tolerances varied wildly – but they are also considered by many guitarists to be softer, rounder, and more musical-sounding than the 'harder' silicon devices that followed.

Open up a Fuzz Face for the first time and you're likely to be startled by its simplicity. Other early fuzzes like Maestro's Fuzz-Tone (1963) and Sola Sound's Tone Bender (1965) are equally basic. As far as the Face goes, you'll find fewer than ten components on the board, two of them being those crucial AC128 or NKT275 transistors. Interestingly, the Tone Bender originally used two OC75 germanium transistors made by Mullard, the revered valve (tube) manufacturer.

Later makes of fuzzes – and later generations of those above – moved on to silicon transistors. Many players found the silicon-based models a little harsher sounding, and the legend of the magical germanium transistors began to grow. Even so, plenty of guitarists get along just fine with the silicon variety. Eric Johnson, often credited with ears of canine ability, uses a silicon-transistor Dallas-Arbiter Fuzz Face to drive the dirty rhythm of his famous multi-amped, multi-routed set-up. He also holds the unit together with a rubber band because he says the bottom plate's central mounting screw affects its tone. Make of this what you will...

High-end builders of today have gone back to germanium en masse for their classic fuzz tones, using it in anything from vintage-style units – like Fulltone's '69, Frantone's The Sweet, and Roger Mayer's Spitfire – to way-out updates of the breed, such as Z.Vex's Fuzz Factory. And as we've said, most of them make sure they test their transistors to sort out the few that will do the job correctly.

MODULATION

The modulation category includes phasing, flanging, chorus, vibrato, tremolo, rotary speaker effects, and octave dividers. Later analog versions of the first three use much of the same technology as echo and delay units, although using chips with shorter delay times, but it makes sense to include them here because their obvious sonic characteristics have much in common with other units made from very different kinds of circuits.

The roots of some of these sounds are well documented in Chapter 1. Most stem from the desire to add depth, dimension and movement to the guitar's natural sound without necessarily 'distorting' it. You will have noticed that a couple were also inspired by effects already being used on electric organs.

Phasing [CD tracks 84-86]

We call these boxes 'phase shifters' because they split the guitar signal and shift one path out of phase by from 0 to 360 degrees through the entire range of the frequency spectrum, and blend it back with the dry path so the moving in-phase/out-of-phase relationship can be heard. When the two signals are totally out of phase – meaning any time they are 180 degrees apart from each other in the full cycle of 360 degrees – they cancel each other out, creating what we call a notch. But a number of factors interact to give a phaser its characteristic swooshing sound. They'll be explained here in relatively simple terms, though in many units some pretty clever and complex electronics goes into making all this happen.

When a notch in the frequency response is swept across the frequency spectrum, the most dramatic sonic effect occurs at the peaks between the notches, where both paths are completely in phase, and we have a full-strength signal. But leaving it there would repeatedly emphasize the same low, middle and high-frequency notes – and delete the same notes at the notches – so the phaser circuit also employs an oscillator to continually move (or 'shift') the point at which these notches and peaks occur, so different frequencies are emphasized and de-emphasized at each pass, at a rate determined by the unit's Speed or Rate knob.

We talk about 0 to 360 degrees because that's the simplest way to envision the 'full circle' of the phase relationship, and in reality you can't walk further around anything than a full circle. Unless you're a phase shifter. For these pedals, designers talk in terms of a continual shifting of the phase relationship from 0 to, in theory, infinity, depending on how many shifting stages the circuit contains. The phase shifts by 180 degrees for each stage, so two stages makes the full circle – but with any more than two stages, it takes the signal beyond a full circle. So for the typical simple phaser with four stages, we're looking at from 0 to 720 degrees, with three peaks and two notches along the way, the peaks occurring at 0, 360 and 720 degrees of the out-of-phase signal, and the notches at 180 and 540 degrees. Phasers with six, eight and even ten stages have been built for use with guitar, but the simple four-stage circuit seems generally most appealing.

Much of this appeal is probably thanks to an outdated pedal with a two-function switch labeled Chorus and Vibrato. These words will trigger a sigh of awe and wonder from many a guitarist because, of course, they are the labels on the mode switch of the famous Univox Uni-Vibe. This pedal is a good place to start because it was one of the first of the transistorized effects of this type to become widely available, and it occupies a patch of ground all its own in the world of things that go swoosh.

Despite the labeling, the Uni-Vibe is more akin to a four-stage phaser than what we consider today to be a chorus pedal, even if that's the label on its most-loved setting. The deception is forgivable when you remember that the Uni-Vibe's intention was to reproduce the chorus-type sound – or Chorale sound, as it was often labeled – produced by a Leslie rotating speaker cabinet used with a Hammond organ. Also, the unit existed before there was much categorization of such things: it was a guitar effects footpedal, it had its own sound… and that was all anyone needed to know.

The Uni-Vibe – and the better of the clones that

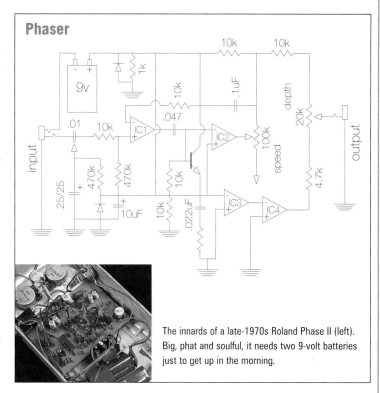

Phaser

The innards of a late-1970s Roland Phase II (left). Big, phat and soulful, it needs two 9-volt batteries just to get up in the morning.

have followed it down the years – is based around a discrete transistorized circuit with four sets of light bulbs and light cells and a low frequency oscillator (LFO) which does the shifting work to move the peaks and notches. But unlike the drawing-board phaser discussed already, the frequencies of each stage of the Uni-Vibe are set differently, so it could be argued there is indeed more of a chorusing of the sound. Disrobed, it's a freakish beast: a complex circuit board with four lamp/photo cell pairings under tiny silver shields at its center, the lamps flashing on and off in series. Archaic, maybe, but even today's top designers swear they can't come close to the soft, lush, hypnotic sound of the original unit without the bulbs and light cells.

Other early phase shifters used field effect transistors (FETs) to control each phasing stage in place of the light bulbs in the 'Vibe, and certainly later units employed opamps with variable resistors (six TL072 dual opamps or similar in the MXR Phase 100, for example). Electro-Harmonix's sweet little Small Stone has a more unusual design which employs five CA3094 type Operational Transconductance Amplifiers (OTAs). The results are similar, but subtly different. Many phasers – such as MXR's Phase 45 and Phase 90, and E-H's Small Stone – carry nothing but a speed control, plus a 'color' switch in the case of the Small Stone. Others have depth, mix and resonance controls; resonance appears on many units with internal feedback loops (the Small Stone and most phasers before it lack this circuitry), and lets the player tweak the degree to which the portion of the signal fed back enhances the frequency peaks.

The gray area between different types of phasers and chorus pedals – and phaser-style chorus pedals versus delay-based chorus pedals – arises probably because designers and manufacturers really have followed two distinct paths in this field. Some phasers have sought to approximate the Uni-Vibe's own approximation of a Leslie cab, and some so-called choruses have done much the same. Other phasers have been designed from the ground up, more from the perspective of phase shifting principles, rather than in an effort to sound like a whirling speaker or any other electromechanical device that's come before. The result means the field is broad and varied, and different phasers (or their related effects) can often have voices with characteristics more distinct than, say, two delays from different makers.

Flanging [CD tracks 87-88]

Usually considered the big brother to the phaser, the flanger is indeed related in some senses, but achieves its heavier (some would say more oppressive) sonic results by imposing more control over its placement of the notches created by the phase relationship, rather than spacing them evenly as the phaser's sweep does.

Much of the basic circuitry behind flanging, to put it very simply, follows the template given above, but requires far more complex engineering to take it where it's going. Pedal-sized units designed to replicate the sound of two big reel-to-reel tape machines sliding in and out of sync weren't possible until larger, more complex ICs became available to help do the job. This extra technology is needed to harmonically tune the out-of-phase notches and, relative to these, the peaks, and it's this harmonic spacing that can make a genuine flanger pedal sound almost like it's actively participating in the note selection of a sequence you are playing. Whereas phasers have from four to ten stages, the individual chips within proper flangers may carry hundreds of stages in themselves. Dizzying stuff.

The A/DA Flanger – not the first commercially available flanger pedal, but probably the first that really worked properly with the full sonic depth of the effect – was made possible by the advent of the SAD1024 chip (others were used through its lifetime, depending upon availability). The A/DA hit the shelves in 1977, and was shortly followed by Electro-Harmonix's equally beloved Electric Mistress, and MXR's big, gray Flanger. Nearly every major maker slapped its own flanger on the butt and sent it toddling down the pike within the next few years.

These were serious pedals in their day, the big boys requiring their own regulated onboard AC power stage to run all that thirsty silicon. Most required a serious investment on behalf of the impoverished guitarist, too: A/DA's unit retailed at $199.95 when introduced, and others went for even more. Not a steal, when you consider that minimum wage was $2.30 an hour in 1977.

The sound blew away guitarists when units first popped up in guitar stores. If the dizzying harmonic swirl didn't make you puke, it really sent you tripping. Interestingly, many tired of it a lot quicker than they did the phaser's subtler, less imposing 'swoosh,' and consequently it's difficult today to name a

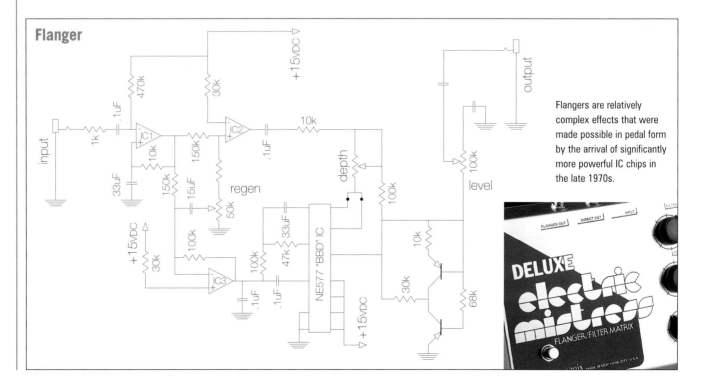

Flanger

Flangers are relatively complex effects that were made possible in pedal form by the arrival of significantly more powerful IC chips in the late 1970s.

fraction as many great guitar tracks with flangers slapped all over them as you can with phasers. For the latter, we've got the Stones' 'Shattered' (or just about anything from *Some Girls*), The Clash's 'Lost In The Supermarket' from *London Calling* and loads from *Sandinista*, and heavier rockers from early Van Halen to recent Foo Fighters. In the flanging corner, we've got The Pat Travers Band's 'Boom Boom, Out Go The Lights' and… well, I'm sure there's another somewhere. OK, maybe the intro lick to Heart's 'Barracuda' redeems it some.

I don't mean to be unfair to the effect (and theoretically this should be a chapter devoid of opinion). Flanging is impressive stuff. It's just that, used heavily at all – where it best shows off its massive harmonics-plinking capabilities – it can become too much for a guitarist to easily play with, which relinquishes it to the realm of background effects and early-1980s electro-pop. Still, plug in and send your brain to space and back.

Chorus [CD tracks 18-26]

While modified four-stage phasers like the Uni-Vibe and its predecessors had sought to evoke a choral-like sound, the chorus pedal as we know it didn't

The chorus pedal as we know it today arrived in the late 1970s, on the back of the revolutionary new short-delay chips that were just then becoming available to manufacturers.

arrive until affordable short-delay chips became widely available in the late 1970s (the function of these delay chips will be explained in more detail in the Echo & Delay section later). This in itself implies that chorus is a type of delay, and indeed it is, but the sonic results of the way these short delays are transformed puts the effect firmly in the modulation camp, so it's easiest to consider it as such.

IC-based chorus effects work in a manner very similar to flangers. The main difference, again put simply, is that the short delays used to create harmonically spaced notches and peaks in the frequency spectrum are manipulated to modulate more tightly above and below specific frequency ranges, rather than shifted to swoosh broadly up and down the entire spectrum. The result, and intention, is a sound like a group of singers or strings, where some voices/strings inevitably waver slightly from those beside them, producing a quivering clash of harmonics that evokes space and dimension when used subtly. The effect is possibly best heard – as pure effect, at least – in stereo, and the nature of the beast lends itself readily to stereo outputs. The broad soundstage and Doppler-like movement that a good stereo chorus can spread out before you (between a pair of well-spaced amps or L-R headphones) make it one of the most spacious, three-dimensional effects available outside of long delays or cavernous reverb settings.

Boss's CE-1 Chorus Ensemble was the first of these types to become commercially available, and is the best remembered of the company's now-archaic-looking early range of die-cast metal pedals. The unit was an instant success when it hit the market in 1976, and was quickly snatched up by a range of major players. Andy Summers used the CE-1 with The Police in the late 1970s and early 1980s, and it's probably most famously heard on the band's big 1979 hit 'Message In A Bottle,' though other players made creative use of it too.

Shortly after the Boss, Electro-Harmonix offered both its Memory Man Stereo Echo/Chorus – which featured a very good, spacious chorus setting that a lot of player's loved – and smaller, stand-alone Small

Clone chorus. Like the Small Stone phaser before it, the Small Clone had a softer, subtler sound than many of the chorus pedals that would soon flood the market, and it too was a huge hit. Kurt Cobain's use of the pedal on 'Teen Spirit' and Chris Novoselic's bass part on 'Come As You Are' from Nirvana's *Nevermind* album shows off how it can add a rich, moving, liquid texture to both clean and distorted parts. MXR, DOD and Ibanez all offered popular early IC-based analog chorus pedals, and today every major mass-manufacturer has a unit on the market.

As these same makers ramped up for digital production, digital choruses naturally joined the team. The effect in its digital form might sound broadly similar, but it is created differently than in the analog circuits. Digital chorus pedals double a signal and add delay and pitch modulation to one path, the latter wobbling below and above the pitch of the unadulterated signal, which produces an audible out-of-tuneness when the paths are blended back together. It's hard to fault the power and range of control that digital technology affords, and this version of the effect has been hugely successful, but many guitarists still prefer the subtle, watery shimmer of the analog version. The same ears might even find the digital variety makes them a little queasy.

Vibrato & Tremolo   [CD tracks 57-63]

True vibrato, as distinct from the volume-chopping tremolo effect often mislabeled as such, is an actual wavering of the note above and below pitch to create a vibrating, warbling effect. Singers do it, and guitarists do it when they wiggle a finger against string and fingerboard, or tremble the arm of a vibrato tailpiece – although the former only vibratos the note from natural to sharp and back, while the latter usually takes it from natural to flat and back, repeatedly in each case. Heavy true vibrato can get a little seasickening, just like heavy digital chorus or flanging, but good implementations of the effect are usually subtle, and can add a gently beautiful movement to a guitar part.

Electronic vibrato was achieved early on with a relatively complex circuit, usually requiring at least two preamp tubes, and was most often installed in amps, though occasionally built as a standalone box – as with Gibson's GA-V1 Vibrato Box. Fender, guilty of mislabeling many amps with a 'vibrato' channel which in fact only carried opto-controlled tremolo, did build a few of its first front-control-mounted brown Tolex amps of the very early 1960s with a subtle form of true vibrato. (Despite its name, the earlier tweed Vibrolux actually carried tremolo, produced by a circuit similar to that used in the slightly larger Tremolux.) As it appeared on the 6G8 Twin and 6G5-A Pro Amp of 1960-61, the vibrato effect required two-and-a-half 12AX7s of the preamp's total of five, excluding the phase inverter (the vibrato circuit 'wasted' half a tube, which was left unused). It also required about as much circuitry again as the rest of that used for the two channels combined, and was clearly a lot of work to build. It sounds fantastic, too, although it's still just barely 'true' vibrato – a subtle example at best. But it simply wasn't worth the effort, apparently, and was dropped after just over a year of production. Ironically the choppier, pulsing tremolo achieved with a single tube and a photo-coupler circuit – as made famous by the blackface amps – has always been more popular, and is more often associated with what we call the 'Fender sound.' Vox, Magnatone, and a few others also offered amps with true vibrato.

The effect is achieved today in solid state guitar pedals with circuits similar to those used for analog chorus units, or sometimes in high-end pedals with fairly complex discrete transistorized designs that are modified variations on early phasers. A few companies, notably boutique amp builder Matchless, have also offered tube-powered units that work along the lines of the shortlived Fender vibrato circuit. When done right, it's a lush, moody effect that adds thickness and motion to any guitar part, as do all of the better analog modulation effects.

Tremolo might not seem like modulation, but you could argue for its inclusion here because, in the literal sense, the effect rapidly modulates a signal from the on state to the off state (or nearly off). Really I'm just sticking it here because I don't feel like creating a one-pedal category to hang tremolo out on its own – or maybe alongside volume pedals, which hardly even seem worth discussing. Not that I, and many others, don't feel tremolo deserves a genre all to itself. We love tremolo, and, as simple as it is, when used correctly it can still be one of the most haunting effects out there.

The advent of tremolo as an amp-based effect was discussed in Chapter 1. As it first appeared in the Fender Tremolux and Vibrolux amps, the tremolo circuit either acted between the phase inverter and power tubes to cut the signal as it entered the output stage of the amp, or else tapped the bias circuit to pulsate the 6V6's on and off, neither of which can be replicated in a pedal. On the other hand, the circuit used in most Fenders from around 1963 onwards, with its atmospheric-sounding lopsided triangular waveform, can be adapted to fit into a pretty small box.

This circuit is based around a photo-coupler made from a small neon lamp and a light-dependent resistor (LDR) coupled together in a small, opaque tube. An oscillator makes the lamp pulse at a speed determined by the effect's 'speed' or 'rate' control, and the LDR – which is in the signal path – injects this pulse into the guitar signal with an intensity determined by the 'depth' control. While most amps of the 1960s and 1970s that carried this effect used a tube to drive the oscillator, pedals that use a photo-coupler convert the drive section to a transistorized stage.

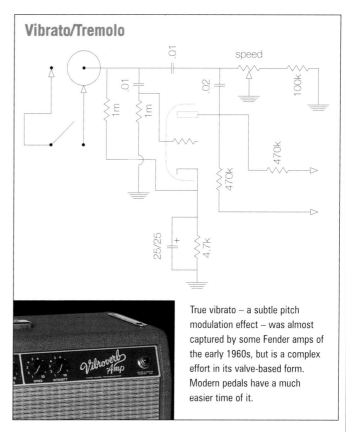

True vibrato – a subtle pitch modulation effect – was almost captured by some Fender amps of the early 1960s, but is a complex effort in its valve-based form. Modern pedals have a much easier time of it.

Most budget to mid-priced pedals do things even more simply. As with the majority of pedals, they use ICs to accomplish all oscillation and modulation tasks, usually with transistorized input and output stage buffers. While purists will argue vehemently for the tonal purity of discrete transistorized circuitry in most applications (meaning without opamps or ICs of any sort), it's probably harder to make the case that a basic dual opamp-based tremolo pedal that effectively pulsates your volume on and off is dramatically inferior to a discrete photo-coupler-based circuit as discussed earlier. Still, use your ears and decide for yourself.

Tremolo dropped from fashion in the late 1970s, through the 1980s and into the 1990s (aside from its use at the hands of a few cool guitarists who always knew what it could do). At the time, it just sounded old-fashioned up against long digital delays, digital chorus and flanging and all the rest of it. But as with so many sonic colors from the early days of rock'n'roll, the effect has built a major new following (the *Twin Peaks* soundtrack from the early 1990s probably reminded a lot of people of its haunting power). Many, many great guitarists now keep a tremolo pedal on their board, or play through an amp with onboard tremolo.

The simple pleasures of tremolo – one of the earliest but most haunting effects for guitar – appear to be with us to stay.

Octave Divider

This is a relatively simple effect, but also one of the freakiest when used right – or, sometimes more so, when used wrong. Like a surprising number of classic sounds, this first came to us via Jimi Hendrix, from a custom-built Roger Mayer Octavia – famously heard on 'Purple Haze,' and plenty of other Hendrix tracks besides. Mayer developed an octave divider with fuzz for Hendrix out of his own experiments with doubling the frequency of a signal in order to make it appear to add a note an octave up from the original, but he never offered the original unit as a commercial item. This left the door open for

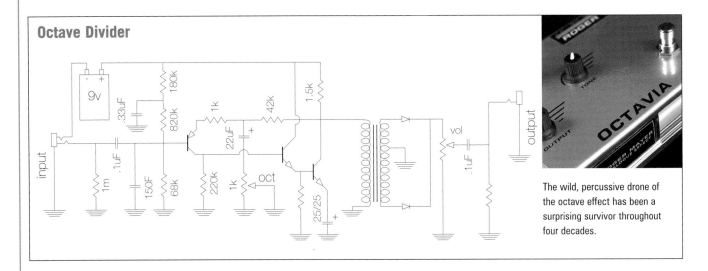

Octave Divider

The wild, percussive drone of the octave effect has been a surprising survivor throughout four decades.

Tycobrahe to offer its own Octavia copy, and that unit was followed by clones from a host of others.

The circuit itself is fairly simple: three transistors, a couple of diodes and an impedance interstage transformer, along with the usual caps and resistors. Primitive stuff, but it has a wild effect on a guitar signal. As Mayer himself puts it, "It doubles the number of images of the note. And that, apparently, makes it sound twice the frequency – whereas it really isn't. Because the signal's going up and down twice as much, even though you've changed the relationship of it, the ear perceives it as twice the frequency." It's like holding something up to a mirror, explains Roger: "You see two of them, but there's still only one." So, a simple circuit, but a complex aural trick.

Octave effects are among the trickier pedals to use well, because the circuit only tracks well if a single, pure, cleanly played note is introduced – and honks into total freakout if it sees an interval. And the fewer harmonics the better, so firm picking on a neck pickup does it the most favors. Again, Hendrix's own playing provides a good lesson in how to use an octave fuzz, and you can usually hear how he cleans up his technique – simplifying the blues slurs, trills and bends that are otherwise plentiful – in order to make the most of the effect.

The octave divider's prevalence in heavy rock of the late 1960s and early 1970s has left it a somewhat dated effect – and a genre-tied sound too (you don't hear it a lot in jazz or country) – but a few adventurous players continue to apply it creatively to perfectly modern music.

Ring Modulators

These units come to us from the world of analog synthesizers, and have far more applications there, but can be useful for the guitarist who needs some wild, wacked-out, totally a-guitaral sonic obliteration every so often. Think in terms of the octave divider's percussive, synthesized octave-up sound, but with more jagged, atonal, random-interval performance. This is another of those tools the flailing guitarist took up in the early 1980s to fight the synth players when electronica promised to take over the world and everyone forgot about 'tone' for a few years. (We lost the battle, but I'd like to think we won the war.)

The ring modulator takes its name from the simplest of its transistorized topologies, consisting of a ring of four diodes and two transformers. Most are somewhat more complex than this. In any case, a ring modulator takes the signals from two sources – either from two separate inputs, or one input and one internal oscillator (called a 'carrier frequency') – and multiplies them to produce a new signal that is totally different from either of the two source signals. The result is a little like an octave divider trying to handle two notes at a time rather than the single, pure note that it's able to deal with, and coughing up a dissonant mess as a result. The ring modulator is designed specifically to cope with these two different signals, but their multiplication produces a new signal with notes at both the sum and difference of the frequencies of the two source signals. Consequently, this output is a mathematical result with no harmonic relationship to the original notes.

Sounds messy, perhaps, and it is – except that most units designed for guitar (or other tonal instruments) generally tap off a portion of the main signal at its input and feed it forward to the output to retain a degree of the original note. This blend of the original guitar signal and the sum-and-difference signal produced by the ring modulation circuit is percussive, jagged, dissonant… and sometimes very effective.

Early and basic ring modulators for guitar generally have a single input and generate their carrier frequency internally, occasionally with user-selectable variations. Some more elaborate models – such as Lovetone's Ring Stinger or Frantone's Glacier – allow for internal oscillation selections and add an extra input for using an external control signal, such as a mike, drum machine, separate line level source, or whatever. What does the sum and difference of your own funk guitar riffs multiplied with a garage drum loop sound like? Chaotic, probably – but possibly like a major hit too.

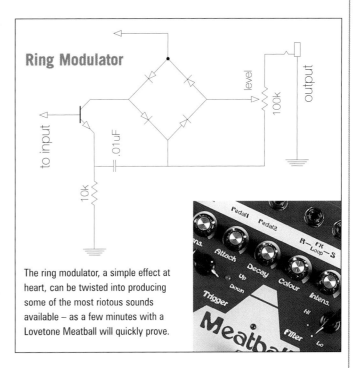

The ring modulator, a simple effect at heart, can be twisted into producing some of the most riotous sounds available – as a few minutes with a Lovetone Meatball will quickly prove.

ECHO & DELAY [CD tracks 64-70]

We all know what this type of effect is like: it replicates, to varying degrees, the sound of playing your guitar in a tiled bathroom, or a cathedral, or mammoth cave, and it has proved itself one of the most atmospheric aural adulterations available. Since none of those real-life locations is entirely gig friendly, our ever-handy techs have bottled the flavor in a reliable, portable form.

This category covers both echo and reverb effects, since they are versions of the same thing. The term 'echo' was used more often in the early days of recorded music – particularly early rock'n'roll – and is sometimes used today to refer to the distinct and distant repeats of a signal; 'delay' could mean anything from the short repeats heard as reverb, to the complex, long, manipulated repeats of an intricate digital delay line. Either way, they are both really the same thing, just used differently.

Analog Delay

The transmogrification of bulky, fiddly tape echo units into transistorized analog echo pedals in the late 1970s is arguably one of the greatest economies the delay-loving guitarists has ever experienced (physically more than financially). Players addicted to anything from slapback echo to the hypnotic sonic cloning of their Echoplexes, Copicats and Space Echoes breathed collective sighs of relief when Electro-Harmonix and MXR introduced relatively affordable analog delay pedals.

By the early 1980s there was barely a rocker alive who would step on-stage without a delay pedal, and every major make offered a model or two. Many players gradually decided that their old tape echoes actually sounded better than the transistorized alternatives, but for convenience sake a majority still stuck with their stompboxes for live work. Opinions on the tonal superiority of tape echo – and especially tube-powered versions – have become even more vehement in recent years, spawning high prices in the used market and even the recent offering of a Tube Tape Echo from boutique pedal maker Fulltone; but many still find tape impractical.

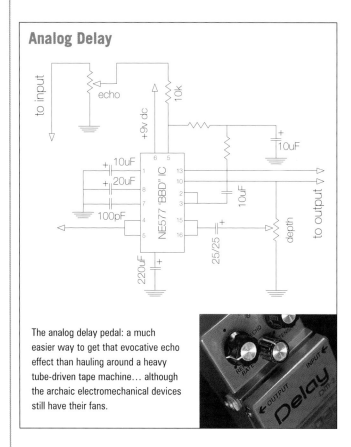

Analog Delay

The analog delay pedal: a much easier way to get that evocative echo effect than hauling around a heavy tube-driven tape machine… although the archaic electromechanical devices still have their fans.

Like so much else, analog delays were first made possible by a shift in the available technology in the mid 1970s, in this case the advent of affordable delay chips. Techies call these 'bucket brigade delay chips' because they pass the signal along in stages from the input pin to the output pin – with anything from 68 to 4096 stages. Inject a signal, govern the speed at which it gets passed from stage to stage, tap the output and, bingo, you've got echo. It's clear from this that the more stages in the chip, the longer the delay the circuit can achieve. The longer the delay, however, the greater the distortion in the wet signal, so most makers compromised to keep maximum settings within acceptable delay/noise ratios.

E-H's Memory Man was one of the most popular solid-state delays ever, and even with its meagre 5 to 320 milliseconds delay time was little short of revolutionary when introduced in 1976. At around $150, it was something of a bargain too, though not dirt-cheap by any means – considering that at the time you could buy a new Fender Stratocaster for just a little over three times that figure. The Memory Man was launched with Reticon SAD1024 chips, but E-H switched to quieter, better sounding and more adaptable Panasonic MN3005 ICs when these became available, and the latter is the chip found in the better-known Stereo Echo/Chorus and Deluxe models.

Different manipulations of similar bucket brigade delay chips were also at the center of the more advanced chorus and flanger pedals that emerged in the late 1970s (as discussed already). With ICs that were themselves capable of creating a controllable time delay in any given signal, the job of harmonically modulating part of a split, delayed signal to produce a warbling chorus or swooshing flange sound became a lot easier.

Digital Delay

The wonders of digital delay arrived on the pedalboard in the early 1980s with what seemed massive capabilities for long delays, clean signal reproductions and the endless fun of one, two, or up to 16 seconds of looping delay. Reproductions often weren't really all that clean (and were colder and harsher too), and many delays were prone to digital distortion if pushed, or poor resolution on the decay of the signal. Even so, the power of the new technology threatened to bury the old analog delay units.

As for the nuts and bolts of digital delays, there isn't space here for a thorough, ground-up explanation (and most people know at least the principle behind binary encoding by now anyway). Simply think of the digital delay pedal as another form of sampler: it makes a small digital recording of your riff, and plays it back at a user-selectable time delay, with depth and number of repeats also more or less selectable. The higher the sample rate, the better the sound quality. Early affordable 8-bit models really did leave a lot to be desired sonically, but as 16, 20 and 24-bit designs emerged, the reproduction of the echoes increased dramatically in quality.

Yet, as with so very many elements in the great world of guitar, once the novelty wore off and we were less awestruck by the new technology – and perhaps came to realize we had little use for two seconds, or even 500 milliseconds of delay time – many of us came to miss the warm, pliable sound of the analog pedals. Today, inevitably, the jury is still out; plenty of great players use each type of pedal, and the music you make with the technology remains more important than the type of technology you choose to make music. Used in isolation, at the same delay settings, each would probably sound just a little different to a guitarist with good ears. At the back end of a pedalboard with eight or ten other effects on it and three or four running at a time, the differences are likely to be negligible.

Reverb

Achieved with springs or plates, as discussed in Chapter 1, reverb is a distinct sound all to itself. The effect has been lured into the delay camp more in modern times because the same bucket brigade analog technology or digital delay technology used to create long echoes can be manipulated to produce a reverb sound too.

Tap the multistage analog delay chip at a very short delay, layer this with further short delays, and a reverb effect is produced. It has something in common with the spring reverb in guitar amps – or old studio plate reverb units – in that both approximate the reverberant sound of a guitar played in an empty, reflective room. While many players make good use of reverb pedals, including anything from Danelectro's newer, far-eastern-built units to old and new Electro-Harmonix and Boss models, most consider the amp-based, tube-driven spring reverb to be the pinnacle of the breed. But there are many great guitar amps out there with no reverb onboard, so for anything from your tweed Fender Bassman to your Marshall JTM45 to your Matchless D/C30, an add-on unit is the only option.

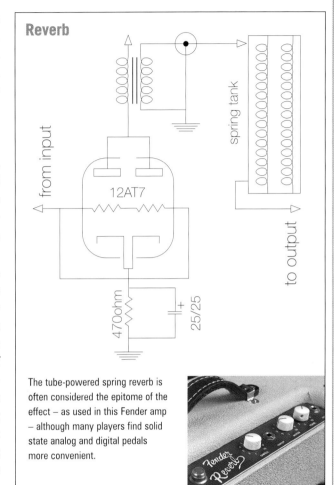

Reverb

12AT7

from input

spring tank

to output

470ohm

25/25

The tube-powered spring reverb is often considered the epitome of the effect – as used in this Fender amp – although many players find solid state analog and digital pedals more convenient.

You couldn't call it a pedal, but Fender's tube reverb, in its original or reissued form, has always been considered one of the best spring reverb units around, and can be added at the front end of any amp (although this isn't ideal if your overdrive sound comes from a channel-switching OD preamp placed after the reverb – most people prefer the sound of reverbed overdrive rather than overdriven reverb). Other amp makers in the USA and the UK also offered standalone reverbs, and the 'How-To' tips in Chapter 5 will offer some advice on making the most of these types.

A spring reverb unit is really a small amplifier in itself, which sends the guitar signal through a tube circuit to a small output transformer (or through a transistorized circuit) and from there to one end of the springs in a spring can rather than to a speaker. This signal vibrates the springs, is picked up by a transducer at their opposite end, and from there is blended back with the dry signal by degrees determined by a 'depth' control, and sent on to the output (or the power tubes, if part of a guitar amp). As you can see, done like this it's a bulky effect, requiring at least a couple of transformers, two or three tube sockets and a spring can, but the circuit itself is fairly simple.

Digital reverbs, like their sibling digital delays, offer more power and a greater variety of settings. And in addition to doing some approximations of spring reverb sounds, digital units usually offer more 'lifelike' reverberation, as heard in anything from a small room to a large concert hall, if you want to add a synthesized 'natural' room sound to your signal rather than merely replicate the classic sproing of springs. A few pedals do this very well, but most such devices are rack units that are best used in an amp's FX loop, and are beyond the scope of this particular book.

FILTERING & EQ

A relatively simple manipulation or filtering of the frequency spectrum in which the guitar operates is capable of producing some of the most emotive effects heard in music. We know this category best in the form of the wah-wah pedal, raised to an art form by guitarists from Jimi Hendrix and Eric Clapton to Slash to Zakk Wylde. Filtering also gives us voltage-controlled envelope-follower auto-wah sounds. Down at the simpler end of the scale, plenty of guitarists seek the aid of an active tone control in the form of a graphic EQ.

Wah-Wah   [CD tracks 31-40]

Wah-wah pedals are often explained to us as being a tone control with a rocking pedal attached, but there's a lot more to it than that. In truth, the wah circuit is a sweepable peaking filter – a bandpass filter that creates a peak in the frequency response which the player can manually (should that be 'pedially'?) sweep up and down the frequency spectrum. When that peak is swept through the portion of the spectrum which contains the notes we are playing, it emphasizes those frequencies and produces the 'wah' sound we hear. The different amounts of resonance produced as this peak is swept also contributes to the characteristic sound of any given wah-wah pedal, and this is something that can vary considerably from model to model.

Because the wah-wah is dealing with guitar, its frequency spectrum usually runs from around 400Hz to about 2.2kHz. This is well within the range of the average sweepable midrange EQ control on a standard mixing desk, and a look at one of these can help you better understand the function of a wah-wah pedal. A common home-recording desk might have an EQ section with a mid frequency sweepable from say 100Hz to 8kHz. Set the Mid boost control to max (most wahs don't allow manual control over the extent to which the peak is boosted – it's preset in the circuit design), then find the range between 400Hz and 2.2kHz on the frequency sweep knob and twist this rapidly up and down between those levels while a friend vamps some guitar riffs through the channel. You should hear a dramatic emphasis when your frequency range hits that of the notes being played.

Of course the bandwidth in a mixing desk EQ control will doubtless be broader than that of the peak produced by most wah-wahs (perhaps 1.5 octaves), so the pedal's frequency emphasis should be more focused, and so more dramatic. Some wah-wahs offer control over this bandwidth – for instance Dunlop's Cry Baby 535Q and the Boss FW-3 Foot Wah.

The most revered wah-wahs of all time, the Vox Wah and Cry Baby of 1967 and 1968 – and Thomas Organ's Clyde McCoy Wah-Wah that preceded them by a year or so – achieve this with a circuit that consists of just a couple of transistors, a coil inductor, a few resistors, and a capacitor. And of

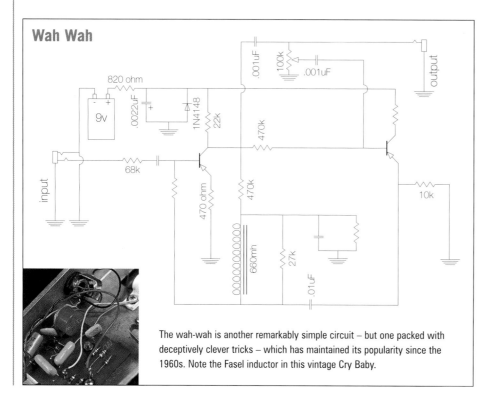

Wah Wah

The wah-wah is another remarkably simple circuit – but one packed with deceptively clever tricks – which has maintained its popularity since the 1960s. Note the Fasel inductor in this vintage Cry Baby.

course a potentiometer with a gear on its shaft so a rocker treadle can set it in motion. Seems like pretty simple stuff, and in principle it is, but there's plenty of magic and mystery associated with good wah-wah circuits, and it can take a lot of effort to get the things sounding just right.

Many players rave about early Italian-made Jen Vox Wahs with Fasel inductors in the circuit, and claim that nothing made after them has sounded as sweet or expressive. There are plenty of myths afloat in guitar gearsville, but some flaw in these early Fasel inductors – or basically just the fact that they were cheap – has been credited with enabling them to achieve asymmetrical clipping with some even-order harmonic content, as opposed to the spikier-sounding odd-order harmonics of other clipping inductors, and this could indeed be responsible for some of the magic. Dunlop has reissued a Cry Baby Classic wah-wah with a Fasel inductor, but this is apparently a new generation of Fasels and I have yet to hear whether they perform the same as the originals. Plenty of guitarists also flip for the silver metal 'trash-can' inductors found in early Cry Baby wahs.

Tweaking and tuning wahs is considered something of a black art, and a number of modifications exist – some user-installable – to help players make the most of both vintage and new models. Roger Mayer's name inevitably crops up in any in-depth discussion of wah-wah modification (yes, him again, but what can you do: the guy was a pioneer, he was in there at the start of transistorized effects, he worked with Hendrix, Jimmy Page, Ernie Isley, Stevie Wonder… and suffice to say he knows his stuff). When they worked in the studio together, Mayer would 'tune' Hendrix's wah-wahs to emphasize the key that the song was in, or tweak the frequency spectrum affected by the travel of the treadle. Today he offers the Red Lion Wah kit that fits into a standard Cry Baby pedal to allow a continually variable sweep.

Many vintage wah-wahs also have a less-than-ideal input impedance for use with guitar, and can be guilty of severe 'tone sucking,' so guitarists also modify them to eliminate this. Boutique maker Fulltone also offers wah-wah mods, and produces its own Clyde Wah clone of the original Thomas Organ Clyde McCoy wah-wah. (See the interview with Mayer towards the end of the book for more in-depth discussion of wahs, and the interview with Mike Fuller of Fulltone for further talk of inductor magic and the wah-wah circuit.)

While the Vox/Cry Baby wah remains the classic template, makers have offered a range of variations on both the circuit and the mechanical operation of the pedal. Morley had an occasionally popular wah in its imposing, chromed range of effects that used quiet photo-resistors instead of potentiometers for sweep control. Roger Mayer's Vision Wah (as we'll see later) is also a potentiometerless pedal, with a low-profile housing and a treadle positioned ergonomically for a more comfortable action while standing. And for pure wild inventiveness, it's hard to beat Z.Vex's Wah Probe, which uses a theremin-type antenna in the form of a copper plate mounted to the sloping front face of the pedal for totally contact-free wah action.

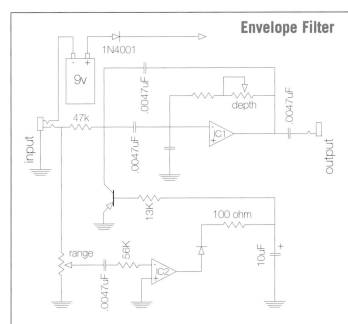

Envelope Filter

The envelope-follower (also called a voltage-controlled filter, or simply auto-wah – or in the case of this Boss pedal, Touch Wah) is the funky, attack-sensitive sibling of the traditional rocker-treadle wah-wah.

Auto-Wah

Of course the king of the treadleless wah-wah is the envelope-follower, voltage-controlled filter, or auto-wah. These effects contain a sweepable peaking filter much like that of the traditional wah-wah, but use the intensity of the incoming signal – in other words the guitarist's pick attack – to generate the control voltage that sends the peak up and down the frequency spectrum. With most such devices, pick lightly and the sound remains bassy and muted; hit the strings hard, and brighter wah-like frequencies leap out.

Musitronics's Mu-Tron III, introduced in 1972, was the first widely available envelope-follower, and remains one of the best-loved. Electro-Harmonix followed with a range of models such as the Doctor Q, Zipper, Bass Balls and Y Triggered Filter, and most major makers of the 1970s joined in.

While the treadle pedal is generally considered the rocker's wah (despite the disco-era's clichéd appropriation of the effect), the envelope-follower auto-wah is the archetypal funk machine. Think Parliament-Funkadelic, just about anything from bassist Bootsy Collins, or Stevie Wonder's 'Higher Ground' (a famous early use of a Clavinet through a Mu-Tron III). As a vocalist, George Clinton would seem to make an unlikely endorser of recent-era E-H's Tube Zipper envelope-follower/distortion pedal – until you consider the man simply oozes more funk than a warehouseful of Mu-Trons, 'mere' singer or not. Overall the effect is probably less expressive than a treadle wah – or, perhaps more accurately, offers less fine manual control over its expressiveness – but is more effective in certain circumstances. Something about the rhythmic way your natural pick attack can induce a pumping feeling in pulsating rhythm parts can often sound more natural than the methodical rocking of the typical disco-wah rhythm guitar part. Outside the realm of the funkateer, though, it's consigned mainly to the 'novelty' shelf.

Graphic EQ

The mini, guitar-pedal-sized equalizer is not an effect as such, but an inline active tone circuit. Still, lots of guitarists have made great use of graphic EQs over the years, so it would seem churlish to ignore it.

The technology behind these units doesn't need a lot of description. We could delve into the intricacies of circuit and design topologies here, but that could get boring fast. Suffice to say a graphic EQ pedal is a multi-band active tone control with sliders rather than rotary potentiometers for graph-style presentation of the equalization settings. The frequency bands assigned to the sliders are fixed, and tailored to be useful to the frequency spectrum in which the guitar operates, and the bands are logarithmically related to correspond to the way the human ear perceives frequencies. As such, they provide a simple, intuitive means of tweaking your tone settings.

Graphic EQs were surprisingly popular in the 1970s and 1980s (when, some would argue, too many new guitars and amps needed severe tweaking to sound decent). Players used them to cure ill-sounding frequency responses, tailor a rig for consistency in differing room acoustics, or provide a boost in specified frequencies for soloing. They were de rigueur on amps around the same time, creeping onto Mesa/ Boogies and other new makes, but when players chose one in pedal form they chose an MXR more often than anything else. The six-band model was the standard for guitar, but players with a chip on their shoulder sometimes insisted on the ten-band model (they usually had Flock-Of-Seagulls hair and secretly knew the guitar was dead, and synth would soon rule the known universe). All the usual suspects of course offered their own versions, so you find these from DOD, Boss, Ibanez, Electro-Harmonix and others.

If there's an unfriendly hump in your frequency response that you just can't find, are loosing bass or treble at the hands of a chain of tone-sucking pedals, or feel your own slice of sonic heaven could lie in a ten-band graphic EQ pattern that emulates the waves of the double-helix of baboon DNA, one of these pedals might be for you. If your guitar, pedalboard and amp are in good shape and well connected, with desirable impedance matches and reasonable cable lengths, and you haven't over-egged the signal chain pudding, you can probably live without a graphic EQ.

Chapter 3
VINTAGE BRANDS

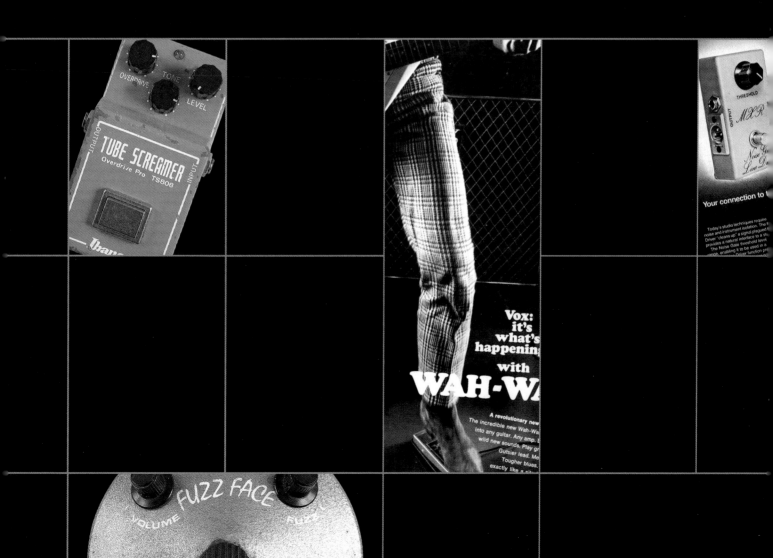

The notion of 'vintage effects pedals' is a relatively recent phenomenon. A fair number of electric and acoustic guitars were recognized as 'vintage' as little as a decade or so after their birth: for instance, pre-CBS Strats and Teles and late 1950s sunburst Gibson Les Paul 'Standards' were already hallowed instruments by the late 1960s, and pre-WWII Martin acoustics had been treasured by players for a lot longer than that. By the time many of the pedals we now consider classics were first hitting the market – hailed as the epitome of the new transistorized technology – specialist vintage guitar dealers were operating across the US, earning significantly higher-than-new prices for scruffy old guitars. Come the mid 1970s, many guitarists realized that the current run of Fender and Marshall amps didn't pack the punch of their tweed, blackface and plexi forerunners. So the vintage amp market was born. But effects? Other than the occasional pricey 1960s Uni-Vibe or some other exotic beast, that Electro-Harmonix Memory Man you bought for $150 in 1976 was probably up for sale in the classifieds for $50 in 1983 when it came time to upgrade to a new one-second digital delay.

Posterity usually learns to appreciate just about anything that proves top of its class, and everything from the Vox Wah-Wah to the Dallas-Arbiter Fuzz Face to the E-H Big Muff to the MXR Dyna Comp eventually attained its rightful place on the tone throne. But more than with guitars and amps, the 'eras' of the classic effects pedals are staggered through the decades – clusters appeared in the 1960s, the mid and late 1970s, the early 1980s and beyond and, I think it's fair to say, are making their way to guitar stores even now. Effects pedals have also arguably been subject more to the 'holy grail' syndrome than guitars and amps – thanks to the inconsistency of pioneering efforts in solid state electronics there are most definitely good'ns and bad'ns of the same make and model, and often they came off the work bench at the same time.

Two of the respected newer makers I interviewed for this book probably sum this up best. First, Zachary Vex recalls the situation when he was getting into the business in the early 1990s:

"People were pulling pedals from underneath their beds that had been there for a couple of decades, just to get the money, because the prices started going up so fast. We would be picking up $25 Thomas Organ Wah-Wahs, and $40 Fuzz Faces – everything was a bargain. Then we would go through them, and we'd sell them to each other to get rid of the ones we didn't like.

"The 'holy grail' at that time was to find one that sounded really great. The Fuzz Faces in particular were put together very slipshod – back then it was just a luck factor to any particular one sounding good. In the vintage and collectable market there's always going to be this holy grail aspect, because so many of the pieces just don't sound 'right,' while some of them sound magical."

Josh Fiden of Voodoo Lab adds this from the perspective of the contemporary effects designer:

"One of the nice things [about building pedals today] is that the tolerances of components have changed over the years. Once upon a time you bought a capacitor, and whatever the stated value, it could be 20 per cent less or 50 per cent greater, and that was considered to be 'in spec.' Now a normal part might have a five or ten per cent tolerance, so you get a lot better consistency. I think that's what happens with those older pedals, in conjunction with the ageing of parts. You get any two specimens and they go from A to Z – one'll sound great and the other will sound terrible."

Undoubtedly part of the fun of tracking down scratched, dusty old pedals is in finding the relatively rare examples that have 'the sound.' With that in mind, be aware that you are likely to encounter significant variations in performance of the models mentioned here. This book is not trying to advise on value or collectability as such – it's too broad a field, and of course values are constantly changing (many going up, but a few even coming down as the arrival of quality 'clones' from younger builders makes certain sounds available again in a new, reliable pedal.) The objective here is merely to point a finger toward some cool oldies, and to provide some specs, details and occasional brief histories.

While this chapter looks at many of the most desirable pedals in the 'classic' category, several of the makers of such classics are still operating today, so under their headings you will also find a wealth of information on newer and even current products. (Consider Boss, for example: the company continues to be one of the world's most popular effects makers, but it would be criminal not to list it as a 'classic' brand, too, for its original Chorus Ensemble and even a number of the early small-box pedals.) Purely contemporary – or at least latter-day – makes will be covered in Chapter 4.

The Sonics comments in the specification boxes aren't intended to be 'reviews' as such – just brief observations on sound types and qualities that each featured pedal provides, which hopefully go some way toward painting the sonic picture.

A/DA

California-based Analog Digital Associates is far and away best known for its Flanger, released as the company's debut product in 1977, but its Final Phase and large, ultra-rare Harmony Synthesizer are also highly regarded. Company founder David Tarnowsky had already designed an early flanger for Seamoon, but in launching his own product under the A/DA banner he set out to seriously improve the breed – and succeeded in spades.

Certain analog effects have proved their worth in the 'classics' category through the ironic twist of appearing on the menus of recent digital modeling amps and multi-FX units. A/DA's Flanger sits on the effects lists of Line 6 products such as the Veta amp and MM4 modulation modeler – and in fact it has been said time and again it's one of the few classic effects that these digi wonders don't perform convincingly (although you will have to let your own ears judge how convincingly any digital emulations emulate the real thing.) While not the very first compact transistorized flanger effect for guitar, most agree the A/DA is the sweetest and lushest of the genre, with an appealing, wide sweep range, and it's therefore probably the most desirable of vintage flangers.

Late-1970s advertisements for the A/DA Flanger called it "the most advanced flanger available today," and it was a fully justifiable claim. Among other features, promo copy also boasted about the pedal's "Even/Odd Harmonic emphasis switch" – certainly a distinguishing feature – and "An automatic sweep that varies between 0.1 to 25 seconds for a complete sweep cycle" – a far wider sweep than any rival pedals. It all came at a price, of course, and the unit retailed for around $200 in 1977, plus $40 if you wanted the Control Pedal A for manual sweep.

The Flanger was originally built with Reticon's SAD1024 'bucket brigade' chip, but later used the Matsushita MN3010. Because the two achieve slightly different sweep ranges, players encountering

---

A/DA Flanger
Made: 1977-1981, reissued c1990s.
Controls: Threshold, Manual, Range, Speed, Enhance; Even/Odd Harmonics switch; on/off stomp switch; single input and output, and jack for control pedal.
Sonics: a versatile and very musical flanger with a wide sweep cycle, adjustable for everything from subtle vibrato to jet-like swoosh to percussive metallic effects.

A/DA Final Phase
Made: 1978-1981, reissued c1990s.
Controls: Sweep Modulation, Sweep Rate, Range Control, Intensity, Overdrive; In/Out (on/off) and Overdrive stomp switches; single input and output, and jack for control pedal.
Sonics: a powerful ten-stage voltage-controlled phaser with steep notches and an almost flanger-like performance, plus added overdrive stage.

vintage models today might find slightly different sonic responses from unit to unit – although A/DA made small circuit changes to evolving versions to try to compensate and restore the impressive 35-to-1 sweep range of the first generation of Flangers. Despite its initial popularity, the original Flanger was discontinued in 1981 after a run of only four years. A reissue was offered in the 1990s.

The Final Phase, released early in 1978, was another serious box along the lines of many heavy-duty phasers of the day. It used a pulse modulator to control the sweep of ten-stages of phase shifting – powerful stuff compared to many of the smaller four-stage phasers available – and included a clipping diode circuit to generate its own distortion. The result of all this is a serious dose of swoosh, and a sound that almost approaches flanging. The Final Phase has also been reissued.

A/DA moved into rack effects in a big way in the 1980s, first analog and then digital, and later became pioneers in the programmable tube preamp market.

ARBITER
(including Dallas-Arbiter, Dallas, CBS-Arbiter)

The Arbiter Group Plc, founded and still run by Ivor Arbiter, remains among the UK's major musical instrument distributors, a position it has held – with occasional ups and downs – for more than four decades. The London-based company has handled brands like Fender, Gretsch, Guild, Vox, Ludwig, JBL and DigiTech (although Fender distribution for Europe has recently moved to Fender Europe), and has manufactured Sound City amplifiers, Hayman drums and other significant makes, often in partnership with Dallas Musical Instruments. Above and beyond any of this, Arbiter will be known to American guitarists mainly thanks to one smiling, round pedal: the Fuzz Face. While the Fuzz Face wasn't the first fuzz pedal to hit the scene, it has arguably enjoyed the most enduring reputation of all the fuzzes introduced in the 1960s.

Arbiter's first Fuzz Face arrived in the company's Sound City music shop in London in 1966, and was soon after picked up by one window-shopper, hanger-outer, and occasional customer by the name of Jimi Hendrix. And the rest – to give an abused cliché a justified outing for a change – is history. This hallowed fuzz went through a variety of minor changes, and a few major, but the best of the early designs sound stunning even by today's broad-eared standards. Yep, I say "the best of…" Vintage pedal collectors have long known that Fuzz Faces, even more than most old effects boxes, need to be carefully selected to sort the few great examples from the many middling units and occasional true duffers in the batch. It's an inconsistency that was with the unit from birth, and Hendrix and other early pro users famously sorted through dozens of pedals at a time to find the best sounding boxes (which, in Hendrix's case, were often further tweaked by Roger Mayer – and of course Hendrix used a variety of production and custom-built fuzzes and overdrives in the studio). Thanks to the wide tolerances in germanium transistors, the tonal heart of this fuzz, and an apparent lack of the will or ability to sort the good from the bad, the gorgeous and 'archetypal' sounding Faces occurred mainly by happy accident, when two relatively correct-value and gain-matched transistors just happened to land in the same pedal.

The guilty parties were the NKT275 transistors supplied by Newmarket (occasionally replaced with AC128s), but don't be too hard on them: for all their inconsistencies, these germanium components yielded a smooth, round, and harmonically pleasing fuzz that seems to be impossible to replicate with parts available today… as proved by the inability of any of the numerous reissues to equal it.

Original units made with NPN silicon transistors rather than PNP germanium are also very good sounding fuzzes (Eric Johnson favors a silicon-transistor Fuzz Face, and you know he tried a few before making his pick). Silicon components offer greater gain, but what some would call a harsher distortion, which certainly makes them suitable for some styles of playing. Aside from the composition of the transistors, original Arbiter Fuzz faces – despite appearing with various logos such as Arbiter-England,

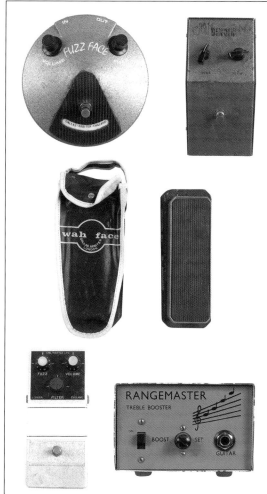

Dallas-Arbiter Fuzz Face [CD track 1]

Made: 1966 to mid 1970s; reissued 1980s, again 1990s to present.
Controls: Volume and Fuzz; stompswitch for on/off.
Sonics: a thick, crackling, saturated fuzz with good dynamics in the better examples.

Dallas-Arbiter Tone-Bender

Made: c1966-67.
Controls: Volume and Fuzz; stompswitch for on/off.
Sonics: a brutal, harsh, but effective fuzz.

Dallas-Arbiter Wah Face (pictured with carrying case)

Made: late 1960/early 1970s.
Controls: rocker treadle for wah-wah, hidden stompswitch for on/off.
Sonics: sweetly vocal, classic wah-wah sounds.

CBS-Arbiter Fuzz King

Made: early 1970s.
Controls: Volume, Tone, Fuzz; stompswitch for on/off.
Sonics: thick, menacing fuzz.

Dallas Rangemaster Treble Booster

Made: mid 1960s.
Controls: single Boost/volume knob, with slide switch for on/off.
Sonics: a treble-emphasizing single-germanium-transistor booster with a sweet, sparkling response, and the ability to drive a tube amp into distortion. Some noise and tone sucking apparent.

Dallas-Arbiter, Dallas Music Industries Ltd, and CBS/Arbiter Ltd between 1966 and around 1975 – shared the same simple circuit of two transistors, three capacitors and four resistors, selected with a sturdy metal DPDT stomp switch for 'true bypass.' Peak under the hood of a vintage unit and codes on the identical pair of transistors will tip you as to germanium or silicon: usually NKT275 or AC128 for the former, or BC108, BC109, BC183 or BC209 for the latter.

While the Fuzz Face was the company's most popular pedal of the day, and remains its most famous, Arbiter was responsible for many other wild and wonderful effects at the dawn of the transistor revolution – some admittedly dire, but others tonal gems. The 'Face' series of the late 1960s and early 1970s also carried pedals such as the Wah Face and Trem Face; the company marketed a vicious Fuzz King in the early 1970s and, like about half a dozen other British makers, offered its own version of the Tone-Bender for a time. (As a kid in the mid 1970s the author purchased an 'NOS' Trem Face from Swallens department store in Cincinnati, OH, for $10 new – they must have discovered a dusty crate of them at the back of a warehouse and been clearing them out cheap – but found the tone decidedly uninspiring. The unit burned out a few weeks later and, this being the height of Peter Frampton's success, was handed over to electronics whiz-kid pal Bob Keyes for conversion to a DIY talk box.)

The American company Crest Audio marketed a reissue of the Fuzz Face in the 1980s, and the Jim Dunlop company took over the brand toward the end of that decade and continues to sell the Fuzz Face today. It carries a later make of germanium transistor, but is constructionally and tonally a somewhat different device. Taking the famed fuzz box full circle, Arbiter also briefly offered its own reissue of the pedal around the turn of the millennium, a version designed with the help of British amp maker and Dallas-Arbiter designer of old, Denis Cornell.

Arbiter's some-time partner Dallas was also behind one of the rarest and most legendary early 'boosters' of all time, the Dallas Rangemaster Treble Booster – a box used by many a major 1960s British guitar slinger to kick his Vox, Marshall or Hiwatt into overdrive.

BOSS
(including Roland)

The Boss name originates in a single product offered by Roland in the late 1970s: The Boss B-100 belt-clip preamp with integral pickup for acoustic guitar. Japanese music electronics firm Roland, established in 1972 by Ikutaro Kakehashi, had already marketed a number of effects for guitar and other instruments, such as the large standalone Space Echo tape delays and RV-100 reverb, and pedals such as the Bee Gee and Bee Baa fuzzes, the AP-2 Phase II, and AS-1 Sustainer. But company heads clearly liked the ring of the shorter name (or were simply serious Springsteen fans), and shifted the pedal line to the Boss brand from around 1976 onward.

A transitional period in around 1975-76 saw now-archaic looking Boss and Roland pedals sharing a uniformity of esthetics in units such as the Roland Phase II and Jet Phaser, and the famous Boss Chorus Ensemble – all housed in large, baked-crackle-finish diecast steel casings. By 1977, however, the familiar small, plate-steel boxes with rubber-cushioned rectangular footswitch were the norm. The same housing design remains in use today, giving Boss pedals stronger direct ties to their roots than virtually any other non-reissue make.

The brand has the association of a mass-market name, yet more pro players than not are likely to be found carrying one or more Boss pedals on their boards. While the Boss name doesn't conjure the same romantic notions as many vintage discrete transistorized pedals of the 1960s or a number of current makes at the center of the 'boutique boom,' it has earned a well-deserved reputation for good sound (though, make no mistake, there is an enthusiastic Cult of Boss out there). Early units like the DS-1 Distortion, DM-3 Delay, DD-2 Digital Delay, CE-2 Chorus and SD-1 Super Overdrive – and others in a range that was broad and varied almost from the start – were instant hits. Even so, players don't discuss the fine points of opamp numbers and circuit evolutions of Boss pedals to quite the extent that they do, for example, Ibanez pedals, which originated at around the same time.

Boss's overdrives quickly earned a major following, including several top names. Although a 'browned out' Marshall half-stack is frequently credited as the center of the Van Halen tone, the godfather of the warp-speed rock hammer-on has used an SD-1 almost from the start to help push his soloing tone into overdrive. And while you might think widdle supremos like Joe Satriani and Steve Vai would employ esoteric handwired boutique pedals to generate their fluid, creamy, sustaining lead sounds, each is a long-time devotee of the DS-1 – Vai even chained a pair of the Boss distortions back-to-back on his pedal board. Arguably more archetypal than either of these, and another rockers' favorite, is the OD-1, a fierce yellow pedal with a razor-sharp treble lift to help you slice through the densest of stage mixes, and no shortage of chunky bottom. Its circuit has employed a number of opamps through the years, but like so many classics of the breed the best of the early units usually carry a JRC4558D chip. It also used a degree of asymmetrical clipping to fill out the sound. The OD-1 pictured in this chapter is a particularly early example, with the 'O' of OD appearing under the 'r' of Drive.

Heavier sounding pedals have joined the Boss ranks through the years to cater for the calcifying tonalities now known as the 'hard rock' or 'heavy metal' sounds. Relatively recent units like the MT-2

Roland AP-2 Phaser [CD track 84]

Made: mid 1970s.

Controls: Rate and Resonance; stompswitch for on/off.

Sonics: a rich, swirling phase with variable harmonic content according to Resonance setting.

Boss Chorus Ensemble CE-1

Made: 1976-1984.

Controls: Level, Chorus Intensity, Vibrato Depth and Rate; High/Low switch; power switch; electrical stomp switches (with metal mechanical appearance) for on/off and Vibrato/Chorus; single input, mono or stereo outputs.

Sonics: a spacious, full-frequency stereo chorus with lovely dimension and musical movement.

Boss Over Drive OD-1 [CD track 47]

Made: 1977-1985; this c1977; currently available as OD-3.

Controls: Level and Over Drive; electrical stompswitch for on/off.

Sonics: a thick and edgy rock overdrive sound fattened by asymmetrical clipping, with fierce, trebly tone lift.

Boss Distortion DS-1 [CD track 76]

Made: 1978-1989.

Controls: Level, Tone and Distortion; electrical stomp-switch for on/off.

Sonics: a sharp, edgy distortion – from light to heavy – which is nevertheless rich in body and has good retention of guitar character.

Boss Super Overdrive SD-1 [CD track 55]

Made: late 1970s to present.

Controls: Level, Tone and Drive; electrical stomp switch for on/off.

Sonics: a smooth yet slightly jagged asymmetrical, full-bodied, medium-gain overdrive with good overall frequency presentation; sounds its best driving a semi-cranked tube amp.

Boss Chorus CE-2 [CD track 24]

Made: 1979-1982; this c1979; closest current model CE-5 .

Controls: Rate and Depth; electrical stompswitch for on/off.

Sonics: a smooth, rounded mono chorus with good depth and lush musical voicing.

Boss Delay DM-2 [CD track 66]

Made: 1981-1984.

Controls: Repeat Rate, Intensity & Echo; electrical stompswitch on/off.

Sonics: a warm, soft mono analog delay with 'tape-like' repeats; capable of good reverb sounds, too, with delay times from 20ms-300ms.

Boss Vibrato VB-2 [CD track 62]

Made: 1982-1986.

Controls: Rate, Depth and Rise Time knobs, Mode switch for Latch/Bypass/Unlatch; electrical stompswitch for on/off.

Sonics: gentle pitch-modulated 'true vibrato' similar to that of some complex vintage units but, of more creative interest, temporary 'vibrato arm-like' effects for emphasis in Unlatch position, with variable rise time.

Boss Digital Delay DD-2 [CD track 68]

Made: 1983-1986.

Controls: E.Level, F.Back, D.Time knobs; Mode switch for maximum 50ms, 200ms or 800ms delay times; single input, mono or stereo outputs; electrical stompswitch for on/off.

Sonics: a warmer-than-usual stereo digital delay, with a good range of delay time options.

Boss Dimension C DC-2

Made: 1985-1989.

Controls: four pushbuttons, labeled 1, 2, 3, 4; electrical stompswitch for on/off; single input, mono or stereo outputs.

Sonics: adds a chorus-like depth and dimension with subtle movement.

Boss Super Distortion & Feedbacker DF-2 [CD track 74]

Made: 1984 to 1994; this c1984.

Controls: Level, Tone, Distortion and Feedback Overtone; electrical stompswitch for on/off.

Sonics: hi-gain, hard-clipping rock distortion unit with heavy crunch and good body, with additional sustained feedback effect produced on second pedal press.

Boss Digital Sampler/Delay DSD-2 [CD track 67]

Made: 1985-1986.

Controls: E.Level, F.Back and Delay Time knobs; Mode switch for 200ms or 800ms delay, Sampler Rec/Play, and Sampler Play Only; single output and input, with Trig.In for external trigger source; electrical stompswitch for on/off.

Sonics: a rich, well-textured digital delay without significant harshness or distortion on note decay, plus sampler function – with tricky external trigger capabilities.

  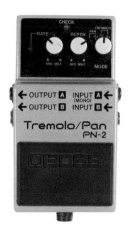 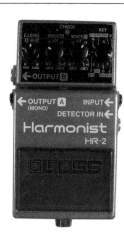

Boss Dynamic Filter FT-2

Made: 1986-1988.

Controls: Sensitivity, Cutoff Frequency, Q knobs; Mode switch for Dynamic Down/Up and Manual/Exp; input for expression pedal to use as standard wah-wah; electrical stompswitch for on/off.

Sonics: a versatile auto-wah with a broad range of tonal variations, plus traditional treadle-wah capabilities.

Boss Digital Dimension DC-3 [CD track 26]

Made: 1988-1993.

Controls: Effect Level, EQ, Rate and Depth; electrical stomp switch for on/off; single input, mono or stereo outputs.

Sonics: from gentle, almost tremolo-like movement to deep, ultra-wide chorus with lush soundstage.

Boss Tremolo/Pan PN-2 [CD track 61]

Made: 1990-1995.

Controls: Rate and Depth, with Mode switch for triangular or square wave in tremolo or pan; dual inputs and outputs; electrical stompswitch for on/off.

Sonics: good traditional tremolo sounds, from smooth to heavy chop, plus unusual bouncing stereo auto-pan effects.

Boss Harmonist HR-2

Made: 1994-1999.

Controls: E.Level (dual ganged pot for A & B), Voice A and Voice B interval select, Key select; guitar input, Detector input, stereo outputs; electrical stompswitch for on/off.

Sonics: selectable dual-pitch harmony sounds.

Metal Zone and MD-2 Mega Distortion each feature a multi-control EQ section for dialing in the requisite low-end girth and high end bite. And the rare, discontinued DF-2 Super Distortion Feedbacker is more far-out than either. Like the name implies, it offers to take care of two of the rocker's most pressing tasks in one box: stomp on the dual-operation footswitch once to engage its classic distortion; stomp it a second time – and hold – to sustain the note you are currently playing, and to coax it into a sweet, hovering harmonic feedback that, if you're lucky, will stay roughly in tune to the riff you carry on with. Potentially a very cool tool for the soloist. (The name later changed to Super Feedbacker & Distortion to avoid infringing on pickup manufacturer DiMarzio's copyright of the 'Super Distortion' name.)

Despite this wide range of distortion devices, Boss is arguably best known for its pioneering range of chorus pedals. As the chorus effect moved away from its roots as a four-stage phaser, Boss set the standard for compact, bucket-brigade analog pedals in the genre. Before this, Roland had pioneered the notion of stereo chorus in a big way, even putting out a large solid state guitar combo devoted to the effect, the JC-120 Jazz Chorus, and Boss took up the flag wholeheartedly. The early big-box CE-1, the industry standard CE-2 mono chorus that followed, the CE-3 stereo chorus, and the later CE-5 stereo Chorus Ensemble and CH-1 stereo Super Chorus hold places on any list of the most popular chorus pedals ever. And although they carried potentially deceptive names, pedals like the DC-2 Dimension C and DC-3 Digital Dimension further expand the chorus roster. Both operate in stereo, of course (hence the 'dimension'), and the former carries the unusual array of four preset pushbuttons – no potentiometers – to access varying degrees of width and depth, while the latter has controls much like a standard chorus. Both are intended to produce the spaciousness of a good stereo chorus, without the potentially nauseating wobble (Boss devotee Mike Fahey points out that with care you can push in two buttons at once on the DC-2 for some multi-chorus mayhem, bending the restrictive preset laws a little).

Down the years, the brand has also introduced more bizarre little sonic smelters than its businesslike image would sometimes imply. Some are unique creative tools, some mere wack-jobs and novelty boxes. The DF-2 discussed above certainly fits this category, as does the HR-2 Harmonist, which squashes many of the capabilities of a big, rack-mounted studio harmonizer into the usual little Boss box. This rare stereo pedal has a stacked (ganged) pot for Level for A and B outputs, Voice controls for each to set the harmony interval to anywhere from a third to an octave, and a Key control to set the effect for operation in any of the 12 major and/or seven common relative minor keys. It doesn't always track perfectly, but it's a powerful sound processor in a floor-friendly package. The contemporary PS-5 Super Shifter pitch shifter/harmonist performs related duties, but carries a Mode control to offer detuned, tremolo arm and flutter effects as well.

Even many of Boss's seemingly straightforward pedals often carry clever twists. The popular but long-deleted PN-2 Panning Tremolo offers good standard triangular or square wave tremolo, or a trippy stereo pan that bounces back and forth between your two-amp setup. The VB-2 Vibrato – one of the most desirable Boss collector pedals – produces pitch-warbling 'true vibrato' rather than mere tremolo that many misnamed pedals offer, but includes two cool twists: an 'Unlatch' mode which lets you trigger the effect to emphasize selected phrases by stepping on the footswitch without latching into constant-on mode, and a Rise Time control that lets you vary the time it takes for the full depth of the vibrato to creep into a sustained note or chord.

From the early 1980s Boss embraced the digital revolution, setting the standard for compact digital delays with pedals like popular DD-3, as well as using the technology to cram some awesome designs into these small, colorful boxes. The DSD-2 Digital Sampler Delay, which, I am told on good authority, is the rarest Boss pedal of all, carries a bizarre and virtually unusable 'external trigger' function in its sampler circuit. Turn the Mode knob to Rec/Play, record a phrase on the guitar, turn again to Play Only, and some time later in the song, gig or century you can trigger that phrase with a keyboard, drum machine, or whatever is plugged into the Trig.In input. Must have sounded amazing on the drawing board, but the live uses are obviously limited, and most studios will have a far more flexible and powerful sampler handy. Never mind. Its delay function (switchable between max delay times of 200ms and 800ms) is sweeter and richer than many digital delays.

Despite the wonders of ones and zeros, Boss hasn't forsaken the analog designs that are closest to many guitarists' hearts, and in fact offers more analog than digital effects in the compact pedal range promoted in the current catalog (the company is now up to *Guide Book Vol 17*). To date, company literature tells us, Boss has sold more than seven million pedals worldwide.

COLORSOUND
(including Sola Sound)
The mid 1960s certainly heralded the era of the fuzz. Hot on the heels of Maestro's revolutionary Fuzz-Tone in the USA came the Sola Sound Tone-Bender and Dallas-Arbiter Fuzz Face in the UK, and then a veritable flood of transistorized noise makers.

Brothers Larry and Joe Macari, proprietors of Macari's Musical Exchange in Denmark Street,

Colorsound Tone Bender Jumbo

Made: late 1960s.

Controls: Volume, Fuzz, Bass-Treble (tone); stompswitch for on/off.

Sonics: a brutal, harsh, razory fuzz capable of stamping its authority all over your tone.

Colorsound Jumbo ToneBender

Made: mid 1970s.

Controls: Volume, Fuzz, Tone; stompswitch for on/off.

Sonics: crunchy, muscular silicon-transistor fuzz tones.

Colorsound Sustain Module

Made: early to mid 1970s.

Controls: Sensitivity, Volume; stompswitch for on/off.

Sonics: a fuzzy-sounding sustainer with no shortage of tonal artefacts.

Colorsound Fuzz Phazer

Made: mid to late 1970s.

Controls: rocker treadle for phase rate, hidden stompswitch for on/off.

Sonics: harsh fuzz sounds plus basic phasing.

Colorsound Overdriver

Made: early to late 1970s.

Controls: Drive, Treble, Bass; stompswitch for on/off.

Sonics: a juicy, compressed overdrive sound bordering on true distortion.

Colorsound Supa ToneBender

Made: early 1970s.

Controls: Volume, Fuzz, Tone; stompswitch for on/off.

Sonics: fierce, crackling silicon-transistor fuzz sounds.

Colorsound Fuzz Wah Swell

Made: early 1970s.

Controls: treadle for wah, stompswitches for fuzz and wah/swell.

Sonics: smooth fuzz tones blended with a round, vocal wah-wah; straight volume pedal as desired.

Colorsound Supa Wah Fuzz Swell

Made: mid to late 1970s.

Controls: Tone, Fuzz & Level knobs, treadle, stompers.

Sonics: as per Fuzz Wah Swell, with more control, give or take a dollop of distortion and a wow of wah.

London (which today remains London's equivalent of New York's 48th Street), saw the tide coming. They commissioned former Vox engineer Gary Hurst to design them a fuzz pedal in 1965, and soon another slice of tone history was born. The Macaris continued to build Tone-Benders under the Sola Sound brand through five different evolutions (MkI, MkII, MkIII, etc), each generally with a differently shaped metal box and a change in legends, logos and colors, until around the end of the 1960s, when the Colorsound name was adopted. Through the late 1960s and into the 1970s they also manufactured a variety of fuzz pedals for other British instrument makers to rebadge as their own, so vintage pedals like the Vox Tone-Bender (second evolution), Marshall SupaFuzz, Barnes & Mullins Champion Fuzz Unit or Park Fuzz Sound are usually electrically identical to Sola Sound or Colorsound Tone-Benders of the same era. Casings and legends are often – though not always – different from brand to brand.

The Tone-Bender contained first two, then three Mullard-made germanium transistors in a basic circuit that is equally simple to that of the Fuzz Face and other fuzzes of the day. It's a somewhat jagged, heavy, brick-wall of a fuzz, without quite the warmth or tactile feel of a good germanium Fuzz Face. But it certainly made an impression on the first few rows of paying customers down at the Marquee on a Saturday night, and became a quick favorite of Jeff Beck and others.

In addition to variety in the early Sola Sound evolutions of the pedal, which saw the effect take on a third knob by the time of the MkIV – adding a Tone control to the Level and Attack (aka 'volume' and 'fuzz' or sometimes 'sustain') – Colorsound further expanded the range to include models like the Supa Tonebender and Tonebender Jumbo (the logos on these apparently losing their hyphen), as well as other effects such as the Overdrive, Fuzz Phazer (sic), Flanger, Sustain Module, Octivider, Ring Modulator, Fuzz Wah Swell, and Supa Fuzz Wah Swell (not just swell, but undoubtedly pretty nifty and neat-o too). All were flashy efforts on the part of the ever-creative Macaris, with blinding orange, yellow and purple boxes and 'whap-bam!' cartoon-style flash graphics. Fun stuff, and certainly destined to make an impact, both visually and sonically.

Competition from compact, modern-styled Japanese pedals dealt Colorsound a heavy blow in the late 1970s, and the company eventually folded in the early 1980s. Larry and Joe Macari's sons, Steve and Anthony, relaunched the brand in the 1990s, and they continue to offer reissues that capture a good portion of the visual vibe and sound of the originals.

A quick footnote on pronunciation: certain dialects of the London accent – and, for that matter, of the coastal north-eastern US – render the pronunciation of Sola Sound as 'solar sound.' You find the wordplay on other stylized British brand names of the era: it crops up again in the Colorsound Supa Tone-Bender and Marshall Supa Fuzz and Supa-Wah. 'Super,' geddit? Also, note that when the Macaris changed their brand name to Colorsound they used the American spelling, rather than the British 'colour.' Hoping for a stab at the US market?

DAN ARMSTRONG

American ex-pats Dan Armstrong and George Merriman began manufacturing their square little plug-in effects boxes in London in the early 1970s, and for a time were responsible for some of the most cost-effective and best-regarded compact units available to the guitarist. In the mid 1970s their units retailed for $29.95 each – pretty good value for such sweet sounding designs.

Dan Armstrong effects were sturdy, simple, and for the most part sounded great – although you couldn't call them 'pedals' as such, since each little metal cube plugged straight into the guitar. It's a format that had been used by others before them – Vox's range of Treble and Bass Boosters come readily to mind – but the defining feature was also their greatest drawback. Players of certain types of guitars, Strats especially, had to rig up adaptor cords to fit them into their recessed jacks, and usually just gave up altogether. Also they were difficult – if not impossible – to chain together in a multi-pedal set-up.

Finally, the effects' diminutive size, while nifty and streamlined on one hand, didn't allow for much more than a mini DPDT switch for on/off or mode toggling, and maybe an added trim pot at best, by way of controls. What you heard when you switched the thing on was pretty much what you got; fortunately, most Dan Armstrong effects sounded damn good, so they were pretty popular despite these ergonomic drawbacks. The boxes had no true bypass either, though, so even when switched off they depleted the guitar's high frequencies somewhat – a fact which is likely to put off the modern breed of tone hound.

Before bumping into transplanted electrician Merriman and launching this army of transistorized metal cubes, Armstrong had already made a name for himself as the designer of the see-through Dan Armstrong lucite guitar, marketed by Ampeg and played for a time by Keith Richards of the Rolling Stones. Armstrong's son Kent, interestingly, has made a major name for himself as a pickup designer and manufacturer.

Armstrong and Merriman's first product was the Green Ringer ring modulator, launched in 1973, and it was soon followed by others such as the Red Ranger (booster), Blue Clipper (distortion), Orange Squeezer (compressor), Yellow Humper (bass EQ), and Purple Peeker (guitar EQ). All were originally made in the UK, but were also manufactured by Mu-Tron in the USA from the mid 1970s.

Each model had its fans, but the Orange Squeezer is probably the best-loved of the bunch, and the one that turns up on the most pros' gear lists. British Stratocaster-picking fingerstylist Mark Knopfler was a user in the early days of Dire Straits, as was – and purportedly still is – studio ace Jay Graydon. His much-raved-about guitar solo on Steely Dan's late-1970s hit 'Peg' from the *Aja* album – using a Gibson ES-335 into an Orange Squeezer into a Rivera-modified Fender Deluxe Reverb – provides a classic example of the unit's ability to add squash and sustain to a guitar's signal without stamping all over its characteristic tone.

The large guitar parts supplier WD Music Products Inc now manufactures and sells a line of similarly styled effects boxes under the same model names, but they have been designed without the input of Armstrong himself and apparently are not sonically identical to the originals.

DOD
(including Digitech)

The pedals' looks and designs has often found them lumped in with classic Japanese makes of the late 1970s and early 1980s like Boss and Ibanez, but DOD originated in Salt Lake City, Utah, and has manufactured pedals in the USA since the mid 1970s. The earliest range, identified by a straightforward name/number system, looked much like rectangular MXR-style boxes but with a contoured front edge and more graphic styling (just), and included what might be the one unarguable DOD 'classic,' the Overdrive Preamp 250. The line-up also included the Phasor 201, FET Preamp 210, Compressor 280, Phasor 401, Studio Bifet Preamp 410, Envelope Filter 440, Mini-Chorus 460, Phasor 490, Flanger 670, Analog Delay 680, and Chorus 690.

These units vanished with the introduction of the Performer range of 1981, which was in turn quickly replaced by the FX range – which is still with us today, in spirit if not always in circuit. Only a few of the original FX models remain in precisely their same shapes nowadays, but the intention of many designs has been retained, with plenty of updates for 'the new music.' Popular pedals of the 1980s and 1990s included Stereo Chorus models FX60 and FX65, Phasor FX20 and Stereo Phasor FX20B, Analog Delays FX90 and FX96, Super Distortion FX55, American Metal FX56, Stereo Flanger FX75 and others. Today's offerings include the Milk Box FX84 compressor, Ice Box FX64 stereo chorus, Stereo Phaser FX20, Flashback Fuzz, FX86 Death Metal distortion, FX69 Grunge distortion, FX75C Stereo Flanger FX66, Vibro Thang FX22, Mystic Blues FX102 overdrive, Equalizer FX40B and Envelope Filter FX25B. Lacking at the time of writing, it appears, are an analog or digital delay, but the company has reissued the classic yellow Overdrive 250.

Under the name of DOD/DigiTech, the company was also one of the more prominent pioneers of

DOD Stereo Chorus FX65 [CD track 21]
Made: circa late 1980s/early 1990s.
Controls: Speed, Delay Time, Depth; electronic stompswitch for on/off; stereo outputs.
Sonics: lush, swirly analog chorus in stereo.

DOD Analog Delay FX96
Made: 1990s.
Controls: Dry/Tape Mix, Delay Time, Regen/Repeat, Tape Quality; electronic stompswitch for on/off.
Sonics: rich analog tape simulation with delay times of up to 800ms; good 'ageing tape' treble-loss simulation from Tape Quality control.

DOD Digital Delay DFX9
Made: circa late 1980s/early 1990s.
Controls: Level, Repeat, Delay and Range/Mode knobs; stompswitch for on/off.
Sonics: from slapback to long delays, with 'infinite repeat' option.

DOD Grunge FX69
Made: 1990s to present.
Controls: Loud, Low, High, Grunge; electronic stompswitch for on/off.
Sonics: fat crunchy distortion with portly low-end response.

DOD Flashback Fuzz FX66
Made: 1990s to present.
Controls: Volume, Low, Tone, Fuzz; electronic stompswitch for on/off.
Sonics: from punchy, crunchy overdrive at low settings to juicy, saturated fuzz with some harsh high-frequency overtones when the knob is cranked up.

DOD Vibro Thang FX22 (not pictured)
Made: 1990s to present.
Controls: Speed, Depth, Doppler and Image; stompswitch for on/off.
Sonics: modulation unit creating vibrato, rotating speaker and vintage-style phasing effects; some depletion of high-frequencies.

pedal-sized digital effects in the early 1980s. Digital Delay models PDS1000 and PDS2000 offered a then-impressive one and two seconds of delay time respectively, and had cool sample/loop facilities in addition to the straightforward echo functions. These were accompanied by the PDS3000 Pedal Verb and a small range of rack-mounted delays, and toward the mid and late 1980s the DigiTech brand concentrated on the burgeoning market for multi-FX units. Eventually DOD and DigiTech went down different paths, and the two are now separate companies.

Though DigiTech has become better known for its multi-FX units, some of its standalone pedals are also considered 'modern classics.' The DigiTech Whammy pedal – in either its WH-1 or XP100 forms – is probably the best loved of these. It uses digital technology to achieve a pedal-controlled divebombing 'vibrato bar' effect that would be difficult if not impossible to get with analog technology (certainly in this compact a form), and has turned up on the pedalboards of Tom Morello, Joe Satriani, Joe Perry, Munky and Head from Korn, and plenty of others.

ELECTRO-HARMONIX

With its roots in the late 1960s and a current line of pedals that is rapidly seeking to outgun the company's numerous wild and wonderful originals, Electro-Harmonix has seen the light of five decades under the control of one man, founder Mike Matthews. Despite a hiccup that saw the brand's disappearance for more than five years, there's got to be a record in there somewhere. Electro-Harmonix (usually 'E-H' from here out) is undoubtedly one of the big cheeses of transistorized wackiness, and perpetrator of an impressive number of sonic marvels besides, including claims to putting the first delay and flanging pedal effects on the market in the mid 1970s.

Brooklyn-born Matthews earned degrees in business and electrical engineering from Cornell University, but first entered into manufacturing guitar effects as a sideline intended to fund his rock'n'roll dreams. Perhaps surprisingly, Matthews was an experienced rock and R&B keyboard player – not a guitarist – and had once even been asked to tour with the Isley Brothers. While working a 'straight' job at IBM in the mid 1960s, he sought to jump on the fuzz box craze by commissioning a contract house to build a run of fuzzes that he could sell to earn a quick hit of cash that would allow him to ditch the coat-and-tie world and try to make it with his band. Guild Guitars bought out the entire run and marketed the unit as its Foxy Lady fuzz pedal, and Matthews moved on to the next quick money maker: a distortion-free sustainer. The idea would not be realized at this time, but the road to creating it led him to stumble on a little wonder of a box that would pave the way for founding the Electro-Harmonix company. As he tells it:

"I asked one of my buddies if he knew a guy who could design this thing for me, and he said, 'Yeah, I know this guy named Bob Meyer, out at Bell Labs.' So I contacted Bob, and he started working on designing this distortion-free sustainer. Then one of the times I went out there to check out the prototype, plugged in in front of it was this little box. I says, 'What's this?' And he says, 'Well, when I designed it I didn't take into account that the guitar pickup put out a lower signal than I had anticipated, so I just put in a little booster there.'

"I plucked the guitar, then I put on the switch on the booster, and all of a sudden the amp was loud as hell. I thought, 'This is really cool.' And that became my first product, the LPB1 Linear Power Booster. In those days, all amps were over-designed with a lot of headroom… But with the LPB1, you could get a hell of a lot more volume, and if you started turning it up you could start to overdrive the amp. That was our first product, and I started to make them while I was at IBM. Then I quit IBM, and that was a big hit product. We sold hundreds of thousands of them, because it really did something and it was really cheap." (See the full interview with Mike Matthews in Chapter 6 for a more detailed account of the Electro-Harmonix story in his own words.)

Electro-Harmonix Big Muff Pi

Made: 1970-1984, reissued 1990.
Controls: Volume, Tone, Sustain.
Sonics: a smooth, thick fuzz tone with excellent sustain; opaque and occasionally woolly, but plenty dynamic with it.

Electro-Harmonix Little Big Muff Pi

Made: early to late 1970s
Controls: single Volume knob plus Tone switch; stompswitch for on/off.
Sonics: a less versatile version of its big brother's fuzz, preset to maximum sustain.

Electro-Harmonix Small Stone

Made: early 1970s to early 1980s; reissued early 1990s.
Controls: Rate knob, Color switch.
Sonics: warm, rich, watery phasing that steers clear of nauseating extremes.

Electro-Harmonix Bad Stone (mid 1970s)

Made: early 1970s to early 1980s.
Controls: Rate and Blend knobs and Color switch on early models; later Rate, Feedback and Manual Shift.
Sonics: phasing variable from a subtle swoosh to a pounding, strident peak.

Electro-Harmonix Deluxe Electric Mistress

Made: 1976-1984, Deluxe reissued c2000
Controls: Rate, Range and Color knobs; Filter Matrix switch; stompswitch for on/off.
Sonics: a musical, harmonically rich flanger when used subtly, capable of notchy extremes and severe oscillation when abused (intentionally or otherwise).

Electro-Harmonix Deluxe Memory Man

Made: late 1970s to early 1980s; reissued c2000.
Controls: Level, Blend, Feedback and Delay, plus Chorus/Vibrato control on five-knob version; former has Squelch switch, latter Chorus/Vibrato switch.
Sonics: a full-sounding, organic analog echo, with rich chorus or vibrato as desired. (NB: Original ads claim "15ms to 4 seconds of delay," although the reissue states "up to 550ms.")

Electro-Harmonix Small Clone

Made: this reissue c2000; originally late 1970s to early 1980s.
Controls: Rate knob and Depth switch.
Sonics: a soothing, fluid chorus; known for Kurt Cobain's guitar sound on the *Nevermind* album.

Matthews founded E-H in 1968, and introduced the LPB1 at that year's *NAMM (North American Music Merchants)* show. The little one-transistor box that plugged straight into a guitar and blasted your amp's front-end gain all to hell and back was an instant hit, and it was onward and upward for the new company – for the next 15 years or so at least.

Most guitarists will know E-H best for its Big Muff Pi, a fat, fully saturated-sounding fuzz box with truckloads of sustain which hit the market in 1970. (Although it's often documented that the pedal was released in 1971, Matthews says a former Manny's salesman reported that Jimi Hendrix bought a Big Muff at the popular NY music store, and he later saw the guitar legend using the pedal in the studio – meaning, if this is true, that its release predated Hendrix's death in August, 1970). The rare first-run Big Muff started life as a slightly smaller pedal than the more familiar larger-box versions that follow it. Referred to by collectors as the 'triangular knob' version because its center control sat a level above the outside two, it is also considered by many to be

the sweetest sounding – although relatively few players have had the opportunity to sample its charms compared to those of later versions. It contained an entirely discrete transistorized circuit, generating its fuzzing and boosting powers from four transistors, all governed by controls for Volume, Tone and Sustain. E-H promos of the 1970s claimed the Big Muff was "high on sustain, low on distortion." Were they listening to their own pedal? It's a smooth fuzz, sure, but don't ever doubt that it ladles the sonic artefacts on good and heavy, and naming its fuzz/drive control 'Sustain' doesn't change that one bit. Still, the all-day sustain generated by the high-gain circuit was a popular feature, and Carlos Santana used the pedal to generate his own famous singing, sustaining tone, until a certain little Mesa/Boogie amp came along (Matthews says Santana bought the pedal from him by mail-order in 1970 or 1971, using a Santana company check).

Further evolutions through the 'straight knob' versions of the mid and late 1970s also retained discrete circuits, although there were some minor changes in design and components. A final evolution of the standard Big Muff pedal in the early 1980s was built around an opamp-based circuit, and that one is considered by most to be inferior to any of the discrete transistorized units.

The Big Muff was a hugely popular fuzz in its own right, but E-H milked the line with a broad range of variations on the theme. The Little Muff and Little Big Muff were trimmed-down versions of the original, while the Muff Fuzz was an ultra-simple, compact fuzz box that plugged straight into either your guitar or your amp. King of the heap, the AC-powered Deluxe Big Muff carried a compressor for added squash and sustain – essentially the Soul Preacher circuit – which could be switched between series and parallel signal paths with the fuzz section in some units, or mixed in with a Blend control in others.

You'd think the Big Muff was E-H's most popular pedal, but apparently the Small Stone phase shifter outsold the fuzz, with the Electric Mistress flanger ranking third and the Memory Man echo fourth behind that. The Small Stone, with its Rate control and Color switch, was an affordable and sweet sounding phaser that landed at the front edge of the boom in the effect's popularity in the mid 1970s. It filled a gap left by the larger, more deluxe units (including E-H's own three-knob Bad Stone) and

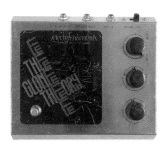

Electro-Harmonix Polyphase

Made: late 1970s to early 1980s.

Controls: Feedback, Speed, Env-Mod, Mod-Speed and Env-Sensitivity knobs; Sweep/Env Mode switch; stompswitch for on/off.

Sonics: versatile and potentially severe multi-stage phasing, though perhaps not as universally appealing as the simple Small Stone.

Electro-Harmonix Doctor Q

Made: mid 1970s (seen here) to early 1980s. Reissued c2001

Controls: unmarked 'depth/sensitivity' knob and Bass switch.

Sonics: round, funky, touch-sensitive auto-wah/envelope-follower sounds.

Electro-Harmonix Clone Theory   [CD track 80]

Made: late 1970s to early 1980s.

Controls: Chorus/Vib, Rate and Depth knobs; Edge switch.

Sonics: a transistorized effort at the Uni-Vibe chorus/vibrato sound, with decent – but sometimes noisy – results.

Electro-Harmonix Full Double Tracking Effect

Made: late 1970s to early 1980s.

Controls: Blend knob, 50/100 ms Delay switch, stompswitch.

Sonics: like it says on the box, a short 'doubling' delay.

Electro-Harmonix Attack Decay

Made: circa mid 1970s.

Controls: Sensitivity, Mix, Attack, Decay and Harmonics knobs; Edge switch; stompswitch for on/off.

Sonics: severe compression/attack-ducking and 'backwards' effects.

Electro-Harmonix Ten-Band Graphic EQ

Made: mid to late 1970s.

Controls: ten sliders for EQ band boost/cut, plus on/off footswitch.

Sonics: active graphic equalization, plus the on/off stompswitch strangely missing from most other makes.

Electro-Harmonix Crying Tone Wah

Made: circa mid 1970s.

Controls: stomp on/off switch, four-position Tone switch, and Reverse switch.

Sonics: variable and broad-voiced traditional wah-wah, plus reverse 'aaw-aaw' sounds.

compact but more expensive MXRs, and at one stage E-H was shipping as many as 8,000 Small Stones a month. The Color switch toggled between a warm, liquid burble and an edgier, more shimmering swoosh; both modes sounded great, and the unit landed on records too numerous to count – or too difficult to accurately track, given its approximate sonic similarity to MXR Phase 45s and Phase 90s and plenty of others, once all the variables of the recording environment are considered. Suffice to say Matthews sold a boatload, and you've probably got one of them.

It was sometimes noisy, possessed some freakish and virtually unusable extremes of operation, and cost as much as a used Pinto with a bald spare, but the Electric Mistress Flanger/Filter Matrix stirred up a serious cloud of freak dust when it landed in around 1976, and spawned more than its share of bad, dope-addled guitar experiments – and a few divine moments besides. The racily named pedal perhaps lacked the added features and 'studio standard' reputation of the A/DA Flanger, but had a crispy, sparkling harmonic response that won it many fans, and a trippy musicality that perhaps better suited some more adventurous-natured guitarists of the day. Also, switching to manually tuned filter matrix allowed you to get your guitar sounding like anything from a tuba down a well to a kazoo in a fishbowl. Unsurprisingly, few players use the feature after that first experimental afternoon.

You really can't say enough about the Memory Man. In an age when other echo units were either unwieldy, expensive, or prone to breakdown – and often all three – it hopped modestly onto studio, stage and practice room floors and completely revolutionized our accessibility to heavenly delay effects. The third-evolution Stereo Echo/Chorus (not the Deluxe, with an echo output and dry output) offered a spacey, ethereal sound between a pair of amps, and an extremely sweet, chewy chorus to boot. And hey, bend a note, drop to your knees, and

"Well Done, Doctor Q."

"By Jove, justice has triumphed again! The resourceful scientists at ELECTRO-HARMONIX have done quite a piece of brilliant work. Without even lurking about in the rain and fog, DOCTOR Q has cut through a seemingly impenetrable maze of clues, and cracked the ring of sinister, greedy villains who have been extorting vast sums of money from needy musicians by forcing them to pay artificially high prices for Envelope Followers (sometimes known under various other sundry aliases). Well done, DOCTOR Q ..."

The new DOCTOR Q from ELECTRO-HARMONIX is a rugged, high quality Envelope Follower with bass equalization and AC/DC operation at a fraction of the cost of other units.

Effects ranging from involuted mellow funk lines to slashing thin chops can be instantaneously and

sensitively controlled through the player's use of attack and decay dynamics. The range of the filter can be preset. And as an added feature,

the bass switch can be used to add a rich bass equalization without losing the thin, whipping Envelope Follower sound on top. This makes the unit excellent for getting potent new sounds from the electric bass, as well as guitar and other amplified instruments.

The DOCTOR Q Envelope Follower is a state-of-the-art, high efficiency unit which represents a significant breakthrough in performance and price. List price is $49.95, but check your local stores. Many of them have the DOCTOR Q on special sale now for less than $39.95. Good show.

To hear the new DOCTOR Q, call (212) 242-7799. Dealer inquiries invited.

electro-harmonix
27 West 23rd Street New York, N.Y. 10010

©1976 Electro-Harmonix, Inc.

twiddle the delay knob to induce mind-melding ray-gun effects that could simultaneously transfix a bewildered audience and send creeping shivers of envy up the spine of that guy playing the monophonic synth at the back of the stage. Most versions were warm, blooming, full voiced echoes – despite a little noise, especially when set toward max delay times – which together ushered in a whole new age of delay for the masses. Never mind that it only offered a maximum 320ms delay time (550ms on the Deluxe that followed). In 1977, that shy third of a second took you to the moon and back. For a time, the pedal was any hip guitarist's must-have; without one, life was merely 2-D.

If these represented the handful of E-H top sellers, there were plenty of worthy 'also-rans' besides. The company brought out so many outrageous and fabulous pedals and related products in the 1970s and early 1980s that Matthews will tell you he can't even recall the existence of a good many of them, much less what they sounded like.

Others that hit the mark included the Small Clone chorus, Zipper and Doctor Q envelope followers, Soul Preacher compressor sustainer, Hot Tubes overdrive, Clone Theory chorus/vibrato, Slapback echo, Screaming Bird and Screaming Tree treble boosters, Mole Bass booster, Octave Multiplexer, Black Finger sustainer, Bass Balls envelope follower, Y-Triggered Filter, Polychorus, Full Double-Tracking Effect, Echoflanger, the 16-Second Digital Delay, and a couple beer crates full of others.

Of equal interest to collectors are the many freakshow efforts that one or another E-H designer over the years briefly hoped might revolutionize the guitar world... and didn't. Any or all of these might occasionally have contributed to some radical experimentalist's ascension to sonic enlightenment, but a distinct lack of sales – and, consequently, their rarity today – tells us they didn't set the guitar world on fire. From their names alone, you know the Pulsar, Knockout Attack Equalizer, Random Tone Generator, Frequency Analyzer, and Micro Synthesizer aim to do something radical to your sound (although, in

their defence, the latter two have recently been reissued, while the first was mainly an exotically named tremolo). To the degree that these over-delivered in aural attack, plenty of their exotically named siblings under-delivered in erotic fulfilment. The Soul Kiss orally triggered wah, Golden Throat mouth tube, and Ambitron exciter could be disappointingly cold company on a lonely Saturday night. And the Big Muff Pi? I'm not even going to go that road, much less probe the thinking behind the Electric Mistress.

The majority of E-H's treadle-pedal designs were marginal effects, too – but they included some unmissably big mutha boxes. Were they really all wearing size 14 shoes in New York City in 1974? Or maybe it was so you could see the pedal past your flares.

The Crying Tone Wah and Muff Fuzz Crying Tone Wah were straightforward enough, and the slightly bizarre Queen Triggered Wah could induce some pretty cool sounds, but the startling Talking Pedal – developed "from advanced research in speech synthesis," apparently – sounds like a wah-wah gone postal right from the start. As for ease of use, an E-H promo tells us that "its critically-tuned resonant filtering of instrument input creates the continuous vowel series 'A-E-I-O-U' at given positions on the pedal sweep." Abuse it just right and I bet it coughs up 'sometimes Y,' too.

Still, none of the above are as musically pointless as the likes of the 3 Phase Liner electronic necklace, the gas-filled Corono Concert 'light show' ball, or the sound-sensitive Domino Theory light tube. Don't ask.

Even the wackiest of these noise makers serves to prove the rule of thumb for Electro-Harmonix design, and the world is probably a jollier place with than without them. As Matthews himself puts it: "My philosophy has always been to leave in as much sound and variety as possible, and always go right to the edge of the effect. And what I mean by that is, like, the Japanese, they'll filter off the noise, compand it and whatever, but when you do that you start to lose dynamics, you start to lose effect.

"I would always leave in the noise if I would lose feeling by taking it out. Of course I didn't like noise, but an effect was an effect, and music is a thing of feeling. Sometimes you'd turn a control up and you'd see that it would begin to oscillate – but sometimes right at the edge of oscillation there are some interesting effects."

All of E-H's more popular pedals evolved through several incarnations, adopting circuit and component changes, revamped graphics, and sometimes new and improved housings. Tracking the changes would warrant a book in itself, and as with most makes, aficionados will point to the most

Electro-Harmonix Volume Pedal (late 1970s)

Made: c1970s

Controls: rocker treadle for volume swell.

Sonics: whatever you put into it, and less.

Electro-Harmonix Talking Pedal

Made: mid to late 1970s.

Controls: Sustain knob and rocker treadle for 'vocal' sounds; hidden stompswitch for on/off.

Sonics: vowel-like 'a-e-i-o-u' frequency notches determined by the pedal position, plus a cut-down version of the Big Muff fuzz sound when selected.

Electro-Harmonix Mini Q-Tron

Made: 2001 to present.

Controls: Drive (filter width), Q and Mode.

Sonics: a versatile auto-wah/envelope-follower with variable filter sweep and Mode settings for low pass, band pass and high pass.

Electro-Harmonix Holy Grail

Made: 2002 to present.

Controls: Reverb depth knob, Spring/Hall/Flerb mode switch.

Sonics: good-sounding and relatively transparent digital simulations of spring and hall reverbs, plus 'flerb' – a preset flange/reverb blend.

Electro-Harmonix Black Finger

Made: 2002 to present.

Controls: Compress, Pre-Gain and Post-Gain knobs; switches for Norm/Sqsh and Lamp/LED knobs; stompswitch for on/off.

Sonics: Smooth, relatively transparent studio-style tube opto compression.

desired and respected versions of many models. As often as not, these are among the earlier designs of each type – but any notions of tonal superiority are inevitably boosted by sentimentality and the vintage patina of age.

The Electro-Harmonix company was dealt a major blow by externally-driven efforts at unionization which began in 1978 and continued again more heavy-handedly in the early 1980s. Matthews and his employees weathered some notoriously aggressive tactics on the part of the would-be organizers (much of it documented on local TV news broadcasts), but in early 1982 the strain eventually led the company – for a time the US's biggest guitar effects manufacturer – to file for bankruptcy. Matthews found the financial support to buy back his assets just a couple months after the closure, and had E-H up and running for another year and a half, until the Japanese competition dealt its death blow in 1984. Business was good, orders were rolling in by the thousands, but a Japanese component supplier reneged

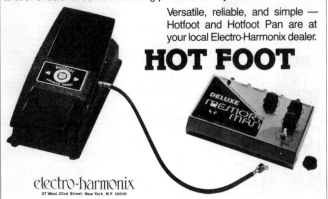
on a purchase order and held back a vital shipment of chips for use in domestic production by E-H rivals. The inability to roll out the stock pulled the rug from under the seemingly revitalized company.

Mike Matthews' adventures in Russian tube manufacturing in the 1980s, under the Sovtek name eventually led to the gradual reintroduction of Electro-Harmonix pedals in 1990. An industrial-looking green-metal Big Muff Pi was followed by a likewise Russian-made Small Stone phaser and Bass Balls twin dynamic filter. New York-made pedals followed in the late 1990s, and E-H has gradually ramped up to production levels on a par with its mid-1970s heyday.

The three Russian pedals are still available, and the US-made line now includes reissues of the Big Muff Pi, Small Stone, Bass Balls, Small Clone, Doctor Q, Deluxe Electric Mistress, Stereo and Deluxe Memory Man, Poly Chorus, Frequency Analyzer, Octave Multiplexer, Micro Synthesizer (guitar and bass versions), and Graphic Fuzz. The company also has new offerings in a range of Q-Tron envelope filters (designed by Mu-Tron III inventor Mike Beigel, and the first totally new E-H design for 15 years), The Worm modulation multi-effects pedal, Holy Grail and Holier Grail digital reverbs, and a pioneering range of tube-powered pedals like the Hot Tubes, Tube Zipper, Wiggler, Black Finger, and LPB 2ube.

Considering Matthews' willingness as a sonic adventurer – and proven knack for hiring cutting-edge designers – these are pretty unlikely to be the last of the newcomers, too.

FENDER

Like every major American guitar and amp manufacturer, Fender marketed its fair share of effects in the Fifties, Sixties, and Seventies – some made by the company, some bought in from other sources. The passive volume pedal, an essential tool for many lap steel players, was one of the first widely used 'effects' (if you can call it such), and many manufacturers offered a version as early as the late 1930s, with Fender following suit in the late 1940s. The first unit in the catalogs was a DeArmond-made pedal, but Fender launched its own version in 1954, and a more complicated Tone & Volume Foot Pedal Control, with side-to-side tone control and rocker volume control, followed shortly after.

The first proper sound-effecting device offered by Fender – other than onboard amp tremolo – was the EccoFonic tape-loop echo unit manufactured by an outside supplier and listed in Fender catalogs of 1958-59. Whether or not the name was intended to ape that of Ray Butts's Echosonic Amp (with its popular built-in echo), as used by Scotty Moore, Chet Atkins and others, the effect landed at the right time to capitalize on a late-1950s craze for the sound. So much so, it would seem, that the manufacturer decided to market the unit for itself in 1959, and the EccoFonic dropped from Fender literature. Apparently they didn't do a great job of it, and this early example of the tube-powered tape echo vanished without trace in the early 1960s.

Fender launched its own solid-state Electronic Echo Chamber tape echo in 1963 and made the unit until 1968, but it was never much of a rival for the Echoplex and other popular versions. The short-lived Soundette echo unit, which used a spinning magnetic drum instead of tape – manufactured by Arbiter Electronics in the UK – joined it around 1967, and vanished by the end of 1968.

Fender's most famous effect, though far from a pedal, is its Reverb Unit, seen as a prototype in 1961 but not widely available until 1962. Gibson, Premier and a few others had included reverb both in amps and external units before Fender first built the effect, but Leo's version would be regarded by most guitarists as the king of sproingsville from the early 1960s onward, whether onboard or separate. The Unit was a three-tube-powered spring reverb with controls labeled Dwell, Mixer and Tone: the first tapped the signal from the 12AT7 preamp tube to send it along to the 6K6 output tube and in turn to the small output transformer (OT) that drove the spring pan much like a guitar amp's OT drives a speaker (the 6K6 is related to the 6V6 output tube, which in fact is used in the reissued 'Tube Reverb'). As such, Dwell sets a rough delay time for the reverb sound, while Mixer, naturally, blends the effected and dry signals; Tone adds highs to the effected sound only.

In this form it's a rich, deep, ethereal effect, equalled in few amps and bettered in fewer still. Originals command big money on the vintage market, and a number of boutique versions have sprung up over the years. Fender's own Reissue '63 Fender Reverb, available since 1994, captures much of the sound, and makes this effect relatively more affordable again.

In genuine pedal territory, Fender doesn't have a lot to offer, but among its few contenders lurk a couple of doozies. A Fuzz-Wah hit the scene in 1968, briefly in prototype as a side-to-side action pedal like the early Volume Pedal but thereafter sold as a traditional treadle-rocker pedal. Both versions had odd and precarious side-mounted stomp switches (or, on occasions, 'stomp them right off' switches) to trigger fuzz and wah effects. The unit doesn't seem to have made a lasting impression on many guitarists, but lingered in the catalog in one form or another until 1984.

Far more lauded than this is the Fender Blender, an extreme and powerful fuzz box with tone boost and, later, an added octave effect. This was a thick, sick and hairy fuzz, not the least bit transparent and blessed with bucketloads of gain, which could play havoc with chords but yielded some soaring solo tones. Robin Trower played a Blender for a time in the 1970s, and Billy Corgan of Smashing Pumpkins apparently used the box on the band's *Gish* album, and occasionally after. A short-lived Phaser joined the Blender in 1975. It was a hefty unit housed in a diecast box not unlike some Roland pedals of the time, and carried only a stomp switch for activation, and a large rotary pad for foot control over the speed of the phasing – plus a hardwired AC cable that extended from the player-side edge of the pedal, where you were most likely to step on it. The little-seen Phaser vanished in 1977 along with the Blender, the latter now a highly sought fuzz in some collectors' circles.

The biggest Fender effect of all – and, after the Reverb Unit, probably the most successful in tonal

played a Blender for a time in the 1970s, and Billy Corgan of Smashing Pumpkins apparently used the box on the band's *Gish* album, and occasionally after. A short-lived Phaser joined the Blender in 1975. It was a hefty unit housed in a diecast box not unlike some Roland pedals of the time, and carried only a stomp switch for activation, and a large rotary pad for foot control over the speed of the phasing – plus a hardwired AC cable that extended from the player-side edge of the pedal, where you were most likely to step on it. The little-seen Phaser vanished in 1977 along with the Blender, the latter now a highly sought fuzz in some collectors' circles.

The biggest Fender effect of all – and, after the Reverb Unit, probably the most successful in tonal terms if not sales – was the Vibratone cabinet, made from 1967 to 1972. It was a rotating speaker unit (or more accurately, rotating baffle) built on the lines of the Leslie Model 16, which had a single vertically-mounted 10″ speaker as opposed to the separate horizontally-mounted speaker and horn arrangement of most Leslies used with Hammond organs. Also, the Vibratone was intended specifically for use with a guitar amplifier, with no internal power amp of its own, as carried in the popular Leslie 122 and 147 models. Its Doppler-inducing whirl is divine in the right hands, and generally better with guitar than the bigger and probably wider-known Leslie horn-and-woofer variant. Stevie Ray Vaughan used a Vibratone all over his *Couldn't Stand The Weather* album – on the title track, more famously on 'Cold Shot,' and elsewhere – and others from Pink Floyd to The Beatles are reported to have employed it too. Given the unit's size – think small fridge – players without their own road crew are more likely to choose a Uni-Vibe clone of some description, despite the Vibratone's righteous sound.

In the 'Weird & Wondrous' category – otherwise known as 'What The Hell Were They Thinking?' – Fender earns a gold star for the bonkers Dimension IV. The whirling oil-filled drum was intended to induce spacey warbling effects when plugged in between guitar and amp, and supposedly sounds pretty damn nifty… if you can find one that hasn't leaked its apparently PCB-laden oil all over the circuitboard.

Fender Reverb Unit (pictured front & back)
Made: 1961-66; reissued 1994.
Controls: Dwell, Mixer, Tone; jack on chassis underside for on/off footswitch.
Sonics: lush, warm and atmospheric tube-powered spring reverb.

Fender Blender
Made: 1968-77
Controls: Volume, Sustain, Tone, Blend knobs (Octave control on late units); stompswitches for on/off and Tone Boost.
Sonics: wild, heavy, ultra-saturated fuzz verging on sick, with a lot of gain. Can make a chaos out of chords. Ringing octave effect with a fairly fast attack and decent tracking.

Fender Phaser (not pictured)
Made: 1975-77
Controls: rotary footpad for Speed; internal trim-pot for Depth; on/off stompswitch.
Sonics: warm, lush analog phasing sounds.

Fender Vibratone (not pictured)
Made: 1967-72
Controls: two-button footswitch for on/off and fast/slow speed selection.
Sonics: the smooth, bubbling whirl of a Leslie cabinet, but with a frequency range better suited to guitar.

FOXX

Foxx was a relatively short-lived brand, but for a time in the early 1970s the California company built some creative and great-sounding pedals, with a few weirdos thrown into the brew for spice. The name is best remembered by many guitarists for the colorful electrostatically fuzz-flocked casings that housed most of the effects, but the circuits that lurked inside many are worthy of attention too.

Effects designer Steve Ridinger founded Foxx in 1970 when he was still in his late teens, and released his first product in 1971 – this was the Tone Machine fuzz box with switchable octave effect (spelled 'Octive' on the unit). He followed with the Wa & Volume Machine, then the Loud Machine volume pedal, Down Machine bass wah-wah, OD Machine overdrive, Clean Machine sustainer, and Fuzz & Wa & Volume pedal.

Other than the Tone Machine, which came in a rectangular shaped pedal with stomp switch, all of these were housed in wah-wah-style rocker-treadle casings. Toward the end of the company's existence the rocker-pedal Guitar Synthesizer I and a phaser also joined the ranks. But in 1975, suffering from poor sales of the newer products and competition from new brands – chiefly MXR – Foxx closed up shop.

Foxx's fuzz effects are generally on the extreme side of the genre, offering dense distortion with crisp, crackling highs. Its wah-wahs set themselves apart early on for having a four-position tone range switch, years before other makers saw the benefit of such a feature. All in all, they were groovy pedals, and taken from us too soon. (Anecdotal Note: as a kid in the mid-1970s, the author briefly owned a Foxx Fuzz & Wa & Volume Machine. It sounded great... until the red fuzz flocking started shedding from the casing and found its way into the treadle wah's potentiometer. Apparently not all pedals suffered the same degree of alopecia, but no doubt there are a few other baldies out there on the vintage market today.)

IBANEZ
(including Maxon)

Sales never quite kept up with the competition from fellow Japanese rival Boss, and all effects carrying the company name were manufactured by an outside supplier, but Ibanez has become the most revered of the Japanese pedal brands of the late 1970s and early 1980s. This reputation comes mostly on the back of the well-known Tube Screamer series of overdrives, but the cachet has rubbed off on other early Ibanez offerings, of which plenty are good sounding units in their own right.

The roots of the Ibanez company reach back more than 100 years. Matsujiro Hoshino opened a book store in the late 1800s, and expanded into a musical division in 1908. But the business as we know it takes its name from the classical guitars it began importing into Japan from Spanish maker Salvador Ibanez around 1930. Although the company's first 30 years or so revolved around acoustics, it was known in the west more as an electric brand by the 1970s, which is where we come in as far as effects pedals are concerned.

By the early 1970s Ibanez was heavily into the business of copying popular American guitars – mainly Gibsons, but a range of others as well – and decided to jump on the effects wagon too. Its guitars were then being made by parent company Fuji Gen Gakki, with electronics supplied by the Nisshin company,

which also marketed its own Maxon effects. It was a natural step for Ibanez to get its effects from Nisshin, too, first repackaging Maxon units, then commissioning some of its own designs.

The company's first inspiration was the newly popular MXR range from the USA. But unusually for Japanese manufacturers of the 'copy era,' Ibanez veered away from marketing exact look-alikes and quickly adopted its own casing design for the units (or its manufacturer's, at least), although some early Maxon pedals do come in a very MXR-like box. The sloping switch surface with recessed control deck of the Ibanez 8 (also called '0'), 9, 'L' and 10 Series pedals is an iconic profile which, in its earliest incarnation in particular, can inspire cold sweats of desire in the lusting collector. Unlike Boss's rigid adherence to the same casing style through the years, the Ibanez box changed its lines with every new series, and the evolution is most notable in the size and positioning of the footswitch – always a rectangular electronic switch in all but the first few units, such as the orange Overdrive and its siblings.

A pair of opamps taken from two different Ibanez TS9 Tube Screamers. The JRC4558D is by far the collector's favorite.

The legendary Tube Screamer is probably both the most-used and most-copied of all overdrives. It is beloved for its juicy midrange and natural, tube-like breakup, which works great in conjunction with a decent tube amp set just loud enough to be on the edge of distortion itself... and booted slightly over the edge when a Tube Screamer is kicked in. Between the late 1970s and mid 1980s, the pedal evolved through the TS-808 (with and without hyphen), TS9 and TS10 versions, and became slightly less desirable with each step along the way. Of the three, however, the TS9 is the most popular in the literal sense of the word – far more TS9s were manufactured than TS-808s, and when it first arrived it wasn't generally considered to be inferior to its forerunner. The TS10 was plentiful, too – and still is relatively so on the second-hand market – but was almost immediately seen by many players as a rung or two down the tonal ladder from the TS9.

As much as the collector crowd salivates over the TS-808, Eric Johnson is known for having favored a TS9 in his time (although his current set-up excludes the Tube Screamer), and Stevie Ray Vaughan is often written of as preferring the TS-808, but a tech of the time reports that he in fact moved on to each

Ibanez TS808 Tube Screamer [CD track 49]
Made: this two-chip small-box version c1979/80, its successor c1980/81.
Controls: Overdrive, Tone, Level; stompswitch for on/off.
Sonics: a creamy, warm, pliant and tube-like overdrive with a distinct mid-hump, relatively low gain, and some loss of low-end body.

Ibanez TS9 Tube Screamer [CD track 50]
Made: 1981/82-1985; this early JRC2043-chip version c1982.
Controls: Drive, Tone, Level; electronic stompswitch for on/off.
Sonics: as per TS-808, with a little less smoothness and a touch more 'chirp' in the high-mids.

Ibanez TS10 Tube Screamer [CD track 51]

Made: mid to late 1990s.
Controls: Drive, Tone, Level; electronic stompswitch for on/off.
Sonics: as per TS9, but perhaps with a little less transparency and 'guitar character' in the tone.

Ibanez ST9 Super Tube Screamer

Made: 1984-1985.
Controls: Drive, Mid Boost, Tone, Level; electronic stompswitch for on/off.
Sonics: as per TS9, with variable mid-range boost.

Ibanez Compressor [CD track 8]

Made: 1979-1980.
Controls: Sustain and Level; mechanical stompswitch for on/off.
Sonics: a soft, well-rounded compression with good attack and note preservation on lower Sustain settings, and plenty of squash when turned up high.

Ibanez CS-505 Chorus [CD track 23]

Made: 1980-1981.
Controls: Speed and Depth; electronic stompswitch; mono/stereo outs; electronic stompswitch for on/off.
Sonics: a deep, plummy stereo chorus with gentle movement and plenty of dimension.

Ibanez AD-80 Analog Delay [CD track 69]

Made: 1980-1981.
Controls: Delay Time, Blend, Repeat; electronic stompswitch; electronic stompswitch for on/off.
Sonics: characterful short to medium echo in mono, with a little noise at longer delays but good analog warmth throughout.

Ibanez AD9 Analog Delay [CD track 64]

Made: 1982-1985.
Controls: Delay Time, Repeats, Delay Level; wet and dry outs; electronic stompswitch for on/off.
Sonics: quality short to medium echo, with good note definition and characteristic analog warmth; improved note definition on AD-80, but a touch less 'rounded.'

Ibanez Phase Tone II

Made: 1979-1981.
Controls: Speed and Feedback knobs; stompswitch for on/off.
Sonics: smooth, liquid phasing sounds.

Ibanez FL9 Flanger

Made: 1982-1985.

Controls: Speed, Width, Regen and Delay Time knobs; stompswitch for on/off.

Sonics: flanging running from warm and sweet to hard and metallic.

Ibanez OD9 Overdrive [CD track 72]

Made: 1982-1984.

Controls: Distortion, Tone, Level; electronic stompswitch for on/off.

Sonics: a spikey, filth-filled distortion with crackling high harmonics throughout the frequency range.

Ibanez BCL Bi-Mode Chorus

Made: 1985-1986.

Controls: Speed and Width twice for band A and B; electronic stompswitch for on/off; dual outs.

Sonics: a lush, sparkling and extremely versatile analog chorus with independent 'dual mono' channels.

Ibanez SS20 Session Man [CD track 71]

Made: c1986-1987.

Controls: Distortion, Dist-Tone, Dist-Level, D-Time; Series/Parallel Mode switch; electronic stompswitch for on/off.

Sonics: a heavy, modern-rock-voiced distortion pedal with variable short delay for 'instant studio sound,' with distortion and delay switchable between series and parallel paths.

Ibanez DFL Digital Flanger [CD track 87]

Made: 1985-1986.

Controls: Speed, Width, Delay Mode, D-Time, Regen; electronic stompswitch; mono in/out.

Sonics: from edgy and metallic to thick and synthetic flanging sounds.

Ibanez TS9DX Turbo Tube Screamer

Made: c1990s-present.

Controls: Drive, Level, Tone and Mode; stompswitch for on/off.

Sonics: from bottomy to middly medium-gain overdrive sounds, depending on Mode setting; generally less smooth than vintage TS9s, but tonally similar.

new model as it came out, upgrading in turn to a TS9 and then a TS10. Take a close look at any of the photos that give you a view of SRV's pedalboard, and many will reveal a clearly distinguishable TS10 plugged in between a Vox Wah-Wah and a Fuzz Face. And tone hound that he was, you know he would have chased down another TS-808 if that was the overdrive he really preferred. Perhaps even more surprisingly, Carlos Santana currently uses a TS9 too, proving that the old Mesa/Boogie – plus, now, Dumble – can't do it all alone.

Famous users aside, the TS-808 is a slightly plummier, rounder overdrive (it's often called 'warmer'), while the TS9 has a little more sparkle through the upper mids – although, as ever, these are tricky things to put into words that mean the same thing to all ears. The circuit changed relatively little through the three model evolutions (and variations within the models), but those few alterations of component values and design are crucial to Screamer aficionados.

The first TS-808s came in a slightly narrower pale-green box than would soon become the norm, which carried a circuit employing two chips, most famously the JRC4558D dual opamp made by Japan Radio Corporation, although one-chip 8s – and certainly 9s and 10s – are the norm after this. The JRC4558D is by far the most revered of the Tube Screamer opamps, although this isn't necessarily because it was consistently used in the production of vintage models. Throughout the era of Tube Screamer manufacture, Maxon used a range of opamps of roughly similar spec, probably whatever the supplier had available when stocks ran low. The 4558 is the most common chip found in the TS-808s made between 1979 and 1981, although other types can be found, and many early TS9s carried JRC2043DDs before the 4558 became standard again, until shortly before the model's demise in 1985, when Maxon switched for a time to the TA75558, the ugly duckling of TS opamps in tonal terms.

After the shortlived 'L' series of 1985/86 – which didn't contain a Tube Screamer – Ibanez brought out the 10 series, and started making effects for themselves. TS10s contain either the beloved 4558 or the loathed TA75558; at the time, the company manufactured its pedals both in Japan and Taiwan, but the stamp of origin on the underplate won't tell you which chip it contains because both factories used both chips, depending on what supplies were available. Some players claim the Japanese TS10s are superior, but the same people usually praise the merits of the JRC4558D – not universally used in those pedals – so go figure.

As the chips varied even within models, other minor circuit changes might be of more use in distinguishing the changes between Tube Screamers of the late 1970s and the 1980s. The TS-808 and TS9 are actually built on the same PCB (printed circuit board) pattern; the component values in the input buffer, clipping, tone and volume stages of each are the same, and the only difference is in the values of two resistors in the output buffer stage. The TS-808 uses a 10k ohm shunt resistor and a 100 ohm series output resistor, where the TS9 uses 100k and 470 ohm resistors respectively. Change these resistors (in the almost tonally insignificant output buffer stage, it should be said) and a TS9 becomes entirely TS-808-spec, or vice versa. The TS10 has one extra resistor each in the input buffer when in bypass (between the input transistor and the JFET switch) and the clipping amp (a 220k series resistor). Remove these and join the gaps, and change the input bias resistor, and a TS10 becomes TS9-spec – and from there's it's two easy changes to the TS-808 circuit, as above. Even so, I wouldn't advise trying it, as these compact circuit boards can easily be ruined by botched 'mod' efforts. It all just goes to show you, though, that there's not a lot between them – other than an easy couple of hundred bucks difference on the vintage market.

As with all things tonal, if you're on the prowl for an original-issue Tube Screamer, it's probably best to apply your ears to any you can track down and sound-sample rather than getting too worried about unscrewing the bottom of each and spilling its guts to see which chip is inside. Certainly a huge mythology has grown up around the JRC4558D, but there are two points of view to consider: on one hand, plenty of knowing players and techs alike will swear by this opamp's prowess; on the other, more than one prominent contemporary manufacturer has told me that exhaustive, lab-conditions A/B sonic testing of the 4558 against other comparable opamps yields no clear winner. The pedal that sounds best to you, and is up for the right price, is the one to spend your hard-earned cash on.

Other early Ibanez pedals have grown highly desirable, too – some because they actually sound very good, some merely because they benefit from the TS-808 and TS9 associations. Collectors go nutzoid over many of the 'other' overdrives, including: the 8 series models labeled simply Over Drive, OD-850 Overdrive, and OD-855 Overdrive II (orange, orange, and snot-green respectively); Maxon's early OD-808; and Ibanez's ultra-rare OD9 Overdrive (rumored to only have been sold in France) and ST9 Super Tube Screamer, the latter with an added Mid Boost control and two chips in the circuit. Early AD-80 and AD9 Analog Delays are very popular, I have tried a great 8 series compressor (or should it be the 'no series,' as the unit bears only the Compressor model name and no alphanumerical designation?), and many of the choruses sound very good, from the early CS-505 to the short-lived mid-1980s 'L' series Bi-Mode Chorus.

The Bi-Mode isn't literally stereo, but dual mono, with two outputs with independent Speed and Width controls for each. Use both outs, and you can set these entirely differently – a fast, narrow chorus into one amp, and a slow, broad chorus into the other, for example. Use the summed out, and the two sides are blended together, so you still get the sound of different bandwidths spinning at different speeds. From the 10 series, though labelled '20,' came the equally original SS20 Session-Man II (I've never seen a version I, but presumably it's out there). The SS20 produces a heavy distortion sound plus a doubling delay effect, and the two can be selected to run in series or parallel, with quite dramatic-sounding differences in each mode. There were also phasers, flangers, graphic EQs, auto filters and a selection of other effects throughout the run of the series.

In the 1990s the 10 series evolved into the plasticky and beatle-like but affordable Soundtank range, or 5 Series. The rounded-off, slightly dumpy boxes are unappealing to most pedal heads, but the TS5 for one carried largely the same Tube Screamer circuit as the TS9 of some years before, although it usually carries a different opamp and has a couple of other minor resistor changes. Ugly, maybe, but second-hand they can be a good, bargain overdrive.

As the 1990s wore on, however, Ibanez became keenly aware of the collector madness bubbling up around its earlier Tube Screamers, and reissued the TS9, along with the TS9DX, with an added mode knob to take you between vintage and turbo modes, but these have been given the unpopular TA75558 opamp rather than the JRC4558D. The reissues, along with the good sounding Tone Lok series, form Ibanez's current offerings in the pedal department. Word has it the company has pledged never to reissue the TS-808.

MAESTRO

Other than two particular vintage effects units, the Maestro name would carry very little clout with guitarists today. Yet the fact is, even aside from the seminal Echoplex and Fuzz Tone, Maestro was a force to be reckoned with in the early days of guitar effects pedals, and a respected high-end brand from the late 1960s to the mid 1970s.

Among guitarists, Maestro has always benefited enormously from associations with Gibson. But rather than all Maestro products being 'made by Gibson,' as more-eager-than-factual music store salesmen were often fond of spouting, the two were siblings under the wing of parent company Chicago Musical Instruments, and later Norlin. In the early 1960s Gibson built many amps that bore the Maestro logo – often the Maestro tube amp was aimed at accordion players, while the near identical Gibson was of course marketed for guitarists – and, apparently, it built some later effects too. But many of the Maestro pedals

were manufactured by outside contract houses which specialized in the type of unit in required.

The first Echoplexes were made in the late 1950s by Market Electronics in Cleveland, Ohio, roughly following the design of the tape echo system Ray Butts built into his amp of the 1950s, as used by Chet Atkins, Scotty Moore, Carl Perkins and others. But the tape echo really hit its stride after the manufacture was taken up by Harris-Teller of Chicago, which produced units marketed by Maestro under its own name. This is another 'not a pedal' effect, but so what – the Maestro Echoplex is widely recognized as the first reliable and professional-grade 'separate' tube tape echo machine available, and set the standard for the effect.

A later solid-state version of the Echoplex, again made by Market Electronics, was sold in the 1970s, but the tube version is the epitome of the breed. The warm, round, thick echo it produces is equaled by few – just possibly by vintage Italian Binson and Meazzi units, and not quite by a Copicat or a Space Echo – and has become one of the most sought-after vintage effects units on the market... on the rare occasion when there is one on the market. A great example of the sound is heard in Jimmy Page's solo on 'Stairway To Heaven,' and near-countless guitarists used it for everything from chugging slapback to spacey multi-tapped long delays throughout the 1960s and 1970s, and continue to do so today.

Maestro scored even more of a 'first' with its Fuzz-Tone of around 1963, widely credit as the first commercially available transistorized fuzz box on the market. It seems bizarre, with hindsight, but the effect wasn't first marketed as a rock'n'roll sound, but – as produced by Maestro and others that followed – was advertised as a way for guitarists to sound like anything from a trombone to a saxophone, and to produce 'endless, singing sustain.' Still, it quickly became one of the rock guitar sounds that defined the decade, and after Keith Richards' use of it on the Rolling Stones' '(I Can't Get No) Satisfaction,' every kid with a 35-buck Silvertone had to have one.

The Fuzz-Tone famously originated from studio engineer Glen Snotty's efforts to replicate the sound of a fritzed tube recording console preamp in a transistorized box. The original Maestro version produced a thick, slablike fuzz that could overwhelm the guitar's own voice and dynamics, but certainly made an impression on the audiences that first heard the thing – and at the dawn of the transistor revolution, that was what really mattered.

Other Maestro products are less famous than these two originators, but many are highly regarded. Tom Oberheim – whose name is better known from the big polyphonic synthesizers that carry it – made the PS-1 Phaser and Ring Modulator for Maestro from the early to mid 1970s. ADT made the

Maestro Fuzz-Tone

Made: 1963 to early 1970s.

Controls: Volume and Attack (fuzz); stompswitch for on/off.

Sonics: thick, jagged, sustaining – a classic 1960s 'swamp your sound' fuzz.

Maestro Echoplex

Made: c1960 to 1970s (in a range of designs); model shown, early 1960s.

Controls: Echo Repeats, Balance, Volume, Echo Delay, Recording Level, Sound On Sound switch; jack for on/off footswitch.

Sonics: rich, warm, full-bodied tape echo. Some noise, of course, but it's the echo sound that analog delay pedals dream of being when they grow up.

Maestro PS-1 Phase Shifter (not pictured)

Made: 1971-1975.

Controls: switches for Slow, Medium or Fast phasing to a preset depth, with on/off rocker switch and mono in/out.

Boomerang volume/wah (or 'wow-wow,' as ads of the day had it), Super Fuzz, SS-2 Sustainer, Octave Box, and a few others. A change of management in the late 1970s saw Maestro shift its contract to Moog Electronics, which manufactured the Fuzz, Phaser, Fuzztain, Stage Phaser and others. These formed a semi-familiar range of rather large pedals with 'foot control' wheels mounted either side plus, on more deluxe units, a rotating toe-pad in the center. Maestro also offered the Rover rotating speaker unit, the guts of which was housed within a stand-mounted circular cage, giving it a very different appearance to the Leslie and Fender Vibratone cabs it followed.

While none of the above have the kudos of the Fuzz-Tone or the Echoplex, or command the same kind of money on the vintage market, most are very good-sounding effects, primarily thanks to Maestro's ability to contract jobs out to creative designers and high-quality makers.

MARSHALL

The grandaddy of the full-stack has made far more significant inroads with effects in recent years than it did back when it was busy launching its classic amp designs. But Jim Marshall's company did market some worthy classics in the 1960s – albeit in units manufactured by other suppliers – and besides, it just wouldn't seem right to list this make anywhere but in the 'Vintage' category.

You can read elsewhere of the birth of Marshall amplifiers in detail (I would point you toward Aspen Pittman's *The Tube Amp Book: Deluxe Revised Edition*, for obvious reasons, and Mike Doyle's book *The History Of Marshall* is another excellent source). In the early 1960s London music shop owner Jim Marshall and colleagues Ken Bran and Dudley Craven identified a need for larger, more powerful British amplifiers than were easily available. They adapted the design of a late 1950s tweed Fender Bassman amp to suit British components, and launched the first commercially-available JTM45 in 1963. As Marshall's 50W half-stacks and, later, 100W full-stacks became the first-choice rig for big rock gigs of the day, the company saw the sense in offering a range of other gizmos to meet musicians' needs.

Newfangled effects pedals like the fuzz box and the wah-wah were an obvious place to start.

The first such product appears to have been the Marshall SupaFuzz, a rebadged version of the MkII Tone-Bender contracted from the Macari brothers at Sola Sound (later Colorsound). The first Marshall version of the pedal is electronically identical to the second version of the Tone-Bender, with three germanium Mullard transistors doing the dirty work, and was housed in a similar shaped 'gravity moulded' metal casing to many Sola Sound units of the time – although it was finished with Marshall-style knobs and a somewhat more businesslike look.

Marshall ads c1967-68 boasted of the pedal's "extra long sustain (15 seconds)," and such was always part of the appeal of early fuzzes, but the effect slathered on the distortion thick and heavy just like any Tone-Bender. Some units had controls marked Volume and Filter, others Volume and Fuzz like the Sola Sound/Colorsound versions, but they all did the same thing.

When the wah-wah craze swept across the UK and the world a couple of years behind the fuzz revolution, the Macaris provided Marshall with, yep, the Supa-Wah.

Like the Sola and Colorsound wah-wahs, the Supa-Wah was a slightly squarer, clumsier-looking affair

Marshall SupaFuzz

Made: circa late 1960s.
Controls: Volume, Fuzz; stompswitch for on/off.
Sonics: a dense, freakish, brickwall of a fuzz identical to the Sola Sound Tone-Bender MkII.

Marshall Supa-Wah

Made: circa late 1960s.
Controls: rocker treadle, with stompswitch for on/off.
Sonics: vintage-voiced wah-wah with a round, vocal, musical response.

Marshall ShredMaster   [CD track 73]

Made: 1990s.
Controls: Gain, Bass, Contour, Treble, Volume; stompswitch for on/off.

Sonics: from crunchy rock rhythm to heavy, saturated lead distortion sounds, at a variety of tonal voicings.

Marshall Bluesbreaker II

Made: 1999 to present.
Controls: Boost/Blues Mode switch, Drive, Tone, Volume; stompswitch for on/off.
Sonics: a loud level boost in Boost mode; juicy but soft overdrive in Blues.

Marshall Guv'Nor Plus

Made: 1999 to present.
Controls: Gain, concentric Bass/Deep and Treble/Mid, Volume; stompswitch for on/off.
Sonics: a fat, chunky overdrive sound intended to replicate a cranked Marshall amp through a closed-back 4x12" cab.

Marshall Jackhammer

Made: 1999 to present.

Controls: OD/Dist Mode switch, concentric Gain/Volume, Treble/Bass, and Freq/Contour knobs; stompswitch for on/off.

Sonics: saturated classic overdrive sounds in OD mode; heavy modern-rock distortion in Dist.

Marshall Edward The Compressor [CD track 16]

Made: 1999 to present.

Controls: Hi/Lo Emphasis, Volume, Attack, Compression; stompswitch for on/off.

Sonics: compression variable from firm and light to heavy and squashing, with some thickening of tone throughout. Emphasis control can be dialed for comp of high or low frequencies, or entire spectrum.

Marshall Supervibe Chorus

Made: 1999 to present.

Controls: Speed, Depth, Wave, Filter; mono and stereo outs; stompswitch for on/off.

Sonics: versatile stereo chorus sounds.

Marshall Vibratrem

Made: 1999 to present.

Controls: Vib/Trem Mode switch, Speed, Depth, Shape (square or triangle wave); mono and stereo outs; stompswitch for on/off.

Sonics: pitch-modulated 'true vibrato' in Vib mode; standard choppy or smooth tremolo in Trem mode.

than the pacesetting Vox and Cry Baby wahs. But it made the right sounds, and no doubt gave the guitar shop sales guys a little extra something to offer in the 'impulse purchase' stakes along with that Plexi stack and SupaFuzz pedal, rather than sending them across the road to the Vox stockist for a wah-wah like Jimi's, or the Arbiter place for a Fuzz Face.

Marshall pedals made more of an impact in their own right when the company introduced its diverse range of chunky, black metal overdrives and distortions in the early 1990s. They were made in the UK, and each was aimed ostensibly at giving you a particular 'Marshall amp' sound at lower volumes – or indeed at higher volumes through another brand of amp, if that was your route. The Bluesbreaker provided subtle drive for the blueser, the DriveMaster soft crunch for the classic rocker, the Guv'Nor aimed for 'cranked 100-watter breakup' – plus a range of lesser sounds – for the Eighties rocker, and the ShredMaster served to please the heavy rocker.

A wide range of design variations achieved these goals with considerable success, according to most players who use them. The easy-going Bluesbreaker employed an opamp and silicon diodes for a very gentle clipping that induced just the slightest, bluesy breakup; the DriveMaster contained a somewhat unusual circuit using LEDs to induce distortion; the Guv'Nor had a circuit not dissimilar to the Drive Master's but tweaked for higher gain, with an added effects loop; and the ShredMaster used the familiar silicon diodes arranged for hard clipping, with a versatile three-band tone stack. The latter provides versatility in a range of heavy rock modes, but it doesn't do the serious gut-busting nu-metal or shred of some contemporary pedals, as the name implies. It did pretty damn fine for Radiohead's huge-sounding 'Creep,' though, so it would probably do for many of your noisemaking concerns, too.

In 1999 Marshall shifted production of its pedals to India, where its budget range of solid state Park amps was also being built, and changed the big wedge-shaped black boxes for little silver metal bricks about half their size. The new – and current – line includes the GV-2 Guv'Nor Plus (with gold-plated controls at Jim Marshall's request, in honor of this revised version of the first Marshall-made pedal), BB-2 Bluesbreaker II, JH-1 Jackhammer, SV-1 Supervibe Chorus, VT-1 Vibratrem, and ED-1 Edward The Compressor. Gone are the DriveMaster and ShredMaster, but of the distortions, the new Jackhammer goes to extremes beyond any previous Marshall pedal. A dual OD/Dist mode allows for classic crunch at the former setting and serious rock noise at the latter, while a four-control EQ section – achieved with two stacked concentric knobs – provides broad tonal variations. Asian production allows for 'competitive pricing' throughout the range – the phrase marketeers generally prefer over 'entry level' or just 'cheap' – but tone obsessives mostly agree that the big black boxes of the early 1990s are the classics of the latter-day Marshalls. Still, the new silver jobbies make all the right sounds, and have already satisfied a great many reviewers and players alike.

MORLEY

If you were a guitarist of the late 1970s who paid any mind to the superlatives of magazine ad men, chances are you were convinced for a time that you just had to have a Morley Wah pedal, perhaps even a Power Wah Fuzz or – gasp, swoon – an immense, imposing EVO-1 Echo/Volume. Morley pedals had a serious mo betta industrial look, photo-resistor control in place of potentiometers for quiet operation, bigger cases and wider rocker treadles than anyone else on the block, were hardwired for AC power, and they had posters with acid-haired and pedal-footed monster guitarists that declared "Morley Men Do It With Their Feet" (an unsavory image in itself, come to think of it,

sonic implications aside. From the look of the guy in the company logo, I always thought he was in the midst of receiving a serious electric shock from an ungrounded pedal – and a spark does seem to be leaping from the corner of the one that forms his right foot – which is maybe why I never bought a Morley). In short, they told us these were the bee's knees in functional modern effects, and it was easy to believe them.

All that over-engineering resulted in some iron-clad pedals that Detroit could have been proud of, and most usually sounded pretty good, but they didn't appeal to everyone. First, the 'new, advanced' circuitry didn't win every guitarist's favor (it never does); second, the 'ergonomic designs' were probably

Morley Pro Phaser (not pictured)

Made: circa late 1970s.

Controls: Center knob, Auto/Foot Mode switch with rocker-treadle for manual sweep control; stompswitch for on/off.

Sonics: rich phasing at desired speed, or switchable to manual for dramatic, vocal-like foot-controlled frequency sweeps.

Morley Bad Horsie Wah

Made: c2000 to present.

Controls: rocker treadle for wah; on/off of effect triggered by foot weight on rocker.

Sonics: a tempered cross between the classic and modern wah-wah voicings, with plenty of screaming highs in the top position.

Morley Pro Series II Wah

Made: circa late 1990s to present.

Controls: rocker treadle, Level knob, Wah stompswitch for effect on/off.

Sonics: a contemporary filter voicing aimed at modern rock, with a bright, almost crispy response.

ergonomic for the guy who designed them, but not for everyone; third, they practically necessitated hiring a second roadie just to carry your pedalboard – most individual Morley pedals weighed in at two or three pounds, and the EVO-1 a whopping eight pounds; and fourth – but in truth, first for most of us – they cost a righteous wad of cash. Clearly those who did bag them loved them (usually they had good day jobs, or prominent record deals), and they spent most of the after-gig party trying to convince their shallower-pocketed pals they should invest in one too, and were dead pleased with all that over-engineering ten years down the road when the Power Wah/Boost was perhaps a little scuffed of chrome, but still smoothly wah-ing and boosting.

Morley arrived in the late 1960s under the banner of Tel-Ray Electronics of Burbank, California, a company founded by brothers Marvin and Raymond Lubow. By the early 1970s the brand was well-established as a professional choice, with a top-shelf image on a par with the likes of MXR, A/DA and Mu-Tron, and units could be found under the feet of everyone from America to Zappa.

Wah-wahs and wah combinations were probably the company's most popular products through the years, and it also offered the usual flock of phasers, flangers, chorus variations and so forth. But there were some inventive – if freakish – effects of other types, too. The monstrous EVO-1 Echo/Volume of course sported the ubiquitous wedge-shaped Morley treadle, but was also a mechanical analog echo built around a spinning electrostatic disk recorder not unlike the Binson Echorec and a few other delays of the 1960s. It probably could have powered your Pinto, too.

The semi-bonkers Electro-Pik pedals such as the Attack, Wah and Percussion had a 'live-wired' metal plectrum grafted on to the hardwired guitar cord that connected you to the unit, which sensed pick attack against string and controlled the effects' attack accordingly. They were interesting designs, and offered some creative alternatives to the norm – but you had to wonder if it was worth adapting your playing style to that triangular metal pick, and what happened when the thing wore down. I guess a lot of guitarists did stop to wonder, 'cos not all that many bought them.

In the 1980s Morley added some 'normal' – meaning rocker/treadleless – pedals to the range. In 1989 the company was sold to Accutronics, and its Sound Enhancements subsidiary continues to make Morley pedals in Cary, Illinois.

The brand is still know for wah-wahs more than anything else, and has revved up its star-artist endorsement program in recent years with products like the Steve Vai Bad Horsie Wah, the Mark Tremonti Power Wah, and the George Lynch Tripler amp selector. The Bad Horsie is a modern-toned switchless wah-wah that toggles between effect on and off by sensing the weight of your foot on the treadle, and has a spring-loaded rocker action to make things easier on your ankle, while the Tremonti Power Wah has up to 20dB of boost in a more traditional package, in Morley terms at least. The Pro Series II Wah and Wah/Volume similarly have Level controls that add boost when the wah-wah sound is kicked in, to lift solos above the level of normal playing, and the Classic Wah is based on the Morley circuit of the 1970s. All the modern offerings are housed in slimmer packages, though they're still solid beasts and chunkier than many. They cost significantly less in real terms than in the old days, too, the Power Wah listing for $199 and the Classic Wah $119.

MU-TRON
(by Musitronics)

The most famous product ever to come from Musitronics's Mu-Tron range carries not a name, but a Roman numeral. Of course nobody would recognize it as simply 'The III.' But mention the Mu-Tron III, and you're talking the grooviest envelope filter of all time – and a pedal so cool the company went right ahead and named everything else after it.

While we think of the envelope filter (or envelope follower, or auto-wah) primarily as a 'funk effect' today, the funk net spread a lot wider in the early and mid 1970s when the Mu-Tron III hit its stride. Jazz and fusion players like Herb Ellis, Pat Martino and Larry Coryell jumped on this and other Mu-Tron effects – Coryell was the company's first endorser – but the III's most famous recorded sound comes courtesy, not of a guitarist, but Stevie Wonder and his Hohner Clavinet track on 'Higher Ground.' Funky? Damn straight, and it created an instant "got to get that pedal!" reaction that shot the young company straight to the higher echelons of quality effects makers.

Musitronics was founded in 1972 by former Guild engineer Aaron Newman and electrical designer Mike Biegel, and developed a strong following quickly on the back of the Mu-Tron III. The funk box wasn't alone for long, though, and the company soon introduced a pair of serious phasers in the form of the large Bi-Phase and the scaled-down Phasor II. The Bi-Phase was, for a time, the phaser lover's 'phasor' (to give it their preferred spelling), and was the most deluxe unit of its kind available. It used the archaic multi-stage variable resistor style circuit of the Uni-Vibe with coupled lamps and photo cells, carried two independent Sweep Generators with both Rate controls and sine/square wave Shape switches, two independent (but syncable) bands with independent Depth and Feedback controls, and more. A monster, and it sounded absolutely gorgeous.

Mu-Tron III

Made: 1972-1979.

Controls: Mode, Peak and Gain knobs; switches for Range, Drive and Power on/off, plus effect on/off stompswitch.

Sonics: a round, funky, organic auto-wah capable of subtle or extreme effects.

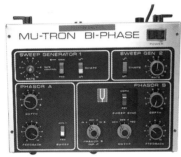

Mu-Tron Bi-Phase

Made: 1974-1979.

Controls: (deep breath...) Rate knob, Man/Ped switch and Shape switch for Sweep Generator 1; Shape switch and Rate knob for Sweep Gen 2; Depth and Feedback knobs for both Phasor A and Phasor B, plus Gen1/Ped Sweep switch for A and Phasor B Input switch, Sweep Sync switch, and Gen1/Gen2/Ped Sweep switch for B; remote two-button stompswitch unit for preset selection and effect on/off.

Sonics: a deep, lush, variable-resistor-based analog phaser with astounding versatility and the added benefit of feedback control.

Respect for the products was near-universal, and it seemed the company could go nowhere but up. Around 1976 Dan Armstrong's former partner George Merriman designed the Octave Divider – with a broader range of control parameters than most Octavia clones on the market – and Mu-Tron also brought out a Volume/Wah with photo-electric control not unlike that of Morley pedals. Around the mid 1970s Musitronics also started manufacturing the little Dan Armstrong plug-into-your-guitar effects

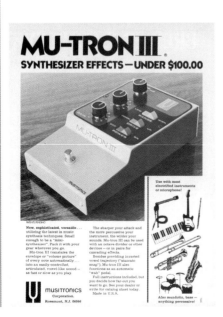

boxes, and in 1977 the company took up production of the seemingly amazing Gizmotron mechanical 'guitar string bowing device'… which is where it all started going south, in a big way.

The Gizmotron, invented by 10cc members Lol Creme and Kevin Godley (who later also had early MTV hits as the duo Godley & Creme), was designed to be mounted to an electric guitar bridge and carried six buttons that triggered individual friction rotors beneath its plastic casing, which rotated against the guitar strings to produce a constantly sustained 'bowed string' sound. Early promos boasted: "When coupled with an electric guitar, the Gizmotron is capable of reproducing virtually every string orchestral sound except that of a grand piano." Surely, you might think, there's a little more variation between the refined designs and tonal subtleties of a violin, viola, cello or bass viol than a Les Paul's solid body, six strings, and 24.75″ scale length could encompass. You're not the only one who thinks so…

It was expected to revolutionize the guitar world, but its spectacular lack of success spelled the end for Musitronics. By the end of the 1970s, the great Mu-Tron name was no more.

MXR

While Electro-Harmonix pedals were tickling the toes of latent hippies, psychedelic rockers and garage-band kids, MXR effects trod the boards with the series rock professionals. This is a generalization of scandalous proportions, of course, but the gist fits the perceived image of the US's two biggest pedal brands of the 1970s. MXR effects were austere, businesslike, and cost a significant chunk more than similar units from some other makers. The company eschewed the multi-surface boxes and colorful graphics of other upmarket makes such as Mu-Tron, Maestro and A/DA, and housed the majority of its clever little effects in the same decoratively minimalistic little bricklike casings, with a double-width but stylistically identical version for the big four-knob units. Man, MXR pedals were serious tools for the serious business of making music.

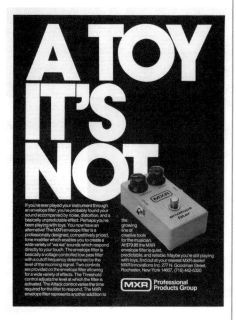

MXR Innovations was founded in 1972 in Rochester, New York, by high-school pals Keith Barr and Terry Sherwood. The company's birth appears to have been quick, straightforward, and relatively painless: hi-fi repairman and fledgling audio designer Barr was driven by that age-old urge to 'build a better pedal,' got captivated by the new phaser effects for guitar that were just appearing, designed the Phase 90, and launched a legend. The ultra-simple but lush-sounding unit, carrying just a knob for Speed and an on/off stomp switch, was an instant hit with local musicians who tried it. The company built up slowly at first, but by the latter end of the mid 1970s MXR had a reputation that would rival the best in the business.

The Phase 90 was soon joined by a range of other popular siblings in the Distortion+, Dyna Comp, Blue Box, Phase 45, Phase 100, Flanger, Analog Delay, Stereo Chorus, 6-Band and 10-Band Graphic Equalizers, Micro Amp, Distortion II, Noise Gate Line Driver and others – each a top-grade example of its type. MXR's circuits were creative and efficient, simple where simple would work (the basic but great-sounding Distortion+, for example), and mostly steered clear of the extreme settings that were of little use to 99 out of 100 guitarists anyway. Similarly, the company released very few of the experimental whacko effects that many others monkeyed around with in the 1970s. At MXR it was all down to business – and business was good.

The Phase 90's success can be pinned down to two factors: lush sound and simplicity. When Barr first started developing his own phaser design, the Maestro Phase Shifter was the effect causing the biggest stir among musicians. But it was a big, awkward slab of a unit designed more as a Leslie simulator for

MXR Phase 90

Made: 1972 to early 1980s (this example c1975-77). Reissued 1990s.

Controls: Speed knob; stompswitch for on/off.

Sonics: a warm, watery swirl of a phaser, staying clear of extreme wobble while maintaining clear, sparkling highs.

MXR Blue Box

Made: 1974 to early 1980s (this example c1976). Reissued 1990s.

Controls: Output and Blend; stompswitch for on/off.

Sonics: fuzzy, occasionally chaotic two-octave-down sounds.

MXR Phase 45 [CD track 85]

Made: 1974 to early 1980s.

Controls: Speed knob; stompswitch for on/off.

Sonics: good phasing with a bubbly, smooth mid-range, but less dimension overall than the Phase 90.

MXR Phase 100

Made: 1974 to early 1980s. Reissued 1990s.

Controls: Intensity and Speed; stompswitch.

Sonics: a lush phaser similar to the Phase 90, but with intensity variable for more or less depth than the one-knob unit.

organ than as a guitar effect, with three switches for 'spin' rate rather than a constantly variable speed control, and no stomp switch that a player could easily trigger in live situations. The Phase 90 housed a relatively simple FET-based circuit in a bulletproof die cast metal box that you could kick across the stage without denting, and produced a sound that was smooth, liquid and rich, but with articulate highs, and which could be set to the tempo of any song you played. Electro-Harmonix's Small Stone equaled it for simplicity, and cost less, but the Phase 90 always seemed that bit more upmarket.

When fuzz was still the norm for distortion devices – along with so-called 'distortion-free sustainers,' which usually distorted like hell too – the Distortion+ offered, in actual fact, less distortion… and many, many guitarists found that to be a very cool thing. Which is not to say the little two-knob box didn't distort your signal; it did for sure but, belying its name, it was really more of a soft-clipping overdrive with just a little fuzz stirred into the brew. With a warm, sizzling heart of germanium (this time 1N270 clipping diodes rather than the transistors of the classic 1960s fuzzes), boosted by a basic IC, it provided a gentler breakup than the opamp and silicon diode distortions that would follow, and could be set for anything from a juicy, saturated squash tone to a light-distortion/high-level booster style signal to drive a tube amp into distortion. Other than the treble boosters of the 1960s – too brash for most ears in the mid 1970s, when rigs retained better fidelity and, hence, more treble of their own – and the simple preamp/line drivers like E-H's LPB1, the Distortion+ was the first widely accepted device that worked in conjunction with a good amp to produce a natural, tubey overdrive at something less than flat-out levels. It was a deserved success.

MXR Distortion+

Made: 1973 to early 1980s. Reissued 1990s.

Controls: Output and Distortion; stompswitch for on/off.

Sonics: a smooth overdrive with an edge of juicy saturation with Distortion knob cranked, but no heavy distortion sounds in modern terms.

MXR Analog Delay [CD track 65]

Made: 1978 to early 1980s. Reissued 1990s.

Controls: Delay, Mix, and Regeneration knobs; stompswitch for on/off.

Sonics: a quality analog delay with some versatility.

MXR Flanger

Made: c1977 to early 1980s. Reissued 1990s.

Controls: Manual, Speed, Width, Regen; stompswitch for on/off.

Sonics: bright, notchy, swirling sounds with some extreme settings available, but good musical middle ground with subtle use.

MXR Micro Amp [CD track 30]

Made: circa mid 1970s to early 1980s. Reissued 1990s.

Controls: Gain; stompswitch for on/off.

Sonics: a fairly linear booster preamp.

MXR Noise Gate/Line Drive

Made: circa late 1970s to early 1980s.

Controls: Threshold; stompswitch for on/off, plus XLR out for DI duties.

Sonics: a transparent unity-gain line driver with noise reduction according to adjustable gate threshold.

MXR 6-Band Graphic Equalizer

Made: circa mid 1970s to early 1980s. Reissued 1990s.

Controls: sliders for boost or cut at 100Hz, 200Hz, 400Hz, 800Hz, 1.6k and 3.2k. No on/off switch.

Sonics: tonal boost or cut, depending upon how you set it.

MXR DD-11 Dime Distortion

Made: 2002 to present.

Controls: Output, Bass, Mid, Treble, Gain; pushbutton mid-scoop switch; stompswitch for on/off.

Sonics: a chunky and searing distortion with boatloads of gain, and good tonal versatility thanks to the three-band EQ.

MXR's delay, chorus and flanger units were all extremely popular, but along with the phaser range and the Distortion+, the Dyna Comp compressor has arguably stood the test of time better than any of the others. This tidy red box has controls for Sensitivity (compression) and Output (level), and adds a nice touch of thickness to the guitar signal along with squashing and sustaining it, according to your Sensitivity setting. It has long been considered one of the Nashville standards, but you'd be hard pressed to find a session guitarist from New York to LA who didn't have a Dyna Comp in his bag of tricks.

Early MXR pedals wore script logos and legends – the first few hundred were even hand-sprayed and silkscreened by Barr and Sherwood themselves – and these are the most desired by collectors. As the company moved to the 'box logo' of the late 1970s and early 1980s, the circuits changed slightly in some models, but the majority largely retained their identifiable MXR sounds. Over the long haul, MXR seems to have altered its designs less than, say, Electro-Harmonix or Ibanez across the life of a model, so box-logo pedals from the original company are also prized pieces, if a little less 'classic' than the script-lettered examples.

A combination of heated Japanese competition and the founders' straying interests ushered in the implosion of MXR in the early 1980s – quite a surprise in hindsight, considering the brand's success and reputation. Keith Barr gathered up his dabblings with digital technology from the latter days of MXR and founded Alesis, while some of the remaining MXR Innovations managers joined together to launch Applied Research & Technology (ART), which pretty rapidly made a name for itself in rack effects.

The Jim Dunlop company bought the rights to the MXR name, and since the 1990s has been offering reissues of many of the brand's classic pedals, along with some recent entirely new models. The former don't always follow the original circuits to the letter, but mostly offer good approximations of their sounds; the latter serve to fill some of the gaps left after the original MXR company's closure and address the needs of the modern rock guitarist.

Some of the new offerings take classic MXR circuits as their templates and update them with added features for more flexibility. The Double Shot Distortion has two channels, the first of which expands upon the Distortion+ for anything from bluesy tones to rock crunch to classic-rock lead tones, while the second provides a meatier modern distortion voice with a chunky low end and cutting highs. Similarly, the Super Comp updates the Dyna Comp idea with an added Attack control to fine-tune its bite/squash ratio.

The Dime Distortion is certainly the most radical of all new MXR offerings. It was designed for super-thrashy Pantera guitarist Dimebag Darrell, and gives the finger to any notions of 'vintage' tone, slapping high-gain filth all up and down your sound – which is obviously what any Pantera-inspired guitarist would want it to do.

PEARL

This company offered a handful of effects pedals in the early 1980s, along with some of its other electronic and audio devices, then vanished again from the guitar scene. But a few of the units have become beloved of the odd guitarist or two, and even verge on B-list collectable, status. Pearl made a range of chorus, flanger, phaser, octave and overdrive units – including multiples of some types – but the most admired appear to be the PH-44 Phaser, CH-02 Chorus, and the occasionally over-the-top FL-01 Flanger.

Pearl CH-02 Chorus [CD track 22]
Made: early 1980s.
Controls: Mix.Bal., Depth, Tone, Speed; stompswitch for on/off.
Sonics: a rich, warbly mono analog chorus with an appealing and musical frequency spectrum.

Pearl FL-01 Flanger
Made: early 1980s.
Controls: Delay Time, Feedback, Modulation, Depth; stompswitch for on/off.
Sonics: a somewhat metallic, chewy flanging sound with emphasis on high-frequencies.

PRO CO

The Pro Co Rat was the first widely available, tonally-successful heavy rock distortion pedal, and it remains a classic of the genre to this day. Pro Co was founded in 1970 out of the ashes of previous music stores and repair shops in Kalamazoo, Michigan, and spent most of the Seventies "striving for the utmost in clean audio gear," as its early Rat ads put it – making cables, DIs, and other non-tonal devices – until engineering director Scott Burnham drew up his wailing, over-the-top distortion circuit. In the realm of things that make noise, Pro Co is known for little else than The Rat and its offspring: the Rat 2, Turbo Rat, and lesser-seen Rat R2DU rack unit. But it's a noisemaking brood to be proud of.

The classic Rat's circuit is roughly similar to that of the MXR Distortion+ that preceded it, but with a few very crucial differences. The Rat uses a pair of 1N4148 silicon diodes rather than the D+'s germanium diodes, for a harder clipping, and it's opamp is an LM308N rather than the MXR's original 741. Probably more significant than either of these differences, however, is an under-valued resistor in the Rat's drive stage, which gives the pedal massive gain and drives the opamp into its own distortion at high settings. The Rat also benefits from a Tone control (called Filter on second-evolution units, although it's just the same thing connected backwards). It's a simple, passive treble-bleed potentiometer, but because of the high high-frequency content of preceding stages of the circuit, it's a more effective tweak tool than the treble-bleeds on many other pedals.

The original production Rats of 1979 and after were 'true bypass' pedals, with no tone-sucking in bypass mode. The Rat 2 of 1987 carried a couple of simple circuit changes and, more significantly, an indicator LED, which required rewiring of the switch, resulting in some loading of the signal in bypass mode and a very slight adulteration of the 'clean' tone. The Vintage Rat reissue of a few years later returned to the original switching arrangement with no LED, to cater for guitarists to whom such things matter. Meanwhile the Turbo Rat was designed with more gain and different diodes, for an even heavier sound.

Pro Co Rat [Rat 2, CD track 75]
Made: 1979 to 1987, and from 1990s to present as Vintage Rat (this example early 1980s).
Controls: Distortion, Filter, Volume; stompswitch for on/off.
Sonics: smooth but heavy distortion with good bottom-end weight and characteristic high-frequency howl when cranked.

Pro Co still offers The Rat 2, Turbo Rat, and Vintage Rat, plus the Juggernaut Bass Rat and the new DeuceTone Rat. The latter is an incredibly versatile unit with two independently switchable Rats in one pedal. They can be used individually, in stereo, or cascaded in series, and each is switchable between four modes: Vintage, Turbo, Clean and Dirty Rat.

ROGER MAYER

He didn't offer effects pedals commercially until the early 1980s, but having built treble boosters and fuzz boxes for London-based guitarists such as Jimmy Page, Jeff Beck, Big Jim Sullivan and others from the early 1960s, and having worked as Jimi Hendrix's main sonic tweaker and custom-effect builder in the late 1960s, Roger Mayer's 'vintage' credentials are assured for all time.

Mayer grew up in Durban, South Africa and, later, southwest London, where he played the guitar in local bands and hung out with prominent musicians on the Kingston and Richmond music scene (for the full story in his own words, and in-depth detail regarding his sonic vision, see the interview in Chapter 6). Having earned a six-year university degree in both mechanical and electrical engineering, Mayer worked a day job reminiscent of Cold War-era James Bond's gizmo lab, as an engineer in a top-secret British Admiralty laboratory doing vibration and acoustic research pertaining to naval underwater warfare. At night, the young scientist went to gigs, and designed and built effects pedals for his more famous pals.

Music electronics was just a sideline, albeit one he took to with major enthusiasm, until Mayer met Jimi Hendrix at a London club in 1967. Hendrix took his new friend into the studio with him two weeks later, where he used one of Mayer's recent

Most Jimi Hendrix fans will be familiar with the famous 'The Experience in the desert' photo shoot, but few will have seen this image, with a young Roger Mayer (far left) popping up alongside the band.

inventions, an octave-up simulating fuzz dubbed the 'Octavia,' to record the solo to 'Purple Haze.' Mayer soon became Hendrix's right-hand tweaker and all-round electronics guru, was present for virtually all of the recording of *Axis Bold As Love* at London's Olympic Studios, and was invited by Hendrix to ride along on the 1968 US tour that followed.

The studio work with Hendrix included not only designing and scratch-building specific effects (the Octavia, again, being the most famous of these), but segmenting out other existing units into separate, heavily tweaked drive, EQ and effect stages, and modifying classic pedals like Jimi's Vox Wahs, Fuzz Faces and Uni-Vibes. Suffice to say that a guitarist buying any of these in standard, original vintage form in an effort to get 'the Hendrix sound' is unlikely to ever quite achieve what we hear as the late guitar legend's tone on record. And of course playing like him is another matter entirely.

After the US tour, Mayer left his job at the Admiralty labs and went to work for Olympic Studios designing and building the facility's custom in-house audio devices (as was done at many major studios of the day). The following year he moved to the US and formed his own company, Roger Mayer

Mayer Rocket Octavia

Made: early 1980s to present (early 1980s version pictured with opto-switching rather than mechanical stompswitch.)

Controls: Drive and Volume; opto switch on early units for on/off, changed to mechanical stompswitch mid 1980s.

Sonics: from subtle to wild simulated octave-doubling effects, with some inherent fuzzing of tone.

Roger Mayer Stone Fuzz

Made: 1999 to present.

Controls: Drive, Volume, stompswitch for on/off.

Sonics: from mild to thick fuzz, with lots of sizzle in the top end and plenty of gain.

Roger Mayer Vision Wah (with underside)

Made: 1999 to present.

Controls: potentiometerless rocker treadle, four pushbuttons for frequency range selection (16 combinations), Volume and Blend controls.

Sonics: many 'classic' round, middly wah-wah sounds, with lower and higher-frequency sweeps selectable.

Roger Mayer Voodoo-1

Made: 2000 to present.

Controls: Gain, Tone, Output; stompswitch for on/off; dual buffered outs for Amp1 and Amp2.

Sonics: a smooth, tube-like distortion pedal ranging from gentle to heavy overdrive sounds, with a considerable level boost available.

Roger Mayer Voodoo-Boost

Made: 2002 to present.

Controls: Gain, Fatness, Output; stompswitch for on/off; dual buffered outs for Amp1 and Amp2.

Sonics: from a clean, unity-gain line driver, to gentle transparent boost, to heavy gain and major level increase.

Roger Mayer Spitfire Fuzz (not pictured)
[CD track 3]

Made: 2002 to present.

Controls: Gain and Volume; stompswitch for on/off.

Sonics: a juicy, sweet, saturated fuzz with a somewhat contemporary voicing but retains classic overtones; stands up well to chords, with good note definition.

Roger Mayer Voodoo-Vibe

Made: c1990s to present.
Controls: Function (Chorus/Vibrato/Tremolo), Range and Fine speed controls (for either sine wave or triangle waveforms), Intensity, Output, Symmetry, Bias; stompswitch for on/off; jack for external speed pedal connection.
Sonics: from watery Hendrix-like Uni-Vibe sounds to heavy 'wop-wop-wop' helicopter effects, and everything in-between, with good clarity and retention of guitar character throughout.

Roger Mayer Voodoo-Axe

Made: 2002 to present.
Controls: Gain, Fatness, Output; stompswitch for on/off; dual buffered outs for Amp1 and Amp2.
Sonics: a razor-sharp fuzz with lots of sizzle and solid body; good dynamics.

Roger Mayer Vision Octavia

Made: 2003 to present.
Controls: Output, Drive, Tone; stompswitch for on/off; three outputs – one hardwired and two buffered.
Sonics: a decently-tracked simulated octave-up sound, with thickening, slightly fuzzy distortion according to Drive settings.

Roger Mayer Vision Voodoo-Vibe Jr [CD track 81]

Made: 2003 to present.
Controls: Sweep, Speed, Vibrato/Chorus Mix, Intensity; stompswitch for on/off; three outputs – one hardwired and two buffered.
Sonics: from the warm, bubbly warble of vintage photocell-based Uni-Vibe chorus sounds to gentle pitch modulation of true vibrato; broad range of selectable speeds, with tweakable frequency spectrum via Sweep.

Roger Mayer Vision Concorde+ Treble Booster [CD tracks 29 & 53]

Made: 2003 to present.
Controls: Output, Drive, Tone; stompswitch for on/off; three outputs – one hardwired and two buffered.
Sonics: from a sweet germanium treble lift with slight gain boost, to a juicy and compressed driven sound with major gain boost, with good transparency and dynamics throughout.

Roger Mayer Red Lion Wah-Wah Kit

Made: 2002 to present.
Controls: PC board-mounted twist-pot for variable frequency sweep; otherwise, replacement board mounts directly into current Cry Baby Wah-Wah housing.
Sonics: bright, clear sweep with slight gain boost; from modern screaming treble to 1960s mid-range tones.

Electronics, building studio equipment such as limiters, equalizers, and complete consoles. The work took him into the studio with the likes of The Isley Brothers, Bob Marley, and Stevie Wonder (for whom he designed and built much of the analog synthesizer used on *Music Of My Mind*, *Talking Book*, and *Innervisions*, all recorded at Electric Ladyland in New York). But alongside the big rocket-science pro audio gear, more and more players were eager to tap his guitar effects knowledge again – and pedals eventually proved the way forward.

Mayer had only built a few custom Octavias in the 1960s, "maybe half a dozen or so," he says, for Hendrix and other friends and artists, and never put the unit on the market commercially at that time. That left the door open for Tycobrahe – and others after them – to pirate both the circuit and the name. But players in-the-know were keen to get back to the source.

In the early 1980s Roger Mayer launched his own Octavia, in the unique and iconic sand-cast 'rocket' casing, and followed that with the Classic Fuzz, his own version of a Fuzz Face modified to Hendrix specs, also in the rocket housing. The similarly shaped Axis Fuzz and Mongoose completed the Rocket Series, and these were followed by the rack-mounted Supervibe, Mayer's version of a Hendrix-modded Uni-Vibe.

In 1989 Mayer returned to England, settling himself and his business back in southwest London, and he has specialized in guitar effects ever since. Despite being one of the originators in this ever-broadening field, he is always striving for the innovation and the new sound rather than recycling his own classic designs ad infinitum. Outspoken and firm in his views (I don't think he'd flinch at being called 'opinionated'), he has little time for guitarists who don't take a similar view with their music, and makes an issue of pressing forward rather than looking backward.

"I've never said that all we do is make a version of our old pedals. We're always constantly evolving," he declares. "New enclosures, new this, new that. We're always using new components. We never make a feature out of using an old component, because years ago most of the components were crap and horrible, and they are better today."

Consequently, Mayer is constantly revising and improving his designs, however well accepted previous versions might have been. His Voodoo series of the 1990s saw the introduction of the Voodoo-Vibe, one of the world's most popular Uni-Vibe style lamp-and-photocell-based chorus/vibe units (in fact, a four-stage phaser). While the Supervibe had been made to the specs of Hendrix's modded Uni-Vibe, Mayer found new ways to improve the effect even further, still with class A discrete analog circuitry. And feeling yet more could be done with the format – or, perhaps more accurately, less – a Voodoo-Vibe Jr has more recently joined the new Vision Series of 2003, with simplified features but all the warm, organic tone of the original (the lamp/photocell phasing stages remain) – at a significantly reduced price compared to the 'Senior.' Both are extremely quiet for this type of effect, a Mayer characteristic, with signal-to-noise ratios of 120dB, which is 12dB better than a standard CD.

The Vision Wah, released in 1999, embodies perhaps better than any other effect Mayer's quest to improve upon the classic sounds of rock, and includes significant ergonomic, functional, and electrical advances on the seminal Vox/Cry Baby format. The top of the carbon-fiber rocker treadle is a full inch lower to the ground than that of a conventional wah-wah, and tipped slightly forward, in an effort to eliminate that hip-ache that can come with too much Cry Baby wailing, while seeking a more natural connection between foot and brain. There's a potentiometerless action, using a 'non-contact position sensor,' and pushbutton EQ switching allows for 16 different frequency sweeps. In addition, there's a volume control and a control to blend the wah'd signal with your straight signal. All this makes for a fairly expensive unit, sure, but the wah-wah connoisseur – or anyone who needs to spend a large portion of stage time rocking away at that treadle – won't want to be without one.

New developments continue to abound. A blood-red Spitfire Fuzz (with classic sizzle but voiced for modern rock applications) recently joined the rocket series; the Octavia has received further updates as a part of the Vision Series; and Mayer has even found a creative way to reinvent the 1960s germanium treble booster – that dodo of the effects world (after all, who needs more treble these days?) – in an astoundingly versatile, toneful Vision Series unit called the Concorde+ Treble Booster. Rather than simply raising a guitar's high-frequency content to ear-spiking levels (as was, believe it or not, pretty useful in the 1960s with all the treble-sapping long, low-quality cables and poorly buffered, or unbuffered, effects chains), the Concorde+ couples the sweetness of a treble-boosting stage containing a carefully selected AC128 germanium transistor with a clever Tone control that returns midrange and low-end body as you wind it up, plus a silicon drive stage for muscle, in a class A discrete transistorized circuit. The results, depending on how you set Tone, Drive, and Output controls, go from sparkling clean level lift, to the tactile fattening of a good booster, to the saturated, compressed drive of a 'boutique' grade overdrive.

Aware of the 'true bypass' debate that continues to rage among players and newer makers alike, Mayer has fitted all of the new Vision Series effects with three separate outputs. The first, labelled 'HW,' is a hard-wired output, which links directly to the input for true bypass in 'off' mode. The second two are both buffered outs that can be used together, if a player is biamping or wants to run parallel signal paths. Which one should be used depends upon where the pedal appears in the set-up and the player's own preferences. Used individually, straight to the amp, Mayer challenges us to hear the difference.

Throughout his work, Meyer's quest for dynamics, musicality, touch-sensitivity, and what he calls "a human quality" overrides all other goals. As he puts it:

"All that stuff that was done with Jimi on all the records, even the stuff that was very distorted, it was very human sounding... You want a tone that's organic. And it's so easy to build a fuzz box or a distortion type of box. You've got many boxes that, to be frank, you put a guitar into it and you wouldn't know what type of guitar it is. The whole tonal quality of that guitar just disappears. It's got 'brick wall' processing in it... Horrendous."

ROSS

Thanks to the fat, squashy, ultra-sustained sounds that Phish guitarist Trey Anastasio elicits from his old Ross Compressor – and the efforts of legion guitar-playing Phishophiles to do the same – this simple, gray, two-knob pedal lodged itself firmly on the 'classics' shelf in the late 1990s. If not for this one pedal's newly stellar reputation, the rest of Ross' effects products would likely be all but forgotten, and the Compressor itself wearing a $15 price sticker in the bargain bin down at your local Music Exchange. Phish or no Phish, it's a great sounding compressor. But the Anastasio connection, and the legend that has built up around it, means the originals are very difficult to get your hands on these days.

In the 1980s Ross manufactured a range of music electronics, from guitar pedals to four-track cassette 'portastudio' style recorders, all of them relatively affordable units compared to the main competition. Although the Compressor is by far the most talked about, most of the pedals of the first series that were manufactured in colored diecast metal casings with recessed 'stove' style knobs have a certain desirability, including the likes of the Distortion, Phaser, and Flanger. Later black-box pedals are also more sought after than many generic effects of the same era, and include – in addition to revised versions of the above – the occasional double-duty oddball like the Phase Distortion.

As for the gray-boxed Compressor, it's essentially an update of the MXR Dyna Comp circuit, and offers a thick, smooth, plummy tone with a somewhat rounded top end and no shortage of squash, along with plenty of breathy dynamics. The 'cult of the Ross Compressor' phenomenon has inspired a few handbuilders to offer their own 'boutique clones' of the original to fill an obvious void in the market. Most notable of these are Robert Keeley, who markets his as the Keeley Compressor, and Analog Man, which sells both a 'CompROSSer' and a Bi-CompROSSer, the latter of which houses the Ross-inspired circuit and a Dan Armstrong Orange Squeezer clone (Juicer) in the same box.

If you don't hear an example of the original Ross Compressor's sound on the accompanying CD, you can blame the author. I found mine in that very bargain bin for $15 in 1995, never used it much, and sold it on eBay in 2001 for $225 – before I knew I was going to write this book. Stupid, huh? Sounded great, too, if a little noisy (though all vintage compressors are), but I never used it much and couldn't resist the 1,500 per cent profit.

Ross Compressor
Made: circa early to mid 1980s.
Controls: Sustain and Level; stompswitch for on/off.
Sonics: a juicy-sounding compressor with plenty of squash and sustain; not entirely transparent, but many players love its thickening effect on their tone.

TUBE WORKS
(also Butronics, Chandler, and Audio Matrix)

Eric Johnson's name has come up already in this chapter: it's little known outside the guitar world, but within it virtually everything he touches turns to gold – in tonal terms, at least. Much like the similarly influential Jimi Hendrix and Stevie Ray Vaughan, Johnson's sound isn't perceived as one heavily laden with effects. Yet his endorsement of a pedal has consistently been a guarantee of 'instant classic' status, making it a must-have for thousands of players. Since early in his career, Johnson has sworn by a Tube Driver pedal, and it has since proven the road to overdrive heaven for plenty of others besides.

The Tube Driver was invented by electronics hobbyist and Hammond organ fanatic Brent Butler in the mid 1970s, when he pirated the guts of his dad's old Westinghouse tube stereo system's preamp to create a budget Leslie drive sound. In 1978 Butler adapted the design for a guitarist pal, and by 1979 he was selling the units by custom order under the Butronics company name.

Early Tube Driver models such as the 201 and 204 carried a 6AV6 single-triode tube (much like half a 12AX7) in their gain stage, with a transistorized compressor stage for added sustain, and just three control knobs: Sustain, Drive, and Gain. Revised Tube Drivers made for Chandler after 1985 used a 12AX7 dual-triode, and carried controls for Tube Drive, Hi and Lo EQ, and Out Level. A range of variations on the two main Tube Driver designs have also been offered, along with the Mini Matrix pedals (originally called Mini Boogee, until Mesa/Boogie stepped in and forced a change) sold in the early 1980s under the Audio Matrix banner. Butler's current company, Tube Works, manufactures a reissue of the original design, plus a range of contemporary adaptations of the theme.

Butronics Tube Driver 201
Made: c1979/1980.
Controls: Sustain, Drive, Gain; stompswitch for on/off.
Sonics: raw tube overdrive with thick, squashy compression.

Chandler Tube Driver
Made: c1985-1989.
Controls: Tube Drive, Hi and Lo EQ, Out Level; stompswitch for on/off.
Sonics: thick tube overdrive, from crunchy to saturated depending on Drive setting.

TYCOBRAHE

Californian PA company Tycobrahe ventured into effects pedals in the early 1970s, sold a few hundred units, went out of business a few years later – and thereby secured its entry in the history books of sound.

They are now about as rare as the proverbial rocking-horse poo. Original Tycobrahe pedals weren't especially well put together, but in the early and mid 1970s, there was no shortage of guitarists looking to cop that Hendrix sound, alongside an inversely proportional shortage of octave pedals that would accurately allow them to do so. Roger Mayer's Octavia had never been available on the market, but after a broken Hendrix unit found its way to Tycobrahe engineers for repair… hey, it soon was. Tycobrahe's Octavia – a transformer-coupled full-wave rectifier circuit that creates simulated octave-up sounds – remains the company's most sought-after effect, while the Pedalflanger and Parapedal wah-wah have benefited from the name's legendary status to enjoy $500-plus prices on the vintage market today.

Tycobrahe effects were housed in heavy, cumbersome, Seventies-clunky, almost DIY-looking steel casings, and shipped in groovy sliding-top redwood mini-crates that you could store your home-grown in after the pedal came out (not unlike those used by Electro-Harmonix in recent years). The circuits inside have been said to be basic and at times even shoddily soldered together, but they found their way beneath the feet of a good few star players, and a run of full-color ads in prominent mags like *Guitar Player* helped to take the message to the masses. Where and why it all went wrong remains a mystery.

Chicago Iron has recently stepped into the void to offer 'hand-matched' clones of original Tycobrahe designs, sold as the Octavian and Parachute.

Tycobrahe Octavia
Made: c1971-1977.
Controls: Volume and Boost; stompswitch for on/off.
Sonics: a dissonant fuzz on low fret/string positions, with simulated octaves on single notes played higher up the neck (especially when used with a Strat's neck pickup with Tone rolled down).

UNIVOX

Univox is far and away most famous for its connection with the Uni-Vibe of the late 1960s and early 1970s – another of the legendary 'Jimi' pedals, but also used to famous effect by Robin Trower and Stevie Ray Vaughan. The brand has appeared in one guise or another on a great number of guitars, amps and related accessories under the umbrella of New York merchandisers Merson Musical Products and, later, Gulf & Western, which continued the name within its Unicord range. None of the parent companies manufactured effects pedals as Univox products, but jobbed out the work to other electronics firms, most famously Shin-Ei of Japan, which made the Uni-Vibe. Korg bought out Unicord in the mid 1980s, and has since superseded the Univox name in the music electronics market.

The Uni-Vibe is a four-stage analog phaser designed by Shin-Ei's Fumio Mieda as a compact transistorized simulation of a Leslie rotating speaker cabinet for organ players. Its warm, rounded, swirling liquid sound was appropriated by guitarists after Hendrix used it so addictively on songs like 'Voodoo Chile,' 'The Wind Cries Mary,' his *Woodstock* performance of 'The Star Spangled Banner,' and plenty of others.

In some senses it's a crude effect, though certainly a complex circuit compared to many guitar pedals. As described in more detail in Chapter 2, the heart of the Uni-Vibe is found in the four lamp/photoresistor pairings that make up the phasing stages, and this discrete and very 1960s circuitry's performance yields a sound that can't accurately be emulated by later 'bucket brigade' IC-based chorus, phaser or vibe designs.

Thanks to its legendary associations and the fact that original units were only manufactured for a few years – and those few years occurred three decades ago – vintage Shin-Ei/Univox Uni-Vibes are extremely hard to come by today, and variable in sound and performance. There are drawbacks associated with the fact that it was designed for organ, too; there's no stomp switch for on/off selection in live performance (although the external speed control pedal has a heel-down 'Cancel' position), and the input impedance isn't optimized for guitar, so a fair amount of treble loss is experienced. On top of that, the original Uni-Vibes lacked a stabilized power source, so their performance could vary greatly depending upon where you plugged in it. But does it matter? A good original one can sound fantastic, which is no doubt why the design has spawned so many excellent clones over the years – most with

guitar-friendly no-load input impedances and on/off stomp switches, and many with vintage/modern switching, too, for a warmer/brighter tonal emphasis respectively.

Not that the Uni-Vibe was the only Univox box on the shelf. A similarly styled Uni-Fuzz was briefly available – again, bizarrely, with only a jack for connection of an external on/off switch. There was also a range of 'amp-head' styled larger effects units that included the EC80 and EC100 Echoes, the UEQ-1 Graphic Equalizer, PHZ-1 Phazer, and U3R Pro Verb reverb. Examples were occasionally seen on B-list stages across the country, but they didn't make a whole lot of impact. As well as this, the mid 1970s witnessed those rectangular metal box effects that some of us will remember, with the knobs on the sides and the big hippy-dippy 'keep on truckin''-era silhouette of a bare foot encircling the stomp switch: the Uni-Comp, Square Wave, Micro Fazer, and Noise Clamp.

Around 1985 Univox effects segued into Korg units and then vanished altogether, but the two brands had collaborated before that time. The Korg-Univox-Synthepedal of around 1976 was a surprisingly Uni-Vibish looking affair, with its master unit/external control pedal setup. Also billed as 'The Wiz' (Korg was fond of these cutesy pet names for a while), it offered "synthesizer oriented" filtering effects through

Univox Uni-Vibe [CD track 19]
Made: circa late 1960s to early 1970s.
Controls: Volume, Intensity, Speed via foot control, Chorus/Vibrato switch, Power Switch; dual inputs, single output.
Sonics: the classic analog rotary speaker simulation – a thick, round, watery phasing with smooth vowel-like peaks at slow to medium speeds, and flutey warbles set faster; causes some treble loss in guitar signal.

a range of 200Hz to 4200Hz. The FK-2 Phaser/Wah/Double-Wah pedal of the same era – 'Mr Multi' to his friends – provided the obvious, plus rocker treadle control of the phaser rate (though no depth control), along with something enigmatically labelled 'double wah.' Above them all, though, the Uni-Vibe still reigns supreme.

VOX
(also Jen and Thomas Organ)

Sure, you'd sell your granny for an original copper-top, red-grillecloth AC30 amplifier (depending on your granny's condition, you might not even raise the current asking price), and that's undoubtedly the baby that secured the Vox name in the tone hall of fame. But the legendary three-letter logo found its way on to numerous other musical instruments and accessories besides – many of them pedals that were likewise conceived by AC15 and AC30 designer Dick Denney, the Muhammad Ali of sonic heavyweights in many guitar players' books.

The original British Vox amps of the late 1950s to the late 1960s were manufactured by Jennings Musical Industries Ltd (JMI), founded by Thomas Jennings, who had run a music shop in Dartford, Kent – just south-east of London – since the 1930s. Jennings himself played the accordion and the organ, and his first major manufacturing efforts revolved around both large and compact versions of the latter in the late 1940s, with amps following in the 1950s as a natural requirement of the portable electric organs.

When a guitar craze swept Britain amid the rock'n'roll boom of the 1950s, Jennings concentrated his efforts on meeting the growing demands for quality amplification. He joined forces with engineer Dick Denney and launched the Vox range in 1956 with the Denney-designed AC15. This 15W class A 1x12" combo, based on a pair of EL84 output valves, is often billed as the first tube amplifier designed specifically for the guitar, rather than adapted from general radio applications as published in guides such as the *RCA Tube Applications Manual*. True or not, there's certainly one irrefutable fact at the center of the Vox legend: Dick Denney had 'the ears,' and time and again he produced designs that have set new standards in rock'n'roll tone. His AC4 and AC10 'student amp' designs are also great sounding recording or certainly small-gig combos, and when bands needed more power at the end of the 1950s, Denney doubled the AC15 to produce the AC30.

Like other guitar-gear manufacturers of the day, Jennings quickly saw the sense of offering a broad accessories line, and from the early 1960s the company had effects in its catalogs, too. Among the first were the standard rocker-treadle Volume Pedal, and the Vibravox, a separate 'head cab' style unit that produced "three degrees of vibrato and three degrees of tremulant (tremolo)," according to Vox promotions of the time. By the mid 1960s, the line-up had multiplied many times over. With Denney's design help, Vox had manufactured its own Tone-Bender fuzz unit in the early 1960s, as well as a Bass Booster, Treble Booster, DeLuxe Distortion Booster, and Bass/Treble Booster (a full-range boost with tone control, really), all in small metal boxes that plugged directly into the guitar. There were tape echo units like the Echo DeLuxe, a Vox Reverb unit, and by the mid 1960s, when it became difficult for Jennings to keep up with production in its Dartford factory, a Sola Sound-made Tone-Bender pedal in the familiar wedge-shaped casing. But of all Vox effects, it was one whose design originated thousands of miles away, in California, that would make the most lasting impression.

In the wake of the British Invasion of the early 1960s and The Beatles' massive popularity in America, Jennings negotiated a deal with Thomas Organ of Sepulveda, California, for distribution and sales of Vox products in the US and Canada. Jennings' belief appears to have been that Thomas Organ would import Vox amps from the UK, but the contract apparently gave the company the right to use the Vox name on its own products, and it swiftly ramped up production on inferior-sounding California-made solid state Vox amps to sell to the thousands of kids that were hot for the 'Beatles sound.' The deal trashed the Vox reputation with plenty of guitarists in the States for many years (at least until they discovered the British-import AC30s), and went a long way toward trashing Jennings's company in the UK too.

The one good thing it did set into motion was a brief sharing of technologies, on the back of which Vox picked up the design for one of rock's great tonal icons: the Vox Wah-Wah pedal.

The history of the development and early production of the wah-wah pedal is sketchy, and the design and manufacture of the effect hopped through a number of evolutions quickly in a few years from the mid to late 1960s. Thomas Organ engineer Brad Plunkett invented the wah-wah around 1965, and it first saw the light of day as The Clyde McCoy Wah-Wah Pedal (named for its imitation of the then-famous trumpeter's mute technique). It evolved down separate but related paths into both the Vox Wah-Wah and the Thomas Organ Cry Baby, with various changes in production location and circuit design along the way. Before manufacturing its own Clyde McCoy, however, Thomas Organ had sent the circuit to Vox in Britain. It was adapted by Denney to make the most of local components for a brief manufacturing run in Jennings's Dartford plant, then jobbed out to Jen Elettronica in Pescara, Italy which was manufacturing other transistorized Vox effects. Some early Clyde McCoys were apparently initially made in California, then Thomas Organ shifted its wah-wah production to Jen, too. In 1968 it launched the famous Cry Baby for US sale, but there were also Vox Cry Baby Wahs sold in the UK in the late 1960s.

Although the pedals had the same design roots, there were distinct differences between them that sent some guitarists to the Vox Wah-Wah camp, and some to the Cry Baby. Hendrix and Clapton used a Vox Wah-Wah for the characteristic singing tone. Plenty of others favored the Cry Baby, with its slightly shorter rocker travel and sweet, fluid sound. Early versions of both featured the famous red Fasel inductor, although Jen later switched to the occasionally derided TDK inductor, making some other circuit changes along with it. Despite the changes, the pedal continued to satisfy thousands of guitarists. But the Fasel-era Jen McCoy/Vox/Cry Baby is undoubtedly the classic… or classics.

Early Vox and Cry Baby wahs lacked 'true bypass' and significantly loaded the guitar's pickups, even

Jen Fuzz

Made: late 1960s.

Controls: Level and Attack knobs; stompswitch for on/off.

Sonics: bright but creamy fuzz tones in the classic 1960s Brit mold… from this Italian-made pedal.

Vox Wah-Wah (original diecast silver, 1966/67)

Made: c1966/67.

Controls: rocker treadle for wah-wah, with unseen stompswitch for on/off.

Sonics: sweet and round frequency range – the original silver diecast UK-made Vox Wah with halo inductor.

Vox Wah-Wah (with interior)

Made: c1967/68.

Controls: rocker treadle for wah-wah, with unseen stompswitch for on/off.

Sonics: fluid, singing wah-wah tones; the 'Hendrix-era' chrome-treadle Italian-made Vox Wah, with Fasel inductor.

Thomas Organ Cry Baby

Made: circa late 1960s.

Controls: rocker treadle for wah-wah, with unseen stompswitch for on/off.

Sonics: sweet and vocal, classic 'American rock' wah-wah; Italian Jen-made with Fasel inductor.

Jen Repeat Percussion (with original box)

Made: mid to late1960s (also as Vox Repeat Percussion).

Controls: Rate knob, slide switch for on/off.

Sonics: a hard-chop, tremolo-like pulsing repeat of your pick attack.

Jen KPS900 Phase Shifter

Made: early to mid 1970s.

Controls: Intensity and Speed knobs, stompswitch for on/off.

Sonics: basic but good-sounding analog phasing.

Vox Chorus

Made: early 1980s.

Controls: Intensity, Speed and Input knobs, stompswitch for on/off.

Sonics: thick, swirling delay-based chorus sounds.

in the off position, keeping the circuit attached to the input at all times. Plenty of players have moaned about the resultant high-frequency loss, in recent years especially, and the 'no-load' wah-wah is a popular mod; but that mellowing of the highs – accomplished even when the vintage wah-wah was in 'bypass' mode – was one of the contributing factors to the warm, gutsy Les Paul/SG-plus-Marshall stack sound of the 1960s.

Vox continued to offer effects through its various corporate incarnations: the square black box Treble/Bass Booster, Distortion Booster, and Repeat Percussion of the early 1970s, the V-shaped white pedals of the Dallas-Arbiter-ownership years of the late 1970s. In recent years Vox – now owned by Korg – has reissued the Wah-Wah and the Tone-Bender, but has concentrated more on capitalizing on its tube amp reissues and new digital amp designs.

WATKINS/WEM

The south London-based Watkins Electric Music was founded in the mid 1950s by accordionist and music shop owner Charlie Watkins. The company is best known for its affordable but good-sounding tube amps – the V-front Dominator being an early classic – and some of its budget guitar line, which fueled British demand in the rock'n'roll years, before Fenders and Gibsons were readily available (or, in later times, often affordable). Like most of the competition, though, Watkins diversified into a few related gizmos and accessories, and deserves an entry here for one in particular: the Copicat Echo Unit.

Watkins developed his simple but effective and relatively compact tube-powered tape echo with the help of engineer Bill Purkis in 1958, and had the unit on the market before other famous European tape delays made by the likes of Binson, Meazzi and Vox. Thanks to some excited word-of-mouth publicity, Watkins sold out the entire debut run of 100 Copicats on the first day they appeared in his record store. More would follow, and its warm, rich echo soon became a major ingredient of the British guitar sound.

In around 1963 or 1964, Watkins started trading under the WEM name – apparently because he liked the look of the distinctive three-letter Vox logo – but the Copicat and most amp designs remained. The echo evolved through a few cosmetic and slight circuit mutations, until the biggest change of all, to solid state, happened in the late 1960s. It will come as no surprise that the tube models are the most desirable (many players like to run their signal through them even with the tape motor disengaged, for the slight thickening the tube circuitry gives the sound), but the solid state models are also very good sounding tape delay units, and a bargain compared to their forerunners. Sound-on-sound and varispeed models also came and went over the years.

Guild also marketed the Watkins/WEM-made Copicat under its own name from the mid 1960s and into the 1970s. Charlie Watkins is now in his eighties, and has continued making updated versions of both the Copicat and the V-front Dominator amp.

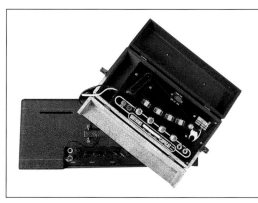

Watkins Copicat Echo Unit
Made: late 1950s to 1970s (first tube-powered, later solid state).
Controls: Swell, Reverb, Gain One and Gain Two knobs; three playback head select buttons (Halo, Echo and Repeat; Motor Off/On switch; dual inputs, single output.
Sonics: a basic but warm, tubey analog tape echo, from slapback to short delays.

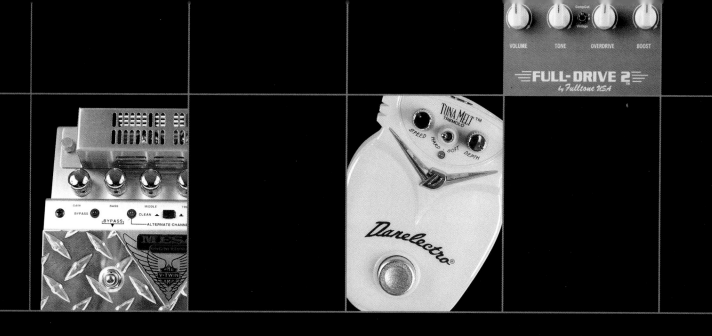

Chapter 4
CONTEMPORARY BRANDS

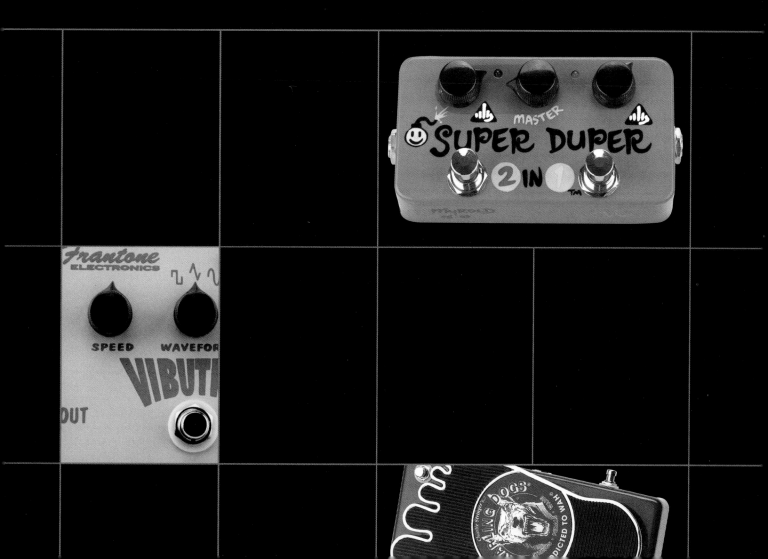

Current makes and models of effects pedals don't quite evoke the romantic images of units from days gone by. Effects from the early years of the 'transistor revolution' – fuzzes with hit-and-miss transistor selection, solid state delays with noisy decay, wah-wahs with severe tone-sucking issues in bypass mode – wear a literal and metaphorical patina that tickles a sentimental bone in many players and collectors alike. Nonetheless a strong case could be argued that many new makes are better pedals. Of the vintage types that are represented by an updated or modified 'clone' or 'homage,' the new version is generally quieter, more versatile and more reliable than the original that inspired it – and equally toneful along with it.

Of course, it's always easier to dissect a groundbreaking design of old and make a few minor improvements to it than it is to draw up that original design from scratch, so I don't mean to imply any disrespect or lack of credit due to the many, many great old effects covered in the previous chapter. But it's important to distinguish what you want out of a pedal and, in many cases, to clearly delineate the lines between players and collectors.

Rather than kick around – and quickly devalue – a $500 original TS-808 (which, in fact, doesn't have quite enough low-end for you anyway, "but hey, it's a *classic*"), maybe you'd be better off gigging with a Hotcakes or a Route 66 at a fraction of the price. Gagging for that juicy, lush Uni-Vibe sound, but not sure the $700 unit you bagged in a recent auction will remain trustworthy on stage? Outstanding, rugged, reliable versions can be had from Fulltone, Sweet Sound, Roger Mayer, Prescription, Voodoo Lab, Foxrox and others. Again, no attempt is being made here to tell you how to spend your money; this is primarily a look at what's out there, with a few notes on sounds and applications.

Some contemporary makers use the past as a springboard and create significantly better products than were ever available before simply by virtue of a few well-chosen modifications. Others do nothing new whatsoever, but just make vanished effects available to the guitarist again. Still others hack out entirely new paths, forging into sonic territory never before explored. And a good few do a little of all three. Each route serves its purpose, and deserves consideration here.

Of course there are also manufacturers out there that churn out lines of cheaply made 'copies of copies' of the better made and slightly upmarket mass manufactured pedals, merely to have something to sell to beginners and players on a tight budget. They serve their purpose, too (we've all got to start somewhere, and the $39 Plastico Stereo Chorus might be just the place), but these are less likely to get coverage here.

By virtue of their youth, the contemporary makers generally have less in the way of history to probe, and fewer 'rock legend' style anecdotes, too, and some of the smaller names are very thinly documented at best. Also, there are more new pedals available today than could ever be covered in one book, with new makes coming to the market all the time, so forgive me if your favorite new chorus or overdrive is absent from these pages.

ANALOG MAN

Before becoming a brand in itself, Analog Man – headed by Analog Mike (Mike Piera) – operated as a vintage pedal dealer and new pedal modder from his shop-cum-workshop in Danbury, Connecticut. The former computer software engineer built up his sideline in effects through the course of the 1990s, which evolved through copying designs from the ground up to building his own modified and/or improved versions of classics. He took up the business full-time in 2000.

Analog Man now offers a range of pedals based on many of the easily defined 'classics' of the 1970s and early 1980s. The CompROSSer is a modified 'clone' of the gray Ross Compressor, while the Bi-CompROSSer houses the same plus a Juicer (an MXR Orange Squeezer comp clone) in the same box. British classics of the 1960s are paid tribute by the Sun Face (a Fuzz Face clone) and Beano Booster (based on the Dallas Rangemaster), and the Clone Chorus offers the round, musical sound of the Electro-Harmonix Small Clone of the 1970s, but with a full-range Depth knob rather than just the switch of the original.

ARION

Yes, this is very likely one of the brands that sprang to mind at my "Plastico Stereo Chorus" quip in the chapter intro above, and the Arion brand certainly resides in the budget camp. They could also easily be placed in the 'vintage' category, having been around since the 1980s. But a couple of the company's units have found their way onto pro pedalboards for years, and much of its affordable range continues to do great service for the shallower-pocketed among us. Sure, they are housed in plastic casings, and the switches and knobs aren't the most kick-proof in the shop, but they are surprisingly sturdy overall (and those casings, plastic or not, take more bashing than you'd first suspect).

I don't have the statistics to hand, but a look at gigging guitarists' set-ups down the years has convinced me that the Arion Stage Tuner is one of the most widely used of such devices out there. Another surprising pro choice is the Stereo Chorus, as used by blueser Jon Amor and LA session guitarist Mike Landau. The Stereo Flanger, Stereo Distortion, SMM-1 Stereo Metal Master, SAD-3 Stereo Delay and a few others also have decent sounds and some clever features – and each is yours off-the-shelf for less than $50. Have a field day.

Arion Stereo Chorus

Made: circa mid 1980s to present.
Controls: Speed, Depth, and Chorus; stompswitch for on/off.
Sonics: a round, musical stereo chorus with good versatility; admirably avoids generic 1980s chorus-itis, and even does good Leslie simulations.

Arion Stage Tuner

Made: circa 1980s to present.
Controls: analog meter, stompswitch to select bypass or mute/tune.
Sonics: magically makes you sound more in-tune if you step on it, then tune your guitar.

BAD CAT

This relatively new Californian boutique amp maker arose in the temporary void left by Matchless when that wonder of tubular class A technology hit the rocks and vanished for the best part of a year around the turn of the Millennium. Bad Cat has featured designs from Matchless co-founder Mark Sampson, whom owner James Heidrich hired as a consultant, and consequently the early look was very much 'rebadged Matchless' – although models and features soon evolved slightly away from that line.

Bad Cat's X-Treme Tone is a two-channel tube overdrive offering a virtually clean boost on Channel One, with high-gain tube overdrive from Channel Two, and the ability to cascade the two channels together. The 2 Tone is a similar-looking pedal (again a tube overdrive with two 12AX7s), but with different intentions: Channel One is a 'tone boost'-style tone shaping channel, while Channel Two provides either gain boost or heavy overdrive. Both have the build quality that players familiar with Bad

Cat amps would expect, and include niceties like internally regulated AC power stages, point-to-point wiring, triple-plated chrome top panels, chicken head knobs, and a full seven pounds of industrial-strength tonal goodness.

BLACKSTONE

The Blackstone Appliances 2SV3 Mosfet Overdrive is a high-grade, hand-built 'boutique' pedal, and the only production unit that New York-based designer/builder Jon Blackstone offers. Despite its diminutive size (4.4″ x 2.4″), the businesslike crinkle-coated metal box carries two footswitches and five slotted potentiometer controls for gain, level and post-OD EQ adjustment of its two channels, plus a further two trimpots inside for fine tuning treble content and mid-range response. The Brown channel caters for softer overdrives from crunchy rhythm to bluesy lead tones, while the Red gets altogether hairier when cranked up, though both stay short of any contemporary heavy rock or metal sounds. Blackstone

Blackstone 2SV3 Mosfet Overdrive [CD track 41]
Made: circa 1990s to present.
Controls: Red Drive, Red Level, Brown Drive, Brown Level and EQ; stompswitches for Channel select and Bypass (on/off).
Sonics: gritty, rich, transparent light crunch from Brown channel, and juicy, tactile overdrive from Red, all with excellent clarity and dynamics.

emphasizes that the 2SV3 is designed to retain the character of whatever guitar you put through it, and advises that the unit "requires unbuffered connection to the guitar" for most effective performance. When used accordingly, the Mosfet Overdrive offers impressive control of distortion levels from the guitar's volume pot. Blackstone might be a one-pedal wonder, but what a pedal.

BUDDA

The staff of Budda Amplification includes one Dan Van Riesen, a former Mesa/Boogie designer responsible for the Triaxis preamp and V-Twin pedal, so the agenda of this purple-hearted California company's first and possibly best-known pedal will come as no surprise. The Phatman is a 2x12AX7-powered tube overdrive pedal with Volume, Treble, Bass and Gain knobs, and a sonic range from juicy blues crunch to vintage overdrive. The similarly styled Zenman is built to the same format, but with more gain for the heavy rock/metal crowd. The company now also offers the Budda Wah and Budda Wah+, the latter switchable for 16dB of clean volume boost.

Budda Phatman
Made: late 1990s to present.
Controls: Volume, Treble, Bass, Gain; stomp switch for on/off.
Sonics: master-volume-style tube preamp for sounds from clean-ish gain boost to crunch to vintage heavy overdrive.

CARL MARTIN

This Danish pedal maker has a reputation for turning out solid, gigworthy units that are both good sounding and admirably versatile, and has developed a 'mainstay' image beyond its years. The Carl Martin brand is a division of East Sound Research, a PA rental company founded in 1990, which hit the scene in a big way in 1993 with its first pedal, the Hot Drive'n Boost – still a very popular 'two-in-one' style unit, now evolved through Mk2 and Mk3 versions.

The Fuzz carries more knobs than any other 'standard' fuzz pedal you're likely to encounter; the Tremo O'Vibe is another two-in-one pedal; the Two Faze offers vintage dual-phase shifting sounds; and the newer Hydra Boost is a simple, discrete transistorized one-knob clean boost pedal. Also available are the self-descriptive Crunch Drive and Heavy Drive overdrive pedals. All carry prices that hover well above the heads of their mass-market rivals from the far East, but they are designed to be solid, professional units and are built to last.

The Fuzz
Made: late 1990s to present (Mk1 unit pictured).
Controls: Level, Deep, High, Gain, Bass, Middle, Treble; stomp switch for on/off.
Sonics: from light, warm fuzz to serious hornet-in-a-tin-can, with a broad range of EQ settings available.

CROWTHER AUDIO

Let a drummer start thinking creatively about anything other than thumping the tubs and you're usually bound for trouble. But when original Split Enz drummer Paul Crowther strayed briefly from skins slapping in the late 1970s to tinker with effects pedal ideas, the eventual result was one of the most highly regarded – though least seen – overdrive pedals on the planet. The Hot Cake carries controls for Gain, Level and Presence, and is beloved for its natural, tubey sounding overdrive which, like pedals of the Tube Screamer variety, sounds best into a somewhat cranked tube amp and doesn't excel at megathrash rock sounds – although the Hot Cakes will do a thicker, fuzzier distortion than TS types when fully floored. The pedal has become a favorite of a long list of players, which includes names as diverse as Sonic Youth, The Melvins, Noel Gallagher of Oasis and Stephen Malkmus of Pavement. Stevie Ray Vaughan is rumored to have owned one for a time before his death, although I haven't found any documented evidence that he ever put it onto record.

Crowther still hand-builds his Hot Cakes in his New Zealand headquarters, and has recently added the Prunes & Custard pedal to the lineup. This one is described as a 'harmonic intermodulator-generator,' with Level, Mix and Drive controls that dial in anything from quirky distortion to near-auto-wah sounds. Characterful pedals from a characterful maker.

DANELECTRO

The Danelectro comeback has been a phenomenal tale of relaunching and then reinventing a vintage brand. Danelectro guitars of the 1950s and 1960s were always budget options, but packed some of the best cool-for-dollar ratios. The original company closed down in 1969, so never really jumped on the pedal revolution of the late 1960s and early 1970s. But after the Evets Corporation acquired the name in 1995, and starting running out good reissues of the guitars three years later, it saw the sense in launching the Danelectro pedal range that 'might have been.'

Dano pedals, all made in China, are definitely of the cheap and cheerful variety – both in cost and construction – but the lineup offers a broad range of units, often with clever designs and useful added features, and has occasionally found fans among a few pro users. The look is irresistible, too, and capitalizes on the 1950s tailfin-chic that always helps to inspire 'classic' associations, linking cars and guitars of the rock'n'roll era.

The debut large-pedal range of 1998 included the Dan-Echo, Daddy O Overdrive, Fab Tone Distortion, Cool Cat Chorus and Dan-O-Matic Stage Tuner. These units, which were discontinued by the end of 2003, were housed in sturdy die-cast metal casings, with plastic 'auto fascia' type inserts to carry the knobs. In another year or so Danelectro really began to hit its stride with the far broader Mini Pedal range. With plastic casings and simplified sonic intentions, these diner-themed pedals are cheaper than their larger brethren, and offer just about every flavor of effect you could imagine. To date, the mini pedal range includes the Pastrami Overdrive, T-Bone Distortion, BLT Slap Echo, Corned Beef Reverb, Tuna Melt Tremolo, Pepperoni Phaser, Milkshake Chorus, Hash Browns Flanger, Surf & Turf Compressor, Grilled Cheese Distortion, Lemon Pitcher Tuner, Chili Dog Octave, French Toast Octave Distortion, Fish & Chips 7-Band EQ, Chicken Salad Vibrato, Bacon 'N Eggs Mini Amp/Distortion, PB & Jelly Delay, Rocky Road Spinning Speaker, Black Coffee Metal Distortion, Black Licorice Beyond Metal Distortion, French Fries Auto Wah, and Blueberry Muffin Chromatic Tuner. Some sound pretty good – others not quite so – but it's a fun array of cute plastic pedals, whatever your ears tell you.

Danelectro's upscale pedal range has also expanded further in the last couple of years. A car-shaped lineup of treadle-style pedals includes the Dan-O-Wah, Shift Daddy echo/pitch shifter, and Trip L Wah. A new 'wide body' sheet-metal-encased range so far includes the Reel Echo tape delay simulator (which recently surfaced in Aerosmith guitarist Brad Whitford's rig) and Spring King spring reverb unit. The large-box range has expanded to include the hippy-themed Free Speech Talk Box, Black Paisley Distortion, Blue Paisley Overdrive, Back Talk Reverse Delay, Sitar Swami sitar simulator, and Psycho Flange pedals. And the newest, up-market Wasabi range includes the AC-1 Chorus-Trem, AD-1 Forward-Reverse Delay, AS-1 Rock-A-Bye, AO-1 Overdrive and AX-1 Distortion. Doesn't look like the new sounds are close to drying up just yet.

Danelectro Black Coffee

Made: 2001 to present.
Controls: Level, Bass and Treble; electronic stompswitch for on/off.
Sounds: somewhat fuzzy distortion, but with a wide range of tonal variation from Bass and Treble controls.

Danelectro Rocky Road [CD track 82]

Made: 2001 to present.
Controls: Speed and Drive knobs, with toggle switch for Fast/Slow Ramp (speed increase/decrease); electronic footswitches for Ramp and on/off.
Sonics: decent budget rotating speaker sounds with gradual ramping between fast and slow selection on the footswitch, though not an especially accurate 'Leslie simulator;' slightly cheesy Drive sounds.

Danelectro BLT

Made: 2001 to present.
Controls: Mix and Repeat; electronic stompswitch for on/off.
Sonics: short slapback echoes at variable depth and repeats.

Danelectro Chili Dog

Made: 2001 to present.

Controls: Oct 2, Direct, Oct 1; electronic stompswitch for on/off.

Sonics: good sounding one and/or two-octave-below effects, with particularly decent tracking of Oct 1.

Danelectro PB&J

Made: 2001 to present.

Controls: Mix, Speed (delay time), Repeats; electronic footswitches for Long/Short echo and On/Off.

Sonics: fairly warm, if slightly lo-fi, short to medium delays.

Danelectro Black Licorice

Made: 2001 to present.

Controls: Level and Bass knobs, toggle switch for Octave On/Off; electronic stompswitch for on/off.

Sonics: filthy, evil heavy metal distortion sounds with added octave effect when desired.

Danelectro French Fries

Made: 2001 to present.

Controls: Resonance knob, toggle switch for Lo/Hi Range (sweep); electronic stompswitch for on/off.

Sonics: somewhat limited but occasionally funky auto-wah sounds.

Danelectro Tuna Melt [CD track 63]

Made: 2001 to present.

Controls: Speed and Depth knobs, toggle switch for Hard/Soft response; electronic stompswitch for on/off.

Sonics: effective tremolo effects, with slight 'honk' at peak of pulse, even on soft settings.

Danelectro Trip L Wah

Made: 2002 to present.

Controls: rocker treadle; electronic stompswitches for effect on/off and selection of three tonal options.

Sonics: decently musical vintage to contemporary wah voices.

 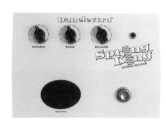  

Danelectro Reel Echo [CD track 70]

Made: 2002 to present.

Controls: Mix, Lo-Fi and Repeats knobs; toggle switches for Solid State/Tube Tone and Warble On/Off; slider for Speed Range (delay), from 0 to 1500 milliseconds; electronic stompswitches for Sound On Sound and On/Off; Stereo (dry) and Main outputs.

Sonics: a broad range of warm, rich tape echo simulations, with added subtle vibrato from the Warble feature, plus Sound On Sound tape-looping.

Danelectro Spring King

Made: 2002 to present.

Controls: Volume, Tone and Reverb (depth); Kick Pad; electronic stompswitch for on/off.

Sonics: budget-toned short-spring boing with a reasonable range of depth and tone, plus added 'oops, I bumped the amp' fun from the rubber Kick Pad.

Danelectro Free Speech

Made: 2002 to present.

Controls: Volume and Growl; electronic stompswitch for on/off; plus attached plastic 'voice tube' with dual attached mini mikes.

Sonics: traditional talk box wah and pseudo-speech sounds, but with unusual built-in microphone for playback straight into guitar amp; as such, occasionally prone to feedback.

Danelectro Blue Paisley

Made: 2002 to present.

Controls: Level, Tone, Single/Hum and Drive knobs; toggle switch for Mid-range Boost/Off/Cut; electronic stompswitch for on/off.

Sonics: tonally flexible vintage tube-style overdrive with a round, juicy voice.

DEMETER

Demeter Amplification of Van Nuys, California, is more widely know for its pro audio gear – which includes a range of rack-mount effects and tube preamps – and also has a good reputation for its guitar amps and speaker cabinets. But the company's limited original line of two guitar pedals has earned it some devoted followers from that camp too. Eric Clapton is a long-time user of the TRM-1 Tremulator, which is one of the few pedals in his set-up. The effect is designed to reproduce the smooth but deep triangular wave tremolo of blackface Fender amps, and plenty of players swear it's the closest you can get short of carting around an old Twin or Super Reverb. Demeter has cleverly added a small 1dB gain boost circuit to the tremolo to counteract the perceived volume-loss that occurs when many tremolos are switched in, so you can also turn the Depth to zero and use it as a low-level booster/buffer pedal.

The COMP-1 Opto Compulator is a little bit special in the realm of compressor pedals, and does its thing via a compact version of the optical compression circuit at the heart of many classic solid state studio compressors. In addition to its Compress and Volume controls, it carries a trim pot (accessed through a hole in the side) that can be used to adjust the gain of the unit's preamp. These two have

Demeter TRM-1 The Tremulator [CD track 58]

Made: c1990s to present.

Controls: Depth and Speed; mechanical stompswitch for on/off.

Sonics: rich, round tube-amp style tremolo with excellent depth and a broad range of speed selection.

Demeter COMP-1 Opto Compulator [CD track 12]

Made: c1990s to present.

Controls: Compress and Volume, plus Gain trimpot; mechanical stompswitch for on/off.

Sonics: warm, plummy, but generally transparent compression, tweakable for anything from subtle sustain to attack-gobbling squash, with some 'swelling and pumping' effects at more extreme Compress settings.

recently also been joined by a pedal version of the Demeter Fat Control, previously available only as an onboard mid boost/buffer for guitar.

DINOSAURAL

Dan Coggins was the chief designer and co-founder of Britain's Lovetone pedals – for whom he retains the service contract – but he has recently branched out by himself, gradually introducing his own pedals under the name Dinosaural. The first of these is the Dinosaural Tube Bender overdrive, co-designed by David Petersen (a London amp tech and co-author of the book *The Vox Story* with Dick Denney). The design first saw the light of day as a DIY kit offered to readers of *The Guitar Magazine* (UK), and is a take on a 'best of both world's' blend of Tube Screamer-esque overdrive leaning towards Tone Bender fuzz/distortion. The totally discrete transistorized class A circuit in the hand-made production model runs from chunky boost to high-gain distortion, but with good clarity, dynamics and frequency response throughout the range. What this mainly means is that the Tube Bender retains a

Dinosaural Tube Bender [CD track 63]

Made: late 2003 to present.

Controls: Drive, Tone and Output knobs; Tone Shift switch; stompswitch for on/off.

Sonics: from crunchy, dynamic overdrive to thick, fat distortion, all with good body and excellent retention of guitar character.

firm low end and more transparent mids – factors that many detractors say are missing from even the best of Tube Screamers. Coggins' pedigree with Lovetone is impressive, so look for more Dinosaural pedals to come. (For more detail on the birth of Lovetone and effects philosophy in general, see the interview with Dan Coggins in Chapter 6.)

DUNLOP

The Jim Dunlop company has its roots in quality guitar accessories such as capos, plectrums and bottleneck slides, but has also carved out a business in recent years by buying up the rights to the brand names of many defunct classic pedals and marketing reissues of the same. Current-production Cry Baby, Fuzz Face, MXR, Uni-Vibe and Heil Talkbox models hale from the Dunlop camp, along with own-brand pedals such as the Rotovibe, Tremolo Stereo Pan, and Jimi Hendrix System range.

Dunlop, a Scottish immigrant, established his company in California as a supplier of guitar parts and accessories, and today it's the largest source of almost anything from fret wire to fingerboard lube. The early histories of Dunlop's reissue model effects will be documented in detail under their original names in Chapter 3: the Fuzz Face under Arbiter, the MXR range under MXR, the Cry Baby Wah Wah under Vox, and so on. The same applies to some extent to the Univox Uni-Vibe too, but the Dunlop Uni-Vibe is so different that it should probably be considered to exist in name only and not as a strict 'reissue' of the original (and in fact some other manufacturers' Uni-Vibe 'clones' come closer in sound and construction than the correctly named Dunlop Uni-Vibe of today). The current Dunlop Uni-Vibe does carry a photocell-based four-stage phasing circuit like the original – housed beneath a little silver foil box mounted at the center of the circuit board – although its little brother, the Uni-Vibe Stereo Chorus, does not, and has a totally IC-based circuit instead.

As well as all of the above, there are the company's own current models, and those which carry the names of vintage designs but have been evolved by Dunlop Manufacturing to meet the demands of modern music. Overall, Dunlop has developed a reputation for robust construction, although many of the circuits – and the components in them – have been altered from the originals.

Cry Baby is one of Dunlop's longest-standing 'classic' brands (launched around 1990), and one of its most diversified ranges, too. The company continues to offer the Cry Baby Classic Model GCB-95F, which once again carries the long-unavailable Italian Fasel inductor (or at least an Italian-made coil with the name 'Fasel' on the outside of it), but this old standby is just the tip of the wah-wah iceberg. There's also the Cry Baby 95Q with adjustable gain boost and Q controls; the Cry Baby 535Q with Q and gain (although even more gain boost) plus six-position rotary voicing switch; DB-01 Dimebag Signature 'Cry Baby From Hell' with extended sweep range, five-way frequency range selector and camouflage housing; the DB-02 Dimebag Custom, hardwired for the Pantera guitarist's favorite setting as a lower price; the GCB-100 and 105Q Bass Cry Baby Wahs; the BB-535 Cry Baby Series Wah for bass and guitar; the EW-95V Mister Cry Baby Volume Wah; DCR-1SR Cry Baby Rack – as used by Slash – which has multiple settings and is capable of taking input from multiple footcontrollers placed around the stage; and the QZ1 Crybaby Q Zone auto-wah.

The company's Jimi Hendrix System includes a range of pedals designed to give the player 'that Hendrix sound' in reliable new packages that provide an alternative to hunting down vintage examples of Hendrix's effects chain. The frequency of the JH-1 Wah-Wah's operating range has been lowered to yield a more 'open' sound; the JH-2S Classic Fuzz carries germanium transistors for a soft, vintage 1960s fuzz sound; the JH-1FW Fuzz Wah combines the two effects; and the JH-3S Octave Fuzz adds the simulated octave-up Octavia sound to the fuzz.

Dunlop Cry Baby 535Q [CD track 33]

Made: 1998 to present.
Controls: rocker treadle for wah-wah, six-way rotary EQ selector, bottom-mounted trim pots for Variable Q and Boost.
Sonics: from mid-voiced vintage wah-wah sounds to more extreme screaming treble voices, with boost as desired.

Dunlop Uni-Vibe [CD track 83]

Made: circa early 1990s to present.

Controls: Speed, Volume and Intensity knobs; Chorus/Vibrato switch; stompswitches for on/off and Chorus/Vibrato mode; optional external footcontroller for Speed control.

Sonics: rotating speaker simulation with a pronounced 'choppy,' lopsided edge in Chorus mode; true vibrato with subtle pitch modulation in Vibrato mode.

Dunlop Uni-Vibe Stereo Chorus (not pictured) [CD track 19]

Made: 2000 to present.

Controls: Mix, Speed and Intensity; stompswitch for on/off; mono input and stereo outputs.

Sonics: a smooth, warbly stereo chorus or subtle vibrato, with 'vintage' tonality (ie considerable loss of high frequencies).

Dunlop Tremolo Stereo Pan

Made: circa 1990s to present.

Controls: Intensity, Shape and Speed; stompswitches for Mono/Stereo and on/off; stereo outputs.

Sonics: wide-ranging tremolo effects plus stereo 'ping-pong' panning.

Dunlop Jimi Hendrix System Classic Fuzz

Made: late 1990s to present.

Controls: Volume and Fuzz; stompswitch for on/off.

Sonics: juicy, squashy fuzz tones in the 1960s germanium vein.

Dunlop Jimi Hendrix System Octave Fuzz

Made: late 1990s to present.

Controls: Volume and Tone; stompswitch for on/off.

Sonics: thick, somewhat soft fuzz with good sustain, effect.

FOXROX

As a young mixing console quality control technician for Crest Audio, Dave Fox – a guitarist and pedalhead on the side – was the man behind the mid-1980s Crest reissue of the Dallas-Arbiter Fuzz Face (Dallas Music Industries had evolved into Crest Audio some years before). He launched his own Foxrox effects company in 1992, and debuted with the Provibe, a Uni-Vibe clone built by Fox after his examination of a vintage unit. Early models were silk screened in the kitchen of his New Jersey home and wired up in the bedroom, but the Provibe's sonic reputation far exceeds its humble origins, and it has since found its way to the pedalboards of Joe Perry, Steve Lukather and Lenny Kravitz, among others. Fox's sometimes quirky but versatile and toneful units aren't widely seen, but have built up quite a following since the days of the Provibe.

The Paradox TZF is a pedal offering 'through-zero flanging' of the variety achieved in the studio in the 1960s and 1970s with a pair of synched – and then carefully un-synched – reel-to-reel tape decks. Rather than the constant swirl of the standard flanger pedal, it produces a sound that not only sweeps down the frequency spectrum of 360 to 0 degrees, but continues through the '0' to yield a rich, fat, musical sweep through the 'negative' degrees beyond zero. The unit also has a Negative TZF mode that produces deep frequency cancellations (or notches) with an extreme sound and occasionally radical low-end reduction.

Fox's Captain Coconut, developed with the help of Mike Piera from Analog Man, is a transistorized homage to 'The Hendrix Sound.' This three-part pedal – perhaps 'analog multi-effects unit' would be a better description – groups Fuzz Face, Uni-Vibe and Octavia clones (dubbed FuzzFoot, Provibe and Octave) in the same housing. The effects can be used individually or together and, impressively, the FuzzFoot section in the Mk2 model comes with interchangeable plug-in circuit cards to let you fine-tune your fuzz. Blues virtuoso Kenny Wayne Shepherd has become a big fan of the Captain Coconut in the last couple years. Foxrox has also recently introduced the ZIM dual-overdrive pedal, with independent Drive and Volume controls for two separate (but chainable) channels, and a plug-in circuit card swapping system similar to that of the more recent Captain Coconuts.

FRANTONE

Pedal designer Fran Blanche founded Frantone in Brooklyn, New York, in 1994, and with the help of Mia Theodoratus has built it into one of the better-respected 'boutique' pedalmakers operating today. Frantone pedals are built to original designs and totally hand-made in New York City, where the small staff personally prints, etches, drills and solders every one of the circuit boards, and machines, silk screens and finishes the cast aluminum casings. The pedals have built up an excellent reputation for their sonic individuality, and their colorful looks – which usually include brightly enameled cases, custom-molded color-matched bakelite knobs and contrasting status LEDs – have been turning heads from the start. All pedals incorporate military spec circuit boards, and are hooked up with aircraft-grade silver-teflon wire. (For more Frantone history and design details see the full interview with Mia Theodoratus in Chapter 6.)

Blanche was the brain behind Electro-Harmonix's NYC Big Muff reissue of 2000, and she has made a name for herself as a designer of overdrives and fuzzes in particular, although she doesn't recycle the E-H design in any of her own current pedals – and in fact Frantone generally steers clear of cloning or copying models from the past.

Frantone's first commercial release was the two-knob HepCat, an overdrive with a juicy, transparent sound that won it plenty of followers. The HepCat was recently superseded by the cobalt-blue Brooklyn Overdrive, which has the same tonality but carries an added Tone control, and has been given more gain. The Peachfuzz – a distortion-cum-fuzz box intended for lead guitar – has also recently been reintroduced in a three-knob format, with 50 per cent extra gain. On the other hand, the evocatively dressed pink casing/white knobbed Cream Puff (billed by Frantone as "the first pedal designed especially for the chick rocker!"), provides a thick, creamy overdrive intended specifically for fat, chunky rhythm work – achieved via controls for Volume, Tone and Fluff (fuzz).

Of all the Frantone dirt boxes, The Sweet is arguably the best loved. This all-transistor germanium fuzz box has a lush, smooth, creamy, full-bodied sound with impressive sustain, crisp highs, and relatively good transparency for the breed, and gets compared to anything from an original 'triangle knob' Big Muff Pi to a good Fuzz Face. Fran Blanche herself feels this is the best fuzz she has ever designed, and it seems plenty of players would agree with her.

Frantone has a few interesting offerings outside the filth zone as well. The recently issued Vibutron emulates vintage amp tremolo effects (as opposed to pitch-modulating 'true vibrato'), but with the added feature of a Waveform control to select between square, triangular or sine wave. The most way-out of the bunch is undoubtedly the Glacier Hyper Modulator, an advanced ring modulator which allows for selectable 'Y' from three different waveforms or a Line/Mic input – this can be used to trigger the effect from a drum machine, keyboard, vocal microphone or whatever you can dig up that produces a signal, with some wild results when used right – and indeed even moreso when it's used wrong.

Frantone Brooklyn Overdrive [CD track 48]
Made: 2003 to present.
Controls: Drive, Tone and Volume; stompswitch for on/off.
Sonics: runs to anything from relatively clean and transparent boost, to thick crunch, to juicy overdrive verging on distortion, all with good dynamics and retention of guitar character.

Frantone Vibutron [CD track 60]
Made: 2003 to present.
Controls: Speed, Waveform, Depth; stompswitch for on/off.
Sonics: warm, rich tremolo effects ranging from smooth pulse (sine wave) to heavy gated chop (square wave), with classic Fender-style amp trem (triangular wave) in-between, plus a good range of Speed and Depth settings.

FULLTONE

The next stop on the 'tone trail takes us to one of the foremost names in boutique effects, and one of the longest-standing of the genre. Mike Fuller has been the man to beat in the pedal business ever since 1993, when he won *Guitar Player* magazine's 'Ultimate Guitarist' competition, and began selling fuzz boxes to keen readers eager to cop his bluesy, driven tone. A year later he founded Fulltone, and the first-version Full-Drive soon became one of the best respected pro overdrives. Since then Fulltone has expanded on its reputation for quality with an ever-broadening range of effects. (For a behind-the-scenes look at the Fulltone story, see the complete interview with Mike Fuller in Chapter 6.)

Fuller evolved his Full-Drive design from the industry standard Tube Screamer style circuits to have more gain, fatter lows, and far broader drive and tone ranges. The pedal also carries an extra channel with Boost switch and Drive knob to let you push that solo into, well, overdrive. Inside the robust blue-steel casing lies a circuit that differs significantly from the TS-808/TS9 clones of this world by using asymmetrical clipping to distort each side of the waveform differently, thereby fattening up the sound. It does carry the legendary JRC4558D chip – as do so many overdrives these days – but the circuit departs in many other ways. Some find the results of asymmetrical clipping jagged and a little dissonant; many others, clearly, love what it does for their tone. Note, however, that it wasn't an entirely new idea even in the early 1990s – Boss' seminal SD-1 used it, as have others.

Ten years down the road, Fuller has seen fit to partially redesign his first big hitter yet again as the Full-Drive 2. The upgraded version adds a three-way mini-switch to the early design, which allows for a Vintage mode like the original's with a juicy mid-range hump, a more transparent FM (flat mid-range) mode like the second-evolution F-D, and a Comp Cut mode for tighter, more articulate in-yer-face modern distortion tones. The F-D2 has true bypass switching, as seems to be a 'must' for the boutique brigade these days.

Other distortions include the Soul-Bender, '69 and '70 fuzzes, the Octafuzz, and the more recently offered Distortion Pro. The Soul-Bender is based on the Sola/Colorsound Tone-Bender of the late 1960s, while the '69 is essentially a modded germanium Fuzz Face clone, with two gain-matched NKT275 transistors in the circuit. The '70 is a modded silicone-transistor Fuzz Face-style effect with intentionally mismatched transistors for extra "snarl and spit," as Fuller puts it. The Octavfuzz is a bid for that 'Jimi sound' that probably needs no introduction – although it's worth noting that Fulltone info states it is, "the only exact circuit copy of the legendary Tycobrahe Octavia" – while the Distortion Pro is aimed at the heavy rocker, and produces more gain and drive than the Full-Drive is capable of. For relatively clean boost with some thickening of tone, there's also the Fat-Boost, which is capable of a 30dB level lift.

Fuller has lately been building a reputation for effects outside the overdrive arena too. Fulltone's original Deja-Vibe was one of the pedals that helped set the standards for functional and great-sounding modern Uni-Vibe-style effects – along with Roger Mayer's Supervibe and later Voodoo-Vibe, the less-seen Prescription Electronics' Vibe Unit, and perhaps a few small-run models like the Sweet Sound Mojo Vibe and Foxrox Provibe. The Deja-Vibe has always been made with a very close approximation of the original Uni-Vibe's discrete transistorised circuit, at the heart of which lie four lamp-and-photocell couplings for the effect's four-stage phasing. The recent Deja-Vibe 2 upgrade carries the original's Intensity knob, switches for Chorus/Vibrato Mode and rocker treadle for Speed (allowing on-the-fly rate changes as with the Uni-Vibe's external foot controller), plus a Modern/Vintage Mode switch for toggling between mellow treble roll-off or full-frequency sounds. The same sound is also available in the simplified and more affordable Mini-Deja-Vibe format.

The Clyde Wah is a recent Fulltone offering, an homage to the seminal Vox/Thomas Organ Clyde McCoy Wah-Wah developed from Fuller's dissection of his 25-strong personal vintage Vox wah collection in an effort to recreate the wailer favored by both Jimi Hendrix and Eric Clapton in the late 1960s. But as with most of his effects that are inspired by vintage designs, the Clyde is no slavish copy. The quest for wah-wah perfection led him to commissioning custom-built 'tuned core' inductors (the heart of any wah-wah, though usually more random and certainly not tuned), redesigning the treadle for more sweep range, and adding true bypass switching, eradicating most players' main gripe about 'tone-sucking' vintage wahs.

Other alternative sounds are available from the self-descriptive Fulltone Supa-Trem, ChoralFlange,

Fulltone Full-Drive 2 [CD track 43]

Made: 1995 to present (first as 'vintage' model).
Controls: Volume, Tone, Overdrive, Boost; toggle switch for Vintage/Flat Mids/Comp Cut; stompswitches for Boost and on/off.
Sonics: a thick, gritty overdrive with good presentation through the frequency spectrum and a somewhat spikey edge.

Fulltone Fat-Boost [CD track 27]

Made: 2000 to present.
Controls: Volume, Tone, Drive; stompswitch for on/off.
Sonics: a relatively clean signal boost at lower drive levels, though with some thickening of tone; produces some overdrive sounds when cranked.

Ultimate Octave and Bass-Drive pedals. But the most radical Fuller creation of all could well be a brand new model based on one of the most archaic of effects devices: the tube-powered tape delay. The Fulltone TTE (for Tube Tape Echo) is essentially a much-upgraded Maestro Echoplex, with a pair of 12AX7s and one 12AT7 in its glowing heart, and a rotating loop of tape for thick, rich analog delay.

"I'm really, really excited about this next phase that we're going into," says Fuller of the TTE's development. "It's the first thing I've ever made with moving parts that's musical. I feel like I'm ten years old again. I'll be happy when everything I play is something that I built... and then I can retire."

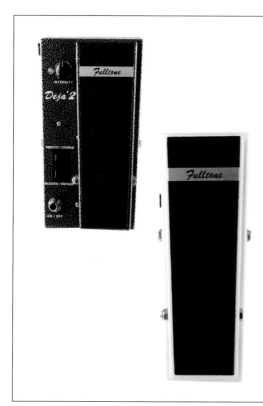

Fulltone Distortion Pro (not pictured)
Made: 2001 to present.
Controls: Volume, Distortion, Resonance, Voicing, Highs, Saturation; stompswitch for on/off.
Sonics: a heavy, jagged rock distortion sound with serious saturation and liquid sustain.

Fulltone Deja-Vibe 2 [CD track 77]
Made: 1996 to present (originally as 'Mk1' model).
Controls: Intensity knob, rocker treadle for Speed control; switches for Chorus/Vibrato and Vintage/Modern modes; stompswitch for on/off.
Sonics: warm, bubbly, watery Uni-Vibe-like chorus/vibe sounds, or subtle pitch modulating 'true vibrato;' some high-end loss in Vintage mode, but good frequency retention in Modern mode.

Fulltone Clyde Wah [CD track 35]
Made: 1997 to present.
Controls: rocker treadle for wah-wah; stompswitch for on/off.
Sonics: crisp and flutey with musical high-frequency peaks, and pronounced vocal 'wah' sounds.

GUYATONE

The cute, tiny Guyatone Micro Effects Series from Japan preceded Danelectro's wide range of shrunken pedals, and has provided many players in need of compact and affordable sounds with some useful alternatives to 'standard' size pedals of the Boss/DOD/Ibanez mold. Unlike many downmarket plastic effects, the sturdy units are housed in metal cases and carry steel stompswitches to trigger their electronic on/off switching. They are, unsurprisingly, short on features, and the sonic offerings of many are quite limited, but they can make a quick solution for a player who only needs one occasional sound from a particular effect, and either doesn't want to spend the money on a more deluxe make or can't spare the pedalboard space to fit a larger unit.

The full range currently includes the WR2 Wah Rocker, HD2 Harmonic Distortion, TZ2 The Fuzz, MC2 Micro Chorus, ST2 Compression/Sustainer, SV2 Slow Volume, FL3 Flanger, OD2 Overdrive, VT3 Vintage Tremolo, MD3 Micro Digital Delay, ME2 Micro Equalizer, MT3 Micro Tuner, NR2 Noise Reduction, PS3 Phase Shifter and SD2 Sustainer D, plus bass pedals BB2 Bottom Blaster (oh yes), BE2 Bottom Equalizer, BL2 Bottom Limiter, and BR2 Bottom Wah Rocker.

A few have even turned up on professional pedalboards, and two or three units have developed reputations beyond the general run of the range. The VT3 Vintage Tremolo yields a smooth, amp-like pulse that won it a coveted *Guitar Player* magazine 'Editor's Pick' (along with its sibling the OD2 Overdrive), and the WR2 Wah Rocker has turned up under the toes of Steve Salas and Lenny Kravitz.

Guyatone has also recently introduced its Flip Series Tube Effects. The VT-X Vintage Tremolo, FB-X Funky Box, MM-X Metal Monster and OD-X Overdrive are housed in larger, folded metal casings and each contain 12AX7 dual-triode preamp tubes.

Guyatone HD2 Harmonic Distortion
Made: circa mid 1990s to present.
Controls: Level and Distortion; stompswitch for on/off.
Sonics: thick, harsh, filthy distortion sounds.

Guyatone WR2 Wah Rocker
Made: circa mid 1990s to present.
Controls: Threshold and Decay; stompswitch for on/off.
Sonics: auto-wah sounds with characteristic quacking mid-range response.

HOMEBREW ELECTRONICS

Arizona-based HomeBrew Electronics (HBE) hand-builds a line of hardwired, point-to-point 'boutique' style analog effects pedals that mostly follows a range of acknowledged classic designs. The Germania is an update of the classic Dallas Rangemaster germanium-resistor treble booster, with Gain control and hi-fi/lo-fi switch; the ComPressor Retro offers a somewhat quieter update of the gray Ross Compressor of the early 1980s; and the Power Screamer is a heavily modded update of the Ibanez TS-808 Tube Screamer (containing a JRC4558D opamp), with added Boost stompswitch and switchable diode modes. The Tramp is an entirely original design merging a tremolo and preamp in a single pedal, while the UFO Fuzz (as in 'ultimate fuzz octave') marries independently selectable 1960s-style fuzz and octave-up effects with added sustain switch. All are well-built units that are gradually gaining deserved support.

HomeBrew Electronics Power Screamer [CD track 46]
Made: 2002 to present.
Controls: Gain, Tone and Level; Diode Select toggle switch for Tight/Vintage/Heavy Comp; stompswitches for Boost and on/off.
Sonics: versatile and wide-ranging overdrive sounds in the TS-808 mold and beyond, with excellent dynamics and better transparency than the standard Tube Screamers.

HUGHES & KETTNER

In Germany, Hughes & Kettner has long been the big boy in home-grown tube amp production; in the USA, the company is perhaps better known for tube-loaded effects pedals such as the Tube Rotosphere rotating speaker simulator and Tube Factor preamp/overdrive. The former goes to greater lengths than most – even the seminal Uni-Vibe – to capture the sound of a genuine Leslie cab, with a drive control for simulated tube preamp overload, a Breaker switch to suspend the 'rotor motors' while still playing through the effect, a Rotor Balance control to emphasize either LF (woofer) or HF (horn), and a Slow/Fast switch that ramps gradually between speeds, with the 'woofer' and 'horn' frequencies accelerating and decelerating at different rates just like the real thing. Some players have complained of the effect's high noise content, but the original Leslie was no silent operator either.

The Tube Factor has footswitches and controls to select either clean boost or tube overdrive, and purportedly runs its 12AX7 tube at a whopping 290VAC for, as H&K puts it, "more overtones, more sensitive response, easier playability and enhanced tone." H&K appears to achieve all this with a single dual-triode preamp tube – with two gain stages to its name – where tube overdrives from Mesa/Boogie, Matchless, Budda and some others all use a pair of 12AX7s (while the early Tube Works Tube Driver did indeed use a single-triode preamp tube coupled to a transistorized compression stage). Make of this what you will.

The chunky, roadworthy range also includes the Tubeman 'Guitar Recording Station,' a three-channel, one-tube preamp with speaker simulation and both Mixer and Amp outputs; and the tube/digital hybrid Replex reverb and tape-delay simulator.

Hughes & Kettner Tube Rotosphere
Made: circa early 1990s to present (MkII version since 2003).
Controls: Drive, Output and Rotor Balance knobs; stompswitches for Bypass (on/off), Breaker and Slow/Fast; switch for guitar or keyboard input level; stereo inputs and outputs.
Sonics: mellow, swirling rotating speaker simulation with gritty, slightly 'tizzy' distortion from Drive control; some background noise.

Hughes & Kettner Tube Factor
Made: circa early 1990s to present.
Controls: Drive, Output, Voicing; stompswitches for Factor 1/2 and on/off.
Sonics: clean level boost or saturated overdrive with decent transparency.

JACQUES STOMPBOXES

French pedal-maker Jacques Charbit has been raising quite a stir in the more esoteric reaches of the effects world since offering the hand-made Fuse Blower in 1999 as his first commercial pedal – and for good reason. He has dissected a selection of classic designs with such gusto that at least a couple of his pedals frequently vie for 'best of breed' honors on various internet chatboards and magazine pages.

Jacques offers two ranges of effects: the Factory Made series is built to quality but mass-manufactured style, and offers pedals housed in casings that sit comfortably beside popular models from the likes of Boss, Ibanez, DOD, and so forth. His Hand Made series is just that: effects housed in plate-metal 'project boxes' with red and black legends and logos scrawled in indelible marker and discrete, hand-wired point-to-point circuits within, all made by Charbit's own hands. The Tube Blower from the former range has been one of the best-received evolutions of the Tube Screamer circuit in recent years, and carries modifications which cleverly counter virtually every drawback to the original design. It has much of the vintage TS series' plummy, juicy drive tones, but with far more transparency, a greatly extended gain range (which takes you both to lower levels – for clean boost – and higher levels, for rockier distortions), and active bass and treble boosters. (Jacques is such a Tube Screamer enthusiast that he has bagged the address www.TS808.com for his website, which displays his vintage TS collection alongside his own pedals.) Also in the Factory range are the Meistersinger Chorus, Bat Fuzz, and the Fat Burner compressor/sustainer/headphone amp.

The hand-made Fuse Blower is a radical fuzz box that offers a lush, dynamic and powerful version of the classic effect, plus an added 'Blow' mode, which triggers a virtually indescribable boost sound with massive gain and a broad, open, but far from clean voice. The Handmade Series is rounded out by the Mercer Box germanium distortion, the Aquamarine cascading tube amp-style overdrive; the all-tube Tube Blower; the Sleep Talker overdrive; the Spin Acher tremolo/Leslie simulator, Singing Geisha Wah-Fuzz-Synth, and the DD Cup double germanium booster. Throughout, it's hard to fault Jacques' vision – or his enthusiasm.

Jacques Tube Blower [CD track 45]

Made: 2001 to present.

Controls: Low, High, Drive and Level; stompswitch for on/off.

Sonics: from a virtually transparent level boost to razory fuzz-edged distortion with excellent juicy, dynamic overdrive sounds in-between; in the TS-808 camp, but with firmer low end and somewhat improved clarity.

Jacques Fuse Blower [CD track 2]

Made: 1999 to present.

Controls: Vol and Fuz (sic); stompswitches for on/off and Blow.

Sonics: a thick, creamy fuzz with an enticing smoothness and better note definition to chords than many; mega-boost in Blow mode, with alternative fuzz sounds according to Vol/Fuz relationship.

KLON

Klon exists for one purpose: to bring you the Centaur pedal, a 'boutique' overdrive that has become legendary since it first hit the scene around 1994. Strictly speaking it's not an overdrive pedal like most of the breed, but a unit intended to drive a quality tube amp so you can achieve saturation and tubey overdrive quicker; the goal is to make a good amp sound great, a big amp sound bigger, and any guitar sound more dynamic, responsive and 'alive.' Most Centaur owners would agree that the pedal achieves these aims in spades. That said, however impressive its transparency and dynamics, the pedal can of course achieve some distortion of its own when you max out Gain relative to a low Output setting (as can most master-volume-loaded pedals from boosters to overdrives). But with Gain set to minimum and

Treble at noon, the pedal offers an entirely transparent boost, which can indeed drive a tube amp into beefy distortion, but doesn't itself color or distort your guitar's signal.

Each Centaur is hand-built by designer Bill Finnegan, and unless you find one used or stocked in a guitar store that's hip to the tip, you have to join a waiting list. The design's inner strengths (housed in a circuit covered in epoxy to scare off the clone brigade) are echoed in a robust gold-anodized casing of sand-cast aluminum with stencilled centaur 'man-beast' graphic – although newer models are available in silver too, and with or without the ponyboy motif. As should be expected at the price (currently $279 retail), Finnegan uses quality parts such as Switchcraft jacks, CTS pots and a Carling switch, and there's no shortage of wizardry within the circuit itself. One trick is the use of a dual-ganged pot as the Gain control; the first pot of the pair controls the drive level while the second simultaneously tweaks the unit's tonal response to best suit that drive level. Despite the price, Finnegan tells us he has sold verging on 5,000 units, and the orders are still coming in.

Klon Centaur [CD track 42]
Made: 1994 to present.
Controls: Gain, Treble and Output; stompswitch for on/off.
Sonics: broad-frequencied and full-bodied overdrive with solid, spanking low-end response and shimmering, crystalline treble; excellent dynamics and retention of guitar and amp character.

LOVETONE

In his search for the ultimate envelope follower, pro guitarist Vlad Naslas encountered designer and repairman Dan Coggins around 1994 and set him the task of building a pedal "with the most knobs ever." The technician soldered and tweaked and revised the thing during quieter moments in his nightshifts as a BBC studio engineer, and in a matter of weeks the Meatball was born. Vlad loved it, and every musician he loaned it to wanted one. In the partnership of Coggins and Naslas, Britain's Lovetone was born, and since the mid 1990s has grown to be one the most innovative and best-respected boutique effects makers on the scene. (For more on the Lovetone vibe, see the interview with Dan Coggins in Chapter 6.)

The Meatball does in fact carry ten knobs, among them the more standard (though rarely seen all together) controls for Sensitivity, Attack and Decay, Range, and Resonance. Lovetone is quick to point out that the unit will happily bag you any ultra-funky Bootsy style auto-wah sounds you might be in search of, but can also be tuned in for anything from subtle aural enhancement to wild frequency peaks, to full analog synth performance. Wackier still, Lovetone's Ring Stinger – a ring modulator of ultra-tweakable proportions – brings you, in the company promo's own entirely accurate words, the sounds of "klangs, bells, metallic effects, pseudo vocoder effects, dalek noises, sci-fi atmospherics, spooky warbling, trem arpeggios, tonal toggling, touch sensitive keying, pitch crossfiring, microtonal and atonal effects, evolving drones, digeridoo effects and, not least, the meanest graunchiest octave fuzz ever."

Other Lovetone pedals are less extreme, but equally original and innovative. The Brown Source is a 'brown-sound' overdrive inspired by the cranked Marshall sound of the late 1960s and early 1970s, the Big Cheese does a filthy vintage fuzz, the Doppelganger is a twin-oscillator phaser/vibrato, the mysterious '?' is better discerned by its subtitle 'The Flange With No Name,' and the Wobulator is a deluxe-featured tremolo, capable of stereo tremolo selectable for split high pass/low pass, modulating anti-phase panning, vibrato and other effects, in addition to a vintage-style tremolo. All are totally analog and hand-built in England, and the high construction quality and versatile sonics have earned Lovetone an impressive roster of pro players for a maker of its size. Bootsy Collins, Flood, Billy Duffy, Larry Graham, Johnny Marr, J. Mascis, Jimmy Page and players from Radiohead all attend the Lovetone love-in – and, word has it, have all purchased their own pedals, since the company operates a non-endorsement policy. At the time of writing, Dan Coggins has departed to run his own operation, Dinosaural (see the entry earlier in this chapter), where he looks after Lovetone servicing and makes new pedal models under his own brand.

Lovetone Wobulator

Made: mid 1990s to present.

Controls: LFO1 Rate, LFO2 Rate, and L Depth, R Depth, four-way waveform and function selector switches; phase switch knobs for each channel; stompswitches for L Enable and R Enable; stereo outputs, inputs for external trigger and external footcontroller.

Tones: warm, rich tremolo with an impressive array of deluxe stereo modes.

Lovetone Doppelganger

Made: late 1990s to present.

Controls: LFO1 Rate, LFO2 Rate, LF Span, HF Span, Colour, and Blend, switches for waveform and True/Spectral Phase; stompswitches for Phase/Vib, LFO1/Dual LFO, and Bypass (on/off).

Sonics: lush vintage phasing and good rotary effects, with a broad and versatile range of variations on these themes.

MATCHLESS

The first word in boutique amplifiers throughout the 1990s, Matchless was founded by Mark Sampson and Rick Perrotta in 1989, and rapidly set the standards for contemporary, hand-made all-tube amps

Matchless Hot Box

Made: mid to late 1990s.

Controls: Gain Ch2, Bass, Treble, Output Level Ch2 and Clean Volume knobs; stompswitch for channel selection.

Sonics: versatile two-channel real-tube overdrive with excellent transparency and good dynamics.

Matchless Vibro Box

Made: mid to late 1990s.

Controls: Volume, Tone, Speed and Depth knobs; switch for Master Speed, stompswitch for on/off.

Sonics: vintage-style tube tremolo with a broad range of controls, plus Tone and some boosting as desired.

built to vintage tonal ideals. As models such as the D/C30, Chieftain and Clubman 35 rapidly became the combos of many players' dreams – and somewhat fewer's realities, thanks to sky-high prices – the company diversified into the pedal market with a limited range of point-to-point, all-tube units.

The 'Box Series' appears to have comprised six units at its peak in the late 1990s. The two-channel Hot Box was the Matchless take on a primo tube overdrive on one channel, with clean boost on the other, while the Dirt Box offered a single bypassable channel for boost and overdrive sounds. The Vibro Box provided vintage amp tremolo sounds; the Cool Box was a clean line driver/buffer, while the Split Box and Mix Box did A/B/Y splitting and 4/2/1 mixing/merging respectively. The California company closed briefly in 1999, at which time both founders joined up with the new and similarly themed Bad Cat amp company. Matchless is going strong once again, but it appears that the pedals are not among the company's current offerings.

MESA/BOOGIE

The story of how San Francisco Bay Area amp tech Randall Smith hotrodded Fender Princetons in the early 1970s to launch what would become the Mesa/Boogie empire is amplifier legend by now. The Boogie MkI ushered in the era of 'factory hotrodded' guitar combos, and soon nearly every big name offered a similar 'cascading gain' tube amp to rival the hot new contender.

In the early 1990s the Mesa/Boogie folks put the same super-hot preamp idea into the V-Twin tube overdrive pedal, designed by Dan Riesen (now of Budda). It was – and still is – built like a tank, carries a pair of 12AX7 tubes, and has two footswitchable channels (with three modes plus bypass) for everything from bluesy crunch to searing rock lead overdrive. And because the Boogie sound had always

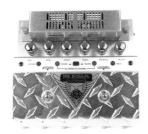

Mesa/Boogie V-Twin

Made: early 1990s to present.

Controls: Gain, Master, Bass, Mid, Treble and Presence; Blues/Clean mode switch; stompswitches for Ch1/Ch2 and on/off; standard and Record/Headphone output.

Sonics: crunchy vintage overdrive tones on Ch1; high-gain rock distortion on Ch2, with characteristic Boogie saturation and sustain.

Mesa/Boogie V-1 Bottle Rocket

Made: 2000 to present.

Controls: Gain, Bass, Treble and Output; stompswitch for on/off.

Sonics: fat and chunky medium-gain overdrive with tactile compression and plenty of drive.

come largely from preamp distortion anyway, the V-Twin offers a more affordable fast-track to that high-gain sound from a small box. The V-1 Bottle Rocket followed in 2000. This 2 x 12AX7 box is more straightforward, with just a single channel and hard-bypass on/off switch, and a gain voicing that runs from blues to classic rock overdrive sounds. Boogie's Triaxis programmable preamp has also won a lot of fans, but that takes us into rack territory and away from the scope of this book.

NOBELS

While it is distinctly a 'budget' range brand, the German-designed and Korean-built Nobels pedals have earned a reputation that rises above some others in their price range, and appearances on quite a few pro pedalboards to boot. The TR-X Tremolo is one that turns up time and again, and is a multi-featured unit with controls for Effect Level, Tone, Speed and Intensity, as well as a four-way switch to select 'master intensity,' if you will, between two shades of square and sine wave modulation.

On top of this, the company offers the full range of flavors, including the CH-D Digital Chorus, CO-2 Compressor, DD-800 Digital Delay, FU-Z Fuzz, DT-1 Distortion, DT-SN Distortion Special, four varieties of guitar and bass overdrive, and AB-1 Switcher line selector. An easy-access top-mounted battery compartment and rugged die-cast metal casing not a mile from the Boss format completes the picture.

Nobels TR-X Tremolo [CD track 59]

Made: c1990s to present.
Controls: Eff. Level, Speed, Tone, Intensity knobs; four-way Mode switch; output for remote switching; stompswitch for on/off.
Sonics: a quiet, transparent tremolo effect with a broad range of speeds and depths.

PETE CORNISH

Englishman Pete Cornish is best known for the big effects rigs he builds for major star clients, and until recently his own pedals were only available as integral parts of those large, multi-pedal set-ups. We're including him here in the 'Contemporary' rather than the 'Vintage' chapter because, although he has been one of the foremost names in guitar effects for more than 30 years, standalone units made by Pete and wife Lydia Cornish have only been available to the average player – independent of his massive pro systems – for the last few of those years. (See the interview with Pete Cornish in Chapter 6 for more detail on his history and philosophy.)

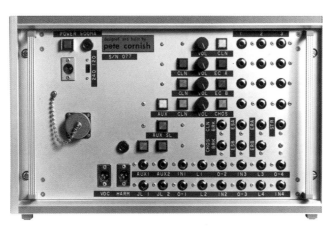

The rigs on the right were made by Pete Cornish for Brian May of Queen, and show the type of large, professional stage set-ups with which he made his name. Note the vintage Vox Wah-Wah mounted at the right side of the floorboard.

Cornish was an electronics hobbyist as a kid and received his professional training as an engineer through an apprenticeship with the British Ministry of Aviation. Not unlike the career path taken by fellow Englishman Roger Mayer, he took his military-grade expertise into the rock world when his interest in music electronics overwhelmed the lure of a steady day job. He worked for a time as a tech at London's legendary Sound City store – where the general poor quality of most of the gear he encountered disgusted him, and spawned an early desire to "build it better." Cornish's first major adventure into the land of noise came in the early 1970s when Peter Banks of Yes commissioned him to build what

Pete Cornish Linear Boost/Mute

Made: as a standalone product, late 1990s to present.
Controls: Boost knob (0dB to +27dB); stompswitches for Mute (switching to Tuner Out) and Boost on/off.
Sonics: a totally transparent boost of from unity gain to 27dB, capable of functioning as a linear line drive or boosting a tube amp into distortion.

Pete Cornish Soft Sustain-2

Made: as a standalone product, late 1990s to present.
Controls: Volume, Tone, Sustain; stompswitch for on/off.
Sonics: a blend of tone-thickening soft distortion and compression, with excellent dynamics and clarity (think Dave Gilmour...).

Pete Cornish P-2 Fuzz

Made: as a standalone product, late 1990s to present.
Controls: Volume, Tone, Sustain; stompswitch for on/off.
Sonics: from chunky overdrive sounds to fat, swampy, full-on fuzz; no pretensions of transparency, but low noise and great rejection of RF for a fuzz box.

was essentially, says Cornish, "the world's first AC-powered multi-effects unit," and the orders came in from there.

His client list, past and present, is awesome by any standards, and includes The Police, The Strokes, Queen, Pink Floyd, Bryan Adams, Lou Reed, Roxy Music, Dire Straits, Paul McCartney, Sting, Jimmy Page, Judas Priest, Black Sabbath, Iron Maiden, Mutt Lange, The Pretenders, The Moody Blues, Stereophonics, Black Crowes, and many, many more. And remember, these aren't people who have been handed a free pedal to join the list, or even bought one or two, but rather have commissioned Cornish to custom-build multi-thousand-dollar effects systems that generally consist of a range of vintage and contemporary pedals (often stored in rack shelves at the backline), plus elaborate routing networks, footcontrollers, and hand-built buffers, splitters, A/B/C/Y selectors and line drivers and so forth... along with the occasional Cornish Custom fuzz or sustainer thrown in as a bonus. It should come as no surprise that, stemming from this experience, Cornish takes a firm stance in the buffer versus true bypass debate, and insists that a quality buffer/line driver of the correct input impedance is an essential first stage for any large professional rig.

The range of standalone effects is made up mostly of booster-based devices – including anything from line drivers to sustainers to overdrives and fuzzes – and switching and buffered splitter boxes. All have the serious custom-workshop look to them that many players will recognize from the Cornish effects systems that have featured in guitar mag pages over the years – Hammerite finished metal boxes with 'Letraset' type legends, metal stompswitches and chickenhead control knobs. All are hand-made in the UK using top-quality components, and engineered for low noise, clarity, and preservation of guitar character and dynamics. Which comes at a price, of course – for example £329 (approximately $525) for a G-2 Fuzz – but hey, you're getting the same custom-built sonic secrets that grace the rigs of David Gilmour, Lou Reed and Jimmy Page. You don't even want to know what the AC Wah/Linear Boost/Mute/Three-Way Splitter costs (OK, it's £964.95, or approximately $1,543).

PHARAOH

Matt Farrow's Raleigh, North Carolina-based company started life as an amp and electronics repairshop and has moved into small-run effects manufacturing in recent years. The pedals definitely have a 'kitchen sink' look to them – with their hand-painted cast-aluminum hobby-box casings and stick-on logos and legends – but the workmanship inside is excellent, of those the author has seen at least, and the range offers some exciting sounds. Distortions are catered for by the Sweet Cheetah 2 'high gain distortion' and the Midnight Cruiser, with the Rodeo Drive and Magnolia taking gentler overdrive duties. The former carries an internal IC socket to allow the user to fine-tune the sound by swapping the

Pharaoh Sweet Cheetah 2

Made: 2002 to present.
Controls: Gain, Volume, Tone; stompswitch for on/off.
Sonics: a beefy, thudding distortion effect with good frequency response and fine dynamics, though more a hot overdrive than a mega-rock distortion character; Tone control offers treble bleed, with muddiness when rolled off slightly.

Pharaoh Rodeo Drive

Made: 2003 to present.
Controls: Drive, Level and Tone; stompswitch for on/off.
Sonics: a thick, plummy medium-gain overdrive, with significant level boost on tap.

included JRC4558D for an LM1458, LF353, LM358, TL072, or other compatible type. The Rodeo Drive employs a unique CMOS integrated circuit that produces a soft overdrive that Pharaoh claims closely emulates the breakup of a vintage Fender tweed amp. The range is completed by the Class-A Boost Pro booster, Tone Engine germanium transistor-powered booster, Uptown Fuzz germanium and silicon fuzz box, Downtown Fuzz, and Monument compressor.

PRESCRIPTION

Prescription Electronics was one of the first 'boutique' pedal brands of the early 1990s boom, and the Portland, Oregon-based company remains one of the most respected of the breed to this day. Like many others in the small-run, hand-made pedal world, a good number of Prescription's models are based on vintage pedals that are no longer available in their original form – although slight modifications and updates are made to most of them for improved performance and reliability.

Prescription Vibe-Unit

Made: early 1990s to present.
Controls: Intensity, Volume, Speed; toggle switch for Chorus/Vibrato; stompswitch for on/off.
Sonics: the warm, lush, liquid swirling sounds of a vintage Uni-Vibe, from gentle pulse to throbbing chop.

Probably the best-known of the range is the Vibe-Unit, a vintage photocell chorus/vibe effect (a four-stage phaser, really) based directly on the original Univox Uni-Vibe circuit. The Vibe-Unit won *Guitar Player* magazine's 'Uni-Vibe Shootout' a few years back, and it's hard to beat for authenticity of tone.

Other 'homages' to the classics include the Yardbox (think Yardbirds), a copy of the original germanium-transistor Sola Sound Tone Bender fuzz; the RxOverdriver, patterned on the Colorsound Overdriver; the Facelift, a modded Fuzz Face in either germanium or silicon flavors, with added selectable octave effect; the Depth Charge bass overdrive, based on the Maestro Bass Brassmaster; and the Throb, based on Electro-Harmonix's esoteric Pulsar tremolo.

Prescription also offers a selection of more original designs. The Dual-Tone is a two-channel overdrive/distortion with added footswitchable tone boost section, while the COB (Clean Octave Blend) does a traditional octave-up sound, with added control to blend back the desired amount of clean guitar signal to the output. The Experience does a Jimi-esque fuzz plus octave effect, with added Swell function for simulated reverse-tape effect. Finally, there's the Germ pedal – a mysteriously named two-channel pedal with a transparent clean boost plus a sweet, open, but potentially fierce overdrive.

SNARLING DOGS

The Snarling Dogs brand was launched as a range of strings by the late Charlie Stringer, who expanded into a line of wild and wacky effects pedals in the mid 1990s with the help of designer Kenny Segall. The brand is currently owned by D'Andrea Inc. These pedals were notable from the start for both their out-there sonics and bright, funky looks – including the trademark foot-shaped rocker treadle on the wah-wahs. The latter was a brainstorm of Segall, who picked up a similarly shaped accelerator pedal at a car hotrodding shop, stuck it on a prototype wah-wah, and liked the look. Snarling Dogs has grabbed more attention for its wahs than for anything else – the current lineup includes seven, plus many still-noteworthy but discontinued models – but the company offers a comprehensive range of overdrives too.

For straightahead wah-wah, the Wonder Wah (now in Mk2 form) is about as 'standard' as it gets for Snarling Dogs. It is hardwired for the company's 'White Room' preset, with a slightly wider frequency response than the traditional vintage wah-wah. The Black Bawl is the same circuit plus preamp boost, and from here things get a little crazy, with features piled on thick and fast. Blue Bawls: three-way selectable wah sound between White Room/Voo Doo/Shaft, volume boost, plus Dist and Vol

Snarling Dogs Fire Bawl 2 Alarm Wah
Made: circa late 1990s to 2002.
Controls: rocker treadle for wah-wah and Volume knob for boost; stompswitch for on/off.
Sonics: wailing, honky wah-wah tones with long travel (and, therefore, broad frequency range), plus variable level boost.

Snarling Dogs Mold Spore Wah
Made: late 1990s to present.
Controls: rocker treadle and three-way tone switch for wah-wah; Volume knob for boost; Freakwincy, Straight Jacket Vol and Psychoscumation knobs for ring modulator; stompswitches for wah-wah and Mold Spore (ring mod).
Sonics: broad-voiced wah-wah sounds ranging from warm, middly vintage rock to peaky funk sounds, plus dissonant, metalic ring modulation sounds.

Snarling Dogs Erogenous Moan

Made: circa late 1990s to 2002.

Controls: rocker treadle, stompswitches for on/off and Mode.

Sonics: standard volume swell with long rocker travel, plus selectable 'reverse tape' simulation for live performance (with automatic 'pick click' sound at end of phrase).

Snarling Dogs SPD-4 Blue Doo

Made: late 1990s to present.

Controls: Vol/Gain, Tone, and OD/Dist knobs, switches for Attack Control and Tone Bypass, stompswitch for on/off.

Sonics: from mild boost to extreme overdrive, in the 'cranked 6V6 amp' mold.

controls for integral Blue Doo overdrive; Super Bawl Whine-O-Wah: three-way tone selector, switchable for twin/single inductor, and two Hormone boost selections (Testosterone and Estrogen, naturally); and the Mold Spore Psycho-Scumatic Wah, with three-way tone selector, boost, and integral ring modulator. There's also a Bawl Buster bass wah-wah with drive control and the three-way tone switch. The discontinued Fire Bawl wah/booster and Erogenous Moan volume/backwards tape effect have their fans, too.

Snarling Dogs' non-wah pedals come in three varieties of overdrive, plus a booster/varitone pedal. The Bloo Doo is a bluesy toned 'tube distortion' emulator that seeks to replicate a hard-driven 6V6 output tube for anything from warm, smooth crunch to snarling high-gain bite. The Tweed E. Bird is a 'tweed sound' emulator that seeks to put a cranked 1950s Fender into whatever amp you're using, while the Black Dog (named after the Zep song) does something of the inverse, purportedly giving any American-voiced amp the thudding bottom and crackly top of an EL34-powered stack. The Very Tone Dog is the odd one out, a simple but unusual pedal that delivers a 'Vari-Tone in a box' – approximating the five-position selector on some old Gibson guitars and amps of that name. Its Tone Selector has five notch-filter settings plus bypass, with a preamp for boost and a two-position Snarl/Bite Attack Control switch. All are housed in large, rugged, folded-steel casings with mechanical 'true bypass' switching and the Snarling Dog logo with red LED eyes when the effect is on, as featured on the wah-wahs too.

SWEET SOUND

Another of the small but well-respected boutique makers, Sweet Sound – of Pompano Beach, Florida –

Sweet Sound Mojo Vibe   [CD track 79]

Made: c2002 to present.

Controls: Volume, Intensity, Speed knobs; switch for Chorus/Vibrato and internal switch for Modern/Vintage mode; stompswitch for on/off; input for speed control pedal.

Sonics: a smooth, warm, round and bubbly rotating speaker simulation with excellent depth and dimension.

is best known for its take on the Uni-Vibe sound. The Ultra Vibe is a full-featured 'clone,' with all the smooth, liquid four-stage analog phasing of the original, while the scaled-down Mojo Vibe houses the same circuitry in a trimmer and more affordable package. Both have found favor with a number of discerning pros. In addition to the 'vibe' units, Sweet Sound also offers a transistor booster pedal, called the Booster, which is capable of delivering up to 26dB of gain.

T.C. ELECTRONIC

Denmark's T.C. Electronic has all but entirely phased out its guitar pedals in favor of big digital effects and dynamic processors both in hardware and software form, but the company has offered a couple of units worth noting in the context of this book. Have I mentioned Eric Johnson in these pages yet? Yeah, I thought so. The T.C. Electronic Stereo Chorus is the one piece of his current effects set-up that we haven't covered yet, and he has been a fan of the pedal for years. Actually it's the 'Stereo Chorus+ Pitch Modulator & Flanger,' to give it its full name, a full-featured and versatile unit indeed, as that mouthful implies. The unit was an impressive and technically advanced chorus (etc) when introduced some 25 years ago, and remains a top-notch effect today.

T.C. Electronic Stereo Chorus + Pitch Modulator & Flanger
[CD track 20]
Made: circa late 1970s to present.
Controls: Speed, Width and Intensity knobs; Mode switch for Chorus/PM/Flanger and Input Sensitivity switch (Input Gain trimmer in newer units); stompswitch for on/off; stereo outputs.
Sonics: a broad, sweet, sparkling stereo chorus sound, plus basic pitch modulation or thick, sweeping flanger sounds.

T.C. Electronics Sustainer+ Parametric EQ
Made: circa 1980s to 1990s.
Controls: Sustain, Gain, Function, Center, and Noise Suppressor knobs; switches for preset EQ selection and Distortion on/off; stompswitch on/off.
Sonics: fairly transparent compression with substantial swell in certain modes, plus noise gate; some noise with gate 'out,' major softening of attack with gate 'in.'

Another deluxe and versatile T.C. pedal was the Sustainer+ Parametric EQ – these T.C. folks were clearly not happy with single-function effects – but that has apparently fallen by the wayside. The company now concentrates more on digital sound processors such as the G-Force and G-Major rackmounted multi-FX units for guitar, and the Finalizer, a popular and powerful studio-quality digital mastering tool, along with rackmount and plug-in software reverbs and other effects.

T-REX

Another Danish 'T' in the effects business, T-Rex has been building a reputation in the Scandinavian market since 1995, but has only recently begun to create a buzz in the USA and other parts of Europe. T-Rex pedals are all hand-made, and the current lineup follows many of the traditional categories but with a few original features and twists. The brand has already won favor with a few name players, including blueser Debbie Davies and alt-rocker Matthew Sweet.

The Mudhoney distortion carries a Boost mode which, when engaged, takes the otherwise smooth, medium-gain pedal into thick, heavy saturated filth-rock territory; the Alberta, on the other hand, is a more vintage-leaning overdrive in the Tube Screamer vein, which seeks to emulate classic tube amp breakup. The Comp-Nova is an extremely transparent compressor, the Betavibe is T-Rex's take on the Uni-Vibe-style rotating speaker effect with added Fast/Slow switching; and the Tremster does both tremolo and vibrato, with some added preset boost to avoid the perceived volume drop associated with some other trem-based effects. Finally, the Replex is a clever delay pedal that offers sounds ranging from warm vintage tape echo to bright, crisp digital delay.

VISUAL SOUND

Bob Weil's road to founding Visual Sound started in 1988 with his own quest for the perfect volume pedal – namely a unit with some form of visual reference to tell you where your level was set relative to full-whack. With no engineering background (he was working in sales and marketing at the time, with a degree in business administration), he set out to design and build a pedal with a 10-LED level scale, eventually got the ball rolling, and launched his own company in 1994.

His debutante, the Visual Volume, proved to be a rather nifty but less-than-profitable product, and eventually fell off the haycart – the company's blatant 'visual' theme all but leaping off with it – and other early products like the Visual Wah-Wah, Visual Metal and Pure Tone buffer equally failed to fly off the guitar-store shelves.

From the late 1990s onward, however, Visual Sound has developed an excellent reputation on the back of a pair of home-base-shaped overdrives, a chorus/delay, and a very clever little power supply unit, which could well have saved the company's bacon. (For more on the Visual Sound story, see the interview with Bob Weil in Chapter 6.)

The Jeckyll & Hyde 'Ultimate Overdrive' carries two independent circuits: Jeckyll for classic TS808-toned overdrive (with the assistance of that JRC4558D opamp we keep bumping into); and Hyde, for rabid over-the-top rock distortion. While the Jeckyll circuit carries the standard Tube Screamer tone shapers of Drive, Tone and Volume, the Hyde adds to its own complement of these an EQ control – to

Visual Sound Visual Volume

Made: 1994-1998.

Controls: rocker treadle for passive volume control, with ten-LED status indicator.

Sound: whatever you plug into it, or quieter… and with lights.

Visual Sound Route 66 [CD tracks 14 & 52]

Made: 2000 to present.

Controls: Sustain, Tone and Gain for Compression; Drive, Tone and Vol knobs plus Bass Boost switch for Overdrive; stompswitches for both Comp and OD on/off.

Sonics: thick, sustaining 'vintage compressor pedal' sounds with lots of gain and a wide range of tone settings; thick, creamy, medium-gain overdrive sounds with slight but punchy mid-range hump, and selectable Bass Boost for fat, solid lows; effects used independently or together.

wind it from flat to scooped mids – and a Sharp/Blunt switch for a bright and edgy or more compressed and mellow sound. The two can be used independently or together, for anything from mellow, crunchy boosts to extreme and ballsy grunge-o-rama.

The Route 66 'American Overdrive' follows a similar two-in-one theme, but this time pairs a compressor at the front end with an overdrive at the back – again selectable independently or together. The former treads ground not far from MXR's classic Dyna Comp but with an added Tone control, while the latter employs the J&H's TS808-style circuit but adds a Bass Boost switch to eradicate a common Tube Screamer weak point. Finally, the H2O Liquid Chorus & Echo pairs, yep, these two popular delay-based effects (the first circuit analog, the second 'analog voiced' digital for up to 800ms delay) in the same single, five-sided sheet-metal housing, with three knobs each and dual stompswitches for independent or in-series use.

As for the bypass/buffer debate, Weil lands in the latter camp with both feet: each of these effects carries his Pure Tone buffering circuit at its input stage, and he insists this greatly improves not only their own performance in 'off' mode, but the sound of your entire effects chain, especially when the Jeckyll & Hyde or Route 66 is first in line.

Visual Sound's relatively recent 1 Spot is a cleverly designed low-noise, voltage-regulated, switching power supply for 9V pedals that is small enough to take up only one socket on your wall outlet or power strip, but powerful enough to run a sizeable pedalboard. No, I know this isn't *The Power Supply Book*, and I haven't covered them universally in these pages, but given many players' loathing of bulky wallwarts, this is one that's nifty enough to mention.

VOODOO LAB

The Voodoo Lab company, a division of Digital Music Corp, is another that grew parallel to the 'boutique' pedal boom of the early 1990s, but has always combined elements of the boutique ethos with more mass-market prices and objectives. When DMC opened shop in 1986, Josh Fiden was making memory expansion cartridges for digital synths and had moved on to MIDI patchbays by the late 1980s when the proliferation of rackmounted multi-FX units inspired him to build "a great footcontroller" so guitarists could get something out of the digital wonders too. The widely used Ground Control switching unit was the result.

But being a guitarist himself, Fiden had an itch to build something that actually made some noise. Vintage pedals were selling like hotcakes, although many of them were becoming harder and harder to get your hands on... and a move into the pedal effects market seemed a natural step. (For more on Voodoo Lab history and some of the thinking behind the effects, see the interview with Josh Fiden in Chapter 6.)

Early Voodoo Lab pedals were largely emulations of vintage effects that are widely acknowledged as classics of 1960s and 1970s rock, and three of the four debut models can easily be traced to their roots. The Proctavia was inspired by the Tycobrahe Octavia, the Overdrive by the DOD 250, and the Bosstone by the Jordan Boss Tone (albeit with added features). The Tremolo was simply an effort to emulate a Fender amp-style tremolo in a stompbox. Each was housed in a sturdy cast-aluminum casing with hip and colorful logos and its own characteristic stylized design motif of soundwaves, squiggles, whatever (I'll let Fiden tell you later in his own words what inspired the Proctavia design).

The cosmetic theme has remained consistent to the current products – along with the hand-wired board-to-controls connections and true bypass switching that were there from the start. Success was near instant, and good reviews and word-of-mouth player vibes spread the name quickly.

From these 'cloning' origins, Voodoo Lab ventured into territory that required more original thinking, but still used classic designs as a springboard to get there. In 1986 the range expanded to include the Micro Vibe, a pedal designed to capture the best part of the sound of a vintage Uni-Vibe – complete with real photocell circuitry – but in a more compact package, and one more affordable than

Voodoo Lab Proctavia

Made: 1995 to present.
Controls: Volume and Boost; stompswitch for on/off.
Sonics: wirey and somewhat metalic simulated octave-up fuzz sounds.

Voodoo Lab Tremolo

Made: 1998 to present.
Controls: Intensity, Slope, Speed, Volume; stompswitch for on/off.
Sonics: from smooth, amp-like triangular wave tremolo to hard square-wave chop, depending upon Slope setting, with variable output level.

Voodoo Lab Micro Vibe [CD track 78]

Made: 1996 to present.
Controls: Intensity and Speed; stompswitch for on/off.
Sonics: a smooth and warm but somewhat warbling Uni-Vibe-style rotating speaker simulation.

Voodoo Lab Superfuzz [CD track 5]

Made: 1998 to present.
Controls: Volume, Resonance, Tone and Attack (fuzz); stompswitch for on/off.
Sonics: a widely tweakable range of fuzz tones, from thin, acerbic dentist's drill to thick, beefy, almost bluesy-edged fuzz with loads of sustain – and much in-between.

Voodoo Lab Sparkle Drive [CD track 44]

Made: 2000 to present.
Controls: Gain, Tone, Clean and Volume; stompswitch for on/off.
Sonics: classic early 1980s medium-gain tube overdrive sounds with plummy mid-range response, and added crispness and clarity according to Clean knob setting.

the boutique 'Vibe clones of most the competition. The unit propeled Voodoo Lab to even greater recognition. Though the Superfuzz that followed derived its core fuzz box tone from the Jordan Boss Tone, as had the earlier Bosstone pedal, it carried a full complement of Volume, Resonance, Tone and Attack controls for extreme shaping of the effect.

Following this, the Sparkle Drive – another unit to garner rave reviews and a lot of player attention – took a raw Tube Screamer-type overdrive circuit and added a parallel clean boost to the effect, which could be blended in as desired by the player to add clarity and firmness to the sound. The company also offers the Analog Chorus, a newer and more deluxe four-knob Tremolo, and in early 2004 was in development on a wah-wah pedal.

In the evolution from near outright cloning to more of an inspired build-it-better approach to effects designing, Voodoo Lab seems to have found a healthy perspective on pedal building, and an ethos that has won it many fans. A big part of all that, according to Fiden, appears to lie in knowing which vintage ingredients are essential, and which can be scaled down or improved upon.

"It's getting into that mindset where you can say, 'Right, I'm OK if we don't replicate every last detail, because we're smarter than that,'" he states. "We can figure out what's important to make it sound right, and what's not important. And by having a better understanding of it that way, we can improve things."

WAY HUGE

Another limited-run, hand-wired boutique maker of the 1990s, Jeorge Tripps earned appropriately large respect for his Way Huge pedals before closing shop to go and work for Line 6 in 1999. His units were well built, offered many outrageous and fulsome tones, and now – thanks as ever to the laws of supply and demand – usually command way huge prices on the used market. They have appeared under the toes of pro players such as Lyle Workman, Pete Anderson, Matthew Sweet, Mike Landau, Dean Wareham, John Fogerty and others.

The Way Huge lineup was fairly diverse at the time of the company's closure, but Tripps seems to have been a specialist in fuzz more than anything else, and his Swollen Pickle Jumbo Fuzz – described as "a Seventies-style fuzz that goes from mild crunch to Armageddon" – has received enormous plaudits from those who have been able to get their hands on it. The Foot Pig Fuzz (yeah, really) was an even more obnoxious germanium-transistor design, while the Red Llama and Green Rhino handled smoother, tubier overdrive sounds.

Descendants of Octavia came in the form of the Purple Platypus Octidrive ("a symphonic overdrive and frequency doubler") and the self-descriptive Piercing Moose Octifuzz. The Way Huge range was rounded off by the Saffron Squeeze Compressor, Tone Leper Midboost, Blue Hippo analog chorus and Aqua-Puss analog delay. Keep your eyes peeled for the used Way Huges still floating out there in the auctions classified ads; pick one up, plug it in, and it will probably peel your ears for you.

XOTIC EFFECTS

Xotic Effects is a division of Prosound Communications Inc, a Los Angeles company that deals mainly

Xotic Effects Robotalk Envelope Filter + Random Arrpegiator
[CD track 37]

Made: 1999 to present.

Controls: Volume, Rate, Range and Freq; stompswitches for mode and on/off; mono in/out plus input for external footcontroller.

Sonics: as Envelope Filter, it offers round, funky auto-wah sounds with plump, musical peaks; as Random Arrpegiator, a bubbling, bleeping blend of tremolo and peaking tone filter.

in exporting high-end guitar gear to Japan. PCI launched the Xotic brand with the Robotalk Envelope Filter + Random Arrpegiator (sic) in 1999, and followed with the AC Booster and RC Booster three years later. The range has remained small, but these hand-wired, US-made pedals have earned a fair amount of respect both at home and abroad.

The Robotalk is a quirky freak of a thing that can achieve much of the weirdness that its name implies, but also functions as a phat and funky auto-wah – which is how I would imagine most guitarists would use it after tinkering with the more novelty-oriented tricks that lie beneath the surface. In 'random arpeggiator' mode (to give it the correct spelling) the degree and frequency range of the standard auto-wah function are, well, randomly arpeggiating, and throwing out frequency peaks that are as much a surprise to the player as to the audience.

Fun stuff, but equally likely to throw out an occasional clunker as they are to produce a sonic epiphany. For an added bonus, there's a jack to connect an external footcontroller (like an ordinary volume pedal) to use the Robotalk as a basic treadle-operated wah-wah.

The AC Booster is a booster-cum-overdrive with Gain, Volume, Treble and Bass controls, while the RC Booster stays more in the 'fat booster' camp, offering anything from unity gain line driver/buffer duties to amp-driving volume boost, with the same controls as its AC.

Z.VEX

The last thing you can call this final entry in our A-to-Z.Vex listing of contemporary makers is a copyist. Zachary Vex represents the ultimate embodiment of the wild and wacky fringes of the fab pedal renaissance of the 1990s and 2000s, and rather than cloning the classics like so many of his competitors in the 'boutique' effects market, he does so by taking a hyper-creative approach to sonic design to bring us many sounds that have literally never existed before.

Z.Vex effects are cute, compact, built like bullets, explore to the Nth degree the extreme potential of otherwise archetypal designs and, for all that, drain so little power from their 9-volt DC cells that many have run for years without their owners ever needing to remove the bottom plate. Also, they are just very cool looking, very individual in construction, with sort of acid-infused-art-commune designs hand-painted by J. Myrold.

For this author – and for plenty of other players – it all makes Z.Vex arguably the ultimate embodiment of the quality, hand-made effects movement. All of which resonates with the spirit of adventure in the first real transistorized effects boom of the early to mid 1970s. (For the full scoop on Z.Vex history and philosophy, see the interview with Zachary Vex in Chapter 6.)

Zachary Vex was a guitar-playing kid and electronics tinkerer in Minneapolis during the aforementioned pedal craze of the 1970s. He ran his own 16-track recording studio in the city from 1985 to 1991, then became a freelance engineer after the 'affordable-quality' home recording boom of the early 1990s effectively put him out of business, along with countless other small studios around the country. The night job segued into an effects business around 1995 when, during a hiatus in work, he built what would become the first Z.Vex pedal, the Octane octave fuzz – wired up, no doubt like so many others' boutique prototypes, at his kitchen table.

The Octane tickled the interest of local guitar stores and musicians, and Z.Vex followed it with the Fuzz Factory, which is arguably his most famous pedal to date. The Fuzz Factory caused even more of a buzz (in every sense), the sales network blossomed from local to regional to national, and a new business was born. At the time of writing, Z.Vex offers 12 effects and one pedal-sized, real-tube guitar amp.

The Fuzz Factory was born out of the crazy notion of cramming as many knobs as possible onto a small metal box (and Z.Vex boxes are sub-MXR small) in order to control every controllable parameter of a 1960s-style germanium fuzz (complete with NOS 'new old stock' transistors). Rather than just the Fuzz (gain) and Volume knobs of the standard fuzz tone, the Fuzz Factory carries Vol, Gate, Comp, Drive and Stab (for stability) knobs; set them right – or maybe wrong – and the thing literally plays itself.

The added bonus of all this is that the player can control the bias point of the transistors, set the unit for extreme compression like the sound of a Fuzz Face running on a dying carbon zinc battery, and much, much more. All this and it even runs on a current of less than 3mA (for comparison, a Tube Screamer runs on nearly 40mA) – giving it such a low draw that Z.Vex is confident in being one of the only high-end makers to build pedals without AC/DC wallwart inputs as standard.

Put as simply as possible, the Fuzz Probe attaches a theremin-like RF 'antenna' in the form of a rectangular copper plate to the side of a Fuzz Factor for freakish manual control over the Stab (stability) control. Set the thing for semi-standard fuzz, pump your foot towards it, and watch out. With a little work the player can get it to create pulsing intermodulations of the fuzz sound, brief stabbing squeals, and plenty more.

The Super Hard On (usually just 'SHO' in polite company) is a very transparent but high-gain booster pedal based on a negative-feedback preamp design, so its single level control gives a 'crackling'

Z.Vex Fuzz Factory [CD tracks 4 & 7]

Made: 1996 to present.

Controls: Vol, Gate, Comp, Drive and Stab; stompswitch for on/off.

Sounds: from bayou-thick to asteroid-bright fuzz, with infinite – and often unstable – permutations in-between; many with surprisingly good character and dynamics.

Z.Vex Super Duper 2-in-1 [CD track 28]

Made: c2001 to present.

Controls: 'the finger,' Master, 'the finger' (ie: Gain, Volume, Gain); stompswitches for on/off of both channels.

Sonics: from a transparent, 'sound enlarging' boost with excellent clarity to amp-slamming gain leap on Ch1 alone; the same plus Master-controlled transistorized overdrive on Ch2, and various levels of selectable two-setting boost or floored filth when used in series.

Z.Vex Seek Wah [CD track 39]

Made: circa late 1990s to present.

Controls: sub-miniature knobs for speed and one to set the filter frequency for each of up to eight pulse points; three-way toggle switch to set 4/8/6 pulses; stompswitch for on/off.

Sonics: anything from sweetly hypnotic techno-style pulses to haunting tone-tweaked arpeggios.

Z.Vex Wah Probe

Made: c2000 to present.

Controls: Drive knob and 'probe' proximity wah control; stompswitch for on/off.

Sonics: occasionally wild but often musical wah-wah with potentially freakish peaks, and major signal boost when desired.

sound when adjusted – and is therefore labeled "Crackle OK" to let users know not to sweat. The Super Duper 2-in-1 is a surprisingly versatile coupling of two SHOs in one small box, which can be used independently or in series, with a master volume control at the output of the second circuit to allow for overdrive-like sounds.

Vex seems to love the unconventional take on wah-wah, and offers the Seek Wah, Ooh Wah and Wah Probe, but no conventional rocker-treadle version. The Wah Probe is the closest he comes – a wah circuit fronted with an SHO booster, and the copper sensor plate for controlling frequency sweep. The Seek is some bastard combination of a trem, arpeggiator and auto-wah that – courtesy of nine micro-pots – can be set to hit chosen frequency peaks at the desired speed through a constantly cycling 4/4, 8/4 or 6/4 tempo, while the Ooh does the same plus random arpeggiation through the bandpass filter. Yeah, honestly. And a lot of people even use 'em… and love 'em.

The Z.Vex pedal lineup is completed by the Woolly Mammoth bass fuzz, Machine distortion/filthifier unit (actually "a dual frequency-tripler circuit that uses crossover distortion for the first time in any pedal, ever," and carries a Z.Vex guarantee to cut through any sound), the Trem Probe (theremin-style probe controlled SHO booster circuit), and Lo-Fi Loop Junky, a trashy sounding but highly effective 20-second looper unit.

And, although it's not an effect, the Nano Head amp deserves a mention for sheer inventiveness. This pedal-sized recording/practice amp head contains a pair of genuine, sub-miniature 6021W tubes and a real output transformer to generate a full half-watt of cranked stack tone, in sub-miniature.

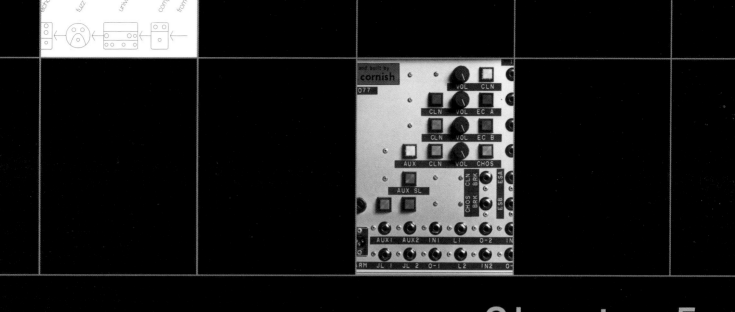

Chapter 5
TIPS, TRICKS & TONE

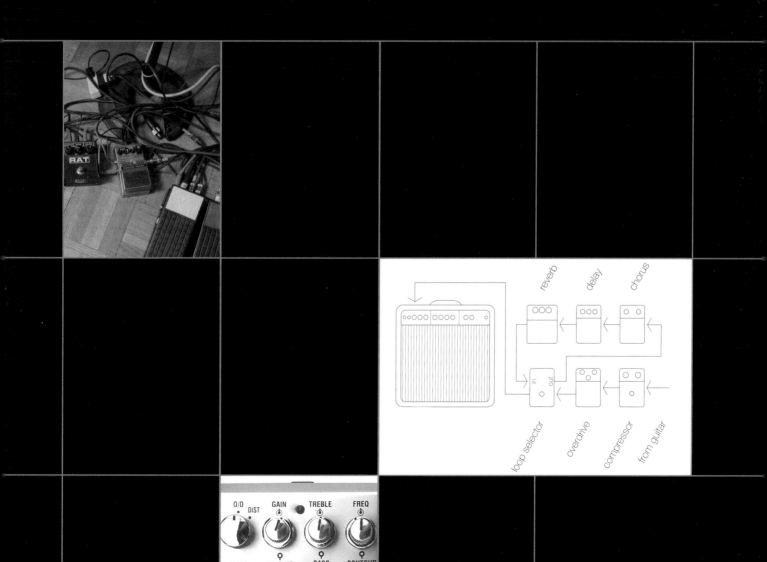

Tone. It has to be the most abused word in the guitarist's lexicon. We've made it a holy grail unto itself, and yet so many different types of sounds seem to qualify for the tag – and, to be honest, guitar players are probably the most wishy-washy when it comes to defining what the simple word 'tone' really means.

Jazz buffs speak of Coltrane's tenor tone; the purity of acoustic tone of a Steinway grand piano, or a Ramîrez classical guitar, or a Benedetto archtop is indisputable. Most listeners could even agree that, say, a tweed Fender Bassman or JMI Vox AC30 tube amp running 'clean' but just on the edge of harmonic breakup contains a universally appealing element accurately described as 'good tone.' But how about the foundation-shaking distortion in a heavily pushed Marshall Plexi 100, the rich squash of a gray Ross Compressor, the hypnotic swirl of a Uni-Vibe, or the fat throaty crunch of a Hot Cake pedal? Can such diversity of sound all hover under the umbrella of the same four-letter word?

Regarding pure sonic content, the simple definition is probably that 'tone' describes a sound's balance of bass and treble frequencies and harmonic overtones. Electric guitarists expand the definition by listening for harmonic distortion content, and indeed for many the THD (total harmonic distortion) is the primary defining factor in achieving a great, playable tone.

Leo Fender's tube amp creations of the 1950s are some of the greatest tone machines of all time, yet Fender and his designers were unhappy with an amp's performance at the point that it broke into distortion – which is going to be anywhere from 3 to 6 on a tweed amp's dial of 12 – and constantly redesigned their products for more headroom and less distortion. Is it just a happy accident that Leo Fender, who undoubtedly knew good tone when he heard it, gave birth to some of the world's greatest guitar tones when his amps did the opposite of what he was designing them to do? (Or, more accurately, when they were abused by guitarists who wanted them to do so?) And of course you could insert the Vox/Tom Jennings/Dick Denney names here with the same results.

The more you puzzle it out, the more convoluted and indefinable this thing 'tone' becomes. But most of us agree on one thing: a pure, clinical, 'clean' guitar sound – a truly hi-fi sound, if you will, with minimal harmonic distortion – does not make for great guitar tone. Play that original 1954 Fender Stratocaster through a modern mixing desk into a solid state Crown power amp, and you'll quickly wonder who robbed your $25,000-worth of tone.

All this considered, those with ears attuned to the subtleties can spot the gradations of something we can indeed classify as 'great tone' in all of the above forms of distorted and altered sound. They can also spot bad tone in plenty of other such sounds. It's not purely subjective, I believe, but can be defined and observed. That said, it's not a scientific phenomenon to the extent that it can be mathematically quantified, and I'll be damned if I – or anyone – can put it into words that do justice to what our ears perceive. (As the sage has said: "Talking about music is like dancing about architecture" – attributed freely to Frank Zappa, Thelonious Monk, Martin Mull, Laurie Anderson, Charles Mingus, Steve Martin, Elvis Costello… take your pick.)

However you slice it, though, our hunt for satisfying, usable effects pedals is all part of this same grand quest for tone, and for many the makeup of the pedalboard ends up being the main, clinching ingredient in the whole tone stew.

For example, choose just three or four pedals that sound good to you, that perform as they should, and are right for your music, and you've got a limitless palette of sonic variations in a rig that will actually feel easier to play. Hitch up some real duffers – or use good pedals, but use them poorly and connect them wrongly – and the best guitar-and-amp combination in the world will sound dead and lifeless, and suddenly seem a real bear to play.

It all works together, and any one ingredient along the way that underperforms and sucks the life from your tone is robbing that tone from the rest of the chain; you can't replace it once it's gone, it won't make it to your amp, and it won't get to your ears, or your listeners'.

THE BIG PICTURE

Tone-conscious players – and the more conscientious designers and manufacturers out there – approach guitar effects with the whole rig in mind. Electric guitar equipment setups are interactive things, and unless you put each individual pedal on its own switchable loop, everything you put in the chain is going to effect the sound of everything else. Even a bypassed pedal placed after a unit that's switched in can affect the performance of the active unit, by introducing noise, sucking tone, sapping signal level, and so forth. The permutations of rig combinations are endless, and every little change in connection order will affect the overall sound – if only slightly – so even individual pedals should be approached with consideration to their sound and performance as part of a group. But no single pedal is likely to be your 'sound savior' if you're jacking it into an already weak setup – unless, perhaps, it's a booster, buffer, or line driver at the front of an impedance-loaded signal chain, or in some cases a noise gate at the end of a noisy one.

Effects that are used well, and that are injected into an amp that's set up to maximize what they do, become a huge part of what our listeners will identify simply as 'great tone' – even when they're alternately hearing contributions from very different sounds, like the bounce of a slapback echo, the swirl of a vintage phaser, or the velvety distortion of a germanium fuzz. Make a list of some of the most legendary pedal-using guitarists of all time, and chances are they're not players whom people generally consider to be 'effects heavy.' Guitarists like Jimi Hendrix, Eric Johnson, Stevie Ray Vaughan, Billy Gibbons, David Gilmour and Eddie Van Halen – the ones who keep popping up in the magazine articles and web site chat rooms that analyze the 'sound secrets of the stars' – all use or used more than a few effects pedals in their setups and, more to the point, almost always have one or two switched in at the times that we really notice their playing most, but we just think of them as having 'great tone'… along with stunning technique. None uses an effect for effect's sake, as novelty, and you can bet each thought long and hard about the big picture when selecting and testing each individual pedal to add to their rig. But overall, the last thing we think of any of these guys being is 'heavily processed,' however heavy their sonic processing. This seems like a laudable goal for any guitarist; on the other hand, if your thing is to craft wild effects into an avant garde a-guitaral slab, that's its own kind of art too.

There are players who are definitely known for their extreme use of effects, who are known more as warpers of guitar sounds, and might even be considered more sonic sculptors than guitarists. I'm thinking of the likes of Adrian Belew, Robert Fripp, Tom Morello, Reeves Gabrels, many of the more adventurous Nu-Metal players… all of whom are the authors of some nut-house sounds, for sure. Great, very effective musicians, too, and they make up another group of guitarists who know how to use effects pedals very well. (Of course we less often think of these as players who simply have 'great tone' – but listen closely, and very often they do.) Again, whether they're a tone hound or a sonic mangler, you can bet all the most respected of the great-sounding pros have put a lot of thought into how each link in the chain affects the sound as a whole.

The main point to consider in all of this is that whether your guitar is a PRS Artist III, Fender Telecaster, Gibson ES-335, Jackson Stealth, Parker Fly, Yamaha SG2000 or Danelectro U2, played through a Marshall JCM800, Fender Super Reverb, Soldano Lucky 13, Peavey Bandit, Vox AC10, Mesa/Boogie Rect-O-Verb or Victoria Double Deluxe – mix'n'match at random – you're going to need to approach your selection and use of effects pedals differently.

GETTING THE FILTH

The majority of guitarists spend more time crafting distortion sounds than chasing any other single sonic goal. There's an infinity of ways to achieve good overdrive and distortion sounds, when you extrapolate from the possible combinations of pedals and amps and high-output pickups and so on. But you could group the majority of these into sounds associated with the era from which they originated: 1) 1950s-1960s – cranked tube amps; 2) 1970s – a 100-watter and a fuzz box; 3) 1980s – cascading-gain preamp into master-vol distortion; 4) 1990s high-gain channel-switching preamp and effects loop; 5) today – all of the above, but for the tone-conscious, often a selection of quality fuzz/overdrive/ distortions into a good 50W tube combo or head'n'cab set to just the edge of breakup.

Whichever variation of these you use, the main thing to remember is that your distortion results from a combination of elements, and if you change these elements, the old combination and new combination are not likely to work their best simultaneously. To look at it a different way, it's almost impossible to get the best of all these types of overdrive sounds from just one rig, either combined in one sound or in succession at the stomp of a switch. Appropriately enough for our purposes here, the closest approximation of the full range can usually be had from a range of carefully chosen and set up pedals. We can analyze each type of distortion in a little more detail.

Let's face it: if it was possible or practical, most of us would get our overdrive sounds from method number one, a cranked vintage amp yielding a luscious, tactile, harmonically rich distortion from its hard-pushed output tubes. It's important to know, though, that even if you're able to go this route, you won't also be able to get a sweet, bright clean sound from the same setup without some knob twiddling, or for that matter a tight, thick, undistorted echo or chorus, and so forth.

If the distortion is coming from the amp itself, there's nothing you can do in front of the inputs to make the setup instantly offer the same kind of clean sound as a loud-clean tube amp. Certainly just winding down the guitar's volume when plugged into a distorting vintage amp can often give you some gorgeous clean tones, and that's how it was often done in the good old days. But in doing so you usually bleed off some of the guitar's own inherent brightness, and – for example – the result of putting a Les Paul Jr on 5 into a Deluxe Reverb on 10 is certainly different than putting a Les Paul Jr on 10 into a Super Reverb on 5, even if the resultant decibel level is exactly the same (I'm just guesstimating here, but you get the idea).

The 'Super on 5' scenario is also probably going to make a bolder, sharper, punchier template for whatever effects pedals you're going to put in front of the amp. But put a Tube Screamer or Route 66 or Jacques Tube Blower in front of the Super Reverb on 5, and you'll get a sound that's not all that far from the Deluxe on 10, with one of the world's tastiest clean sounds at the tap of a foot when you switch the pedal out. In a smaller room, the same principal applies to the scenario of putting the pedal in front of the 22W Deluxe Reverb set to 4 or 5, rather than getting your distortion from a cranked Princeton, for example.

The high-gain channel-switching thing done by the likes of a Boogie Rectifier, Peavey 5150, Carvin Legacy, Bogner Ecstasy and so forth yields a form of preamp distortion that is de rigueur for many modern rock styles. If this is your chosen breed of filth, you can greatly expand your distortion textures by using a selection of overdrives and distortions into the front end of the amp, switching them in when the amp's 'clean' channel is selected. A low to medium-gain overdrive can even juice up a channel-switcher's 'lead' channel pretty nicely in some circumstances, giving it that extra goose… something a lot of amp makers are achieving with a footswitchable 'Boost' feature. But efforts to get some ultimate over-the-top aural assault from a high-gain distortion pedal or two injected into a saturated high-gain amp's cranked lead channel usually just result in a wall-of-mud tone with little definition or dynamics, and often plenty of extra noise.

The more you distort a signal before it hits the amp input, the more you deplete its definition and attack. When you're talking about the input of the lead channel in a modern channel-switching amp – a design that chains together a series of ultra-high-gain tube preamp stages – this means mega-amplification of a signal that has already lost much of the guitar's original character and dynamics, and is destined to lose even more on its way to the output stage. This might work as a whole other sound unto itself, but for big, bold, dynamic and over-the-top excess you'd probably do better with a distortion or two set for high gain and full body, and injected into a powerful, tight-bottomed amp with a full voice and firm, fast response. A low-gain overdrive or booster into a high-gain distortion can make a great setup for three switchable intensities of dirt, plus instant clean – voila, a four-channel amp, with better rhythm sounds than many of the breed.

The implications of these channel-switcher scenarios bring up further questions regarding the best placement of modulation and delay effects in the chain. At the very least, you need to compute all the variations in sounds of echoes and tremolos and choruses and so forth when placed before the input and, therefore, in front of the amp's own distortion, but still behind your pedal-generated distortion, or in the amp's effects loop to take the preamp sound.

As for these amps' overdrive channels themselves, the high-gain sounds supplied by modern channel-switching amps are achieved with preamp tube distortion (most of them variations on the classic Mesa/Boogie cascading gain topology). The high-saturation, almost buzzy distortion this provides has become a standard of modern rock. On the other hand, the vintage overdrive sounds that many guitarists lust after were the products of power tube distortion; 'classic rock' sounds were often created with a booster, fuzz box, or distortion pedal in front of a big Marshall or Fender Bassman or something of that ilk.

Such pedals don't turn a vintage-style, low-gain preamp design into a Boogie, but they boost the amp's front end enough to drive the output stage into distortion. It may be an overdrive sound helped along by solid state circuitry, but it possesses so much of the richness and juiciness of the output tube distortion responsible for many of the best overdrive sounds of all time: any of the great heavy sounds of Jimi Hendrix, Bluesbreakers or Cream-era Clapton, Jimmy Page, Eddie Van Halen, Slash, Randy Rhoads, and plenty of others.

Many boost and overdrive pedals (as opposed to fuzz or distortion pedals) really want to drive a tube amp to sound their best. They aren't designed to be juicy, toneful devices on their own, but want to interact with your amp, helping to push your output tubes closer to distortion, as discussed above. Consequently, they often don't perform their best plugged into a solid state amp, and even sound different when played through the high-gain tube preamp in a channel-switching amp.

To test this at the extreme, try DI'ing an Ibanez Tube Screamer, a Klon Centaur or a Crowther Hot Cake – all respected overdrives – or indeed a boost pedal like the MXR Micro Amp, Fulltone's Fat Boost or Z.Vex's Super Hard On. Inject them into any ordinary mixing desk, and monitor through speakers or headphones. The sound will probably be far from what you would hope for in such a pedal. Definitely un-tubey. Played through a quality solid state amp that's cranked up pretty high, they will certainly sound better, but still not their best. Plug them into a decent tube amp, though – even one set very clean – and these can yield a distinctly tube-like overdrive sound. That's what they're built to do, but it only works under the right conditions.

Many heavier fuzz boxes or hard-rock/metal distortion pedals, on the other hand, generate their full palette of distortion within themselves, getting a lot closer to doing their thing even when DI'd, and can sound damn fine through a big, firm tranny amp. Try MXR's signature Dimebag Darrell Dime Distortion pedal through Randall's 300W solid state Dimebag Warhead stack and you'll get a quick taste of the potential mayhem in such a rig. Of course these pedals will also push a tube amp into serious OD, so the options abound.

Given a free choice, most players who need a distorted 'lead guitar' type of sound would probably still get it from a Marshall Plexi 50W on 10, a Fender Bassman on 12, or a Vox AC30 – or for that matter Matchless D/C30 or TopHat King Royale – cranked up to quittin' time. But it just ain't gonna happen for most of us, at least not down at McMurphy's Tavern on a Friday night, the low-ceilinged billiards room packed to its 125-body standing room capacity and the vocal PA gagged down to about 3.5 to keep the lid on the squealing feedback. The best we can probably hope for – with a sledge-fisted drummer and a healthy-lunged vocalist alongside us – is our dream crunchy-to-clean sound from a good 50W tubester set at 11 o'clock, and a choice selection of overdrives and the rest to lend us that drive, saturation and sustain when required.

Of course if the gig just doesn't call for a clean sound, whack up that tweed Deluxe or Bad Cat Cub 15 and count your blessings – you're in distortion-tone heaven. In most cases, though, pedals are what give the rest of us the instant-switchability of sounds, even if we only need to go between clean and a couple flavors of distortion, while enabling a retention of the truest, richest canvas possible in a base-sound.

There's a certain machismo in guitar circles today in playing straight to the amp, getting your clean/distortion sounds from the guitar volume as discussed above, and pretty much saying, "Hey, these crunchy-sweet blues riffs I'm squeezing out sound so damn fine that I just don't need any echo/phaser/chorus/vibe, so screw 'em." A lot of guitarists go out of their way to avoid using pedals – overdrives in particular – when to do so could be the quickest way to a rewarding, consistent and playable guitar sound.

There is also the view that the best of both worlds can be had by switching between a big clean and a small distorted amp for 'pure tube tone' at the required volume. Great if you can manage it, and plenty of touring guitarists have done this for years, but what a headache – especially if you haven't got your own traveling guitar tech and roadie. Trouble finding quality amp switchers, hassles with ground loops, the expense, the sheer weight… they all add up to make such setups prohibitive for many of us. But if you can pull it off, it's a cool way to go, and your effects can be routed separately or together.

Neil Young's setup makes an interesting example of one exception that proves the rule. He uses a mechanical automated system dubbed 'The Whizzer' to make instantaneous changes to the two Volume and one Tone controls on his tweed Fender Deluxe amp – effectively turning a 50-year-old, 15W 1x12″combo with only three knobs to its name into a channel switcher offering clean (well, semi-clean), crunch and searing lead sounds at the stomp of a switch. And all this without modification to the vintage circuit within the amp itself. This allows him to avoid the use of any overdrive or distortion pedals – and certainly any modern, high-gain amps – to continue playing through the little 1950s Fender he loves so much, and still attain a sound that has led many to christen him the 'godfather of grunge.'

Admittedly he does use a variety of pedals for other sounds: a Maestro tape echo, a Uni-Vibe, even a digital delay for an extreme, chopping echo sound, so he's not taking some faux-Luddite 'no pedals' stance by any means. Just achieving the best possible sounds for his playing purposes, by whatever means he can devise.

I don't know where you'd even begin to get your hands on your own Whizzer, or the cash for a vintage Deluxe in good condition; but stick a booster and an overdrive into a Fender Blues Junior or something – along with whatever other pedals you want for echoes and swirls – and you've got a versatile and selectable range of sounds not too far off the mark for just a few hundred bucks.

'STANDARD' PEDAL ORDER

There is an accepted 'correct' order in which to chain pedals together for the best interaction and sound, but this subject should only be approached in the knowledge that whatever order gives you the most desirable sound for your own style, or for a particular song, is clearly the correct order for you. Who cares how the latest guitar hero does it, or how the books and magazines tell you it should be done, if the sound you're getting from an unconventional effects line-up really rocks your world and makes your guitar easier and more fun to play?

That said, it's worth knowing the rules before you set out to obliterate them, and understanding how

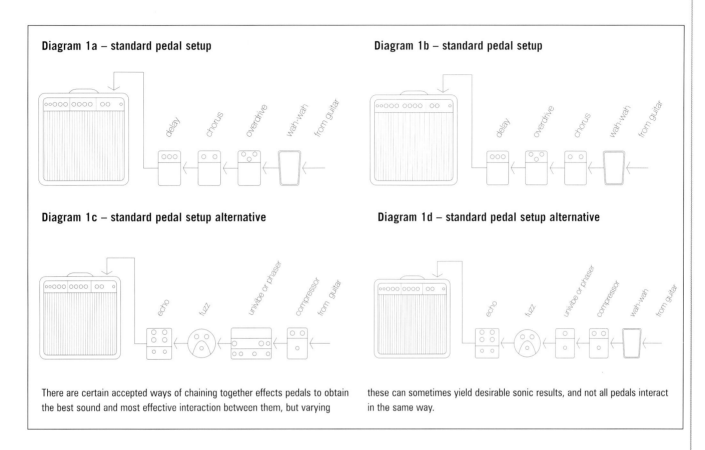

Diagram 1a – standard pedal setup

Diagram 1b – standard pedal setup

Diagram 1c – standard pedal setup alternative

Diagram 1d – standard pedal setup alternative

There are certain accepted ways of chaining together effects pedals to obtain the best sound and most effective interaction between them, but varying these can sometimes yield desirable sonic results, and not all pedals interact in the same way.

certain effects interact makes it a lot easier to craft your sound without resorting to sheer guesswork, and perhaps missing out entirely on some very cool tones. Just remember, these aren't very hard and fast rules, breaking them incurs no financial penalties or prison terms, and you can feel free to toss them out the window at will.

The short-form guide to chaining effects pedals says you put tone filters and EQs first, boosters and overdrives second, modulation devices third, and delays fourth. With this line-up, you filter or EQ the raw guitar before distorting and boosting it, distort and boost it before making it spin or wobble (thereby spinning or wobbling the fully-driven sound), and finally, echo or reverberate all that's come before. A common variation on this, one that certainly works best with certain types of pedals, is to swap the middle two of these four stages.

Some modulation devices, such as vintage-style analog choruses, phasers or Uni-Vibes and their clones, do their best work when put before overdrive or fuzz pedals. This is mostly because their function and sound includes an element of filtering-type tone shifting, sweeping frequency notches or out-of-phase signal paths; sending an already distorted signal into this frequency-twisting mayhem can just cough up hairballs of atonal mush, but injecting the ethereal swirl into an overdrive or fuzz that follows it works a certain magic.

The diagrams in this section show a few variations on 'standard' routing, with certain ingredients added and subtracted, plus some alternatives. Of course there are other exceptions to the rules, and in some cases you might find that there really is no 'perfect' order in which to chain the six effects on your pedalboard, because perhaps two of them want to perform their best in the same position, while the stereo chorus might sound better before the fuzz, but you want it at the end of the chain to split your entire effected sound to a pair of amps for proper stereo projection. Play around with what you've got, try it all in every conceivable combination, and go with what sounds best. You might have to make some

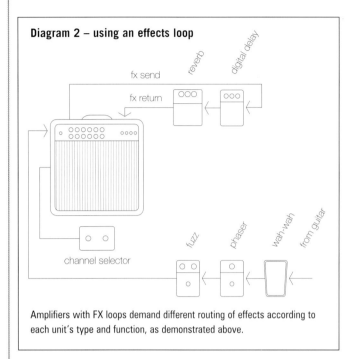

Diagram 2 – using an effects loop

fx send

reverb

digital delay

fx return

channel selector

fuzz

phaser

wah-wah

from guitar

Amplifiers with FX loops demand different routing of effects according to each unit's type and function, as demonstrated above.

compromises and use a pedal in a position that doesn't offer its optimum performance, but which yields the best performance from the entire setup.

Certain effects are likely to perform their best in the effects loops of modern amps. Delays, reverbs and some modern-style choruses might prefer to sit here, where they can be used post-distortion when you're playing through the amp's own lead channel (these effects loops invariably sit between preamp and power amp). Amps with parallel rather than series effects loops – in the former a portion of the sound enters the loop, as opposed to the entire sound in the latter – and with a related effects-out level or mix control, are a real bonus here: many of the devices you would insert in such a loop can be sensitive to high input levels, throwing up nasty distortion – often particularly nasty digital distortion – if you slam them too hard.

Work carefully with the units in the loop, start the effects-out signal at its minimum and work gradually upward until you get just a hint of input distortion, then back it down into the clean zone. In time you'll learn just how much the in-loop effects can take; you'll sound better, and the units themselves will enjoy longer lives, free from the stresses of input overload.

Trouble in deciding your signal-chain order can arise with certain effects that get some of their 'bonus' functions from a direct interaction with your pickups' impedance, or with those that really insist on sitting before or after other effects to sound any good at all. Many good fuzz boxes like to be first in the chain, not only to sound their best but to allow the player the useful utility of turning down the guitar's volume control in order to clean up the distortion some, the result being a lot more tonal flexibility than merely 'fuzz pedal on/fuzz pedal off.' Put the fuzz after another pedal or two – especially a buffered pedal – and you often lose that element of interaction, even when the preceding pedals are switched off. Some overdrives behave much the same; Blackstone's 2S Mosfet Overdrive, for example, carries the advice "Requires unbuffered connection to the guitar" printed right on the front of it.

For the best 'vocal,' musical performance, wah-wahs invariably like to sit first in the chain too. The traditional usage allows the wah-wah to frequency-filter a clean, untainted guitar sound and then pass it down the chain, where the round, expressive 'voweling' of the sound can then be fuzzed or overdriven or echoed or what have you. Of course, as ever, there's a 'what-the-hell' exception, and a freaky wah'd fuzz (as opposed to fuzzed wah) can produce wild, woolly-to-razory frequency swoops and shifting notches that are extremely cool in the right application. In the end, if you've got a Fuzz Face, a Cry Baby and a Blackstone on your pedalboard, you're going to have to make some compromises somewhere down the line.

Everyone from Jimi Hendrix to Eric Johnson to Yngwie Malmsteen to J. Mascis to Joey Santiago used or uses their wah-wah first in line, while Carlos Santana sticks a Tube Screamer before his, Brian May puts his treble booster first, Steve Vai has wahs both before and after his Boss DS-1, and I've seen a few players put a Digitech whammy in front of their wahs (although I can't discern whether they're using the two switched in together at any time).

Plenty of other name artists flout the conventions in small or large ways, and you can check them out to discover a little about how it sounds to bend or break the rules. While the convention says you want echo to follow just about everything else but reverb, Dave Grohl of the Foo Fighters – for most of his live work – uses the extremely simple line-up of delay pedal into MXR Phase 90 into amp. Early on he used a Boss DD-3 Digital Delay, with a Mesa/Boogie Dual Rectifier or two at the end of the chain; his admiration for Queen guitarist Brian May's singing Vox tone has more recently led him to acquire a pair of AC30s to partner with the Boogies – A/B'd to select the former for clean, the latter for overdrive – and he seems to now be using a Boss DM-3 Analog Delay rather than the digital DD-3. Pearl Jam's Mike McCready also positions his Boss DM-3 somewhat unconventionally, after his Dunlop Uni-Vibe and 535Q Cry Baby, and before his MXR Phase 90, volume pedal, and TS9 Tube Screamer.

Around the time of the groundbreaking *OK Computer* album, Radiohead's Johnny Greenwood placed his Boss RV-3 Reverb/Delay after a Marshall ShredMaster (the first pedal in his line-up) but before his second overdrive, a Boss SD-1, from which point the signal split straight to one amp (a Vox AC30) or on to a second – a solid-state Fender – via a DigiTech Whammy, a tremolo unit (unconventional placement number two), a DOD envelope filter, an Electro-Harmonix Small Stone phaser (unconventional placement number three), a Roland Space Echo, and a Mutronics Mutator. Plenty of rules broken here, for sure, but his sound can be otherworldly, verging on the divine.

Of course it doesn't matter so much what order you connect the pedals if you're only ever switching in one unit at a time, but most players who string together more than a few will invariably use a couple or more together to elicit some unconventional results. Even Jimi Hendrix flouted convention to some extent by putting his Univox Uni-Vibe last in the chain, when today 'Vibe-type effects are usually placed first, or near the front at least. Hendrix's signal chain went: Vox Wah-Wah, Dallas-Arbiter Fuzz Face, Roger Mayer custom-built Octavia, and Uni-Vibe... and that fuzzed and sometimes even wah'd watery swirl running through the 'Vibe sounded gorgeous time and again.

This segués well into another lesson: seeking out a particular pedal because you heard or read that so-and-so plays one on such-and-such track can often backfire. Try the thing out, sure, but don't buy anything on hearsay alone, and certainly think twice before basing your own precious sound on whispers of rumors of gear used by others – or at least don't be surprised when the sound just ain't quite what you hoped. While some players' signature sounds remain consistent, any seasoned pro will tell you that equal doses of trickery and experimentation go into getting new and different sounds in the studio, and these aren't always as easy to replicate as plugging X guitar into Y pedal into Z amp. Even written reports in players' own words offer no guarantee of taking you there either; by the time guitar mag interviews come around, the big artists are often promoting an album that was recorded months before. Could you remember precisely what ingredients went into making the 'guitar solo sound on track 11' of a recording made six months ago, late at night in a smokey studio, with a warehouse full of effects, guitars and amps at your disposal, having had maybe 15 attempts (and as many different pedal combinations) before the final successful take? Most people couldn't.

Also, although it's relatively easy, in the information age, to get your hands on the effects line-ups that plenty of big-name pros tour with, few artists stick religiously to the same rig both live and in the studio. You might see the guy touring with a Voodoo Lab Superfuzz because it gives him a good and versatile all-around fuzz tone, but chances are he tried a vintage Fuzz Face, Tone-Bender, Fuzz-Tone, Big Muff and half a dozen others in the studio before honing in on that plummy, warm fuzz-guitar solo you have just fallen in love with.

Take the case of Jimmy Page; he went a long way toward helping to sell Les Pauls and Marshall stacks, even though a Tele and a small Supro amp were responsible for some of the finest recorded sounds the man ever made in the earlier days of Led Zeppelin. Still, there's nothing wrong with taking a respected artist's use of an item of equipment to heart, and it often makes a good starting point in your own sound search. Just keep the near-infinite variables and the 'big picture' in mind at all times.

You might set off down a road that intends to explore the conventions, and end up at a place that indicates there really are none. That's fine, and it goes to show once again that the only reliable way to find your own sound is to try out whatever pedals you can get your hands on, and explore them to the extreme, in all imaginable positions and at all possible settings. After you put the time in, the choices are simple: use what sounds good to you.

SIGNAL SAVIORS

Long or convoluted signal chains can often use some help in getting your sound from guitar to amp in the best possible condition, and there are a number of avenues you can explore here. There's a big fondness for 'true bypass' these days, especially among fans and makers of many 'boutique' pedals, and I'll look at that in a little more detail in a minute, as it applies to both individual pedals and entire pedalboards. There's little argument about the fact that, with no effects engaged, most of us would prefer to be plugged straight into the amp with a relatively short cord/lead. But the majority of players these days have at least one effect switched in more often than not, and any gigging guitarist knows your lead can only be so short… without eventually pulling the amp down on your head.

For many players, buffers or line drivers are a big help in getting the signal from the guitar through six or ten pedals and a Hail Mary's worth of cable and finally to the amp with as little degradation as possible. In simple terms, they condition the signal, drop it to low impedance to keep both your pickups and your amp's input happy, and give it a gentle kick in the ass to help scoot it along the wire. "But I don't like buffers," you say, "they interfere with my guitar's natural sound, make it trebly and thin, and add noise." It's a common argument, in reply to which I can only say, "Try a good one."

First, get your hands on a decent, transparent, unity gain buffer or line driver, but don't hook it up just yet. Unplug yourself from your pedalboard, and stick you guitar straight into the amp via a short cable of 10′ or 15′. Sounds great, right? Now connect the buffer/driver at the front of your pedal chain, plug into it with the same cable, and connect the whole line-up back to the amp from the last pedal on the board, but with none of the pedals switched on yet, except for the buffer. With a good quality buffer/driver, your sound should be not too far from the direct-to-amp sound – although you might not realize the full weight of the improvement until you remove the buffer from the chain again and listen to things as you had them before. There's a selection of tracks on the accompanying CD that do this for you, as well as testing the merits of true bypass as used in certain setups.

The truth is, a good buffer should help get your guitar tone to the amp sounding much more like itself than that same tone passing through six pedals and many yards of wire. We all need a shoulder to lean on sometimes, and a good buffer can make an excellent, transparent crutch for your precious guitar signal. There's no shame in it. And if you've got eight or ten or more pedals in your chain, the way many players do these days, your straight, clean sound is very likely suffering badly without one. Many, many players benefit from buffers without even knowing it. All Boss and the bulk of Ibanez and DOD pedals contain a buffer stage, for example, as do pedals from Visual Sound, many from Roger Mayer, and plenty of other quality makes, so if you've got one of these at or near the front of your pedalboard you are benefiting from this already.

The popularity of onboard preamps and other forms of active electronics in the late 1970s and 1980s saw many players carrying buffers right on their guitars, although when used as a separate unit most will place them in front of the first effect in the chain – unless they've got something that they really want to connect straight to the guitar first. There might still be some marginal treble loss due to the loading of whatever cable and switching comes before the buffer, but it should still get you pretty close to a straight-to-amp sound. Also, be aware that many guitarists' ears are attuned to the slight 'warming' and 'rounding off' that a little high-end loss at the hands of long lengths of wire contributes to their sound; going too hi-fi all at once – as if there was nothing but a couple inches of wire between guitar and amp – could take you off in the wrong direction.

ROUTING AND PARALLEL PATHS

While the simplest and most obvious way to route your guitar and effects is still to plug your guitar into the first unit, run a jumper cable between each in succession, then hitch the last to the amp, a look at the rigs used by plenty of pros, both live and in the studio, will show you there are many more creative ways to pass your signal down the chain. The plethora of stereo pedals available obviously points to the notion of routing the sound to two amps standing side-by-side (see Diagram 3) – identical amps, preferably, if you're looking for 'true stereo,' although a mix'n'match combination can also help to fill out the sound and add texture. Either way, this is really not much different than the first, straight-through setup, with all pedals sitting successively in a chain and two amps at the end of it to take the stereo split, from a chorus or delay or reverb or whatever stereo pedal you place last. Of course many players also switch entirely between two amps with an A/B selector (commonly for 'clean' or 'lead' sounds), rather than splitting to stereo. In this case they either place all effects in front of the splitter to have them available with both sounds, or group their 'clean effects' and 'lead effects' separately – for example, a compressor and chorus in the former chain, a wah-wah and fuzz box in the latter. Both routing paths can be very effective, but there are still more inventive multi-path options than these.

Plenty of good players will split their signal far earlier in the chain (as in Diagram 4 on the next page) – after a buffer or booster or line driver, or possibly after a stereo pedal placed only second or third on a board of several. One path goes straight to an amp that's kept either 'dry' (totally without effects), or nearly so, with maybe just an overdrive and phaser or chorus in front of it. The second path then goes on through a number of other effects to a different amp, which obviously carries the bulk of the 'wet' sound when pedals are switched in. This is a great setup in a number of situations; perhaps the 'dry' amp is a smaller amp cranked to a relatively higher volume setting – or a vintage tweed or Vox or something – that keeps an edge of plummy output-tube distortion in your sound at all times. Such sounds often don't handle effects very well, and don't

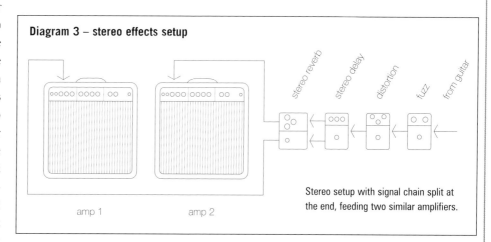

Diagram 3 – stereo effects setup

amp 1   amp 2

stereo reverb   stereo delay   distortion   fuzz   from guitar

Stereo setup with signal chain split at the end, feeding two similar amplifiers.

need any pedal-overdrive – so don't give them any. Routing the bulk of the echoes and wobbles and swirls, along with any heavy pedal-generated distortion, to a larger, tighter amp with more headroom and a good, bright clean sound takes care of the wet signal – and the blend of the two, set correctly, can be absolutely gorgeous.

This setup also offers a range of textures you can only achieve quite right with two amps: the 'crunch' amp keeps that broken-up texture in the sound at all times, even when you are playing parts perceived mainly as clean (thanks to the headroom of the bigger amp), or step on a distortion pedal running to the big amp to shift the relationship to heavy overdrive from the big amp, blended with crispy crunch from the smaller one. You can even place a volume pedal after the signal split going to the small, cranked amp to back off its distortion content a little. To expand upon this, if you're lucky to have three great-sounding amps of different distortion characteristics to hand, you can place an A/B pedal after the first split and route it to your 'crunch' and 'full-whack' amps, either of which is on at all times, with the rest of the wet signal again going to a larger, clean amp. With any of these, however, you really do need a buffer or line driver at the start of the chain to avoid losing signal level, and you might find yourself

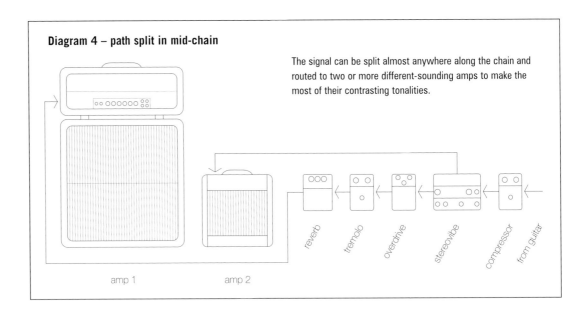

Diagram 4 – path split in mid-chain

The signal can be split almost anywhere along the chain and routed to two or more different-sounding amps to make the most of their contrasting tonalities.

reverb · tremolo · overdrive · stereovibe · compressor · from guitar

amp 1   amp 2

having to deal with ground loops (quality splitter boxes will often have 'ground lift' switching on one signal path to take care of this for you; otherwise you will have to investigate safe techniques for doing it for yourself).

Even with one amp you can take advantage of parallel-path signal routing (as in Diagram 5 at the top of page 145) to either preserve some direct, fully analog signal at the amp, or to re-route effects whose sounds you want to sit beside each other rather than run through each other. Genuine two-channel amps – with two channels active at the same time – are rarer things today, but they were commonplace from the 1950s right up through the 1970s, when manufacturers finally worked out that not many hip beat combos were all playing and singing through the same amplifier any more. In many ways that's a shame, because they're great for running parallel paths into just one amp; consequently most vintage Gibson, Fender, Traynor, Sunn, Marshall or Vox amps and many others are good choices for such setups. It's very much like the two-amp split above, taking off one 'dry' path early in the signal chain to keep a portion of the toneful, dynamic, responsive sound you get by plugging straight into the amp, and running the second path through whatever effects you need to get the job done.

Using a parallel path is a really good technique to employ when you've got a pedal or two that are on one hand indispensable to your sound, but which sap the virtue of your natural tone more than you'd prefer; many digital effects, some vintage tape delays and outboard spring reverbs and a few other types are commonly guilty of this. (Of course many of the latter two types can sound great even when switched out, but they still taint your signal and sound different than straight-to-amp; Fender Tube Reverbs, for example, despite the tube reverb-driver stages, actually impose some signal loss on your sound.)

On vintage-style two-channel amps you can set EQs and volume levels to maximize the performance of each signal path, but it's a routing you can achieve with some success even on many one-channel amps, provided they have dual inputs (usually hi and low sensitivity). In the case of one-channel amps, you're stuck with one shared level setting – which will of course usually be a little lower-gain in the number two input – but the two paths blend together naturally. Even on a one-channel, one-input amp you could use a Y-splitter to join the two signal paths together again. If you have a pedal (or more than one) in your chain that you feel depletes the quality of your dry tone somewhat, try this. Or give it a shot if you think you'd benefit from simply having a little more direct sound from guitar to amp. Remember to tweak your effects' balance, mix, or blend controls to account for the fact that you're halving their presence in the mix, and the results can be seamless and really satisfying.

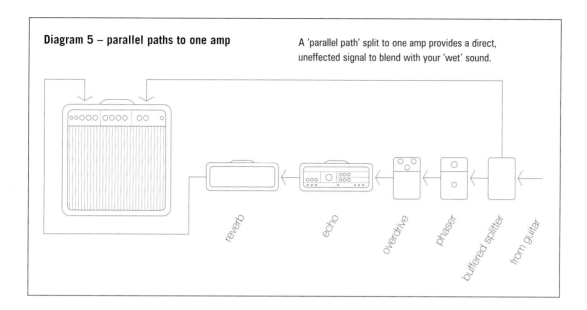

Diagram 5 – parallel paths to one amp

A 'parallel path' split to one amp provides a direct, uneffected signal to blend with your 'wet' sound.

reverb · echo · overdrive · phaser · buffered splitter · from guitar

Keep in mind, though, that possible phase cancelations – caused by a signal split into two paths that arrive at an amplifier at different times (due to slight but sometimes perceptible delays caused by differing cable and chain lengths) – can sometimes cause a depletion of tone, especially in the low end. Check out the variables for yourself before gigging or recording with any new setup.

Many players also use 'loop' or 'routing' pedals within the pedal chain (as shown in Diagram 6), even when going to just one amp, and this is another way of splitting off an effect or group of effects that deplete the quality of your clean signal when kept constantly in the path. You might run your compressor, phaser and overdrive at the start of the chain, and make them always available for use, but at the same time split off a digital delay and vintage reverb unit through a footswitchable loop that accesses them only when they're needed. This is also a great way of switching in a bank of sounds that are to be used together whenever they're used at all, such as a chorus/delay/reverb sound – too many footswitches for a two-footed guitarist to stomp on together, but one click of a loop selector brings them all in and out at once.

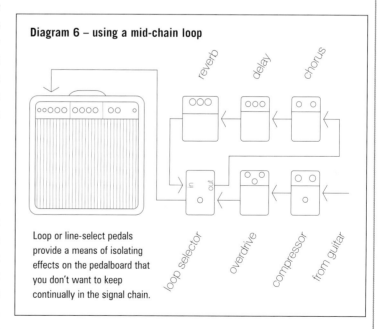

Diagram 6 – using a mid-chain loop

reverb · delay · chorus

loop selector · overdrive · compressor · from guitar

Loop or line-select pedals provide a means of isolating effects on the pedalboard that you don't want to keep continually in the signal chain.

TRUE BYPASS

The phrase 'true bypass' (also referred to as 'hard-wired') is used to describe a pedal switching format that routes the signal directly from input to output when the effect is in off/bypass mode, rather than sending it through a buffer or leaving part of the effects circuit hanging off it. Some vintage pedals had this from the start, although many did not. In any case, until recently, it was a thing impossible to achieve in pedals that also carried status LEDs because the switches available to manufacturers only carried enough connections to allow either a direct bypass wiring or a wiring that switched the on/off light while routing the signal through a buffer at all times. The availability of 'triple-pole, double-throw' switches (also called '3PDT')

– some of good quality, some dubious, all relatively expensive – has made true bypass switching a more achievable reality in recent years, and it has become the mainstay of the majority of boutique manufacturers.

The 'true bypass' issue has evolved into a thorny subject, and there are plenty of cases for and against. On the surface it sounds a great thing: switch your pedal out, and hey, you're connected straight to the amp. And with short cable runs and just a pedal or two on the floor, it probably is the best way to go. But get up to five or six pedals, all with true bypass switching, and other considerations come into play. Think back to what was discussed before, regarding buffers and line drivers – a 20′ cord from guitar to a buffered pedal in position one, then jumpers between six others, and another 20′ cord from the last pedal to the amp leaves you with only the loading of the first 20′ cord. Remove the buffer – and switch off all six of your true bypass pedals – and suddenly you've got close to 50′ of wire hanging between guitar and amp. Can you say "treble loss?" I thought you could.

Again, there's a few tracks on the accompanying CD that display this: the same riff is played straight to the amp, then 'dry' three times through a multi-pedal chain – one time fronted with a buffered Roger Mayer pedal, once fronted with a buffered Visual Sound pedal, and once with no buffer at all, just the switched-out true bypass units. (See the interviews with Roger Mayer, Pete Cornish, and Bob Weil in Chapter 6; they address this subject with more authority than I ever could.)

Almost all effects contain an element of signal buffering when switched in, so the all-true-bypass pedalboard also offers the oddity of constantly switching between buffered, unbuffered, and buffered signals, which can make it especially difficult to set your treble levels at the amp. For most players with more than one or two effects on the floor, a blend of buffering at the front of the chain and some true bypass working within it – if you like the sounds of the pedals that offer the feature (admittedly, many are among the finest being made today) – will probably offer the best results. It's something you really have to try for yourself, and then make your judgement according to the results with your rig and your fingers. It's another good reason to keep the 'big picture' in mind, and never select a pedal in isolation without trying it in position with the rest of your setup.

As with most of what has been discussed here, the key is probably in locating a transparent, high-quality buffering stage, if you find you need one at all, and work toward getting the through-the-pedalboard sound as close to your straight-to-amp (with short cord) sound as possible. (A good buffer, by the way, should get your sound safely through up to ten pedals.) As with every aspect of your pedal search, hunt, test, hunt again, and test some more – always with a guitar and amp as close to the types you are using, if not your very own, and playing the music you plan to play through them.

There are a lot of great sounds out there, and there's a lot of fun to be had tracking them down.

Chapter 6
MEET THE MAKERS

f you want the inside scoop on any type of equipment, it often helps to go to the makers themselves. Eight prominent figures in the effects world – Mike Matthews of Electro-Harmonix, Roger Mayer, Pete Cornish, Mike Fuller of Fulltone, Josh Fiden of Voodoo Lab, Dan Coggins of Lovetone & Dinosaural, Zachary Vex of Z.Vex, Bob Weil of Visual Sound, and Mia Theodoratus of Frantone – were kind enough to open their hearts and minds to the author on the subject, in the process offering candid glimpses from the workshop perspective that aren't often available to the average player. All interviews were extremely informal – casual chats even – with the subjects left free to veer off track whenever an interesting thought might lead them astray. At some points the discussions are very in-depth and technical, at others basic and accessible. Each conversation is presented Q&A style to allow the reader to dip in wherever a question or response catches your attention. The interviewees are presented in an approximate chronological order, assembled roughly according to the time they entered the business in a commercial sense – no 'ranking' or 'merit' is applied to the order in which they appear.

MIKE MATTHEWS, OF ELECTRO-HARMONIX

The effects business has taken Electro-Harmonix founder Mike Matthews from his New York roots all the way to Russia – where his 'second wind' gusted in the form of the Sovtek tube company – and back again. He spoke to me from his office back in the Big Apple, where the majority of Electro-Harmonix pedals are made once again, and where the company's owner of more than 35 (slightly segmented) years actually lives and sleeps during the workweek, in an apartment within the factory itself.

Electro-Harmonix founder Mike Matthews, with P-Funker George Clinton and an E-H Tube Zipper.

What got you started in effects?

I was a pretty good rock'n'roll keyboard player back in the 1960s. I had that glory dream, I had it in my blood, and I wanted to go out and make it. I also promoted a lot of rock'n'roll shows. The Isley Brothers wanted me to quit school and join them on the road, and Hendrix wanted to form a band with me ... When I knew him he was Jimmy James ... But the only regret I had was not trying it with The Isley Brothers, because that was my bag, that R&B bag of the early Sixties. Hendrix and I, we were just buddies.

At that time I was working for IBM, and I wanted to quit and spend some time trying to make it with the band. I was married, so I thought, "Let me try and make a shot of money on the side, and then I can give it a go with the band and my wife would have a little security." Fuzz tones were real hot at the time, and people just couldn't make them fast enough. The Stones just came off their blockbuster hit 'Satisfaction' that was Number One for something like 13 weeks. A guy I knew had a plan for a fuzz tone and we were going to make them together; we started, and then he just disappeared. This was maybe 1966-67. So I was stuck. I made them at a contract house, and Al Dronge, the founder and owner of Guild Guitars, wanted them all. They were branded Foxy Lady. This wasn't any one of our early designs, but that's how I got started.

Then suddenly everybody wanted to play like Hendrix – he was able to get this great sustain out of his guitar, by just vibrating his long, supple fingers. So everybody thought they wanted a distortion-free sustainer. I asked one of my buddies if he knew a guy who could design this thing for me, and he said, "Yeah, I know this guy named Bob Meyer, out at Bell Labs." So I contacted Bob, and he started working on designing this distortion-free sustainer. Then one of the times I went out there to check out the prototype, there was this little box plugged in in front of it. I says, "What's this?" and he says, "Well, when I designed it I didn't take into account that the guitar pickup put out a lower signal than I had anticipated, so I just put a little booster in there."

I plucked the guitar, then I put on the switch on the booster, and all of a sudden the amp was loud as hell. I thought, "This is really cool." And that became my first product, the LPB1 Linear Power Booster. In those days, all amps were over-designed with a lot of headroom. You turned an amp up to ten, and it wouldn't distort unless the speaker was a little ratty, or unless you were using an external distortion box. But with the LPB1, you could get a hell of a lot more volume, and if you turned it up you could start to overdrive the amp. That was the first item ever to do that – and it was a big hit. That was our first product, and we sold hundreds of thousands of them, because it really did something and it was really cheap.

So I quit IBM. I had no experience in manufacturing, but that product was so simple – it only had one transistor. So it gave me a chance to learn on a simple product, and we took off from there.

What size company was E-H when you first got started?

I started with just one guy but we kept hiring people as the need grew. Being in the middle of New York City, it was pretty easy getting workers, with such a huge labor pool. My first loft was only 150 square feet. We started with $1,000 capital and the company grew to $5,000,000 a year and we became leaders in introducing many different sound effects.

Later on, Electro-Harmonix was first in the world to introduce an inexpensive flanger, the Electric Mistress. We had the biggest seller of 1976 and 1977, the Small Stone phase shifter, we were first in the world with analog delay with the Memory Man, first in the world with cheap digital delay, the Two-Second Digital Delay, and later this was expanded to the 16-Second Digital Delay. Initially we only built about 800 units of that effect, which we have not reissued, and now the vintage units sell for over $1,000 each. Electro-Harmonix was also first in the world with cheap samplers, the Instant Replay and then the Super Replay – I later gave this technology to Akai.

How technically involved are you in the designs themselves…

Well, I am an electrical engineer, but mostly I'm a promoter and businessman. And I'm not a guitar player, I'm a keyboard player. But once they'd presented me with a new technology, I was good at selecting what was good to move on. As a result, we were first with a lot of things.

Didn't you hand-wire a lot of the earlier effects?

Yes, but only at the start – the early boosters and even the first few thousand of the Big Muff.

Do you find there are any essential ingredients in a good-sounding analog effects pedal?

Yeah. My philosophy has always been to leave in as much sound and variety as possible, and always go right to the edge of the effect. The Japanese, they'll filter off the noise, compand it and whatever, but when you do that you start to lose dynamics, you start to lose effect. I would always leave in the noise if I would lose feeling by taking it out. Of course I didn't like noise, but an effect was an effect, and your music is a thing of feeling. That was always my philosophy. Sometimes you'd turn a control up and you'd see it would begin to oscillate – but sometimes right at the edge of oscillation there are some interesting effects. Sometimes that interacts with other things. A lot of companies would take that out, so that the user wouldn't get a shitty sound, but I would leave that in and leave it up to the user to get a fringe effect.

With your experience over the years, have you identified certain ingredients that really make a difference?

They all make differences, and all those differences add up. But the ingredients were always changing.

And as hard as you work to stay on top of it, you make a little change that you don't even think about, and it changes something. At first you might not hear it, and then you change something else, and these compound and add up.

It must be the same from any manufacturer's perspective: Leo Fender, Jim Marshall or anybody. They're not trying to make a thing less desirable, they're just developing…
And sometimes when companies get bigger, they start to concentrate on profits … They try to cut costs, and they think they're still preserving the sound…

I know many 'boutique' pedal-makers are trying to recapture the best early sounds by using some archaic technology and even NOS components, but supplies of some of these are drying up. Are there any crucial ingredients in reissued E-H effects that you eventually just won't be able to get.
There's nothing that should give us supply problems in the next two or three years, at least. BBD [bucket brigade device] delay chips aren't in production any more, but I have a few hundred thousand different types, so I can keep my customers satisfied for a few more years.

When it comes to players preferring earlier pedals, maybe it's partly just that people get used to the sound of the first models. If they'd had the later ones first, they might have thought those were the great ones.
Yeah, well, sometimes we improve them. We worked very hard at preserving the sound, and we have a lot of musicians in the company and we're very careful. And we're doing real well now with our reissues.

What's cool is that we're still selling thousands of the Big Muff that I brought out in 1970. And here it is 33 years later – I mean, that's rare in electronics, to be still selling the same thing.

Settle a long-standing mystery among many guitarists: how did you come up with the name for the Big Muff Pi?
Well, first of all, since I had the small box for the LPB1 I tried to make a few other products in the same box. So I came up with the Screaming Bird treble booster, the Mole bass booster, the EGO microphone booster and the Muff Fuzz. These early Muff Fuzzes had two transistors; the other boosters had just one transistor. I called this fuzz 'Muff' Fuzz because it had a funky, soft, 'muffled' sound.

About a year later, I asked Bob Meyer to make me a unique distortion box, and he designed for me what became the 'Big' Muff. I spent weeks tweaking the unit, changing the value of a capacitor here a resistor there… back and forth until I got down to the smooth sounding, sweet sustaining Big Muff Pi.

I still have a copy of an order where Carlos Santana bought a Big Muff from us mail order back in around 1970, with a Santana check. And I saw Jimi using it in the studio. He used to invite me to all his recording sessions when he was in New York, and one day Henry at Manny's Music told me he just sold a Big Muff to Jimi, and I went down to the studio to show him something else, this early version of the distortion-free sustainer, and I saw he had the Big Muff on the floor of the studio. I know early on he used the Fuzz Faces, but he did eventually use a Big Muff.

Things sure boomed from there. Do you recall how many models you were offering at the peak of the first incarnation of Electro-Harmonix?
I don't remember exactly how many models we had in the late 1970s and early 1980s, but it was maybe about 50 different items. We had plenty that never even came into production, but I just can't remember them all. Of course I do remember the big ones. The Small Stone was our number one seller, the LPB1 was number two, and Big Muff was number three biggest seller.

A lot of people like the unique sounds we had in our products, partly because of our philosophy, and partly because we had great designers – the greatest of whom is an English dude, David Cockerell. He went on to design all of the Akai samplers, but he's back working for us full-time now, so we're going to have some blockbuster stuff coming out in the future.

Tell me a little about the fall and rise of Electro-Harmonix, via the Sovtek days.

We went bankrupt in 1984, and after that I helped Akai get their sampler program off the ground and developed some wireless products. Then I got sidetracked and involved with vacuum tubes from Russia. I was the first American allowed to visit some Russian all-military cities, and the first foreigner to sign direct contracts with Russian tube factories. All of this used to be only through the electronics ministry in the central government.

So I started getting tubes from Russia, and my new girlfriend Irusha – who was Russian and lived in St Petersburg, ran my Russian business. Her father was the co-inventor of the hydrogen bomb. He was higher up than Sakarov, and the two of them used to chase women together when they weren't working on the H-bomb. At this time, which was around 1990, I learned that most all of the old Electro-Harmonix pedals I made were selling for a lot more money than in the old days, on what they called the 'vintage market.' Since I was just getting established in Russia, and since the Russians needed work as they were converting from a military economy to a consumer economy, it was easy to release the first few E-H pedals as made in Russia. We still make Russian versions of Big Muff, Bassballs and Small Stone, but now we also make USA versions of these, and of plenty more. We now also own the largest vacuum tube factory in the world. It's a dying technology, but still in demand by most guitarists.

Do you have any strong views on analog versus digital sound quality?

Analog in general preserves the feeling, but with digital of course there's a lot of things you can do that you just can't do in analog. But, you know, you take a digital modelling pedal that says "this is a Big Muff," and when you listen to it it might have a tone close to a Big Muff, but when you play it it just doesn't feel like it, you know. You chop up the sound and compress it, and no matter how many bits you use, you start to lose some stuff.

If you have a really good designer like David Cockerell, you can get some really good stuff. One of the products that we're going to be bringing out soon is an updated version of the 16-Second Delay, and that sounded real good. The aim is to preserve maximum feeling with the dynamics – like when your pick plucks the string and in the first fraction of a second you get that sprinkling of high harmonics… You know, the simpler the product, the less stages it's going through, the less transistors it's passing through, the more you really preserve that feeling.

You hear that principle most easily in old tube amps. The simpler they are, the better they usually sound.

Yeah, you have those tube amps with switching channels and overdrive and all that shit… You're adding stages, and you start to lose some clarity.

Do you have any views on 'true bypass' in pedals?

It all depends on the circuit. Without true bypass, if you have the right impedance then it approaches the sound of true bypass. So it varies from circuit to circuit how much you need true bypass. Our old pedals didn't have true bypass in the old days, but you didn't need it. But now on all the pedals we're building, we have triple-pole/double-throw footswitches, really good ones, and we have true bypass on everything. It does make a difference in a percentage of the circuits.

ROGER MAYER

The well-informed and ever-effusive Roger Mayer and I met up in my local pub, The Lion in Teddington, SW London. There couldn't have been a more appropriate location for a heads-down chat with this pedal guru: he used to pass here on his way to work at the Admiralty Research Laboratories on the other side of Teddington; Kingston and Richmond – the nexus of the British R&B scene of the mid 1960s – are just across the Thames; Eel Pie Island, where The Rolling Stones and others got their start, is just up river; and Mayer's own current home and workshop is only a couple miles east of here. Oh, and they serve great beer.

Roger Mayer with a
Spitfire Fuzz.

Let's have a little bit about your background. What first got you started on effects?

When I was growing up – not far from here – some of the guys who played in the local bands I got to meet were Jeff Beck and Jimmy Page. Playing blues. I play the guitar myself, so when I started hanging out with them we were always interested in what made the American records sound different. We were listening to people like Freddie King and all kinds of different people, kinds of music that not a lot of other people were listening to because it wasn't on the radio. Stuff from Chess Records in Chicago and some of the American stuff, James Brown and that, and those records were really hard to find in England.

Even before that, when I was still in school, I had started making treble boosters and playing around with different guitar tones ... I later did six years of university and studied mechanical engineering and electrical engineering at the same time, then I worked at the Admiralty Research Laboratories, just down the road...

...It's a spooky-looking place – these huge airplane hangers and such...

Yeah – the Admiralty was a top-secret establishment. We were involved in vibrational acoustic analysis, which is half engineering and half electronics, because all the measurements you do are electronic, and you've got all the subsequent vibrational and acoustical analysis of it using pickups, using all sorts of transducers and different equipment.

It's all even related to electric guitars, if in a very broad sense.

Well, it is allied. Say in the case of submarine detection, which is done by listening underwater through hydrophones, underwater microphones, the techniques used for listening to the sound and picking up the sound were always state-of-the-art then – they always are – and we were involved with that.

And you were getting heavily involved with the music scene at the same time.

Oh yeah. That was the daytime job. I had a lot of friends who were professional musicians who were making different sounds. Obviously you were actively encouraged to have hobbies to help you at work.

Who was the first person you started building things for.

I suppose really it was Jimmy Page. Jimmy Page and Big Jim Sullivan in the early years. In fact one of the fuzz boxes I designed and made in 1964 was on a Number One record – 'Hold Me' by P.J. Proby. That was the first fuzz box recorded in England.

Everybody argues about where the first fuzz and amp distortions came from...

Put it this way: anybody who turns a guitar amplifier up loud is gonna hear distortion. Anybody who had a car radio back then would have heard distortion. You know what I mean? Electronic amplifiers way back then were not that great.

But turn them up 'too loud' and often they did sound great.

Well... yeah. There's always an optimum window for things to operate in, and they weren't designed for that [being pushed into distortion]. Traditionally you'd have that classic rockabilly sound, or at the other end of the spectrum you'd have your jazz tone, Charlie Christian and that kind of stuff.

It always occurred to me – despite all the early rock'n'rollers arguing about who played the first distorted tone – that early jazz and blues electric guitarists like Christian and T-Bone Walker and others certainly would have cranked those little amps up well into distortion when they were jamming at home or in small clubs, even if they weren't allowed to do so on the bandstand.

I would imagine so, yeah. Down at the juke joint or wherever. Quite naturally, if someone's going to get an amplifier the first thing they're going to do is turn it up, especially if you're a player like that. To imagine that someone didn't explore the boundaries of it is crazy.

A fuzz tone is a little different than amplifier distortion, obviously, but as a way of getting that tone at different volume levels it must have its roots in the same desires for a particular sound.

It's not so much even getting that tone at different volume levels. The important thing in the beginning was actually producing the sound to be on the record. Because once you've got it on the record, people can play it at any level and it's going to sound right, isn't it. So I started off making stuff that was used on records. It obviously worked live as well, but that's really what I'm probably most known for – making pedals and devices that were used on records.

Most of the guitar players I met way back then would want me to make a pedal or something that had a different sound on it, because that was the important thing. Playing live was of secondary importance, because you ain't going to get the gigs unless you've got a hit record, and if you want to break new ground you want to get your recording sound right. I still think that holds true today, of any artist. If you listen to a record and in the first five seconds you go, "Who the hell is that making that sound?" – you've got them.

Sure, and if the kids find out what gear they used they'll run out and buy the thing, too.

To some extent. But that's really a marketing exercise of the manufacturers jumping on the bandwagon, which really didn't happen so much back then. But yeah, of course.

It always amazes me how many young guitarists don't realize that the way they should set up to play in the studio is very different from the way they set up live.

Oh, there's no comparison. None at all. The actual goal when you're recording is to get the sound on tape so it can be played back through the loudspeakers, and then go back through the whole mastering process. What you've actually recorded – on tape or digital, it doesn't matter, that's only a recording medium – it has to go through broadcasting, mastering, CD, vinyl, whatever process you're using, and it has to stand up.

Go way back. If you listen to an early Elvis Presley record with Scotty Moore playing, the sound of the guitar playing still comes through. If you're listening to it in a '57 Chevy on an AM radio, it's still a hit record, it still sounds cool, it still sounds rock'n'roll. And that's with limited bandwidth and all... that's, shall we say, the lo-fi of it, that's not hi-fi. But the sound, the intrinsic heart and soul of the sound, still is maintained. That doesn't hold true for an awful lot of modern sounds, for many reasons.

If you're going to make a sound that's going to be recorded, that's completely different than if you are going to make a guitar tone that will suit a small pub. Then you've got another further scenario of a major stadium rock band. Then you have to make the sound on-stage, which then has to be amplified by a microphone to go upstairs to the big rigs so everyone else can hear it. And that's another problem. That's a cross between recording and playing live. It's another tone you would require, because the actual tone is coming out of the speaker cabinet – picked up by an SM57 or whatever they're using – and then it's going through huge linear transistor amplifiers and upstairs to the speaker rigs.

If you see ZZ Top or Aerosmith or any other big band live, are you really hearing the guitar amp? I don't know. You are hearing a sound that originated from a guitar amp, but it's had a lot of subsequent processing done to it. It's gone from an electronic signal, into a loudspeaker, into the air, into a microphone, into a whole other bunch of preamps and EQ and maybe compression, into another power amp and into a huge set of loudspeakers overhead, and then it's propagated through a huge auditorium before it hits the ears of the punter.

And that only highlights the conundrum a lot of players get into in their search for a certain pedal which they believe some guitar hero or other uses to get a particular sound. They often get the impression that this magic effect will give them 'that sound' in all circumstances…
What they are forgetting – and this is where some understanding of the science of hearing has to be thought about – is, for instance, there's a whole set of perceived frequency response curves of the ear at different sound pressure levels, and these are reasonably well documented. They're called Fletcher-Munsen Curves. Basically the ear perceives different frequencies differently at different sound pressure levels. So as it gets louder, you need more and more top end, and so on. The actual EQ you perceive – and I'm not saying what's coming out of the loudspeaker, but the EQ that you yourself perceive – changes. It changes with the sound pressure level, and it also changes, too, with the duration that you've been listening to a loud sound.

If you're subjected to continuous high sound pressure levels, say if you're in the studio all the time, your high frequency starts to pack up, and you compensate and compensate. And this is why people can walk out of a mix – and this is not even talking about other substances, drugs or whatever, which distort it even further – and not be aware of what they've ended up with. Your perception changes with time, and it changes with how loud it is.

You've also got the variables, of course, that the loudspeakers in the amplifier do not respond the same at different volume levels. There are so many variables. And then someone can take an amplifier into a different acoustic room, and the effect of the room is different. You can do a soundcheck in a room without any people and then come on and play when the room has filled up, and it's dramatically different. It's almost a waste of time doing one. Rooms even sound different in the winter than in the summer, because people wear different clothes. It's all to do with applied acoustics.

The point being that there are no universals: you might find some favorite pedals that do the best for you in certain situations, but they're never going to sound the same for you in every circumstance in which you use them, or the same as when your hero uses them.
Exactly.

Looking a little more at your own career as it developed, what was your first commercial pedal product? Was it the Octavia?
Well, I never originally offered that commercially as such, I just made them for a few select people. They were like prototypes. What happened was, I was working with Jimi [Hendrix], making all the different sounds. When I made the Octavia for him we made a few, like maybe a half a dozen or so, but when I went to live in America I went straight into manufacturing recording studio electronics. Making studio

CHAPTER 6 ■ MEET THE MAKERS

consoles and equalizers and being involved in the start-up of Record Plant and Electric Ladyland and all that sort of stuff, so I wasn't into making little guitar boxes. The only time we'd make a few guitar boxes for people would be for famous players, not anything available commercially in the music store.

When you were working with Hendrix, he obviously couldn't just go to the shop and pick up different boxes for different sounds because the effects just weren't there. But better than that, he had you in the studio working right along with him. What was the process like?

The process started, basically, where Jimi's got a particular song, and there'd always be an emotion that he wanted to portray in the song. If you get an idea what the song's about... like, Jimi and I would spend a lot of time around the flat or at the Speakeasy discussing what sounds we might want to do. If you were going to use echo on it that would be one sound, or if you wanted the guitar to appear to disappear then come back...

The sound that you're ultimately going to put on the record is going to depend on a couple of things, isn't it: what's the song about – you're not going to put an inappropriate sound on it; what key's the song in, because you can then voice the box differently. You might want to tune a wah-wah differently for it...

Would you go as far as tuning in resonant frequencies and such?

Oh yeah, yeah. We'd got one amp, two amps, we had multiple-path techniques of processing because we were only recording to four-track, so it had to be done pretty well immediately. I'd go back to the control room and have a listen and then...

...And then get out your soldering iron...

[Laughs] Yeah, well, we'd got the room at the back there, the maintenance room, where we could go and change that. But you'd take a few different things to the studio that you wouldn't have on-stage – different driving stages to put in front of the fuzz boxes, different equalizing stages, different voltages you're using on the fuzz boxes. You segment the stages out.

You've got the interesting case of pre and post-equalization. So you can equalize the fuzz box before you turn it on, and afterwards, and both, so you've got an infinite number of variables. Then the different amplifiers, the miking techniques, it goes on and on. As I said in the beginning, we are only concerned with making a good sound that goes onto tape, and we're going to use anything we can to get it.

And you don't have to repeat it on stage...

No, no – because that's irrelevant. Because when you actually go on stage the public can only appreciate about three different sounds. They will be much more concerned with the energy on stage, whether he took his jacket off, changed his guitar, and so forth, because they're getting caught up in the hysteria and the noise. It's not technical.

Did Hendrix enjoy recording?

Up to even the *Axis Bold As Love* album he was very shy in the studio. He didn't think he could sing. All the lights would have to be out, he'd sing with his back to the control room, he was very shy. He needed a lot of encouragement.

As well as the technical side, one of my jobs with Jimi was to help get that three minutes or so of magic. That's the end, the goal. The whole day has to lead up to that, whatever your job is, engineer or making the sandwiches or whatever, your objective is to capture 200 seconds of magic.

Jimi would cut a solo and I might be sitting next to him on the floor of the studio, and he'd say, "Go and listen to that, Roger." He wouldn't even bother to come back in. I'd listen to it, and Jimi'd go on the intercom to the studio and go, "How was that?" Chas would go, "That's great, Jimi, that's a take." And then he [Hendrix] would say to me, "What do you think?" I'd say, "Take one more, Jimi." Then he'd do what would end up as the actual solo, and people's jaws would just drop. You see, I knew him, and I knew what he could do. He was just messing around, and that solo wasn't the one.

I guess Chas had some other considerations, too.

As a producer in the studio, Chas was very, very good, but he was always watching the wallet. Jimi would happily spend all day in the studio but Chas was always in a hurry to get it done. The production work in the studio was all done between Chas and Jimi, I handled the guitar sounds, and Eddie Kramer really was the engineer. He had no idea what the song was going to be until Jimi was finished with it. No one did, really, then they totally couldn't believe it, because we were breaking new ground.

Which I guess is partly why people constantly come back to Hendrix, they come back to The Beatles, they come back to Elvis or The Rolling Stones...

Because we didn't have CDs we would listen to and say, "We want to sound like that." We had records we'd say, "We don't want to sound like that." When Eric Clapton and Cream came out with *Disraeli Gears*, Eric was pissed off because we came out with *Are You Experienced*, because that blew him away, and he knew he could never sound like Jimi.

He went out and got permed.

Yeah [laughs], you know what I'm saying? It was a completely different spirit of breaking new ground, and it was totally on the edge of making new sounds.

Hendrix was working very much at the dawn of transistorized effects, and he used them well, but when we think of Jimi Hendrix's playing we don't think of a player getting his sound by running through a big pile of effects. You think of his Strat, a cranked-up amp, and a lot of feeling and tone.

Oh yeah, yeah – exactly. That's the whole point. You see, that is the true measure of doing the job right: that people don't think of it as an 'effects' sound. Any song you hear with Jimi playing the guitar, OK, yeah, he's got a great sound, but you don't think, "Oh, it's gimmicky." That means the job's done well.

And the songs where people get the sound totally from an extreme use of effects often do come out as gimmicky, usually one-hit wonders.

Or hit and shit, as we used to say.

Something like where a guy has just discovered a flanger, so the whole song is washed in flanger.

Yeah, over-used.

Or, as you put it, the brick wall effects, which don't allow a player's own dynamics and emotion to be a part of the sound.

And then the band becomes anonymous. If the particular effect is not sensitive to the player, then the band becomes anonymous behind it. The band achieves total mediocrity instantly, because the sound is shit. On our website, for example, we've got eight seconds to impress somebody with a guitar tone, no more. And in the first 30 seconds of watching a guitar player, people can usually work out whether they can play or not.

And if you've got a piece of gear with which anyone who plugs into it sounds exactly the same...

Which they don't with Jimi's rig, because I've experienced people come up to Jimi's rig and plug into it, and they sounded horrible.

After your days of making studio equipment, working with the Isleys and Bob Marley and Stevie Wonder, what got you back into guitar effects pedals.

It got to about 1980 or so and people started to ask for my effects a bit more, and that's when I designed the rocket-shaped enclosure...

...Which is now such a distinctive thing.

It's an icon, really. The actual reason I designed it was because I wanted to have a pedal that when anyone looked at it they knew it was mine. You didn't have to put any writing on the box. That kind of thinking came about from the automobile industry. People look down the road and you don't have to see the label of the car, it's all shape recognition. And also the shape of the rocket has a lot of ergonomic considerations: it's got the fins on the back that protect the knobs from anyone putting their foot on them, you can drop the box and never hit the knobs, and you can also hit the footswitch from any angle – back, front, sideways. So that enclosure was a culmination of a lot of design parameters.

What did you first put into that enclosure?

The Octavia. But when we first made it we did it with an optical switch, it didn't have a snap-action switch in it. We put those out, and after a period some people said they liked the snap-action of the switch and this and that, so we put a different switch in it, which was slightly cheaper to produce than the optical switch anyway.

And your stuff's been more or less available since that time?

Yeah, since the early 1980s. We had the Axis Fuzz, a Metal Fuzz, and the Mongoose pedal.

It seems, if anything, you've had more of a boom again just recently.

What I started doing, when we came back to England, was I stopped making any specialized rack-mounted equipment for different people, and I concentrated on getting worldwide distribution. Japan's always been our biggest customer. We're very well known in Japan.

In Japan the equipment is perceived in a different way. The multi-FX digital pedals are really perceived as amateur pedals, they're not used by professional rock musicians at all, or very, very rarely. And then all the cheaper types of Chinese and Korean pedals and all that, they're strictly entry level pedals for beginners. And the mass-produced Japanese pedals are considered not quite the professional level... so it's just perceived differently. Our pedals, in Japan, are one of the best-selling of the high-end pedals. We're probably about number six in the whole of Japan.

What do you think of the whole so-called 'boutique' pedal market?

Boutique pedal market? I don't consider myself in that market. Most of them are just clones and rip-off merchants. Most aren't designing anything new. They're not putting any R&D into it, they're not designing their own enclosures, and they're not making anything new. And I'm getting tired of being ripped off.

But since you were one of the first builders, it's probably hard to follow you without building something that is at least vaguely similar to a pedal you have done yourself. Like with the Octavia, which you never offered commercially the first time round...

Yeah, but that type of market is charging someone a lot of money for rubbish. What I'm saying is they're not spending any real money on R&D, are they? They're really not taking it any further. And also, continuously going back to the past and not evolving is bad. It's not investing in the future.

In any publicity, I've never said that all we do is make a version of our old pedals. We're always constantly evolving: new enclosures, new this, new that. We're always using new components. We never make a feature out of using an old component, because years ago most of the components were crap and horrible, and they are better today.

So many people make a big deal about dredging out old vintage germanium transistors and this and that...

We use germanium transistors in a couple of designs. But the reality is that you've got to buy thousands of them, then you've got to sit down and test them all, and you're only going to come up with a small percentage that are any good.

How bad are the tolerances?

There's maybe 30 per cent that you can use. But it was always like that. The tolerance on the gain of a germanium transistor can go from 20 to 600. That's 30-to-1. You always had to select them, and in these simple circuits you spend more time biasing than you do making them.

And, of course, what you're buying today, because they're not made any more, is you're buying old transistors. It's like buying old capacitors – they're rubbish. Even if you bought an old fuzz box, all the electrolytic capacitors are going to be dried out, gone. And today all the resistors are much better.

So you don't think there's anything in carbon comp resistors, or...

No. Rubbish. That's just myth. Noooo... rubbish. A resistor doesn't do anything. There is nothing in the composition of a carbon comp resistor versus a metal film resistor that is going to add or subtract any harmonics to the signal. It's the same as audiophiles in hi-fi talking about different types of copper and speaker cable. That is unbelievable... and it's the people they're selling it to, the mugs. I'm a scientist, and copper is copper. More copper is better than less copper, but there's no such thing as great 'northern Italian copper' and all this rubbish. That is the biggest load of bollocks I've ever heard in my life. Absolutely unsubstantiated snake oil.

So you feel you can almost always do the job with new and improved technology?

The only exception you have to that would be in transformers, in transformer steel – talking about valve amplifiers in particular. Certain types of laminations used back then are a different shape than they use today, but they were less economical to produce than they are today and the steel was slightly better.

So your output transformers would sound a little different.

Yeah, and you might like that. And with the old loudspeakers, the lighter alnico magnets used to sound different of course, but now they're horrendously expensive. But when it comes to resistors and capacitors, there's nothing you can put on the bench with all the most sophisticated analytical equipment and find that one bit of mylar capacitor is different from another.

What about differences between different types of op amps on the market?

Well, then you get into design, and actually knowing what's inside the operational amplifier. That's where you really have to know your beans. If you're going to use an operational amplifier, it's not what they put on the specification sheet, it's what they don't put on it. And that – when you're an electronic designer and not an experimenter – that's an art form. If you're writing a specification sheet, it's what you *don't* put on it.

If you're on the cutting edge, as manufacturers, when we're using a different component we actually have to go to the manufacturer of that component and speak to the design engineer to get the information we want. And then he puts you on the shortlist, so you give him feedback from your experiments. Because if you're on the cutting edge, you're always going to be in an area that's not even written down. They're only going to write the specification generally: the car's got four wheels, it does 100 miles per hour. Things like that. They're not going to tell you what happens if you operate it at this voltage rather than that voltage, all these other things. There are so many exceptions, you see. And to produce distortion, you've got to know how to bend the parameters to get what you want.

And dealing with guitar tone, it might often be that in the exceptions to the rules is where you find the cool sounds.

Oh, the most important thing you don't realize about sound is that music, by definition, is a non-repetitive waveform. It doesn't repeat.

Though when you get it represented in the usual waveform diagram it's always illustrated as if it is repeating. So tell us why it's not...

Because it's not repetitive. Music is not a repetitive waveform. Once the brain hears a repetitive waveform, like a door chime or a drum machine pattern, it immediately categorizes that as not being music. It becomes a mechanical pattern, and we are programmed to recognize it. We can sit on a train and hear the rhythm of a train, and we hear it as a mechanical rhythm. Say you listen to a dance record, you immediately work out what's done by a machine and what isn't, if it's repetitive. You'll categorize a repetitive pattern like that as being non-musical.

But getting back to the technical side of a repetitive waveform – music doesn't repeat itself, no two cycles of music are the same. When you start using techniques such as electronic feedback and so forth, they don't necessarily work. Because feedback is a process – and I don't mean squealing and howling, but electrical feedback as a corrective process. The point is, that because the waveform has changed by the time you apply feedback, there is a finite time delay: you are time-smearing it. So what happens is the electronics you require to accurately reproduce amplifier distortion and so forth have got to be incredibly quick, and have to have a huge bandwidth to faithfully reproduce what's going on, because once you start applying feedback to limit the bandwith, it gets distorted, in the truest sense, because it gets altered into something it never was.

That's one thing. So any analysis technique you apply to music using sine waves is limited, because it doesn't give you the dynamic response. It doesn't give you the true technical response of what's going on.

So what do you do? Just play the thing?

What you do is use every tool in your arsenal, whether it's conventional distortion analyzers, time domain analysis, and all these different techniques to look at the waveform to see what the harmonic content is. But these are only ever guidelines, because it's the instantaneous dynamic response of the amplifier or effect that you're interested in. I've always specialized in designs where we use a lot of different techniques. We use a lot of feed-forward in my designs, which means you're taking information from the input or the guitar to modify the circuit. So all this is changing in real time: how hard you play, how soft you play, all the subtleties and the nuances are changing. It's impossible for someone to really analyze this, because they have to know what you're trying to do to start with before they can even decipher it.

A simple circuit, if it's designed in a certain way, becomes a very complex thing analytically. It does not become that simple. But it becomes organic, so the actual sound itself then begins to take on a human quality, because quite naturally you are taking information from the [guitarist's playing technique] or from the input, and that's control in itself, that's determining its own output. It hasn't had an algorithm or a set of parameters placed on it to predetermine the sound.

And that's where your dynamics and your touch-sensitivity come from…
Exactly.

Which end up being the sounds people really like, even if they don't know exactly why.
Because they're not repetitive and they're constantly changing – then it takes on an organic quality, a very human type of sound. Even though it's distorted, it's not the same type of distortion. You know, all that stuff that was done with Jimi on all the records, even the stuff that was very distorted, it was very human sounding. The sounds take you out into space and they take you back, and you relate to it better.

If you listen to the classic 'brick wall' effect of a fuzz box on something like, say, 'Summer Breeze' [by The Isley Brothers], that's got one tone on it and that's it. You might like what it's playing, but it's got no human quality to it.

It's the 'can of bees' sound.
Exactly. And I've always stayed clear of making any of that kind of thing.

Whereas your goal would be to build a fuzz that you can play with, not one that's just a wall-of-mush fuzz.
Yeah, you want a tone that's organic. And it's so easy to build a fuzz box or a distortion type of box. You've got many boxes that, to be frank, you put a guitar into it and you wouldn't know what type of guitar it is. The whole tonal quality of that guitar just disappears. It's got 'brick wall' processing in it, and this is ever so true of some of these cheaper multi-FX processors. Horrendous…

What are your feelings about digital pedals?
It basically boils down to these actual factors. Number one, when it comes to digital sound there are several major differences. The sampling rate is one. The actual sampling rate will never be high enough to capture the analog sound. The other major difference is that the resolution of a digital signal gets worse and worse as the signal gets softer, as it decays. It might start off at 24 bits, but you can't use all 24 bits because then you get into digital distortion. So then you get down to 20, and as the signal decays you might get down to 10, and it's not that clever.

That's where I often hear the flaws, on the note decay.
That's where you always hear it, especially on digital echoes. I worked in the studio years ago when digital echoes were first coming out, and they were ferociously expensive – I'm talking about studio echoes that cost about $20,000 – and, naaah… They didn't sound any good.

The best digital echo you can get is using Pro Tools and some of this stuff, but that's using a very fast processor, and it's got the benefit of buffering the signal before you process it. And it's not in real time. The whole thing about digital processing in real time is that you're always going to have at least one sample delay before you can do anything to it. It's quite a delay. And the other thing about using digital processing is you've got to decide exactly what you're going to do to the signal before you do it. You cannot use feed-forward techniques, you cannot use the input of the signal to suddenly modify the algorithm as the signal is changing. You're stuck with it. And digital [emulations of] distortion are not proper… digital modeling of amplifiers does not sound that clever.

The whole problem with the digital thing is you can't put enough processing into it for the money. When it comes to cheap digital products, you simply can't put enough processing into it. They'd all like you to believe you can, but you can't. The amount of processing you need to do the job properly is enormous. The difference with the computer stuff is you're not doing it in real time. They can put a buffer in of half a second, they can use the latency in the processing to their advantage. You've got this latency, which makes these hard disk systems work. But when you're playing live, you can't play with 30 or 40 milliseconds of latency. It's just not quick enough.

The other thing you don't want to do, is you don't want to go in and out of the digital domain more than once, if you can help it. If you can record digitally, OK. But then transfer digitally, master digitally, and then make the CD digitally and bring it back to analog one time, when you listen it. You don't want to go in and out two or three times. You don't want to have a digital stomp box on the bloody floor, plug into a digital guitar amp, then go into a microphone that's recording on digital, then go back out to mix it in analog and record on another digital recorder, all this and that. You've got a complete nightmare of approximation.

You're losing bits all over the place...
Exactly. Once again, it comes down to a simple test that anyone can do. If you roll off treble from your signal source, you can't add it back again to your original sound source. And that's in the analog domain. Once you've done a digital process to something, how's it going to know where it was before? The info's gone, lost, finished. You cannot know.

It's not like video. See, video's a different aspect where digital works, because you're surrounded by other information from the pixels around it. You can make an educated guess at to what the picture should be. But you can't do that with audio, because it's changed. Once again, you go back to the definition: music is non-repetitive.

And the artefacts in digital, once they go down to a certain level, become very grainy. It gets a bit annoying on the old ears. People call it coldness, hardness, listening fatigue, all kinds of stuff. It's literally attributed to the fact that the brain is having to do too much processing. If you are listening to a telephone conversation or even someone talking in a rock club, and it's very very loud, and you have to keep straining to hear what they're saying, after a couple of minutes you're going to tell them to shut up and let's wait until we can hear one another. Because the brain is using so much processing power to screen out all the background noise to try and understand what they are saying. You don't realize it is going on, but it is, and it's very tiring on the old brain – and after a while it goes, "Oh, bollocks!" It can't be bothered to deal with it.

This occurs to me time and again when I've tested or reviewed a digital modeling guitar amp. Maybe it has 16 amp models and 20 effects on it, and you'd think a guitarist would enjoy playing with that all day, but more often than not I want to put the guitar down after 30 minutes or an hour. My ears are tired, I feel like I'm getting a headache, and I'm just not enjoying playing. Give me a little 15W tube amp, though, even a cheap little thing, and I'll play it all day.
That's because your brain is totally dissatisfied with the work it has to do listening to the digital amp.

It always struck me that way – and it's not that I have any prejudice against modeling amps or anything.
Oh, no, no, no – that's exactly what it is. Your brain is worn out by it. It's an interesting thing. Look at it like this. Imagine walking in a jungle. We are conditioned, through millions of years of evolution, to detect a stick breaking, in amongst all the other noises, as a danger signal. Piece of glass breaks, you turn around. We've got all these inbuilt danger signals. That's what you're hearing, without you realizing it. When you hear sounds that are artificial, they stand out to you. When you hear a synthesizer rendition of an actual instrument trying to sound like something, your brain rejects it. It says, "That's not real."

And the synths that worked best were – and are – often analog synths, that are not trying to sound like something, but generating a sound in their own right.

Yeah, and the actual sound source was analog. I did three albums with Stevie Wonder: *Music Of My Mind*, *Innervisions*… We used analog synthesizers. I built them, and we were using analog sound sources and modifying them. Sounds great. Those types of analog sounds that are developed, even though they're synthetic, sit in the mix. You can mix them in. Whereas when they first came out with certain types of digital synthesizers, maybe DX7s and that, you could identify any DX7 sound. Didn't matter what they were set like. You'd go, "That's a DX7, that's an M1." Now, isn't it funny that the brain can identify the algorithm the bloody thing was based upon and categorize it, just like that? The brain's got a huge machinery.

To get back to effects, the best effects are the ones that sound human, and blend into the music, become part of the music.

Do you feel you're best known for any one particular pedal?

I suppose the most unique pedal is the Octavia, which is the frequency doubling one that Jimi used on 'Purple Haze.' And that's the one that's probably been ripped off the most [laughs].

Had anybody done anything like that before you?

Nah. I was just thinking about doubling the frequency and different electronic techniques. And we came across a technique that, looking at it simplistically, it almost acts like a mirror. It doubles the number of images of the note. And that, apparently, makes it sound twice the frequency – whereas it really isn't, but it does [laughs].

Because the signal's going up and down twice as much, even though you've changed the relationship of it, the ear perceives it as twice the frequency. It's much like putting a picture up to a mirror and you see two of them, but there's still only one real picture. Reflection of sound is much like that in a room. You can make it sound louder. When you mix two signals together, you've got two mathematical variables: one is the sum of the signal, and the other is the difference. Now if you get two frequencies and mix them together, you get the sum and the difference.

Going back to the digital side, that's why you need a huge bandwidth. If you're making an analog mixing console, the actual mixing amplifier needs to have a frequency response of up the 300 kilocycles, because it's mixing together all the tracks, and it couldn't mix them together properly unless it had a huge bandwidth. You would lose all the air and the definition between the signals. Everyone says, "You can't hear more than 20kHz," but that's a sine wave – we're talking about the subtle variations in the music, and you can hear those.

That's a great point that doesn't get said much: things happening in a sonic realm beyond the capabilities of our hearing can still affect the reproduction of the parts of the sound we do hear.

Well, it's amazing what you perceive. One of the most frequent comments that you get from engineers when they use digital on a microphone is that they lose what they say is 'the air' around a recording. You hear the actual sound, but you don't hear the ambience. So you're not hearing the tiny subtleties.

And one of the tricks of good engineering is capturing the ambience.

Once you've lost detail in an audio signal, it's gone forever. It's like in a guitar: once you've lost the high frequency from a guitar in a pickup, you can't get it back. The detail is gone. And that's what you're struggling to maintain.

Do you ever wish you'd put out the Octavia commercially yourself back in the late 1960s, and so undercut the copyists who came along soon after?

Nah. I had my other work, and besides, the interesting thing is that the copies never quite did it right.

But I've got no sour grapes about any of that. The one matter about infringing the copyright, though, is they should at least pay respect, you know? If you're making a copy of something, don't tell me the copy's better than the original, when all you're doing is ripping something off.

You see, that's the problem with all these retro, reintroduced pedals – they're not doing anyone any favors. They're not doing the musician a favor, they're not taking anything forward.

Which of your own newer designs has excited you the most?
Recently, an updated version of the Octavia. That's good. I think the most universally used pedal is the Voodoo-Vibe – that's been used by all kinds of people. Now we've just recently come up with a smaller version of the pedal called the Voodoo-Vibe Jr, in the new Vision enclosure. See, this is the new enclosure [removes a new Vision Octavia from its box]. The battery door slides like this… [demonstrates]. I designed this enclosure. That's a proper piece of engineering, see. That's not a *'boutique'* pedal…

I know people who have enjoyed the Voodoo-Boost a lot.
Yeah, that's a good pedal. That works. It's the perfect example of a good silicon circuit driving a tube amplifier. It'll interface perfectly for that.

Plenty of players will swear by tubes – they don't want anything but tubes amplifying their sound – and I'm more of a tube-freak than most – but put a good solid state booster pedal in front of their favorite vintage tube amp and suddenly they're in tone heaven…
They do benefit from some preamplification. The 12AX7 is very limited in what you can do with it, in terms of getting good distortion. I don't like the sound of 12AX7s distorting much. Pretty horrible, actually. It's very, very nasal.

I'm almost always disappointed by the proper tube-based distortion pedals out there, except sometimes when used for that massive, cascading-drive modern rock sound.
Yeah. They don't sound right. And once again, that's the properties of the preamplifier tube. The preamplifier tube is fine for amplification and a little bit of distortion, but for the subtleties of it, no.

And the distortion we usually like most – whether we know it or not – is output tube distortion.
Yeah, but it helps to do something before that stage. The type of [solid state pedal] circuitry we use works better than tubes – and I've tried both.

Do you find certain types of amps get the best sound from good pedals?
I personally design my pedals on a Fender amplifier, a very clean amplifier. I want a reference tone that I'm voicing for. I tend to voice the pedals from a clean amplifier so that someone can go from clean to distorted. I use a '57 Fender Super. It's a classic amp – I've put Celestions in and boxed up the Jensens to avoid buggering them up. Then I'll also try the pedals out with the Fender distorted as well, and that gives me a very good basis. A Marshall amplifier is very hard to design on, because it never goes clean enough, so you can never hear the subtleties.

Amps like that Super of yours sound great clean, but even the beauty of their clean settings are generated by subtle degrees of distortion.
Yeah. And you can listen to it all day, as well. It's a very good frame of reference.

Which other designs are you pleased with?
I designed my Vision Wah because the traditional wah was designed to be played from a sitting position.

When you play the traditional treadle wah standing up, it puts your hip at a funny angle, you're off balance, you can't stand on it. But my basic aim with the Vision Wah, from an ergonomic standpoint, was to connect the foot to the brain with a more transparent medium. The actual pedal goes slightly forward at an angle. It's still got the same travel, but it's more comfortable, and it's the ultimate low-profile device, so that when you put your foot on it it's as close to standing on nothing as you can get.

See, you've got to connect your brain to your foot. From an ergonomic standpoint, I looked at the foot and the bones and the way they moved, and we went from the angles to create the wah at the minimum height. The Vision Wah is a full inch lower than any other wah. It doesn't use potentiometers, no moving parts, no moving switches. It's all electronically adjustable, and it's very high tech. I went to the top people who do all the composite work for aerospace, and that's where we designed the carbon fiber top plate.

That's a lot of work...

You're talking a lot of money. Upwards of £100,000 [approximately $160,000] in development for that pedal. And the whole point of that is to develop a transparent interface from the pedal to the brain, to make a pedal that the musician can use – and a lot of people use them now. Santana bought six. It's a cool pedal, and it was a very, very satisfying piece of design to do. The actual position of the pedal is sensed electromagnetically. There's no parts to wear out, and the switch action... as the pedal comes to rest on a piece of rubber, we still measured the angle of the pedal, but then we measured the little change of the angle of the pedal as the little piece of rubber compresses, and that triggers the switch. Then you can adjust how much you press down on the rubber, so the switch pressure's adjustable.

Sounds like you should be in aerospace or something.

Yeah, well, I come from that kind of thing... But my pleasure is hearing the stuff used on records, and getting to meet great guitar players and being their friend.

Financially, I could probably have made more money by having my stuff made in some Chinese sweat shop or in Taiwan or something. Like everybody else does.

But you probably wouldn't be happy with your work.

Exactly. I can still eat a steak when I want to eat one. I bump into a lot of other manufacturers at a lot of trade shows, and I'm not envious of them at all. It's the other way round. I look at them and I say, "So, how's your Taiwanese manufacturer doing?" 'Cos I know that they're going to be put through the mangle, whereas I know that our stuff is all made in the UK. We just hand it out to the top people, a certain niche of people that's going to pay for it, and that's it.

Tell me a little about the circuitry inside a traditional wah-wah pedal. People usually get the short explanation, that it's a tone control with a rocker pedal on top.

No, no. It's a bit more than that. Basically, the wah-wah circuitry is a filter. It's a peaking type of filter that is swept roughly in about a two-and-a-half octave range. Maybe from 400Hz up to 2.2kHz. Now, there's a couple of variables in the circuitry that make the difference. You have a virtually infinite number of values of coil inductors and capacitance that will give the same sweep range. Because of the mathematics of it, you can still get the same sweep range using different coil values and capacitor values. But this then, in turn, changes the actual fatness of the curve, so the actual EQ curve then starts to change in character. In other words, the Q of the curve gets broader or it gets narrower.

So you've got quite a few variables to tune in a wah-wah. Not only in the sweep range – what the frequency begins at and what it ends at – but also in the fatness of the curve. This makes a big difference on the actual perceived sound of the wah. To make matters even worse, I found early on – like, with Jimi

– that if you started varying the actual quality of the magnetics you use in the coil, that also changed some of the distortions produced in the circuit itself. In actual fact, tuning wah-wahs is quite a black art, of which I am probably considered one of the masters.

I used to spend quite a bit of time back then… I didn't actually wind too many new coils, but we spent a lot of time playing around with different coils and different capacitors to tune the wah-wah for different songs.

Just to get it to react better in the key of each individual song?

Yeah. Because, if you imagine that you've got a song where you don't want to use the whole travel of the wah-wah, you can adjust the wah-wah so the actual travel doesn't operate the whole sweep, you see? It makes it more expressive from your own brain-to-foot connection. It really becomes an exercise in fine-tuning what your foot does and what you hear. And that will depend on what shoes you're wearing and all this kind of shit.

And this still applies to the stuff you build today, even the Vision Wah?

Yeah, but it's been taken to the nth degree. We do make a kit today called the Red Lion Wah, which has got continuously variable sweep on it with one potentiometer, and that goes into a standard Cry Baby housing – but our new one, which will probably be based on the Vision Wah carbon fiber housing, will have an even more extended sweep. Once again, it's tuning the sweep and the frequency of the sweep to what people want to hear.

The Vision Wah that we introduced a few years ago has an additional feature based on something that we did in the studio with Jimi, which is to blend the original guitar back in with the wah-wah, to lessen the effect of the wah. You've got a wah-wah going on, but if you blend the guitar back in it softens it down. We just used a parallel path, with one signal going straight back into the studio. You could try it at home: you have one guitar that's clean, one that's distorted with wah-wah, and you mix them back together.

That's something I've found makes sense with a lot of effects; if you feel you're losing too much of the dynamics, split the signal before the pedal and take one path straight into the second channel on your amp, or to another amp.

Yeah, exactly. That's why our Voodoo and Vision effects have two outputs, so you can parallel-path all the time.

Plus, your current stuff is a lot quieter than most of the older, vintage pedals anyway.

Yeah, and that's because up until the early 1970s, low-noise transistors were nearly non-existent and extremely expensive. They just weren't being manufactured.

What's your view on the whole 'true bypass' issue?

What a lot of manufacturers are trying to do is make something of the fact that bypassing the effect with a piece of wire is a feature. Well, look at it like this: the best signal path from a guitar to an amplifier is a short piece of wire. In many cases this is impossible. So if you go into an effect and then bypass the effect with another piece of wire, then come out with a 20′ lead, in a stage environment you might be better off using a buffer, because that will eliminate any stage vibration, cable noise, whatever. And the amplifiers like to be driven from a low source impedance. Many amplifiers do not like to see a long cable with a guitar pickup on the end of it. The amplifier starts oscillating. So, you know, buffers are useful in many instances. Our latest Vision Series of pedals has one hard-wired and two buffered outputs, so you can choose the output you prefer. But which is best depends upon a lot of things…

...Such as how many pedals you've got in the chain?

Yeah, and where you use the buffer in the chain. But listen to the Vision Octavia on the buffer and on the hard-wired output, and with short cables I defy you to hear the difference. On a long cable, that's where the difference comes in.

The whole true bypass thing came from one person in America who started selling three-pole double-throw switches and wanted to make that a feature. It's marketing. It's not based upon any technical advantage whatsoever. It was based upon a myth of many years ago that some pedals had a very low input impedance and sucked the tone from the guitar, even when they were off – but modern pedals, nah.

And wouldn't it be true that if you've got a long chain of pedals that all have true bypass, you're going to be changing the impedance load every time you switch pedals, whether you've got one pedal on, or two or three on together, or none.

Yeah, of course you are. The actual fact of the matter is that most tube amplifiers do not like seeing an inductive coil at the end of a cable. They're not that thrilled with it.

And that's where the buffer helps.

Yeah. Some amplifiers go unstable without them. Some of the American boutique amplifiers are built without the grid resistor, the 68k resistor, and they've just decided they don't need that for some reason. But without it, the amp can start to oscillate wildly.

Let's talk some more about your Voodoo Vibe. I understand a good 'Vibe-type pedal is a tricky effect to build.

That was an evolution... it all started off with Jimi and his Uni-Vibes, you know. The Uni-Vibe was developed by a Japanese company, primarily for keyboards to start with, to simulate the Leslie sound. It's almost like a four-stage phaser, in a way, but the frequencies are set differently so you get this chorusing effect from the unit. When we started using it with Jimi, there was no stabilized power supply within the unit, so the operation went up and down with any variation in the mains voltage, which is quite substantial in America. And the input impedance of them wasn't that great.

The first ones, yeah, they were OK. Then after a while in the States people asked me about them, and I made another version of it for myself, called the Super-Vibe, which Stevie Ray and Robin Trower and other people used. That was another evolution of the effect that addressed some of the problems of the earlier one. After the Super Vibe, I developed the circuit even further.

I took a lot more care in matching and selecting all the light cells, because once again it's a swept filter that's using a light source and light dependent resistors. The secret to making them work well is to have a good matched set of light cells, which you need in groups of four, and then just keep tuning them.

I took this to the ultimate, really, because we had variations for everything: the type of waveform we used – we could use a sine, we could use a triangle – we could modify the symmetry of the waveform to modify the rise and fall times, to give you helicopter effects and this and that. Lots of different speed ranges of the unit, and a footcontrol for the speed too. The trick with them, because you've got quite a few variables, is to find a really good starting point. To find a ballpark in terms of what type of sweep you want. On the Voodoo Vibe, you can change the way it sweeps, not to mention the speed and the waveform, so it's quite complicated to use really.

But a lot of players seem to have been happy with it.

Yeah, it's probably the most successful of all the vibe-type units, certainly in terms of sales. In Japan and

Europe, more of those have been sold than any other clone that's been produced. And part of that is because our one isn't a clone of the original. We're not trying to make it a clone, we've taken the downfalls of the original one and improved upon them. Some worked, some didn't, because they weren't that well selected. And they used light bulbs whose characteristics varied with age. And the original Uni-Vibe also had a light cell that used a particular toxic form of cadmium sulphide that you can't use any more, because you can't get rid of the toxic waste because it's bloody lethal, you know. So the chances of you finding an old Uni-Vibe that really works well are practically zero.

We use a modern type of light cell – once again they have to be carefully selected. There's about a six-to-one spread in the light cells, so we buy literally 10,000 at a time and they're all selected out. The batches are put together, then they're matched with selected batches of LEDs, and then each unit is voiced individually. That's part of what makes their success, that the unit is voiced.

That's what you're paying for, really. The chances of you buying a bag of LEDs and a bag of light cells and putting them together and making it work is nil. I mean, it might work, it might not, but it's not going to sound great. The people who use our pedal acknowledge it, studio wise, as the one to have.

We've just come out with the Vibe Jr, which is a slightly cut-down version of it. It's got four knobs, we've dropped the tremolo function which was just a plus that wasn't on the original, and we've got a wide-range speed control. It's been designed as a plug-in-and-go version, so musicians can leave the knobs at 12 o'clock and it's going to sound cool. It's got exactly the same circuitry as the other one, just that it's got a Speed knob rather than multiple speed ranges – which will cover 90 per cent of what people used anyway – and we've got rid of the triangle wave form, which most people didn't use. The Symmetry control we got rid of, which was most useful on tremolo effects. So we just got rid of two knobs. Plus it's got hardwire bypass and two buffered outputs. And ours is all class A discrete circuitry, no opamps in it, which can't be said for a lot of them. That also maintains the transparency and detail all the way throughout the range.

Do you ever think back to the heyday of working with Hendrix and miss those times?
The thing I miss probably most of all about Jimi is that he was up for anything. If you came up with a new idea and it appealed to him and he could imagine it, he'd say, "Let's do it!" The enthusiasm he exhibited for doing something new and exciting and innovative was great. Nowadays you speak to a lot of the people and... you know, any guitar player who cannot be bothered enough to sort himself out and thinks the roadie can do it for him, in my book, he's not even interested.

It would be like a Formula One driver totally trusting his test driver to select the car for him. If he can't be arsed... Do you know what I mean? Some of these people imagine that by reading a few magazines, reading a few reviews, they can go and emulate a great sound. The problem is, even if they can emulate a great sound, it would always be in the past, they'd always be six months, a year, behind what could be in the future. So they're not really breaking any new ground. I very rarely get asked questions by guitar players about breaking new ground. It amazes me that they're not even interested.

I find a lot of the guitar players nowadays are extraordinarily conservative. The sad fact of the matter is that unless they've got any vision to aspire to a future, all they're going to be doing is duplicating something that happened 30 years ago, which to me is sad.

And that's kind of what spawned effects pedals in the first place. You get this box with two or three knobs on it, and by the time you figure in all the variables you can always do something that sounds different from everybody else.
When it comes to guitar effects, the sky is the limit. Believe you me. You can paint a sonic picture between someone's ears that will blow their mind. If they've got the vision, and they've got the balls to follow it.

Guitar playing does not have to appear to come from one place in the mix. Jimi's never did; it went from left to right, backwards and forwards. It took you to dimensions – your mind traveled with the sound. He took you out with the music, out into space and back again. He painted a very, very colorful picture in your own mind's eye of what was going on. It wasn't one-dimensional.

PETE CORNISH

Since the early 1970s Pete Cornish has specialized in building large effects-routing and switching systems for major artists to use in live performance, and his individual effect units have been made available on the commercial market only relatively recently. The Cornish client list, past and present, includes Brian May, David Gilmour, Bryan Adams, The Pretenders, The Police, Jimmy Page, Iron Maiden, The Strokes, and dozens of other big names.

How did you learn your trade?

I served a craft apprenticeship with the [UK] Ministry Of Aviation, at the same time studying for an HNC in Telecommunications.

What first got you interested in effects pedals?

Of necessity, when I was requested by Peter Banks of Yes to build the first AC-powered integrated multi-effects system in the early 1970s. My first pedal design was the Cornish Custom Fuzz, which was integrated into many of the early effects systems I built.

When did you decide you could make better pedals than were already out there?

The main problem with commercially available units was the unreliability. My training with the Ministry Of Aviation showed the way to making the existing units more reliable, and this naturally progressed to designing my own effects units which, initially, were only available as part of my multi-effects systems.

These days pedal connoisseurs rave about everything from JRC4558 chips to AC128 and NKT275 germanium transistors. Do you believe there are any specific essential ingredients in a good-sounding analog effects pedal?

No, I think this is all hype; a good design will sound good no matter which brand of components are used. The trick is in the maths and understanding of component tolerances, such as gain spreads with transistors.

Do you have any overriding goals that you keep in mind when designing or building a new unit?

My first consideration is not to lose the tone and dynamics of the guitar when one of our effects is used. The tone and 'playability' of and instrument/amp combination is something that's often ignored by other designers, which is why everyone can end up sounding the same. My effects allow the musician's personality to show through, but with added tonal enhancement, rather than a signature 'Pete Cornish Sound.'

The signal-to-noise ratio is another major consideration when designing effects with lots of gain, or those to be used with high-gain amps.

Are there any enduring 'pedal myths' you could help to debunk?

My main contention is with the myth of 'true bypass.' The true bypass function, which is promoted by some, can create dreadful problems with a system that uses many pedals. Take for instance a 15′ guitar cable linked to six pedals, each linked by a 2′ cable, and then on to the amp by say a 30′ cable. If all pedals have 'true bypass,' and are off, then the total cable length hanging on the guitar output will be

55′. This will cause a huge loss of tone and signal level, particularly if the guitar is a vintage type with low output. The amp volume is then turned up and the treble control increased to compensate for the losses. The inherent background noise now increases by the amount of the gain and treble increase and is usually, in my experience, too bad for serious work.

If one of the pedals is now switched on, then its high input impedance – and, usually, low output impedance – will buffer all the output cables from the guitar and the signal level will rise due to the removal of some of the load on the pickups. So it's like you're suddenly playing through 17′ instead of 55′ of cable. The treble will rise and the tone will not be as before. If that pedal was, say, a chorus or delay – devices which are usually unity gain – then your overall signal level and tone will vary each time an effect is added. Not a very good idea.

My system, which I devised in the early 1970s, is to feed the guitar into a fixed high impedance load which is identical to the amp input and then distribute the signal to the various effects and amps by low impedance buffered feeds. This gives a constant signal level and tonal characteristics which do not change at all when effects are added. The proof that this works are in the recordings of my clients...

Pete Cornish
(PHOTO BY LYNDA CORNISH)

Do you have any strong convictions one way or the other in the analog/digital debate?

Our ears tell us that a good quality guitar feeding into a correctly designed tube amp is a sound that cannot be improved upon. My effects systems, which usually incorporate some digital effect such as delays, reverbs etc, all feature a true analog main signal chain with all the digital stuff in a side chain so that the main signal path from guitar to amp is not degraded by passing through several analog-to-digital converters and, of necessity, digital-to-analog converters on the way out.

Do certain pedals – or maybe all effects pedals – work best or sound best into certain types of amps? Is the average guitar amp input stage optimized for linking pedals, or could there be a more suitable 'pedal amp' input stage design?

I have found that all distortion type effects work best into a low gain, clean, full-frequency range tube amp. The effects that use delay in its many forms – chorus, vibrato, echo, reverb, etc – seem to work best at high signal level between the preamp and power amp sections of amplifiers, where possible.

Do you have any advice on the use of batteries versus large converters to power multiple pedals?

Batteries are very useful as they can't create ground loops when used in multi-effects systems. AC/DC converters should be used with care, and the only sure way to avoid ground loop problems is to use a separate converter for each pedal.

What are your favorite 'classic' or 'vintage' pedals?

The Roland CE-1 [Chorus Ensemble] is my absolute favorite, especially when I upgrade it to rackmount. Same goes for the original Uni-Vibe.

Have any newer effects models from other makers caught your attention?

We seem to only get asked to incorporate the older type of effects into our systems. One great unit that we have added to systems is the Dynachord CLS222 Leslie Effect.

What are some of your favorite examples of effects used well?

My work with David Gilmour, both with Pink Floyd and his later solo *In Concert* shows, demonstrates the use of effects to create great beauty.

Are there some artists using your own specific pedals on record that we can listen out for?

The Pete Cornish NG Fuzz is the ultimate in rude distortion – it can be heard on Lou Reed's *Ecstasy* album in the 15-minute track 'Like A Possum.' When Lou used it during his *Ecstasy* tour he was assailed by one guy who was convinced Lou's gear was about to blow up. It's been nicknamed 'the Death Pedal' and is for serious distortion fans. On a technical level, the distortion circuit is all vintage germanium but we have fitted a modern drive preamp to ensure that none of the noise problems that occurred with the vintage pedals are repeated.

On 'Big Sky' Lou uses my P-2 Fuzz and G-2 Fuzz and adds the Pete Cornish LouTone near the end (6:04). This part is double-tracked and the LouTone is added to the G-2 Fuzz while the P-2 carries on without change. At 6:20 Lou finds the exact pitch for the feedback on the G-2 Fuzz which he holds to the end, when he hits the Mute pedal.

Any final tips?
Clean the plugs to free the tone.

MICHAEL FULLER, OF FULLTONE

Michael Fuller started to make a name for himself in the early 1990s when he combined his playing and vintage pedal-chasing efforts with a knack for modding and electronic experimenting, and launched what is now arguably the world's most successful 'boutique' brand, Fulltone. He spoke to me from his California home, where he was clearly bubbling with enthusiasm for his latest endeavor: the Fulltone TTE 'Tube Tape Echo.'

What first got you interested in pedals?
I'd always been a big fan of the old Marshall and Fender amps, and Voxes, and Echoplexes and Fuzz Faces and Vox Wah-Wahs, so I used to go around buying and selling them, before it was real popular. We're talking about the mid 1980s, before the prices went crazy. I would go to guitar shows and load up on Vibratone and Leslie speakers, reverb units, Fender amps – well, Fender amps were big, but everybody was focusing on just the amps and guitars. For me, I would go and clean up on all the effects. I'd get them home and they didn't work, and I'd notice with all these different Fuzz Faces how they varied greatly.

Pretty soon I had to learn how to fix them, then I guess I started stumbling on how to improve them, or how to make them sound a little different. Then I discovered, "Wow, I can sell this Fuzz Face I picked up for $35 for $550. And if I could put out a more reliable, smaller version that was maybe a little more reliable, a bit more tweakable…" So I started making the '69 pedal, which is a germanium fuzz. I followed that up with the Octafuzz, which was a remake of that incredibly rare Tycobrahe Octavia. And that took off… well, I shouldn't say it "took off" – I started running ads in *Vintage Guitar* magazine. This was about 1991.

And then in 1993 *Guitar Player* magazine did a small article on my guitar playing: I won a competition they had, the 'Ultimate Guitarist' – I won the blues category. At the time I was mainly just selling used pedals, but they kind of got the text wrong and implied I was making pedals – and because my address was published I started getting letters and letters and letters every week. I thought, "This is interesting, people obviously want this stuff." So I decided I could go into business making these things.

Then a buddy of mine did an article on me in *Vintage Guitar*. Dealers started calling, and pretty soon I had to hire people, and soon I had to turn down the meagre session jobs I was playing on, little trailers, commercials and stuff like that. That was in around 1995. So I got serious about it, I borrowed $10,000 and bought $9,000-worth of parts and just started building.

My impression was always that you developed a very good reputation pretty quickly, though maybe it didn't feel like that to you at the time.

Yeah. Thanks to *Guitar Player* magazine. I remember a buddy of mine kept calling me and saying, "Man, you've got to send those three pedals." He was referring to the '69, the Octafuzz, and the Deja-Vibe. He said, "You've got to send those to *Guitar Player*." I kept saying, "You're kidding, they're going to rip me a new a-hole. I'm not going to do that," you know?

So I sent them in, and in the January 1995 issue they did a very, very glowing review – I think it was their first 'Cool Pedal Alert' – they gave me this incredible review. Basically, the artists started calling, like Billy Gibbons and Eric Johnson, Joe Satriani, Robin Trower. I never advertised. They would do their articles and say, "I'm using the so-and-so by Mike Fuller," and the word just got out there. It really wasn't a conscious effort. I got busy, and hired someone to help me, then hired another person, and another person. It really was the crash-course in how to run a business. Right now we're at ten full-time employees, and we're probably doing about $2.2million a year in sales.

That sounds like a nice way to get into business, to let it just grow of its own accord.

Yeah, not trying to force it. I have never, ever called a dealer and said, "Will you carry my pedal?" They called me and said, "I want to carry your pedal" – and some would call and say they wanted them, and I'd say, "You know what, unless you've got two or three people a week asking for it, don't waste your money." They kind of appreciated that, and I've built a really loyal dealer base, which to this day is probably about 150 dealers.

That's got to be important.

It's tough. At that time, there was only myself and Prescription Electronics as the boutique guys. As you know now, my god, there's pedals that very much resemble the Full-Drive. The Full-Drive was the thing that really put me on the map. I think there are 15,000 of those things sold so far.

Clearly your biggest seller.

By far.

I would guess distortion and overdrive and fuzz pedals probably sell more industry-wide than all other types of pedals combined.

I think you're right. As far as I go, anyway, it's about ten to one.

I certainly started noticing how prominent the Full-Drive was when, working as a guitar journalist even five or six years ago, photographers would come back from one shoot after another of stars' rigs, and more often than not there'd be a Full-Drive pedal on the pedalboard.

Cool. That's a great, amazing thing. I look at that thing as an essential tool. It's a hammer to a carpenter. And if I can outfit the working guitar player I'm happy.

How did you learn your electronics skills?

I don't have any formal training. I had the kind of dad who would come out on a Saturday and say, "OK Mike, we're putting a new transmission in the Pontiac." You know, and we didn't know what we were doing, but he had that spirit. We built go-carts, and I used to race motorcycles… all kinda do-it-yourself. I used to make little electronic devices, to try to bring tarantulas back to life and stuff like that…

I learned music electronics mainly just from reading articles in *Vintage Guitar* and studying books and stuff. You know, my knowledge is a lot less than my ears, development wise. There was something

Fulltone's Michael Fuller, and fully analog Harley.

with the Full-Drive about five years ago. I really wanted it to be more open sounding. So I'd just open it up and literally just take some caps and resistors and start poking around. You know, nine volts isn't going to hurt you. So I'd come across these things that a guy who really knew what he was doing wouldn't try, because it defies accepted logic.

I think most of the better things that I've done are just through luck. I have this method where I'll just try every possible thing for five hours straight and find out what's best. It's just tenacity, I guess.

Which seems to be how a lot of good rock'n'roll sounds evolved anyway. It's got to appeal to the ears, rather than just 'work' on paper.

Yeah. I used to bias amps, and if you look at a standard method of biasing amps, they want to get zero crossover distortion. And what that ends up with is probably the coldest sound you've ever heard. I found if I under-biased my amps so that they're running hot, if you looked at that on a scope it was outa whack, it was asymmetrical. But it sounded great. I've always loved asymmetrical clipping, because generally when you have mismatched tubes and an amp running a little too hot, a class A/B amp running practically into class A, you get these overtones that I always love. You can make a Fender amp or a Marshall amp almost sound like a Vox amp.

I wanted to try and get that asymmetry in the Full-Drive, so I made the clipping a little different. All these overdrives and Tube Screamers and things are symmetrically clipped. And so I started experimenting with ways to whack it out and throw it off-kilter, to where some of those even overtones would come through. What that did was produce a pedal that, if a guy had a pretty good ear, he'd say, "You know, that sounds more amp-like."

Some guys hate that. Some guys really like symmetrically clipped distortion. They want to hear some of the odd overtones, or whatever. A certain fight between the notes. Almost like tuning a guitar. If the guitar's too much in tune, it's almost boring.

What I love is, you get a good maple-neck Strat and play a complex chord on a nice, clean amp, and you get these magical overtones that make it fatter than it really is. That's what draws me to a sound; the complexity of it, as opposed to raw distortion. I really don't use a heck of a lot of distortion in my own playing. It's more about fatness and overtones.

Do you have any great beliefs in 'essential ingredients' in classic pedals?

Not really. I think the simpler the better. You can name any amplifier – and I think of a pedal as just a miniature amplifier – and which are the most pure and open-sounding ones? Is it the one with four or five controls, or is it the one with pull-pots and 12 sends? You know, you start killing the sound... It's like a river: if it branches off into too many tributaries it gets weak.

I'm not a big fan of 'band aids,' meaning if you have a bad tone at the first stage, you go to the second stage and try to fix that tone. Never do it. I'm always interested in a really raw, great sound that's as unfiltered as possible. If it's too bright or too ugly, then go back to the drawing board and start at that first stage again. Because a lot of devices are simply, "Let's create X amount of gain, then we'll filter it, then we'll clip it again..." And you end up with just a very flat sound.

As for components, sometimes the cheapest components sound great. I remember when I first started making a wah-wah, I thought, "I'm going to use Wima capacitors and polypropylene caps, and that's going to be great..." Then when I first hooked a couple of them up, I though, "Oh my god..." You know, a wah-wah's such a raw circuit. When you try to put a tuxedo on a homeless guy, it might not fit. It's just not the way to do it. I just have that method of trying every single component, and it doesn't matter what brand or what type it is, as long as it sounds good.

Which has got to be the whole point. And I think more and more players are coming around to

realizing that simplicity, in amps or pedals or whatever, can yield the best sonic results. Everybody went through that high-gain, channel-switching, effects-loop stage…

Yuck!

…And recently there's been a lot more appreciation of simplicity, and of trying to get your signal to the output with the least amount of crap in the way.

Yeah. It's funny, you know, I've had guys who either hate my stuff, or they get it and they can use it, and sometimes they even love it. If I walked up to a blackface Fender Deluxe Reverb, I would put the treble on three. I feel like I get plenty of brightness out of it. I see guys who would go up to that amp and put the treble on seven or eight… And if you're that person, you wouldn't even want to buy my stuff, because it's not trebly enough. I like a certain EQ, I guess.

Or maybe their ears are just shot from too much volume, so they're compensating.

[Laughs] Yeah… I don't know, man. I'll tell you, it amazes me when I hear something that I've designed in use and it just sounds so bad. I want to go, *"Please!"* But you know what's weird? You can't control that. The biggest problem I have had to overcome is that you cannot control how your children turn out. You give them all their training and send them out into the world, and hopefully they'll make good of themselves. But I can't control how they're used, so I just let go of that.

You know, I'm really, really excited about this next phase that we're going into. We're doing that TTE, a tape echo. It's the first thing I've ever made with moving parts that's musical. I feel like I'm ten years old again. You tell the metal shop, "No, let's make it 0.21″ shorter and bend it this way." It's really exciting. You go to the next step, then the next step. We're getting so close to the thing being ready to be released, and it's really cool because I can do whatever I want with this. It's the first time, I think, where I've ever had enough funding. I tooled up for the tape cartridge, and I didn't like the way that the lid snapped on, it broke, and I wanted you to be able to reload the tape. So I changed the tabs, and… just going through all the little details. And when you finally see this thing show up, you cannot believe that you actually designed it.

There must be so much more to think about with a product like that.

Oh, it's crazy. We've got it to the point now where you can put it next to any delay pedal, turn the amp on ten, and the TTE has less noise and hiss than the delay pedal. It's really cool, man. Basically, I'll be happy when everything I play is something that I built, and then I can retire.

I've always had these Echoplexes, and even if the echo's not on heavy, I just love what it does to the tone. The day that I get to play a gig with my own echo, I'll probably just quit.

This must be one of the last things missing, though, from your chain.

Yeah. You know, my interests are very much in the studio as well. I have a pretty elaborate 24-track, 16-track, an automated Studio Tech, George Massenburg faders and all that. Sometimes I tweak and do little preamps and stuff. So I think maybe the next step to do is some mike pres and stuff for the studio.

That's something else people are starting to appreciate more. Everyone can record to 24-bits on hard disk, but they're plugging in cold and then wondering why their recordings don't sound like their favorite records.

Oh, man, have you ever tried putting together a digital recording system? I do have a digital part to my studios, and the alchemy of the German RME card if you try to put in a MOTU MIDI thing and they start crashing…

They can be a real pain in the ass. But just making it sound good can be the biggest trick. You've got a medium that is supposedly high quality, but you still have to put a good sound into it.

Well, you've got so much clarity. We're so used to distortion. The bottom line for me, my whole life, is distortion. You've never heard a clean tone. Unless you've taken a Stratocaster and plugged it into a Yamaha power amp, you've never heard clean. Clean tones, for guitarists, are varying degrees of distortion, ie harmonics, overtones. Same thing with a great recording chain: tube mike, a little bit of grit; Neve preamp, more grit, overtones. If you use all that stuff going into a digital [recorder] you can actually approximate a great sound; but if you just go cold into some sound card, digital doesn't work.

For ten years I've been going into 2″ tape, you've got it biased for plus-six, you've got the meters pegged into the red. What do you have? You're adding compression, you're adding distortion – and of course people perceive that as a great guitar tone, fat sounding or whatever. So that's where my interests are going, into recording. Because digital is here to stay.

Yeah, we've pretty much been landed with it.

I'd like to try and really get some organic tones out of digital, which is my goal.

It would be a service to the world.

Oh, record drums through a digital system, you can be like, "What happened?" You can't compress it and distort it enough to resemble what tape does to it, so we have to manufacture the crud [laughs]. Put some crud on it before it goes in.

I don't have enough knowledge to really get into the digital world. But I have these really esoteric Mytek digital converters, and I open them up and go, "Hmm, that ain't that hard." I look at what are used for the coupling caps, all that stuff, so you never know. I would be thrilled to maybe make some converters that were just bitchin' sounding.

And it's such a young industry still, as far as digital sound goes.

I have an example for you, and this applies to effects. There are techs, and there are musicians. I think if there is any reason for success on my part it's because I don't have a lot of the tech, but I hopefully have some of the musician. I had these wah-wah inductors hand-wound for me by a very brilliant transformer maker, inductor maker, and he's schooled, he's pure school. So I get the first batch of these inductors a few years ago, and I notice they're microphonic and they don't sound that good. So I call him up and go, "Hey, Sergio, these things are microphonic."

"Impossible. You can't make microphonic inductors, it's physically impossible."

So I say, "OK." I take identical wah-wahs, mark them A and B, I put an old-style inductor in one and the inductor he sent me in the other one. B is completely microphonic. I send them to him, and I say, "Sergio, I want you to plug these two wah-wahs in, try them, and then what I want you to do is change the inductor, nothing else." He does it, puts A into B, tries them, and guess what? Now A is microphonic. He calls me back and just goes, "I… I… I…" You know? So I guess what helps me is my ignorance.

Going by your ears, rather than by the drawing board.

Yeah. There's something in the Full-Drive that actually taps off part of the circuit and spills it back on the clipping circuit. I call it a 'turbo charger.' I have a very good tech called Kiyoshi Sasaki, and he says, "Hey, you can't do that." But we plug it in, and there it is, there's what we call the FM in my Full-Drive. So the new one has a switch so you can go from the old-style Full-Drive with lots of mid-range, to the new style without the mid hump. It works. But he's like, "That should not work, you're putting DC onto AC." But it works, it's not blowing up or anything.

That's the kind of thing that makes guitar gear fun. If it sounds right – and it ain't gonna blow up – who cares.

You know, there are some guys over the years who just had the ears for great distortion sounds. Dick Denney, who designed the Vox AC15 – man, I have an old, fawn-colored AC15 that I buddy of mine sent me from England for $800, and that is the best sounding thing I have ever heard. It is the best distortion device ever made. That, and some of the Sola Sound and Colorsound Tone Bender pedals, the Tone Bender MkIII in particular… These things just have a sound. Some of these guys really knew what they were doing.

You clearly have a major interest in amplifiers, too.

I have probably 45 vintage amps. Basically every good Marshall and every good Fender. Marshall, I stop at 1973. All the Fenders, some of them in duplicate, all the blackface series and all the tweeds. They all sit in the studio along the wall and I have a big rolling boom stand that I roll around and listen to the sound.

It sounds like the pedal business has provided a great opportunity to be able to do some things like that.

I'm extremely fortunate to be able to do that. Ten years ago I was making $300 a month teaching guitar. I'm extremely happy to have these opportunities.

Are there any people who helped you along the way with your early development, with gaining your knowledge?

I used to go over to Groove Tubes when Red Rhodes was still there, and ask him, "What do you think of that?" And he would sit down and talk about bias, or this or that, and he was absolutely just a genius.

Apparently the man had a great sense for good sound.

He was a great steel player. He was old school, and he was always helpful. There were also some local guys, over at Caruthers Guitar Shop, a guy named Big Jim. This guy was 6'7", 340lbs, ex-Navy electronics engineer. I'd go pick his brains, and I always was able to get free rein on these places. I'd get to know all the parts outlets and get friendly with them. They'd say, "Oh, go on, go ahead and look back there." And I'd pick through these bits – they had no idea that these germanium transistors and great old pots were worth having. And I'd just grab a tube, "These KT66s – I'll give you three bucks for 'em."

It's kinda sad now, because Radio Shack now is a place to buy a boom box. There are no tube testers, there are no parts. I used to be able to go to Radio Shack and go through their drawer and find Mullard 'lifetime' tubes that were branded as Radio Shack for a couple of bucks. I've always collected the tubes. I put them in these road cases and match them with my old tube tester, and get out my Sharpee and mark them.

All of which further proves the point that it's worthwhile for any guitarist to get to know every element in his sound chain.

Absolutely.

Do you find any particular amps are better as 'pedal amps' than others?

I really do. I have some extremely strong views on this. As a matter of fact, my products are not made for 'insert name of popular high-gain amp here,' you know. I have never owned one, I have never played one. I have tried to play them, but, preamp rackmount and so forth, no. My architecture for the way I get my best sounds is for a tube amp with a lot of head room and a great clean tone.

People think of Marshalls, unfortunately, in the last 20 years, as buzz boxes. And a Marshall to me is an overblown tweed Fender. It's a four-input thing that you turn up loud enough to where you get that 4x12 pushing a little bit of air. I never turn an amp to ten, man, unless it's a Vox. But put it on four or five on the volume, and then you have this incredible platform that, if you have a good pedal, you can take it in increments as far as you need to take it.

That's the way I approach it. That's the way I test, that's the way I design. So I wouldn't be surprised if my stuff sounds like crap in certain amps, and I'm sure it does, and I've heard about it from people. There's a small section of the world who appreciate that: a good clean tone with a little edge on it. Turn it right to there, and then my job is, incrementally, to take it as far over the top as we can get it.

It's no coincidence, I'm sure, that we saw the return of the really cool, simple vintage-style non-master volume amps – not necessarily old amps, but new boutique makes – at about the same time that the old pedals began to be appreciated again.
You are 100 per cent correct. It's all correlated. And it's really cool to hear this new generation of people coming in that want that sound. I talk to them every day, and they're the ones buying my stuff. The other guys are scratching their heads and going, "What's that?"

Sure, and wondering why people are charging $300 for an overdrive pedal.
Yeah, it's so hard to answer that.

I guess if they buy something they don't like they can always sell the pedal on again.
And luckily since my pedals usually hold their value, they can get their money back out of it.

JOSH FIDEN, OF VOODOO LAB

Voodoo Lab was born out of California's Digital Music Corp when founder Josh Fiden, a guitarist himself, wanted to build a few pedals that made some noise, rather than just MIDI patchbays/jackfields and footcontrollers that helped people switch the noise around. Since the mid 1990s, Voodoo Lab units have found their own niche by blending vintage sounds with updated, often simplified functions – a marriage which has resulted in a popular range of practical, playable pedals.

Tell me how you got started in this wonderful world of effects pedals.
I was working for a computer company as a software engineer, and I had a friend I was working with and we were both guitar players. We hated the computer stuff because it was just boring as hell – too many guys with suits and all that – but there was another fella we knew who was really involved in the up-and-coming MIDI stuff, so we got involved with him. When the company started out, I was making memory expansion cartridges for DX7s and Casio synths, and then started doing MIDI patchbays, and that's what we did until the end of the Eighties.

It wasn't until the tail end of 1989 or the beginning of 1990 that I came around to thinking, "You know what, I don't really like MIDI and keyboards and all that stuff. I play guitar, this isn't any fun." Actually what gave me the first idea to get into guitar products was I had a roommate who brought home an Alesis Quadraverb, which of course in 1989 and 1990 was the thing to have. At that point there were a few MIDI footcontrollers out, but it just hadn't really clicked with me. Prior to that the only effects I'd been using were stompboxes, basically. I had a couple old Boss pedals, and the Maestro Phaser – the big box with all the colors. Oh, and a Vox Tone-Bender. So he brought home this Quadraverb, and it just clicked. I thought, "Hey, here's this thing, it's neat, it's got some good sounds – but you can't use it without a footcontroller, if you play guitar." So that sent me off on that idea: "I'm going to make a footcontroller, I'm going to make a great footcontroller." And that's where the Ground Control came from.

Then I think it was 1994 or so – the whole boutique pedal thing was just getting going. And what first caught my attention was that they were starting to get astronomical money for some of the really cool older effects. And you know, a lot of it was magazine reviews. Things like switching systems always kind of took back seat to the stuff that actually makes the sound. And what used to really piss me off is that they would do articles about artists and what stuff they were using, and of course by the mid 1990s we had a lot of pro touring artists using our switching systems. So often they'd interview the guy, and they wouldn't even mention what switching system they were using.

Josh Fiden at work in the Voodoo Lab.

So you wanted better billing.

Yeah... [laughs]. You know, they'd say what effects and what amps they were using, and even though the center of their live rig was our switching systems making all that stuff work, they would either gloss over it or not mention it at all. It kinda felt like you were getting brushed off. Like, if you don't actually make the sound, you're not that important.

So it was a combination of those things, and of seeing these cool effects going for that amount of money and thinking, "That's silly. There's no reason why someone should be paying $800 for a Tycobrahe Octavia, if what they want is the sound." You know. It's one thing if you're a collector – and I came across one in the original wooden box after we started making our reissue of it, and it's something that I'm very happy to have, but I'd certainly never play it, and I think anyone who would is silly. Why take a pedal that's a collector's thing worth $600 or $800 and take it out on a gig and have somebody pour beer on it?

It does get crazy. It becomes like the whole pre-CBS Strat thing. Why is it worth $20,000 when a very well-made Custom Shop Strat will only cost you $2,500 or something.

Yeah, or a Tom Anderson or Don Grosh guitar or that sort of thing. And then you just worry if it's going to be stolen. But anyway, it was a means to make some of those things more accessible. That's been sort of a theme of how I've done a lot of things, like with the MIDI footcontroller. I go and look at what's already out there, at what sort of products already exist and what they do. That's the starting point that you want to build upon, and then try and go outside the box and not think from the perspective of what that is, but if we started with a clean slate, what would you want? And then take the engineering background and see what's really possible.

So with the pedal effects, it was looking at things like the Tycobrahe Octavia, and the little Jordan Bosstone – the little box that plugs right into the guitar. They're virtually unusable as they are, but wow, it's a really cool sounding fuzz. So we thought we would come out with some pedals, and we needed a handful to get started. I started asking around to see what people thought was a really cool fuzz, and the Jordan Bosstone was enthusiastically brought to my attention. Then I played it and thought, "Wow, this thing really is cool." And they're so esoteric. If you want one, they're not easy to come by. So that was really it.

The original four were the Overdrive pedal, which was taken from the original DOD 250; the Tremolo, which was really just intended to sound like a Fender amp tremolo; the Proctavia, which is our Tycobrahe Octavia, and the Boss Tone. And add true bypass, because that's what people want – well, not just what people want, but what you should have if the idea is to make stuff sound good. And then we just used good quality parts – in some cases we upgraded stuff. We started selling the first four pedals in 1995, so I might have started working on them in 1994.

So from the start it was a combination of thinking partly that you could make these things better, but also an effort just to make them available at all?

Yeah. Absolutely. The idea is, "Wait a minute, why should somebody pay $800 for a Tycobrahe Octavia when I can offer the same pedal that's better made, it has better parts, it sounds virtually identical, plus it has true bypass and good connectors and so forth, and I can sell it for $150 retail. That seemed like a good thing that people would like, and it was fun for me. I like pedals. Coming from this background of making MIDI patchbays, the Groundcontrols and switching systems… they're really cool, and they serve a function, and the people that use them need them. But I'm not one of those people. Those aren't really the sounds that I like.

It seems like you gained some respect and some good reviews pretty quickly.

Yes. I would say that things were fairly well received from the very beginning. Reviews were pretty good. Although what really put us on the map was the Micro Vibe. You know, even before that, with the Proctavia … it's kind of an interesting story. Ah, I probably shouldn't even say this…

Oh, go ahead.

Well… when we're working on stuff here, we often have little pet names for products, generally not intended for public consumption, and not always very tasteful. So when we were working on the Octavia, we had yet to to come up with a name for it, and we started calling it the Proctavia, because of the proctological significance of it. We just thought it was funny. It wasn't intended to be a name to release the product under. You know, until you get the idea of what Octavias are – you just pick one up, turn the knobs up and play it – it kinda sounds like shit, doesn't it? [Laughs.]

And so when the thing was done and we had to come up with a name for the product, the problem was we had spent months calling it the Proctavia, and nothing else sounded right. So we just thought, "What the hell, we'll go with it. And if anybody asks we'll just tell them it's a contraction of 'Pro Octavia.' And plenty of people thought that. But it's not, it's just Proctavia, and to go with that theme, it's the black powder-coated box, and we have patterns that we created for each of the pedals, and that one has the little brown swirls…

Turds?

Well, little… brown… sphincters. That's something that doesn't usually go outside the office.

Time to blow the lid off that one.

Yeah. I think most people would find it funny, as we did.

I do remember there being a lot of sensation over the Micro Vibe.

Yeah, the Micro Vibe came out later. We were working on it in November of 1995, so I guess it came out in early 1996. That was actually different from the first four. It was the slow metamorphosis of what we were doing. The first four pedals were utterly unoriginal, other than going, "Let's see, they used a ceramic disc cap here, but that's probably because metalized polyester capacitors didn't exist yet when they did this in 1968, so why don't we try some different parts and see what we think sounds the best…" So we made some changes like that, and just using some better components in some cases, and things that just didn't exist when the originals were made. And one of the nice things [about building pedals today] is that the tolerances of components have changed over the years. Once upon a time you bought a capacitor, and whatever the stated value, it could be 20 per cent less or 20 per cent greater and that was considered to be in spec. Now a normal part might be a five or ten per cent tolerance, so you get a lot better consistency. I think that, in conjunction with the ageing of parts, is what happens with those older pedals. You get any two specimens and they go from A to Z, one'll sound great and the other will sound terrible.

The Micro Vibe was really the first departure from that where we didn't just take something and make an exact duplicate of it. Of course a Uni-Vibe is a big tank of a thing, and it doesn't run on a battery. So we thought that would be a cool enhancement, if we could make a pedal that sounds just like a Uni-Vibe, but it's compact like the rest of our pedals and you could run it on a 9V battery.

We chased our tails with that one for a while. What we finally came up with was that the incandescent lamp and the CDS photo cells were so integral to what it sounded like, that trying to replace those with something else was way more effort than it was to just put them in. But the whole discrete transistor circuit, that could be very easily replaced with an opamp circuit that did exactly the same thing. And so the advantage of it is that it's more compact and we could make the thing draw less power. It really required a significant amount of engineering work to do it – to do the analysis of the original one to see what it did, and then come up with a new circuit that exactly replicated what it is.

Of course Uni-Vibes are all over the place, but if you take a really good sounding Uni-Vibe that you really, really like, and put that in one loop, and the thing that you're working on in another loop, then you can A/B. And with the Micro Vibe we ended up with something that was absolutely indistinguishable from what we consider to be the best Uni-Vibe we ever heard. I think that was reflected in a *Guitar Player* magazine review where they did a Uni-Vibe shoot-out. Things really exploded after that. As I recall, the Prescription Electronics Vibe Unit was overall favorite.

It's kind of a funny thing: when we select a reference pedal that's the best sounding of its type, we always refer to it as 'god.' For Uni-Vibes, what we actually came up with as 'god' was a Prescription Electronics Vibe Unit. And I mean it's an identical circuit – he [Jack from Prescription] made an exact copy of the original Uni-Vibe.

We had three original Uni-Vibes, and a Fulltone Deja Vibe which had come out not too long before, and we sat down and found the best Prescription Vibe Unit out of about ten or 12 we tried, and that was the cream of the cream, it sounded better than any of the original Uni-Vibes we tried. So we used that as the model.

The review came out, and it said: "We loved the Vibe Unit, however, the Micro Vibe sounds the same, and it costs half as much." Jack at Prescription Electronics told me that when that review came out, his sales just plummeted on that particular product.

Oh no…

Well, Jack is about the nicest guy that ever lived, and he told me that without the slightest bit of hostility. But it only makes sense, when a magazine review says, "This product's just as good, and it only costs half as much."

It's going to happen.

Yeah. In part, I think, because they were expensive – they were $400 or $500 for a Vibe Unit. Ours is more compact, it runs on a battery, and list price is around $200.

Players are more aware of the ins and outs of classic effects today than ever before, and they talk up all sorts of fine points of circuitry and components. Do you think there's much to the 'vintage ingredients' in a lot of pedals, or is it all snake oil?

There's a little of both in there. With the Micro Vibe, for example, we found we needed to keep the photo cells and the incandescent lamp. And there was a very specific reason for that: the way an incandescent lamp works is it's a filament that, when you put a bunch of juice through it, it heats up. It's the temperature of it that makes it glow, that makes the photons. So the way it does that is crucial to the way a Uni-Vibe sounds. You have an oscillator that's driving it, which in the case of a Uni-Vibe is a true sine wave oscillator. And on top of the sine waves you're overlaying the characteristics of the response of an incandescent lamp – you put a current through it and it heats up relatively quickly, but you take the current away, and it cools down much more slowly than it heats up. Since what affects the sound of the pedal is how much light is emitted by the thing, the change in illumination from the bulb is a very odd waveform. It's this sine wave overlaid on top of the characteristics of the filament. So you get a sine wave that's kind of this weird, lopsided distorted thing.

Then you have a third thing that's overlaid on top, which is that the CDS photo cells don't respond instantaneously either. This is a device that, depending upon how much illumination it gets, changes its resistance. But they don't do that linearly. As you illuminate it, the resistance goes down relatively quickly, but the resistance goes back up relatively slowly.

So there's an inconsistency there such as that which, surprisingly often, seems to create great sounds in rock'n'roll.

Yeah, but there's even more to it. The last thing related to that is that the photo cell is not a very precise part. One photo cell doesn't really work exactly the same as the next. In the case of a Uni-Vibe you have four photo cells, and they're all going to respond slightly differently. Each one is going to lead or lag what the other photo cells are doing. What you end up with – and maybe this is what you're getting at but in different words – is a very organic process, where you have something that's not precise. It's not at all what you're going to get out of a digital effect where it's very precise and it always does the same thing. This thing is like an instrument made out of wood, or something involving sticks and mud, you know. It has more of a natural feel to it because of those imperfections.

That seems to be what works for electric guitarists, though. That's often where the magical sounds come from.

Well, this is the way we develop anything. It's going on as we speak – we're working on a wah right now – and, especially if you're trying to do something a little bit new, you look at it and you try to come up with your first approximation of what you think are the important characteristics in the design to make it sound like what you want. Then you make that, and you listen to it, and you compare it to those things you think sound really good. You listen critically to it and you go, "Well, this aspect of it, we really caught it there," or sometimes you go, "Ooh, listen to what that's doing, I like that even better." It can be different from the original, but different in a good way. But the thing is to listen and work out what sounds right, and what doesn't. Like with the Micro Vibe again, we tried to replace the lamps and photo cells and it just didn't sound right. There was a sterile character to it, and the original just feels juicy.

It's getting into that mindset where you can say, "Right, I'm OK if we don't replicate every last detail, because we're smarter than that." We can figure out what's important to make it sound right, and what's not important. And by having a better understanding of it that way, we can improve things.

And the result is often that you can compact down the less important parts of the circuit, and make it more affordable.

And that's good. It's that kind of thing that really put us on the map.

Do you feel there are any great myths afloat in the world of effects, vintage or current?

Yeah, I think there's a lot of them... There's a lot of myths about certain things, and in general it simply comes from a point of – I almost hate to use the word, because it's kind of demeaning, but – ignorance. It's when you hear something and you decide you're going to take the source of this as being credible and you just go with it, where it hasn't really been proved.

And not that the 'ignorance' is the fault of guitarists who have often just been misled – by marketing departments or reviews or whatever – or poorly informed, at least.

Exactly. And it's very difficult, because most people, if you don't do this as an occupation, you don't have the opportunity to get a bunch of stuff together and A/B things, and say, "Well, these people say this opamp sounds better than that opamp, so let's go to the manufacturers and buy a bunch of parts of every opamp people have said is good, or that we think, from looking at the specs, should sound good." But we can stick a socket in a pedal and spend a day swapping opamps. And we'll get a tube of each one, so when we find ones we like we can determine how much difference there is from one to the next of this particular part, because maybe they don't all sound the same – and they don't. So you end up coming up with, "This thing does matter, but this other thing doesn't matter."

The original Voodoo Lab pedals had the switch and the jacks hand-wired to the circuit board, and it wasn't very much fun to do. The only reason why we did it was because we thought that's what people wanted, and a certain number of people to this day will tell you that the hand-wired ones sound better. But I will tell you that I think the hand-wired ones do not sound better, and the reality of a lot of hand-wired things is that there's an inconsistency there.

The first thing we found was that the way you wired them altered how they sounded, meaning how the wires were actually routed. Because you don't want coupling between certain things – and also when you have two conductors near each other you've created a capacitor so, depending on how close the wiring is to the grounded case, in effect you're adding a capacitor to that part of the circuit, albeit a small one. But guitar stuff, when you're talking about low-level signals and one meg impedances, can be quite sensitive. With hand-wiring there's a lot more variation from one thing to the next, versus something that's laid out on a circuit board where you were very careful about the traces on the board, so everything was laid out the way you want it and the things that need to be carefully separated were. I think that's something that is certainly a myth some people need to still hold, which is that hand-wired things are inherently better than PC-mounted.

Which probably applies even more in the boutique amp world. Although maybe the myth propagates because many hand-wired amps have had a lot of careful attention put into them in other areas, and not merely because of the hand-wiring.

Sure. But you get a lot of amps that are great-sounding amps and they're built with PCBs. I mean, who's going to tell you that a Bogner is a crappy amp because it's got a printed circuit board.

Sure, or a Soldano or something. It's a tricky world for the gear-buyer. You need to read up and do a lot of research before you put your money down.

And not only that, but just being able to hear the stuff before they buy it. A lot of people are making purchase decisions on hearsay, instead of hearing. As for myself, I have to live with something before I know whether it's right for me. Maybe there are people who are better at that than me and can sit down with something and make a decision. Sometimes, sure, right away I hate something or right away I love it, but more often than not I have to take something home and get comfortable with it and really fiddle with it and spend a few hours of quality time to really get what I like or don't like about it.

Do you have any advice regarding pedal setups? For example, do you believe it's worth having

a bypass route or a loop switcher or something to get around your three or four pedals when you're not playing through them?

That's something that's going to vary from pedal to pedal, depending on what you're using. What I would do is just play through all the pedals, with all of them on bypass, then plug into the amp and listen to it straight. If there's no real difference, don't worry about it. But pedals are all so different that you can't just generalize on something like that.

It depends on what they're doing. Like, a typical Boss pedal is buffered, it's going through an active buffer and some FET switching all the time. So that is going to have a different effect than, say, a typical wah pedal that doesn't have true bypass. The way it works is that, in effect, it hard-bypasses around the pedal, but it doesn't disconnect the input of the circuit. What that means is you don't get the coloration of going through active opamp circuits and FETs and stuff, but the detrimental effect is that you've thrown an additional load across there.

It's generally accepted that guitar pickups sound best with a one-meg load on. It's a reasonable assumption; one meg is the typical input impedance of most guitar amps. As you lower that impedance and put a bigger load on your guitar pickups, you roll off the high end a little bit and start to muddy up in the mids. That's what you're going to see with a pedal with that sort of design. That's completely different from either the buffered scenario or the true bypass scenario. It's something where you have to actually listen to what you have, and decide if that's something you can live with. And, you know, what's the application, what are you doing with it? How much do you care? You know, if you're really, really anal retentive, then maybe any little coloration is unacceptable. But if it's this little pedalboard you're taking out and playing in a bar band, nobody's going to know – and probably you don't even notice, in the context of a bar band. Because when you start talking about switching systems or complex routing, you get into some considerable amounts of money. You may be buying something that costs as much as the four effects you're playing through.

And if you always play with one pedal or another on, as many people do, maybe you shouldn't worry too much if your signal is altered just slightly from the straight-to-amp tone?

Yeah. Way too many people get into this chasing after the 'holy grail,' but they're not doing it with their own ears. They're asking other people, "How should I do this? How should I do that?" It reminds me of a call I got once. I can't remember which pedal it was, but the guy asked me, "How should I set the knobs on this pedal?" Which I always think is pretty idiotic to start with, because most of our products have two or three knobs on them, one of which is volume, so we all understand that. But you've got to tell them something, so I told this guy, "Well, this is a setting that I kind of like: put this one at one o'clock and that one at nine o'clock…" And his response to me was, "Oh, OK, because I had it set at this and this and I really liked it." I said, "Well, then I think you should go with that."

But that's a mentality, it seems, that a lot of guys have. Maybe they're just too timid or they don't have enough experience, but they just don't trust themselves.

Maybe too much is written in guitar magazines and online about how you supposedly should use your gear, or about how 'the stars' set up theirs.

Maybe, but it's *your* sound, and it's always going to be an evolution. Whatever you like today may at some point cease to be inspiring to you, and you'll have to change something.

Any passionate views about analog versus digital?

At this point in time, there are very few digital pedals I have much interest in. I don't view that as, "I'm anti-digital," and I can say unequivocally that it is not Voodoo Lab policy to say, "We're never going to do anything digital." It's more that if we think it sounds good, that's OK. I don't think there's an inherent flaw in digital that says it will never work. And again, you have to look at the application. If you're making recorded music, hey, guess what – it's going to be distributed in a digitized format, so how can you say that everything has to be analog when you're going to take the end product and digitize it?

But right at this moment, are there a lot of digital products out there that I get excited about? Not really. I can get excited about the concepts of what they're doing, and there are things that are really neat from a technology standpoint.

It's the same A/B-ing, interactive, advancing process as we're doing with our own pedal development, where people keep looking at it and go, "OK, maybe this doesn't sound exactly like our holy grail of sound, so what do we need to do? Is the sample rate not high enough, is the bit resolution not high enough, is the bit resolution not accurate enough? Or, on individual effects, where is the algorithm falling down so it doesn't precisely match the real analog thing?" Which again is a very difficult technical problem.

One of the things I've learned in doing this is that the ear is much more sensitive, from an engineering perspective, than you'd ever think it was. It surprises me the subtleties of things you can actually hear. And that gets down to critically listening to stuff, and noticing, "Wow, I can actually hear that." And that's the trouble with modeling something analog in the digital domain, you realize that, "Wow, we can hear a lot." Where the model departs from the analog counterpart can be very subtle, and yet very noticeable.

Speaking of development and new products, your Sparkle Drive of a couple years back really seemed to strike a chord with a lot of people.

I think it did. The Sparkle Drive has its basis in the Tube Screamer, but it's creating something sonically that's no longer a replication of the original. It's thinking, "Well, I don't really like Tube Screamers, so what is it that I don't like about them?" and improving that aspect of it. The whole clean-control Sparkle Drive thing tended to turn the Tube Screamer into a pedal I really like, so that was a cool thing to do.

Which of your own pedals have become dearest to your over the years?

I really love the Superfuzz. I really do. I find, when I actually sit down with it, it's really a lot of fun. And the Sparkle Drive, I love the idea of it. Generally my favorite setup is a Don Grosh Retro-Classic with Fralin pickups, and a '64 Deluxe Reverb, and the Sparkle Drive complements that rig incredibly well. With the clean, it keeps everything I like about the guitar into the amp sound, but at the same time the Tube Screamer part of it seems to take what you like about the amp when it starts to warm up and just fill that out. That, to me, is a spectacular, timeless sound.

With the Superfuzz, I like that with the Resonance control you can get some beef in the bottom end through a lower-gain amp, and the Tone control is pretty much a mids control, which seems to add some coloration to it that's the right thing, where you get different feels. I like that pedal a lot.

DAN COGGINS, OF LOVETONE AND DINOSAURAL

Along with fellow Lovetoner Vlad Naslas, designer Dan Coggins has an ear for extreme sounds, and has developed a reputation for bending classic tones to new and more flexible uses. Coggins has recently branched out on his own to launch the Dinosaural company, whose debut pedal – the handmade Tube Bender overdrive – is now available.

Tell me how you first got into effects.

The first time I was aware of effects pedals, in a strange personal way, was probably because as a child I was interested in electronics. My dad used to give me electric motors and batteries and lightbulbs when

I was quite young… very thoughtful of him. I was addicted to listening to the radiogram, and I got into buying electronics magazines. When I was about eight years old I got *Everyday Electronics*. This would have been about 1977. There were circuits for fuzz boxes, wah-wah pedals and all that stuff in there, and at the same time I was getting interested in guitar.

I couldn't actually play the thing for years, but I'd actually had an electric guitar, and my dad bought me a wah-wah pedal, a Colorsound, when I was about 11, before I had an amplifier. I was playing 'air wah' for a while. Within a few years I was starting to use it, and I built my own fuzz box based on an old *Everyday Electronics* design from about 1978. Good little thing. I added a tone control to it and started messing with some cap values and that, and that was the very early seeds of my involvement with pedals, which was all before the age of 14.

Did you study electronics formally?

I did an HND [diploma] in electronics at Plymouth University (UK). I did start on a degree, but everything was maths – and everyone who did that degree seemed to go on to be doctors and pilots. It was certainly useful to me, the first year on the degree, but I slipped onto the HND and went for that, and that was very useful. And I worked in electronics jobs. I worked with computer printers and early PCs, and I'm not particularly hot on that stuff, to tell you the truth. I had a job with the BBC in the early 1990s as a shift engineer, and that's where I learned a lot about pro audio… and professionalism.

When did you get the idea you could make a better pedal than what was already out there?

I was always making this and that, trem pedals and fuzz pedals for my own use, and eventually I started buying the commercially available stuff because I was in bands and gigging. So I ended up buying in proper pedals. I thought, "These will be the real ones, so they must be better than mine." So for years I was happy to use whatever I was using, Boss pedals probably, along with my wah, tape echoes, valve amps, Fender guitars, that kind of thing.

Then back in 1993 I designed a fuzz pedal for an electronics magazine, and through Dave Petersen [London-based amp tech and co-author of *The Vox Story*, with Dick Denney], who I got to know that year because I wanted some information on how to fix an old Vox Conqueror – that was great, solid state, loads of effects on it – and he was very kind and helped me with my learning curve on amps. He took me to meet Dick Denney, who designed the AC30. Dick was very kind, and he heard my fuzz box, because Dave suggested I bring it along. I said, "Do you really want to hear this?" But I was pleased with it, because I wanted to get that late-Sixties overdriven guitar in a pedal form, and I hadn't yet bought one I felt did that, but this thing was giving me that sound. Dick heard it, and he was very gracious about it. He said, "Wow, blimey cuz, you've got the ears." Something like that. So coming from him, who designed my all-time favorite guitar amp, I thought maybe there's something in this.

It's a pretty good endorsement to have behind you.

It is. Of course the poor chap's gone now – he died a couple of years ago – but he was a very lovely fellow. And a great engineer and innovator, too. It wasn't just the AC30, but the Vib/Trem circuit… well, of course he invented the trem half of it by shorting one half of the modulator with his screwdriver [laughs]. But that whole thing about voicing the tone circuits in all the Vox amps in the 1960s, even the solid state ones, he was way ahead of his time in that respect.

And look what people are paying for old AC15s and AC30s today.

I know. They are wonderful things. But in the end, he said, "it's all in the ears." I remember him saying that very phrase, and I tend to agree with him. Engineering knowledge is important and it does help if you know what you're doing, but it also helps if you're brave enough to do things that aren't in the book, and to rely on your own intuition and what comes through those flaps of skin on the side of your head.

This is the acid test: if I've designed a circuit for a pedal, if I find myself just playing the guitar through it and I can't stop playing the guitar, and an hour's gone by and I'm saying, "Wow! I'm into this." Well, that's the time when you say that it's done.

Did that early fuzz box end up in any of your products?

No. There was a PCB on the front of the magazine and people could build their own, but I never had any feedback on it. And I did a few more designs for a magazine called *Electronics In Action* over the next year or two. But very shortly after that I met Vlad [Naslas, Lovetone co-founder], because I was selling off Fuzz Faces and whatnot. He replied to my ad in the paper, phoned me up, and he said, "Do you know much about pedals then?" I told him I knew a bit, yeah, and he said he was looking for an envelope filter – we're leading to the Meatball here, you see – this was in 1994. He was looking for a serious envelope filter with extended features, and he said to me something like, "I want you to make one not with one or two knobs or three knobs, but with ten knobs." I said, "Yeah, as long as it's a one-off I'll do it." At that point we weren't even thinking of making them. But Vlad's a professional musician, he knows a lot of people in the music biz.

I built this envelope filter when I was still doing my night shift at the BBC. I'd take it to work with me sometimes and fiddle around with it, playing Radio 4 through it. I was tweaking it up, taking it back, and he'd say, "Yeah, that's good" or "I don't like this..." He was always wanting everything more extreme; I think I was being more on the polite side. He tends to shoot for the moon a bit more than me, but over the years those differences have merged, and I'll do some more extreme things myself, but I was probably a bit more conservative then because I was more in the tradition of doing things by the book.

So anyway, we ended up with this thing with ten knobs on it. The prototype. He took it around and showed it to a few people, and everyone said, "I want one, I want one." He said, "How do you fancy making these things?" I was giving up my job anyway – I was going to do amp repairs and fix people's gear – so I thought I'd give it a shot: what have we got to lose?

Dan Coggins of Lovetone and Dinosaural.

It doesn't seem to me like you did lose much. I remember the Lovetone name had a lot of clout pretty quickly.

It was very rapid. I think we officially began in April 1995, and within a month or two we had these things on the market. Only made in small quantities, it's only a very low-key operation and always has been, that's how we've kept it. We're not businessmen in the true sense of the word. We're not in it for making money, just because we like doing it.

Have you identified any elements over the years that contribute to making good-sounding pedals?

Yeah, something I've learned over the years from playing with stuff – I'm always keen to find out what kind of electronics something has in it if I'm at all interested in it, just to see if my theories about sound are reinforced by it. I would say there are three categories of analog sound electronics: valve, we all know that they generally sound very good – I'm a big valve fan, but at the same time I'm not a die-hard fanatic, and I dare say there are some valve things out there that sound pretty dreadful as well. And then you've got transistor technology, what we call discrete transistor circuitry, that was coming in in the mid 1960s and dominated until the mid 1970s. That's the circuitry I particularly like, because it tends to be class A – the small-signal circuitry like you find in pedals – so the sound quality is very good. The distortion tends to be nicer than with, say, opamp circuitry.

From the early 1970s onwards opamps were in everything. I started off using opamps myself, and

I've kind of worked backwards a bit. The problem with opamps is the amount of negative feedback used around them, and the phenomenon known as 'transient intermodulation distortion,' or TID. But I've mainly gone back to discrete transistorized circuits myself.

Do you feel there's much in the notion of some of the 'magic' vintage ingredients people rave about, like germanium transistors for example, such as the AC128 and NKT275s?

Yeah. Those two types of transistors, although they're both germanium, they do sound slightly different because of the geometry of the construction inside them. I've fiddled with old Fuzz Faces that I've fixed for people, and I've put in AC128s because that was all I could get. NKT275s were made by a company called Newmarket in the 1960s, and I managed to track down a handful, which are all gone now. They certainly sounded different, though I don't know if they sounded better. It all depends.

Did those go into a production pedal?

No, no – the only germanium devices we've ever used in any of our pedals have been diodes, only in the Ring Stinger. It's difficult to get them in small quantities, which is a problem for a company like ours. They're getting more and more scarce. They do have a certain sound, because the whole chemical action in them is different, the voltages are different, the steepness of the curve as the characteristics differ, so the distortion is completely different.

In the same way that tubes differ not only from type to type, but from make to make.

Absolutely. The early transistor equipment was designed by people who worked with valves before, and the early transistor circuits that you see in amps and products from the mid 1960s are very much designed as if they were valves. But the transistor actually behaves very differently to the valve. Transistor design came of age in the 1970s as a result of people thinking, "No, you have to do this with a transistor, and it's less noisy, and it does this and that ..."

Being a tube-head myself, it surprised me when I first encountered people raving about, for example, the JRC4558 chips in an original Tube Screamer the way they would about Mullard EL34s in a vintage Marshall Plexi.

Well, I had a Tube Screamer and I tried putting a very ordinary chip in it, and I found it didn't make any difference whatsoever, to my ears. But there you go. Some people can hear it, and who am I to argue with them. On the whole, though, I'm into discrete transistorized electronics.

During the course of Lovetone, going through the naive stuff from the early days, we went through the process of getting into analog synths. Just working out how they did what they did, and applying that concept to the later designs such as the Ring Stinger and that sort of thing. Voltage control and all that – getting into Mini Moogs, VCS3s, Arp Odysseys – that was a big inspiration for finding out how modulation works and stuff like that.

A case in point for a good class A discrete electronic circuit and how wonderful it can sound, and how fast and in-your-face, is the Mini Moog. There's opamps in there, but they're only used to sum control voltages. Every other device in the Mini Moog is a transistor and it sizzles, you know. A very good piece of kit.

Are there any myths you feel obliged to debunk? Anything that gets on your nerves?

The only thing that really gets on my nerves is lack of originality. Adding a knob to a pedal design that's been around for 35 years is not a particularly innovative or creative act. I mean, it is to a small degree, but I think it's good when people do stuff that's very original. I'm not trying to slag other people off, because I don't feel that strongly about other people's pedals anyway. Vlad and I do what we do, and we get by doing it, so it doesn't matter what other people do. There are some good things out there, and people are making useful boxes. I think they're making nice, robust boxes too. In short, I guess I think originality is good, and plagiarism – or just knocking out another slight variation on a Fuzz Face – is a pretty pointless thing to do.

There are plenty of them out there.

Yeah, and they're great pedals, I love Fuzz Faces. Silicon or germanium, they sound completely different from one another but they're both great, wild pedals. Another thing with germanium is the internal capacitance that's on those transistors – there's a leakage capacitance in them that gives them a softer sound, as well as the fact that they distort more gently. And they have less gain, so they don't have as much sustain as a silicon would. But they also varied wildly from device to device.

I understand you have some strong views that players should take their whole sound chain into consideration.

Definitely. The sound chain starts with your instrument; if it's a guitar, how hard you're hitting it, what pickup you're using, what chords you're playing, how complex your sound is to start with. For instance, with a Fender Strat, you've got the gauge of strings you're using, whether you're using old-fashioned pickups or low impedance Lace Sensors or something, your volume and tone pot values – if it's a passive guitar and you've got 250k pots it's going to sound duller than if you've got 500k or 1m pots, which loads the pickups less so they're brighter; then there's the kind of cable you're using – and the capacitance of that can load the pickups and affect the top end seriously, especially when it's a long cable. It's not uncommon for a long guitar cable to have 500 picofarad capacitance, which is massive for a guitar pickup.

Then you're going into either a series of pedals, or to start with, just going into a high impedance amplifier. Your Marshall, your Fender, your Vox, they've all got 1m ohm input impedance, which is good for guitar – it keeps the tone and top end there as well as it can. Then it's straight into your valves and tone circuits and then into your power amp, that all sounds different from amp to amp – though they don't differ all that much, some of them. The old 5F6A Fender Bassman spawned a lot of amps. Of course it's been said that Jim Marshall took a Bassman and stuck British speakers, valves and transformers in it, but that in itself I consider a creative act, because he ended up with a completely different sounding amp.

Then there's the type of speakers you're using, whether they're vintage type speakers that roll off everything above 4kHz, or whether you've got an open or closed back speaker cabinet, which affects the bass and the looseness of the sound…

But it all starts with how hard you hit your guitar, really. That's probably about 80 per cent of your guitar sound, if you're not using so many effects that it all just sounds like mush. I think, despite the technology, the musician's personality is always going to come through. That's not to say the technology isn't important, otherwise what I'm doing for a living wouldn't make sense. But the technology is just adding pepper and salt.

What do you use for testing a new pedal?

Well, whenever I've worked on design, especially for Lovetone, we tend to have a few different guitars and amps for the thing to be tried on. But at the design stage it's very much done with one setup all the time… I'd rather not talk about it. It's just a pretty basic, uninteresting hi-fi setup, just to see how the thing sounds as it is.

I'm always curious to know when designers might have optimized a pedal for a particular

setup, as with some overdrive pedals for example, which sound great with certain amps but not so good with others.

Well, sure – things like overdrive pedals, you have to try them with a few different amps, because some sound so bright. I've got an old AC30 with blue speakers, and it's actually so bright sounding. Ultimately the experience of listening to that amp is it's fairly woolly, but when you're up close and listening to it at low volume, there's a lot of treble there. What I would say is that I design stuff listening at very low volume, and don't turn it up loud. If it sounds good quiet, it's always going to sound better when it's turned up loud. I would say an unforgiving setup reveals all the problems.

Is the average guitar amp input optimized for using pedals, or a chain of pedals?

Yeah. Impedance-wise it is, because it's a high-impedance input, and the basic rule with impedance matching is that a low impedance source will drive any impedance, and a high impedance input will take any impedance to drive it. But reverse those two around and you've got a situation where a high impedance output will only work without loss into a high impedance input, and a low impedance input needs a low impedance source to drive it. Otherwise, you get attenuation of the signal, treble loss, and distortion as well.

So are most pedals conventionally converting to low impedance?

Not necessarily. But a low impedance output in a pedal is good because it will drive long cables without treble loss. That's all well and good – and it tends to be a by-product of having some active circuitry anyway that the output impedance is going to be finite and fairly low. But where the problem lies, certainly in these mass-produced pedals with electronic switching, is that you're going through silicon all the time and you're limited to 9V of headroom maximum, probably less in practice, and that's affecting the transient response of your instrument's clear sound, and it's giving you an unrealistic amount of top end. It's certainly going to sound different than if you didn't have the pedal there.

That's why true bypass has become a big deal, for the tone sucking from the circuit that's still hanging off the footswitch, if you like.

It's a big issue these days. True bypass is very big with a lot of makers, but you get people like Pete Cornish who warn against it…

Yeah, he buffers. We met Pete in the early days just before we were starting out, and he gave us some advice: just build the stuff well, and make it properly. We always did our best to do that, so we thank him for his advice. He's very professional.

So true bypass is certainly a benefit compared to some cheaper pedals or some old tone-sucking designs, but…

Yeah, for instance the old Cry Baby wah had an old single-pole footswitch that didn't enable you to switch out the circuitry in bypass, so you had a slightly dull sound. But some people like that. I believe that people like Eric Clapton and Jimi Hendrix, at the time, were playing with that dullness in the sound, and whacking up the presence on the Marshall to compensate.

And Pete Cornish is thinking very much in terms of a system, where he believes in high input impedance, low output impedance everywhere throughout the system. If you treat every pedal as an individual box within the system then I suppose, yeah, uniformity is good for that, because he's talking about big rigs. It's generally a good thing, but sometimes impedance mismatches can be a good thing, like the DI box situation, where you're playing a guitar into a transformer into a mixing desk, and it's got that slightly dulled sound.

Any strong views one way or the other about analog versus digital sound quality?

I used to be a die-hard analog boy – if it was old and full of valves and on vinyl it was better. But in recent years I've started to question that view. I've got a PC with a soundcard on it, and I think CD players – if they're good ones, and they've got a good analog stage in them – driving good valve amplifiers, is quite a formidable sound. At the same time, vinyl has a physicality to it that CDs don't have. There's definitely a difference. Yeah, it's very subjective. And hi-fi is just like guitar setups: what stylus and what pickup are you using? Or turntable, amplifier, connectors, cables, power amplifiers, preamps, and speakers…?

You don't build any digital pedals, do you?

No, not interested in digital technology as such, not as far as my gainfully employed life. The only digital pedal I've tried was a DigiTech Whammy, and I thought that was a pretty interesting pedal, actually. If it does something extreme that can't be realized in analog… I mean, that's a great example of something you can do fairly easily with digital technology, but my god, you try to do that with analog… You wouldn't want a valve computer, would you? They used to exist, but they had to keep them in warehouses. My god, it must have been warm in there. It's horses for courses, I think.

Which seems to be one of your main points; try the stuff out, in the applications you would need it for, and consider the entire sound chain.

Yes. I think the emphasis as a pedal user should be to try them in different combinations, different orders, with different guitars and different amps. Spend some time fiddling – but at the same time, do some playing as well. It's very important to just see how they all interact with each other, and what combinations work best. That's the great thing about separates – it's the hi-fi argument for separates, really. There are great designs going back to day one when the Maestro Fuzz-Tone came out, and I would kind of go along with most people's perception of what the great boxes were, because I've been lucky enough to hear some of these things when I've had them in for repair. All the old MXR stuff is great, and I love all the old E-H stuff.

But you definitely need to consider your sound objectively, without any preconceptions. If a sound initially seems good, but disturbs you within a minute or two, then it's probably not pleasant for anyone else either. It seems best to embrace sounds that you lose yourself in, and don't want to stop listening to. I know this seems obvious, but I'm talking about the very quality of the sound as well as its EQ, some frequencies being more 'ear friendly' than others. If one piece of gear is causing the ugliness, best to remove or replace it, because it will almost certainly be impossible to hide the ugliness otherwise.

Any favorites of your own pedals?

I do love the Ring Stinger. That's just such a weird box. People like the name as well, because they'd ordered those before they heard them. I like the Meatball as well, because that was our first one. It's like your kids – the oldest kid always has a certain je ne sais quoi, you know. But the Ring Stinger, because it's just so weird and it never fails to surprise. It's also a very crude thing, and that's what I like as well. Ring modulation – I always thought it was something that was just unusable. But the amount of people who enjoy using the Ring Stinger… I don't know what the hell they're doing. They're probably just having a lot of fun making silly noises, I don't know. But it's a musical ring mod because it's got the germanium diodes in it, so it's a very lo-fi, 1960s approach to ring modulation, like an early way of doing it.

As for the Meatball, when Vlad and I were trying out the prototype – after some serious tweaking – in my front room back in early 1995, a cat in the back garden suddenly started miaowing each time we made a sound with the Meatball, as if to mimic it. Then the birds started twittering when we raised the frequencies… This is absolutely true. And at that point, once we'd stopped laughing, we decided to leave the design pretty much alone. After all, what greater vindication is there than nature itself?

ZACHARY VEX, OF Z.VEX

Z.Vex founder Zachary Vex is known for his unique designs and fun, colorful pedal casings, and is undeniably the creator of some of the wildest sounds out there today. He is a confirmed 'night person' (a hangover from his days as a recording studio owner, perhaps), and he spoke to me from his Minneapolis headquarters in the wee hours of the morning… showing no signs of flagging.

What first got you interested in effects pedals?

I grew up during an explosion of interest and popularity in electric guitar. When I was in sixth grade my brother Jim started getting interested: my uncle had a Jordan Bosstone and an ES-335 and this nifty practice amp that was slanted and black – I don't remember the name of it. When we'd go to my uncle's house he would pick it up and play, so most of my interest probably stemmed from that.

When I got into tenth grade, I played in an orchestra and one of the kids in the choir had an electric guitar, and he would bring it along and play it with the singers. He had one of those Jordan Bosstones, but he had put it into a new box. I had been goofing around with electronics a little bit throughout my childhood, and suddenly when I realized you could rebox something it kind of triggered something in me. I built my first fuzz box, and actually sold it to that same guy. That was $10. Then after that I didn't build another fuzz box, but I built some amps – all tube. One was strongly influenced by the Boogie MkI.

Later I had a recording studio and I had to do a lot of repairs and a lot of modifications to gear for that. And I started to really see the need – having a recording studio and working with bands – to have a lot of tricks at your disposal. Because people get kind of scared and depressed that they are spending their life savings trying to make a record and they're not getting the sound that they want, not getting the magic. You can see them sometimes get this exhausted look on their face, like it's hopeless. So I'd take every trick out of the bag all the time, to try to give them some sort of spark to make them interested in their project, to help bring it back to life.

So it really taught me a strong lesson that you need to have a lot of tricks in your bag. I started making a lot of stuff for the studio, but I didn't focus on guitar effects so much as on tricky things for singers to sing through to get strange tones or more colorful tones, or very thick tube tones, and I made two tube mike preamps for singers to use. I also modified a lot of guitar amplifiers so guitarists could get different textures.

I opened a studio in 1985 in my apartment in Minneapolis. I recorded an all-girl band called the Blue Up? – the name ended in a question mark. I almost got kicked out of my apartment for bringing the drummer in there. I was making enough money doing repairs for a big service corporation, repairing high-tech machines, and I opened a little store-front studio in the cheapest space I could find in downtown Minneapolis. I had to put it in the basement, because there were apartments up above.

I started that up, and the lead singer from the first band I recorded, her boyfriend wanted to record with me. He ended up being quite a popular producer in the Minneapolis area, doing a lot of noisepop and British-influenced stuff. His name was Ed Ackerson, and he had a band called Polara. His name has popped up in *Guitar Player* a lot, and he still has a studio here called Flowers. He brought his band in, and they brought other bands in, and pretty soon the studio blossomed. Then my boss found out I had the studio, and he fired me.

No rock'n'roll in this industry…

Yeah, I think it was August of 1986 I got fired. And I worked in that studio until January of 1991, then I shut it down because the popularity of home studios had become so high and equipment had become so inexpensive that a huge number of bands had their own studios at home, and other bands would just go to their homes and pay them the minimum to use them. I had a full 16-track studio here and I just could not compete.

I sold off most of the gear except the really fun stuff, and then I went independent and joined up with one of my competitors until April of 1995. They shut down for what was going to be one month – they had nearly finished the build-out at a new location downtown. Something went terribly wrong, and they ended up being shut down for a full year. So I didn't have anywhere to work. There were so few studios in town and it was all sort of incestuous, and engineers were all lined up for jobs and jealously guarded any work they got.

I was just sitting at home twiddling my thumbs wondering what to do. I had built the Octane, which was my first pedal, sitting at my kitchen table: I'd purchased an octave fuzz – an old Apollo Fuzz Wah – and it was so quiet, I loved the sound but I couldn't do anything with it because the output was just so low. I studied the circuit and decided to build my own booster for it, and modified the tone control, and tweaked the circuit some more, and pretty soon I had my own thing. I stuck it in my own box, and not really having anything else to do I painted it up and labeled it. I took it to show it off at Willie's American Guitars, which is a local vintage guitar shop here – really nice guys. Nate, the owner, asked me for three of them. He really liked them, and he thought people would buy them. I made three more of them, pretty soon they were gone, and he asked for some more. In the meantime I had developed the Fuzz Factory; I gave him one of those, and that ended up being much more popular. After a couple of years, I kept my expenses really low and I was actually able to make a living just making pedals here and there.

I went on a road trip with a friend of mine to sell a large recording console at a studio up in Boston, so we hit as many music shops as we could between Minneapolis and Boston. I went into Rudy's in New York City and I tried to convince Tomo, this salesman they had there, to pick up the line. I brought a backpack and I probably had 15 pedals in it – at that point I had the Octane, the Fuzz Factory and the Super Hard On. I was showing them off to him and he loved the pedals, but he said there was no way he could sell them in New York. He kept saying, "Everybody plays blues here, no one will buy them." He had this thick Eastern European accent. It was kind of depressing because I was surrounded by countertops filled with all these exotic pedals, and I was holding this little hand-painted, hand-built pedal thinking, "God, this is just a pipe dream, thinking I could ever make anything out of these things."

I walked downstairs and left the place, dejected, and I was standing there listening to the sound of New York, when Tomo came out of the store and tapped me on the shoulder and said, "Hey, Zach, I'd like to buy one of those Fuzz Factories from you. I really loved that pedal." So I said, "Why don't you sell them in the store if you like it that much?" He said, "No, no, they'd never sell in the store, but I just want to buy one from you for myself." I said, "Why didn't you ask me up in the store," and he said, "Well, it's 'cos the owners here are really nervous about me. They don't trust me – they think I'm shady or something."

Zachary Vex; the Fuzz Factory speaks for itself.

I pulled out a Fuzz Factory and gave it to him, and he said, "OK, I'll send you a check." I thought, "Oh, great…" I had already dropped off consignments at other stores along the way, so I had all these pedals going out and no money. Sure enough about a month went by and I hadn't heard from the guy, no check, so I figured, "Yeah, I got screwed." And then the phone rings. It was Tomo, and he said, "Did you get the check? Is everything taken care of?" I told him I hadn't, and he said, "Oh, man, my record company was supposed to send you a check…"

But the reason he called me up was that he decided he could sell them, and he wanted to stock the store with them. He placed an order for the next month, and they sold 40 pedals in one month, in January. It was just insane, and for me it was complete salvation. I suddenly could pay off all the mounting debts I had, and I was able to pay back-rent – I was out of trouble, and I had a big smile on my face.

After I did well at Rudy's I picked up a few more stores… Eventually I ended up with 75 stores. But it's taken me a few years.

It seemed like once the word got around, there was a pretty big buzz for your stuff.

There were several years of explosive growth. I grew 100 per cent in sales for three years in a row. After getting into Rudy's, Joe Gore – who was playing with P.J. Harvey at that time – bought a Fuzz Factory and an Octane from there and then reviewed them in a magazine… He had beaten them all up, they were all chipped – luckily they used a pretty small picture so you couldn't tell. I've changed the paint since then so they hold up a lot better. Back then I was using enamels. Anyway, he really loved them and he was such a nice guy. I was so lucky he had come through Rudy's and bought one of those things, or a few of them, and then had such a positive opinion about them – considering they're so strange and wacky – and that he was writing for *Guitar Player*.

And then Art Thompson contacted me and asked me to come to a pedal roundtable they were having at the winter *NAMM* show a few years ago. Basically it was some people from MXR, Charlie Stringer from Snarling Dogs, a lot of the amplifier companies, and a whole bunch of people who were involved in the budding part of the industry; there were just big discussions about what people wanted, what was important, and there was a lot of mayhem – nothing really got accomplished. But I got introduced to a lot of people. I met Jack from Prescription, and Jack steered me to some part numbers to replace a transistor, 'cos I was running out of transistors for the Fuzz Factory. I didn't end up using that part number, but I did use it as a jumping point to find more part numbers…

I guess that's important – gathering the expertise to source parts.

Exactly.

Along those lines, are there any essential parts in a good pedal which, for you, the design just can't do without?

Well, I've had to change the transistors in the Fuzz Factory… Let's see, I started out with the 'spam can' transistors, then I went to an RCA but I had a very small quantity of those – I only made about 50 pedals with those. Those were the reverse-polarity transistors, so I had to make that version of the pedal positive-ground. Jayson [Myrold] had just started working for me, and he painted all the pedals backward so they were mirror-image on the front.

After that I had to switch to yet another transistor, and the fellow who had those had an enormous quantity of them, tens of thousands. And he died. When they cleaned out his belongings they just junked all kinds of stuff. They were gone. I contacted my source and he said, "I can't get those things for you any more." I said, "You promised me I'd be able to get these transistors for years to come." And he said, "Well, I'm sorry, the guy's dead."

And they threw them away? What a crime.

Yeah. So I've switched yet again to a larger package of transistors. I've gone through four or five different kinds of germaniums for the Fuzz Factory, and I've rejected probably 50 different kinds of transistors because they just don't have the right tone.

So you do seem to have some belief in germanium over silicon for fuzzes.

For that particular product, yeah. Just for the Fuzz Factory and the Fuzz Probe. But I'm not absolutely hung up on the concept of germanium being the be-all and end-all for fuzz. I mean, there's an awful lot of fuzz textures. There are so many people making germanium fuzzes that you don't have to worry about that as being some sort of essential thing. Basically, in this industry, for someone to get across now they have to stand up in a new way. There are different approaches people take; some of the new, more prominent guys that are popping up are making pedals with so many knobs you can't adjust them any more. There are fuzzes that have 13 knobs on them – I don't know what you do…

It does seem kind of insane. Then again, I wouldn't want to enter this business today with my heart's desire being to build the best fuzz box, hoping to beat any of the half a dozen or more outstanding ones already out there.

Yeah. But there certainly is room for more distortion boxes. If someone could offer a distortion box that could do the sound of metal, that would do well. There are a few good ones out there, but they haven't quite got it.

And you know, I fully believe you can get a beautiful metal sound with solid state. I have seen it. There's a fellow named Jeff Arnold who lives in Illinois. He drove up here and met me, and he brought two prototypes of a piece he'd made that he worked on for 11 years, and it sounded like metal like you wouldn't believe. We took it from shop to shop, and on the highest-end high-gain tube amps we could find, we switched between the clean channel and the metal channel on the amp, and then between the metal channel and the clean channel with the pedal on – and the pedal just floored everybody in the store. In fact in every store we went into they asked me, "When will we be able to get this? When will this be a Z.Vex product?"

I tried to negotiate with him for a while... and he ended up going to Peavey [Zach laughs]. I don't know when the thing's going to come out, or in what form, but I had a name picked out for it and everything. If the thing comes out and people hear it, Peavey might have a pedal that is actually successful.

They sell a lot of gear, certainly.

I think their point is to sell it as a pedal, not stick it into an amp, because they've stuck so many of those things into amps before. But he's a very, very intelligent man. Applied mathematics is his degree, and he started off not knowing anything about electronics, but he designed it based on math, on theories based around opamps. He had heard that tubes weren't going to be available in the future – and this was back in 1992 – so he thought it was a perfect opportunity to use his applied math to create a solid state circuit that would simulate what tubes were doing. Then he spent 11 years discovering that you can't do it with math, you have to do it with real electronics, then he kept going and going...

It seems engineers who design music products purely on the blackboard often get it wrong – although this guy obviously took the time to revise, and eventually got it very right.

Oh, I've seen very many mistakes made. But it also shows another point, that sometimes it takes an enormous amount of time to come up with something. People are often in such a rush to get a product out to the market, so there's a lot of slipshod stuff that happens. You end up with a shotgun approach, where you get lucky sometimes.

Which is maybe a little bit how Electro-Harmonix did it in their heyday.

Oh, man, they put out so many products. I've talked to Mike Matthews about it and he doesn't remember them. He doesn't know what all these pedals are.

Are there any great myths you can identify that are propagated in the minds of boutique or vintage pedal fanatics?

You can make an enormous amount of great sounding analog equipment without using germanium transistors, for example, which has been the big buzz recently. Anything that's not a fuzz – and there is a way to use silicon transistors to get some beautiful types of fuzz, but you can't necessarily get every part of the sound that you get with germanium.

That's a very interesting question – the holy grail thing. Just prior to getting into this business I had been in a band that used a lot of pedals. I was buying pedals at a store called Hi-Tech Consignments, a store that cropped up here and started selling pedals like crazy. People were pulling pedals from underneath their beds that had been there for a couple of decades, just to get the money because the prices started going up so fast. This was the early end of the 1990s. So we would go into the store every single day. It was almost a race, to see if you could get something before anyone else could. We would be picking up $25 Thomas Organ Wah-Wahs, and $40 Fuzz Faces – everything was a bargain. Then we would go through them, and we'd sell them to each other to get rid of the ones we didn't like.

The holy grail at that time was to find that particular one that sounded really great. The Fuzz Faces in particular were put together very slipshod. They didn't test the two transistors to see which one was high gain and which one was low gain. They didn't sort them, they just threw them in there. If you were lucky you could find one that had the right combination. These days you can go to websites that explain which transistor has to be what gain range, and tell you to stay away from ones that are leaky. And they even tell you how to build circuits you can use to tell which ones are leaky. Back then it was just luck...

The analogy with vintage guitars works pretty well. You can very easily buy a pre-CBS Fender Stratocaster or Tele for $15,000 or more that really doesn't sound or play all that great, and maybe never did, whereas the one hanging next to it might sound like heaven...

Uh-huh. We were very, very lucky that the prices were low enough that we could pick and choose. And if we didn't like something, prices were going up so fast we could bring it back into the store in a couple of months and sell it for 15 bucks more. So it didn't matter if we liked it or not, we just needed to get it before someone else did.

Do you think, on the whole, modern and especially so-called boutique makers are building better and more consistent pedals than many of the vintage classics?

Yeah. I think there's a lot of fuzz makers now that are testing and sorting their transistors really carefully. There is so much information available these days, and I can't believe that anyone would purposefully short-change anybody.

There is sort of a magic quotient in the traditional Fuzz Face circuit. But not everything revolves around the Fuzz Face. There doesn't seem to be any magic quotient around how to build a good wah. They talk about the Fasel inductors, and the halo inductors and all this kind of stuff. But I don't know if anyone's ever revealed a way to test the actual inductors to find the proper one you really want to use. So most of these guys don't want to throw any inductors away because the things cost so much.

And plenty of players hear rumors about magic ingredients and vintage effects – or even new ones – that are tonal nirvana, and end up buying something disappointing.

So much purchasing now is done online or remotely. They make a phone call or look something up online, cross their fingers, and pull out their credit card. And they don't necessarily try and play through the actual item they're going to take.

I had a guy write to me and say that he went into a store and tried a Fuzz Factory and he loved it, so he went home and ordered one online so he could get a better deal. Then the one he got didn't sound the same – the gain was higher, and he couldn't get the low-gain sound that he wanted, that he had gotten at the store. It turned out he had used a completely different type of guitar at the store – a guitar with a really low-gain pickup. So that's where the source of the low-gain was.

When I was still buying gear for myself quite a bit, I definitely would take my own guitar into the store, and would try to play through an amp that was identical to or at least similar to the one I used. With the recording studio, gear was coming in and out all the time, so I would come into contact and would have heard a particular piece and would hear it was for sale later. I could say, "Yeah, I want that." It's that up-close and personal experience you have.

Look at Jimi Hendrix. When he was working with Roger Mayer, Mayer was right there in the studio working with him. Roger would say, "What do you think about this one?" and Jimi would want a little more of this or that, so Roger would go away and make the change. That's really what you need to do – to be in close contact with the device you're going to be playing through.

If you're lucky as a designer, you have so much experience of hearing what people do with things that you can take your own guitar and amp and play with it and get to fall in love with the sound, until finally you've got the sound just right. Then you can release it and feel comfortable that it's a product people are going to want to hear.

Do you think there are any types of amps that pedals sound best with?

There are a lot of classic problems with certain amps. Like Fender Twins – you can hardly make a Fender Twin break up, and by the time you do you've been evicted and your wife and kids have divorced you, and you've got permanent tinnitus. That's the problem dealing with powerful clean amps, is getting them to give you your tube break-up sound, unless they've got a high enough gain that they break up pretty naturally. Somehow the 100-watt Marshalls, even though they're vicious sounding, have a softness to them that makes them sound less aggressive.

The biggest problem I see is that people are trying to get everything out of their amplifier at the same time that they're trying to get everything out of their pedals. They try to get distortion from their amp and from their pedals.

And you have to set things up completely differently to get the best out of either.

Exactly.

A lot of people seem to have trouble getting wah-wahs to work for them in certain rigs.

If you plug a wah into a terribly distorted Marshall, you might get lucky and get a good tone, especially if the harmonics coming out of the guitar are complex enough, such as with a Strat, so there are a lot of them available for the sweep range of the wah and each one of them can spike out. But even with a Les Paul – there's always a difficulty with a Les Paul, especially with the rhythm pickup. "Where did the wah go?" And then you go into a distorted amp, and it becomes even more blurry.

People have begun to insert things into this 'effects loop' in modern amps, and man, that is a whole other conundrum, because now the preamp of your amplifier is acting like a pedal itself. The output of that preamp could be 680 ohms impedance, it might be really low. It doesn't work to take the output of a guitar amp preamp and put it into a fuzz, for example. You can get certain tones, but you'll lose a lot of things.

On a Fuzz Face, the input impedance is so low that when you're playing it wide open on your guitar and you get that terribly distorted sound, if you grab the volume control on your guitar you can turn it down to clean it up so it becomes clean and bright. You can't do that if you go through a preamp first. There's no way. Even if you turn down the preamp, the output impedance on the preamp doesn't change like your guitar volume control does, so it doesn't change the input relationship with the pedal. The Fuzz Face stays fuzzy and it never cleans up, so you have to sacrifice so many of the magical things you get from using a fuzz directly in front of the amp.

So there is definitely a very big, complex problem that has evolved from using effects loops. And, for example, a wah in an effects loop is just the strangest thing. Now you've got complete spectral control over all this fuzz, and the whole power level shifts around on your power amplifier, and the whole relationship becomes very, very strange.

I get questions or even complaints a lot from people who are trying to do impossible combinations of things. They just haven't done enough experimentation to discover that the mistake they're making is they're trying to plug the wrong sound into the wrong sound, or the wrong impedance into the wrong impedance.

Which again, like you said, is trying to get all options from all parts of your sound chain at the same time.

You have to learn how to find the right combination of doing channel-switching to get to the dirty sounds, and then a few effects in the loop that sound best in the loop, and then channel-switching again to get back to your clean sounds to use the effects that sound best in front of the clean part of the amplifier. A big, warm, clear, clean tube amp with just enough breakup to give you some compression seems to be a good starting point for testing out pedals, to see what kind of tones you want to get, and see where you go from there.

Which, if you're a real pedalhead, is probably the best setup for you anyway.

Yeah. I've always loved Marshalls, I've always loved Bassmans, all the amps that have warmth and clarity in the first place, but have the ability to break up without getting like a sledgehammer. Twins are very useful for exquisitely accurate representations of a fuzz. You can almost see square waves coming out of a Twin. But as far as amps that you can get away with using a lot of pedals in front of, to me Marshalls – especially the 50-watters – and Bassmans, of all vintage, they're just spectacular. AC30s confuse me. They seem to have a sort of a hollowness. I've heard such beautiful recordings of them, but I seem to never experience that.

That's another example of a piece of vintage gear that some people will pay crazy money for, but which might not be set up right or in the right condition to give them what they're hoping to get.

I remember before they were reissued – before the latest reissue at least – there was definitely a holy grail thing associated with AC30s. Guys would be saying, "Oh, I found this AC30 that sounds so great." But they were usually so fragile. You could hear it in the guy's house and pay $2,000 or $3,000 for it, pick it up and put it in your car, and when you got it home it would just go 'kkkcchhh–kkkkccchhhh!' – because that's how they are, that's how they were from the very beginning. The tubes were mounted horizontally...

I think that's one design that some of the boutique amp makers who followed have really improved on, as far as build-quality at least – people like Matchless and TopHat and others...

Yeah, in the electronics in the amp at least. But those Vox blue speakers were such a big part of that sound, and they have to break in, too...

Back with pedals, do you have great belief in batteries over converters?

There are two things people need to know about carbon zinc batteries – and some people have huge beliefs that carbon zinc batteries sound better for fuzzes. Well, carbon zinc batteries have got a very high start voltage. The start voltage in a carbon zinc battery can be ten-and-a-half volts. I've seen them at 10.6 or 10.7 start voltage. You don't see that so much any more. Rockets used to make them that high; I can't seem to get Rockets any more, but I can get ones that are 10.2 or 10.3. At that higher voltage you seem to get a little more 'zip' out of a fuzz.

Alkaline will almost always be delivered at 9.3 or 9.2, so it's a whole volt lower. The output resistance – and batteries do have an output resistance just like a circuit does – for carbon zincs is much higher to start with, and it gets terrible toward the end of its life. It becomes so saggy that if you try to pull any power out of it it just goes, 'ppphhhhh...' – it's almost as though someone's inserted quite a large value resistor between your battery and the circuit.

On the Fuzz Factory I've got that effect: the Stab knob goes up to 10k, and you can insert the resistance that makes it sound as if the battery's about to die. The reason I did that is, when I was testing the circuit I put a couple of batteries in there that were dead, and I loved the sound and decided I would try to simulate it. What that comes from is that the surfaces of the electrodes inside of the battery – which are coated with contaminated chemicals – begin to hold back the ability for the thing to function as it starts to burn out. Less and less electrons can flow cleanly.

Alkalines, even toward the end of their lives, never have such a high resistance, so you never experience them going through the same sort of phases of that output resistance thing, and you also don't see a big spread of voltages over the lifetime of the battery. Alkalines are much more stable, so they're kind of nominal. You see a lot more changes in fuzz pedals over the lifetime of a carbon zinc battery: you'll hear pretty oscillation things you've never heard before, you'll see a roundness to the waves, to the square waves, that you'll never have with an alkaline.

But obviously no player can easily switch from the fresh battery to the nearly-dead battery mid-performance – which I guess is why you built this into the Fuzz Factory..
Yeah, you can use it with a power plate or an alkaline battery and get the same sound you'd get with any carbon zinc.

When I was recording in the studio sometimes we'd get a fuzz sound that was just incredible, and then it was late at night, maybe two o'clock in the morning and we'd have to go home. In order to preserve the sound, so we could continue recording the next day, I would always unplug the fuzz or maybe even pop the battery out to protect it. Then we'd come in and hook it up, and for the first couple of minutes it would be a little brighter, because it comes back to life. There's a change in the chemistry when you take the load off, and for a little while they're a higher voltage. It is kind of creepy.

Do the huge variables in the business drive you crazy sometimes?
They don't bug me too much. What I find is – like you were saying before – there's a mythology associated with these things, and it's because people haven't had enough experience and don't have enough background in what could cause those things to happen, that they don't develop a relationship with the thing and think to themselves, "OK, I should use an alkaline for this pedal or a carbon zinc for that one."

But if you want to know my direct recommendations, I think fuzzes should always use carbon zincs, and if you have a voltage tester yourself, try to find a nice, high voltage on one; if you find one that's terribly high – ten-and-a-half volts or something – listen to it when it's brand new and see if you like it, and that's how you can learn about your fuzz and which battery you like the best. When you're ready to record, you can use it at just the voltage you like best.

Another thing you should know about germaniums is they're terribly temperature sensitive. This is funny, but you should stick your germanium Fuzz Face-type pedal in the fridge. [Laughs.] Leave it there for a few hours, take it out, plug it in, and listen to the way it changes as it warms up – because it'll change a lot. The gain on the transistors will change almost by double, depending on the temperature range. So when it gets to just the right temperature… You could come up with your own little curve, your own little drawing: "After 15 minutes it sounded perfect…"

Or you could devise a little fridge unit to keep it chilled at just the right temperature…
They do. You could get one of those solid state coolers you get to chill a six-pack in your car.

That could be the next thing – have J. Myrold paint one up in Z.Vex graphics…
Exactly. 'Temperature Stabilized.' Then people would need power supplies just to cool their unit…

We've talked a lot about Fuzz Faces. Do you have any other favorite classic pedals?

There's a lot of them that people haven't really noticed over the years. Pearl made a phaser called the PH-44 – just knocked my socks off. The thing sounded like it was chewing gum… Do you remember the synthesizer sounds on Alan Parsons' *I Robot?*

Sure. It was a classic of its time.

Yeah. Well, I'm 44, so there are a lot of kids who have not ever heard that album. And there are a lot of synthesizer tones and textures on that album that are unique for that period. I think it's because there wasn't a huge amount of synthesizer stuff going on, where they really used and explored the textures of synths – except by Pink Floyd, who were produced by Alan Parsons – and if you go backwards you find The Who using synth on songs like 'Baba O'Reilly' or 'Won't Get Fooled Again' – and what you discover is that each one of these bands would be associated with a particular synthesizer. So each one would have a particular texture.

I heard the Alan Parsons Project, and there was something to the voicings of the synthesizers, and the human-ness of the voicings, that made me think of that as soon as I heard the Pearl phaser. I'm sure he didn't use it on that album, though – it sounds like synthetic stuff, but it's also very soft and very pretty. Very few people have heard it; it was never a popular phaser.

What else sticks out in your mind.

The Electro-Harmonix Polyphase. Not the Polyflange or the Polychorus. The Polyphase is much more rare. I don't really like flangers too much. The Polyflange always kind of bugged me. But the softness and gentleness of the Polyphase – it just had, once again, a human voicing to it. It almost had an emotional quality to it, as if it was very sad. It had an oscillator that let you sweep in an up-and-down fashion at the same time as it was sort of triggered like a triggered wah. And it was almost as if it was laughing, or maybe crying. If two people were involved and one was playing, the other could turn the knobs and make it sound as if it was trying to say something… and I really fell in love with that. Like it was trying to communicate or something.

Wow, and random sample-and-hold stuff can be amazing. The Robotalk is amazing. It's like an extreme version of my Ooh-Wah. I have a feeling it's at least partly based on the Maestro Sample & Hold, which was another filter that moved around randomly. But the Robotalk is distributed by my Japanese distributor, Prosound Communications.

Which of your own pedals is closest to your heart?

Well, it's always the simplest. The Wah-Probe. It's not terribly popular, but it's so pretty, and it's got such a nice, wide range. That circuit I use in the Ooh-Wah and the Seek-Wah and the Wah-Probe, you only really get to hear it shifting phase the way it does naturally in the Wah-Probe, as you sweep through it when you move your foot up and down, or your hand up and down, you can hear the phase twist, like it's phase shifting at the same time as it's wah-ing. I guess all the things I've fallen in love with have been phase shifting.

Maybe they have the most going on, short of weirdness.

Yeah. Flange, for example, can be such an extreme effect. And when you think of the great uses of flange they're usually in the midst of song mixes. What do we have? We have 'Life In The Fast Lane,' [The Eagles] which just totally blew me away…

Or 'Itchycoo Park.'

Yeah. And there was another one… 'Listen To The Music' by the Doobie Brothers.

And after those three, anyone who's going to do it again is going to sound like a cliché.

Sure. But there was one bad, bad use of it at the very beginning, and that was 'Sky Pilot.' Do you remember 'Sky Pilot?' It was this terrible song from the 1960s: "Sky pilot, how high can you fly?" [Zach begins to sing it, tapping a hand to the front of his mouth to simulate a flanging sound]. It went like that, up and down, all the way through the sound. Non-stop. You were positively queasy by the end, like a bad carnival ride.

I think that's the difficulty with flanging that goes up and down. Every time it comes up again you feel you've been through this, "Let's hear something else, please." It's not that pretty, it's kind of grating, and it gives you that inside-out kind of queasiness. It's too similar to have something shooting toward you and moving away from you.

Oh, and another thing of my own that's probably my favorite – the Nano-Head. It's my favorite for having accomplished a lot of things at the same time. And it's invisible, you can't see from the outside what kinds of things I had to do to make it possible. I had to make a 230V DC power supply that operated from 12V inside that box, and operated close to high-gain circuitry.

The power supply uses something called 'negistor' technology, and I don't think anyone's ever used a negistor in a commercial product before. Negistors were always circulated in electronics hobby magazines, and I spent my whole childhood reading those things. As I got older and was running out of ideas for my pedals, I would go to the library to look up one thing, but I'd end up reading through a whole year's worth of things.

I stumbled across this thing called 'The Mysterious Negistor,' an article in *Popular Electronics*. The negistor is a modified transistor, where with three components you can make a voltage-controlled oscillator that delivers a perfect sawtooth wave, which is really unusual. It's so simple that I fell in love with the thing.

But it doesn't quite work at 9V, you need just a little more. I was working with 12V for this tube amp because the filaments require 6V each, and there's two of them, and so I strung them together to make 12 and started with that as a basis – that's just enough to get a negistor going. I had developed this complex oscillator-based power supply then found out I couldn't use it, so I kept the oscillator part – because it was a switcher power supply and you had to have an oscillator to get it up to speed (I was running it at 25kHz) and I replaced it with my old favorite, the negistor.

It replaced, like, 15 components with three. It worked perfectly, and it fixed the entire circuit. I thought, "Oh my god, there's got to be some flaw." But there wasn't, it worked perfectly. I was able to squeeze the whole power supply down to 22 components, and no chips. There's one power transistor and one coil, and the rest is a bunch of little parts.

At high gain settings on the Nano-Head, if you put a scope across the output, it's got a full volt of 27kHz noise coming out – which is just above the hearing range of cats and dogs, so it doesn't bother anyone. Except maybe bats. But it's just low enough voltage so that it doesn't interfere with the guitar.

So the kinds of things I had to accomplish in order to figure out how to build the Nano were much more complex and technical than anything I'd ever encountered designing pedals, so I feel proud of that particular piece.

What tubes are in it?

They're tiny, tiny little things. They're 3/8″ in diameter and about an inch tall. They're 6021W, a military tube. I've purchased enough stock to build them for the next ten years, and I did that on purpose so I'd not have to worry that someone would come along and buy up the stock and I wouldn't be able to get them any more.

So if someone needs a new tube you can supply that too.

But that's kind of a weird thing, because from all the research I've done on this particular tube, I don't think anyone's ever going to need a new one.

There was a new technology associated with the coating that was used on the cathodes for these tubes, which was developed in 1960, and it was the last era of the military putting money into developing new tubes, before transistors came in and took over. So the last little bit of money came into developing these reliable, highly miniaturized military tubes, then they were abandoned. But the technology was used to manufacture those tubes all the way up to 1987. So my tubes are all labeled with date codes of 1987, 1986 and 1985.

Oh, also, regarding the negistor – negistors use a quantum physics phenomenon that includes time reversal and absolute-zero stuff as well... which I think is exceedingly cute, to have such a small vacuum-tube guitar amp with a time-travel device inside. You don't get that every day.

BOB WEIL, OF VISUAL SOUND

The quest for the 'perfect visually referenced volume pedal' led Tennessean Bob Weil to found Visual Sound, a company now far better known for pedals that make a serious racket rather than those that merely passively process your volume level. The Jekyll & Hyde and Route 66 are popular two-channel overdrives that have found favor with a lot of players, and provide an alternative to the more expensive 'boutique' makes on the market today.

What first got you interested in effects pedals?

I've been a guitarist since 1980, so I've been using effects for a long time. I didn't start messing around with the circuits of them until around 1995, when I soon got hooked on all the tonal possibilities every pedal seems to have.

Do you remember your first pedal?

An MXR Distortion+. It sounds like garbage to my ears now, but back then there wasn't much else that could really make your amp go over the top.

When did you decide you could make better pedals than were already out there?

That was around 1990, when I bought my first volume pedal, an Ernie Ball. I became frustrated with the abrupt taper of the pot and the lack of a visual reference. I remember thinking, "Shoot, there's only a pot and a string in there... How hard could it be to design something better?"

I was shocked that nobody had ever made a volume pedal with a visual reference, so I set out to learn enough about electronics to design a 'visual' volume pedal. After a few years of studying at the library, asking lots of questions, and experimenting (the internet hadn't been invented yet), I finally learned enough to put together the first prototypes of Visual Volume. They were extremely well received by the musicians I showed them to, so I started Visual Sound based on that one product at the beginning of 1995. I already had a degree in Business and about ten years of sales and marketing experience in other industries.

Do you have any overriding goals that you keep in mind when designing or building a new unit?

It has to be musical. By that I mean the effects have to be something I would use in a live performance myself. It has to create a sound that would enable me to play what I hear in my head and heart, not hinder my playing.

The equipment has to also be pretty bullet-proof. I hate having products coming back to us for repair – and fortunately, not many do come back.

Do you believe there are any specific essential ingredients in a good-sounding analog effects pedal?

We could get into 'exotic' capacitors and old carbon comp resistors, but I would hardly call them 'essential.' A well-designed circuit will still sound very good even with cheap components. Will it sound better with high-priced components? That's subjective. For example, I recently met a guitarist who had Robert Keeley modify the overdrive channel in one of our Route 66 pedals. Keeley had replaced all of the ceramic caps with nice little polyester caps and had replaced the opamp, even though it was already a JRC4558. He had even changed some of the resistor values and used metal-film resistors instead of the standard carbon resistors we use. I did a blind A/B test with this guitarist using a stock Route 66 and the Keeley mod Route 66. Guess which one sounded better to that guitarist? The original one with the 'cheaper' parts... I had to agree as well, even though I was thinking the modded one might sound better before we did the A/B test.

Visual Sound's Bob Weil.

Judging by your Route 66 overdrive, you must be a Tube Screamer fan. Any views on the JRC4558 chips that people rave about in those pedals?

OK, let's kill the mythology about the 4558, shall we? The JRC4558 was never discontinued or changed. It has always been made by Japan Radio Corporation. They changed their name a while back to New Japan Radio, and the part number in various wholesale catalogs changed to NJM4558, but the chip never changed. It still says JRC4558 on the chip, for that matter. I got all this information from an engineering manager at New Japan Radio directly, by the way.

Is there any particular 'snake oil' talked about vintage pedals, or even boutique designs, that gets on your nerves?

The internet has become the ultimate 'urban legend' machine. Someone thinks they heard somebody say something important and they go and put it up on the web for the whole world to see, without checking the facts first. Then the rumor mill gets going and the myth takes on a life of its own. Take true bypass switching, for example. A lot of guys don't even know what it is, but they think it's really important when they're shopping for a new pedal. The fact is, Boss has never had true bypass switching and look how many great guitarists have made great records using Boss pedals. I'm not a big fan of Boss, by the way, but that fact alone has got to make you think a bit.

Visual Sound pedals do not use true bypass switching, because I came up with an excellent buffering system which is better than true bypass. As Bob Bradshaw, Pete Cornish, and other 'rig designers for the stars' found out long ago, true bypass does nothing to help cable capacitance when you've got lots of effects running in series and long cable runs to the guitar and amp. But a good preamp buffer preserves your signal no matter what's in-between you and your amp.

For example, if you have a Route 66 Overdrive/Compression pedal first in your chain of effects, it will make you sound like you're plugged straight into the amp even though you've got several 'tone-killing' pedals and 50' of cable following it... it's a beautiful thing. Another downside to true bypass is the loud mechanical click you get from the 3PDT switch, combined with the electrical pop you get through your amp. The 3PDT switches also tend to be less reliable because there are three separate sections of the switch that can potentially break.

Do you have any opinions one way or the other in the analog/digital sound quality debate?

Yes, definitely. Although digital delay can be made to sound very analog, other effects like overdrive, distortion, chorus, flange, and others really don't sound the same, even with the modern marvel of modeling. You especially notice this in live performance. There's this fake and distant quality to the sound that just doesn't cut it.

What are your views on amps to use with pedals? Are there any 'types' that work consistently well to show off effects in their best light?

The ideal pedal amp, for me, is one that is not inherently bright or high-gain. Obviously tube amps are the best in general. It's all very subjective, but some of my favorites are Fenders or old Marshalls (like the Bluesbreaker). Some of the boutique amps are great, but you tend to pay a lot for them. One of the best sounding pedal-friendly amps I know of in the mass-market, reasonable-price realm is the Fender Hot Rod DeVille 2x12″. It's heavy, but has great overall tone. The Reverend Hellhound and Fender Hot Rod DeLuxe are two other great amps that are reasonably priced and lighter weight. I mention these, not because they are necessarily the 'best amps on the planet,' but because you don't have to spend thousands of dollars to get great tone. Our pedals and these amps prove that. While you can now get tube amps with three or more channels, it's still usually the same basic overdrive tone on all channels at varying levels of distortion. If you really want flexibility, just use an amp that has a great clean channel and get your overdrive/distortion from pedals… The variety is endless.

Any noise-reduction tips for large pedal chains or long cable runs? Do you believe in driving the front of the chain with a unity gain preamp to go HiZ to LoZ, for example?

I don't really believe in that stuff per se. But I can recommend a good noise reduction pedal – the Decimator from ISP Technologies works unusually well. It was designed by the guy who made the Hush system, but it's a much better, more up-to-date circuit. I gave one to Johnny Hiland a while back and he swears by it. If you use something like that, you don't have to get an engineering degree to know how to set up your rig for optimal impedance matching.

Any good pedalboard bypass tricks, or loop tricks, or A/B tricks you can share?

Well, this isn't a trick, but a lot of people don't seem to understand what an effects loop is for on many amps, so I'll tell you. You only need to use your effects loop if you use your amp's overdrive channel. If you only use pedal overdrive/distortion with the clean channel of your amp (like I do), then don't bother with the effects loop. If you do use amplifier overdrive, then you should put delay effects in the loop to keep it from sounding very muddy.

Do you put your faith in batteries or large converters to power multiple pedals?

I've always hated buying and changing batteries, so I've always used adapters. It's also very un-cool to have a battery die in the middle of a gig. The drag about 9V adapters is that they take up too much space on a power strip, the cords are too short, and they only power a few pedals at best. Power 'bricks' are OK, but they're expensive and take up two spaces on your pedalboard. That's why I came up with the 1 Spot. It's a 9V adapter that's so small it only takes up one spot on your power strip, yet it can power an entire pedalboard, no matter how many pedals you have of just about any brand. It also has a 10′ cable and can work anywhere in the world without a transformer. It just solves all those annoying problems that guitarists like me have put up with for years. And it's very inexpensive too.

Are there some artists using your pedals on record that we should listen out for?

The Route 66 pedal was used quite a bit on U2's *All That You Can't Leave Behind* album. Just about everything The Strokes have recorded has gone through Jekyll & Hyde pedals. Johnny Hiland's upcoming CD on Favored Nations will have all our pedals all over it. I've heard that lots of sessions in LA and Nashville have had our pedals on them, but I don't have a catalog of all the songs.

MIA THEODORATUS, OF FRANTONE

Mia Theodoratus is marketing director of New York-based Frantone, a role which – as in most smaller companies – finds her also taking some development duties and even plenty of hands-on work. Theodoratus is a classically trained harpist who now plays a lot of jazz and rock, which gives her some unique views on tone and amplification. She works alongside Frantone founder Fran Blanche who, in addition to her original Frantone designs, has designed major pedals for other manufacturers, including Electro-Harmonix's New York City Big Muff and Frequency Analyzer.

Where did the whole Frantone thing begin?

Fran is probably one of the last people in the United States who started by doing old electronics and Heathkits and things. Before she even played guitar she was messing around with electronics. She started playing and didn't have money to buy equipment, so she started modding out her guitar and building her own effects. She also found work restoring old radios and that kind of thing. That segment of the United States where there used to be electronic hobbyists has almost died out at this point, so Fran's like the last of that line of self-taught electricians with engineering knowledge. Because she started from electronics, everything is more practical. Like, she doesn't think there's some kind of electronic voodoo in different components, like people who think that electronic current isn't a logical force.

Which must give the company an advantage, in the R&D department anyway, over all the people out there that are following the myths that are rife in the pedal world today.

Certainly when there's something wrong with a piece of electronics sometimes it's hard to figure out what's going on. But that's how Fran started; when she needed a new television set, she would have to go and fix one. And then when she went to work for Electro-Harmonix she just got thrown into the gladiators' ring, and learned how to make very quirky designs work with modern components, which pushed her up to the next level.

After she did the New York City Big Muff and made it work – within Mike Matthew's parameters and with the components she was given – that made her top of her game. The two things that have made her unique is that she has an extensive electronic hobbyist's background, and she knows how components work in the real world. There seem to be three camps of people who make effects: there are businesspeople who just want to sell lots of stuff, and there's nothing wrong with that; and then there are engineers who don't really understand musicians, and don't really understand how components work in real life – just because it says something on a schematic doesn't mean it does that all the time, and doesn't mean it *sounds* good. For example, I have to search for this certain PCI capacitor that for some weird, quirky reason sounds better than all the other ones – and none of my suppliers and no engineer understands, but it sounds better, there's something about it. It's not snake oil, it's just made differently.

And then the third group of people who make effects pedals are musicians who don't really have an electronics background, and sort of learn how to fix their own stuff but don't understand basic nuts-and-bolts electronics. Fran is in this weird fourth category – there aren't that many people who have bothered to go back and learn basic electronics.

It does seem to be important to combine the tech knowledge and the musician's sensibilities.

Yeah. And we're also a little different in that we have no ego about what we do. We make product that people buy, and we try to adhere to what people want. The reality of, like, distortion pedals is each guitarist has maybe six to ten, and they're all constantly rotating. So if you make a quality product, there's just as much room on someone's pedalboard for a Frantone Sweet, or a Z.Vex Fuzz Factory, or a Roger Mayer pedal, and the reality is that they switch them in and out all the time.

It's fascinating, isn't it. Something great comes along and suddenly this is 'the best,' and

nobody builds a better whatever – like when vintage pedals started becoming all the rage again and everybody was raving about Ibanez Tube Screamers. Then pretty quickly a lot of makers started improving upon them – and also maybe the ear gets tired of a sound, or just used to it – and all of a sudden something else sounds juicy and huge, and 'the best.'

Yeah. I certainly see that. Our slant on what we do is that we just make usable pedals for rock and blues musicians, that can go extreme if they want to, but everything has a usable, musical setting. And we try to pull different sounds by using different designs and components.

Everything we do is original. Some people seem to think that the Sweet is a Big Muff copy, but we made sure that it has nothing to do with the Big Muff circuit. And the sound of the germanium transistors is just so wonderful. It's like when you get a Fuzz Face – a really good one, that hasn't been tinkered with – and one of the Sweet pedals, they all have that crunch, which is a fantastic sound.

What's your own background?

I started out as a classical harpist and went to a bunch of fancy conservatories, and I have an MFA in music performance. I went electric because I was playing with Charlie Haden and the Liberation Orchestra and I worked *so* hard… I'm sitting there with my acoustic and my little Fishman piezo pickup, and they couldn't hear a damn thing I played, because there were four saxophones. It pissed me off so much, I just decided that if I had been electric I would have been able to go straight to the board and my signal would have been hot enough that I would have stood a chance. So it was like a no-brainer – at that point I started buying electric instruments and messing around with effects pedals when I could afford them.

I played with other jazz people and I played in a bunch of rock bands. Then I got a job selling tubes at New Sensor, and I began noticing a lot of other factors about my sound. Classical musicians don't have a really good ear for tone, they're more into notes, and rock is more into tone. When I started working at New Sensor I really started to hone in on what tone was, and really started learning the difference between the different amps I was using, because my first amp sucked…

So I started experimenting and learning the difference between digital and analog, and started to hone my ear in. I love gear, so I started doing marketing for Fran when she started Frantone running. That was in 2000, but she started making pedals in 1994. She started when the boutique market was really new, with the Hep Cat and the Peachfuzz. People would call her up and call her names because her pedals were too expensive – and she was charging $140 for a Hep Cat.

Which is nothing in today's boutique market…

And now on eBay they go for like $225 used. But the market has changed.

Yeah. Some would say it's gone crazy, but maybe people have just started appreciating what goes into a hand-built pedal.

How I look at it, and what I tell people now, is you can buy a cheap pedal that's made in a country that doesn't really pay their workers very well, and it's going to last you maybe three or four years, and it's not true bypass. Then you're buying something that is throwaway, basically, 'cos that stuff can't be fixed. Or the amount you would spend to buy a quality boutique pedal is usually only $60 to $70 more, and you get true bypass, and all the people I know in our little niche, all the upper ten manufacturers, will repair their stuff for such a minimal charge. And we pay our people a living wage – everyone gets paid except me and Fran [laughs].

Thinking a little more about the whole concept of tone, one of the things that fascinates me, as a guitarist, is the fact that if something sounds good you can stand in a room for two hours and

slam out even the simplest chords and riffs and it's a highly pleasurable experience. So many guitarists seem to have that kind of awareness and deep appreciation of the pure sensuality of tone, and are on that constant search for 'the sweeter sound.' Do you feel as manufacturers you are always chasing some 'holy grail' of tone?

Well, our philosophy is to make tools that people can use, and we aren't trying to impose what we feel is the 'ultimate overdrive' or the 'ultimate fuzz.' What we're trying to do is give people a palette. Rock'n'roll and popular music is not really about what you play, it's about how you say it and the method you use. So what Fran tries to do is, she tries to give the musician a palette to express what they want, with what sort of timbre. It's a different way of looking at it. We tend to have settings that are just very straightahead that people can use in a working situation.

Like, the Peachfuzz is probably one of the most popular working musicians' pedals for sidemen, and it's the one we see at least once a week on late night television and variety shows, where they'll have a singer-songwriter and a group of hired musicians, and there's the Peachfuzz. Because it makes a sound that can accompany a singer-songwriter, it's not too abrasive. With every pedal we try to have a focus like that. The Creampuff is sort of a rhythm focus, and the Peachfuzz really is sort of a 1960s soloing backup. Each one has a specialty or a niche, and we try to make it so there are as many variations within the tone and the bass, so that people can really have a working, reliable unit.

Certainly plenty of companies out there are trying to make the wildest version of this or that, but sometimes you play with them for an afternoon and are impressed with some way-out sounds, but in the end there aren't that many you'd end up using.

Yeah, and for us it's sort of the economics of it. For Fran and I, this is what we do for a living, too. So you have to make things that will work for other people. We do have some things here at the shop that are really outrageous and will make the shingles fly off your house, you know; but we aren't making effects for ourselves, we're making them for other people to use.

It's like when you look at a catwalk, and you see these really skeletal women walking down the catwalk in things that you'd never want to see your mother wearing – or even maybe your girlfriend – and you're like, "What was that designer thinking?" And we would rather be a quality black leather motorcycle jacket, that never really goes out of style, and you can pretty much wear it with anything.

Was there a point when you and Fran looked at the market and said, "We can do it better," something that made you feel that was viable?

We felt there was a need in the market for good, original designs. There are people who do amazing copies of Tube Screamers and Fuzz Faces, and we really thought people would want original designs for different kinds of tones,

Frantone's pedal-playing classical/jazz/fusion/celtic harpist, Mia Theodoratus.

and there was a market for it. After we'd been in this business for three years, and Fran had been in it for six, it was also what we knew how to do, so what else are you going to do?

Of course thinking about tone – and designing – is the fun part. The sexy part is the designing of the concept for the new pedal; but the boring part is, like, nobody wants to drill out 200 cases. And that's the reality of it. The daily drudge is a little daunting. But we saw our niche, and we thought if we acted right now, nobody was really there.

It's surprising that there really aren't more original sounds going out there, considering the sky's the limit electronically. And it has to be said, your pedals look fantastic too.

Thanks. And the other problem some people have is that they do it sort of as a vanity business. But when we're making our 900th Sweet pedal and making that just as good as our first run, that's what counts. It's tiring, and it's a lot of work to make sure every pedal is worth it from the end user's perspective. They save up for this thing, they buy it, and they open it up and it's their little baby. And we have to make sure every pedal lives up to the quality they expect, and that's where the hard part comes.

Fran happens, for better or worse, to have an amazing ear for fuzz and distortion, right up there with Roger Mayer's, and that's really rare. I don't know where one even gets that – just to figure out the different kinds, and know how to create them. She just was born with this ability to figure out different circuits to make great-sounding distortion pedals. But that's sort of the easy part. The hard part is to make sure that every one is as good as the first, especially in an internet society...

The only problem we've ever had with the Sweet pedal was with this guy who had a souped-up Mesa/Boogie he'd tinkered with, and he had really hot pickups on his guitar. He wanted to play at ten with his guitar gain at seven, and then he wanted to fling the Sweet's gain all the way up. You know what that does? It's a huge, massive shrieking feedback. So he got on the internet and was saying all this crap about the pedal... I was on the phone with him for 30 minutes explaining that the nature of the Sweet is that it is high gain, and you just can't do that with it.

Other makers in your market have told me much the same thing; the main problems they get from customers are with players trying to use the pedals in the wrong applications, particularly thinking they can use a fuzz or distortion pedal to kick their already high-gain amp up over the top, and then complaining that it just adds noise, or they can't control the feedback. Ideally, I guess you'd like to tell them to give it to a friend with a Marshall plexi or something.
Yeah [laughs]. Or, you know, if you don't like it, don't buy it. You don't have to like them. Some people like chocolate, some people don't. It doesn't make chocolate bad if you don't happen to like it. Leave it on the shelf.

Overall, though, Frantone seems to have built up a very favorable reputation.
There was one guy who posted a bad review of the Peachfuzz, but we had a feeling he was another manufacturer. He used the name of a really old jazz musician, and we were like, "This guy's not real..."

What has been your most popular pedal?
The two steadiest ones have been Peachfuzzes and Sweets. Probably the Peachfuzz, because it's just such a meat and potatoes pedal, it's a usable tool. But the Brooklyn – we just had our first Brooklyn review out, and we cannot keep the Brooklyn overdrive in stock. I thought the world did not need another overdrive; we had a little meeting and I voted for no Brooklyn – but Fran went ahead and made it. It's really, really good and it sounds nothing like a Tube Screamer, so the Brooklyn is probably going to be our most popular pedal. We just did a new batch, and we're probably going to be out of it in a week.

My own favorite, though, is the Glacier... It's just amazing because, well, Fran was the one who did the update of the [E-H] Frequency Analyzer, and she wanted to make it better but Mike wouldn't upgrade it and spend the money for the parts, so this is like the ultimate version of that. When we first started out Fran used to do mods and repair other people's pedals, and she took all the things that just didn't work well and weren't musical in other people's ring modulators, and fixed all the problems. So it has a regulated power supply, so you always know what your getting; it's full range, it tracks on bass, guitar or keyboards, so it has full scope and doesn't cut out any of your tone; and man, it's crazy. It can get beyond that '(I Can't Get No) Satisfaction' sound by Devo, and then it can go really normal and get a beautiful tremolo with the selectable waveform. And it has an auxiliary input, so you can trigger it from a drum machine or whatever... [laughs]. It's so much fun.

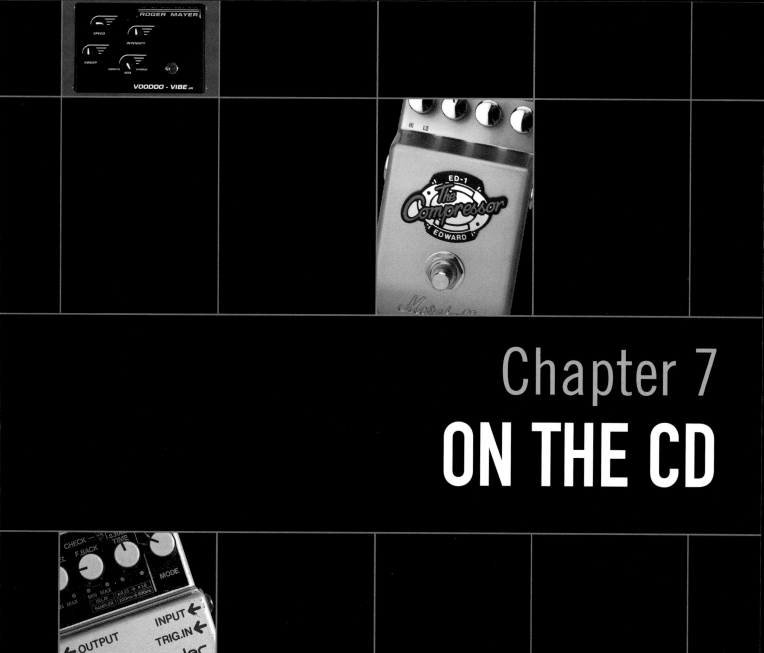

Chapter 7
ON THE CD

The attached sound-samples CD (all 92 tracks of it) has been recorded with the utmost consideration for consistency in sound quality, with a view to making it an accurate and comparative guide to the relative sounds of different types and makes of pedals. To that end, no compression or EQ has been used in the recording process, which was designed to give as much of an in-the-room sound as possible.

The pedal settings in the notes below, as well as the amp settings, are given in the 'o'clock' style – ie 3:00 being a three-quarters rotation of the stated control knob, rather than 3 on a scale of 10 – as this is an easy, universal visual reference. A few exceptions, primarily where an amp or pedal is famous for a printed number scale, are noted where they occur.

The control positions selected for each type of effect were intended to get them as close as possible to the same sonic settings, rather than to simply turn the dials to the exact same positions (recognizing the fact that different makes of the same effect type can sound very different even when set to the exact same control positions). The exception to this rule are the TS-808, TS9 and TS10 Tube Screamers in the Overdrives section, where controls were set identically for direct comparison betwee these three from the Ibanez series.

Recording details:

Amps used

The majority of pedal types, unless otherwise stated, were played through a 20W 1x12″ TopHat Club Royale combo (serial number 666) with EL84 output tubes and Celestion G12H-30 speaker. Controls set as follows: Volume 9:15, Treble 9:15, Mid 2:00, Bass 11:00, Cut 3:30 with Strat (2:00 with Tele), Master 3:00, Boost switch Off. The tremolos and boosters were played through an all-original 18W 1x12″ tweed 1960 Fender Tremolux with 6V6GT output tubes and Jensen speaker – the former in order to compare them to the amp's own tremolo, the latter because it's just fun to boost a good tweed amp – with the Instrument channel Volume set to 4 and the Tone set to 5.5 (in this case these are the markings on the amp's own 1-12 control scale).

Guitars

An original 1957 Fender Telecaster (maple neck, original electronics) and 1964 Stratocaster (rosewood neck, original electronics) were used throughout; the specific guitar and pickup selections are noted at the top of each effect category listing below.

Microphone, preamp, recording system, bits & bobs

The two small, sub-20W combos were employed because this enabled the use of a sensitive figure-eight pattern Coles 4038 ribbon microphone. It's a mike that, I feel, provides a more 'real' and in-the-room sound than almost anything available, short of some multi-thousand-dollar tube capacitor mikes. The Coles was placed approximately 14″ in front of and slightly above the combo speaker, and run through a custom-made 'vintage Altec style' dual channel tube mike preamp, a unit that offers excellent clarity and presence. The mike pre was patched directly into a MOTU 828 converter and each take recorded direct to hard-disk.

Two categories of pedals were DI'd – the choruses and the distortions. This was to enable a clear, perfectly matched stereo image in the stereo versions of the former, and to provide the most untainted picture of 'unit-generated distortion' in the latter, rather than combined amp-overdrive and pedal distortion. The choruses were DI'd through the tube mike pre (which has Hi-Z inputs for that purpose), and the distortions through a PAiA 'Stack In A Box' in order to use its basic speaker emulation facilities.

Connecting cables included 18′ Horizon guitar cords at either end, with 6″ jumpers between pedals where more than one pedal was used at a time. The pick (plectrum) was a medium-weight black Gibson 'teardrop' type.

The riffs

All of the riffs used as examples were played 'live' straight through the effect in question. Recordings made for the purposes of comparing other types of sound equipment sometimes employ 'one take' samples, which are recorded DI'd to disk then routed back through each test item in turn, via a matching transformer – essentially a reverse DI. This works well with other types of gear because it gives a consistent standard; but with guitar pedals, the direct interaction with the guitar's high-impedance pickup is an important factor in each pedal's performance, so I felt it was crucial that each pedal tested here be linked directly to the guitar.

Other than where specifically stated, none have buffers or line drivers or any other effects placed before them. For this reason, there will be some slight variations in the performances, but all are consistent enough for comparative purposes.

The riffs themselves are all original compositions by the author, and mostly intended to emulate a style or styles of playing with which the particular type of effect is most associated. You might detect that a few are 'in the style of' a particular artist known to use such a pedal, but otherwise they are merely intended as brief licks that show off what the effect – rather than the player – can do.

The 92 tracks:

Track number	Length of track

FUZZ BOXES
(TopHat amp, Strat, bridge pickup)

1   Fuzz Face (red, original)   0:51
Volume 11:30, Fuzz 3:00
NOTES: original red Dallas-Arbiter unit with two NKT275
germanium transistors

2   Jacques Fuse Blower (factory)   0:51
Volume 9:30, Fuz (sic) max

3   Roger Mayer Spitfire Fuzz   0:51
Volume 2:00, Drive 3:30

4   Z.Vex Fuzz Factory (fuzz sound)   0:51
Vol 9:00, Gate 10:30, Comp 10:30, Drive 12:00, Stab max

5   Voodoo Lab Super Fuzz   0:51
Volume 10:00, Resonance 1:45, Tone 2:00, Attack (fuzz) 3:00

6   Roger Mayer Voodoo-Axe   0:51
Gain 2:00, Fatness 1:00, Output 1:15

7   **Z.Vex Fuzz Factory (noises)**   0:32
produced by alternately manipulating the Stab,
Drive & Comp controls

COMPRESSORS
(TopHat amp; 'heavy' Tele bridge pickup, 'soft' Strat middle pickup)

8   **Ibanez Compressor (late 1970s)**
heavy – Sustain 3:15, Level 12:00   **0:32**
9   soft – Sustain 10:45, Level 1:00   **0:20**

10   **MXR Dyna Comp (box logo)**
heavy – Output 1:15, Sensitivity 4:00   **0:32**
11   soft – Output 2:00, Sensitivity 10:30   **0:20**

12   **Demeter Compulator**
heavy – Compression 3:00, Volume 3:30   **0:37**
NOTES: the 'sucking' and 'pumping' at the end of this riff are
genuine characteristics of the sustained chord.
13   soft – Compression 10:30, Volume 2:00   **0:21**

14   **Visual Sound Route 66 (compressor side)**
heavy – Sustain 2:00, Tone 12:00, Gain 11:00   **0:33**
15   soft – Sustain 10:00, Tone 11:30, Gain 10:45   **0:20**

16   **Marshall ED-1 Compressor**
heavy – Emphasis 10:30, Vol 10:30, Attack 9:30, Comp 2:30   **0:33**
17   soft – Emphasis 1:30, Vol 12:15, Attack 2:00, Comp 10:30   **0:21**

CHORUSES
(Tele bridge pickup; DI'd, in stereo where applicable)

18   **Ibanez BCL Bi-Mode Chorus**   0:29
Speed A – 2:00 B – 11:00, Width A –11:00 B –2:00

19   **Uni-Vibe Stereo Chorus**   0:29
Mix 8:00 (near max), Speed 11:00, Intensity 1:30

20   **T.C. Electronic Stereo Chorus+ Pitch Mod & Flanger**
Speed 2:00, Width 1:30, Intensity 1:45   0:29

21   **DOD FX65 Chorus**   0:29

22   **Pearl CH-02 Chorus (mono)**   0:29
Speed 11:00, Delay Time 2:00, Depth 3:00

23   **Ibanez CS-505 Chorus (c1980)**   0:25
Speed 11:00, Depth 3:00

24	**Boss CE-2 Chorus (mono)**	**0:25**
	Rate 10:30, Depth 3:15	

25	**Boss DCD-2**	**0:27**
	Mode: 4	

26	**Boss Digital Dimension DC-3**	**0:27**
	E.Level 2:00, EQ 2:00, Rate 10:30, Depth 3:00	

BOOSTERS
(Strat bridge pickup, Tremolux amp Tone 5.5, Vol 4)

27	**Fulltone Fat Boost**	**0:20**
	Vol 1:00, Tone max, Drive 2:00	

28	**Z.Vex Super Duper 2-in-1**	**0:22**
	Ch2 'master' 1:00, 'drive' 1:00; Ch2 'drive' 12:00	

29	**Roger Mayer Concorde+**	**0:21**
	Output 2:15, Drive 10:30, Tone 2:15	
	NOTES: Tone is really a 'fatness' control and works in the reverse way to most, making sound fatter as it's turned up.	

30	**MXR Micro Amp (reissue)**	**0:21**
	Gain 1:15	

WAH-WAHS AND AUTO-WAHS
(funk – straight through, Strat middle p'up; fuzz – Strat bridge p'up, with Roger Mayer Spitfire following the wah, set Vol 2:00 Drive 2:00)

31	**Cry Baby (original Jen, Fasel inductor)**	
	funk	**0:40**
32	fuzz	**0:30**

33	**Dunlop 535Q Cry Baby**	
	funk – Range first position, Q 10:30, Boost 10:30	**0:38**
34	fuzz – Range first position, Q 10:30, Boost 10:30	**0:29**

35	**Fulltone Clyde Wah**	
	funk	**0:37**
36	fuzz	**0:29**

37	**Xotic Effects Robotalk Envelope Filter & Random Arrpegiator (sic)**	
	as auto wah – Vol 12:15, Range 5:00, Freq 12:30 (Strat neck pickup)	**0:30**
38	slow, random arpeggios – Vol 12:15, Range 12:30, Freq 12:30, Rate 11:30 (Strat bridge pickup)	**0:35**

39 Z.Vex Seek Wah
slow arpeggios – four pulses, Speed 11:30, knobs 1-4 set
1:00, 9:00, 1:00, 9:00   **0:41**

40 fast and weird – eight pulses, Speed 9:00, knobs 1-8 set
12:30, 9:00, 12:00, 9:00, 3:15, 12:00, 7:30, 10:30   **0:21**

OVERDRIVES
(soft OD blues riff Strat neck pickup, bypassed @ 0:25, then heavy rock
riff @ 0:38 Strat bridge pickup)

41 Blackstone 2SV3 MOSFET Overdrive   **1:11**
blues (Brown channel) – Level 3:30, Drive 2:00, EQ: 2:00
rock (Red channel) – Level 1:45, Drive 4:00, EQ: 2:00

42 Klon Centaur   **1:11**
blues – Gain 10:00, Treble 12:00, Output 1:15
rock – Gain 3:00, Treble 10:30, Output 11:30

43 Fulltone Full-Drive 2 (Boost off)   **1:11**
blues – Vol 11:00, Tone 2:00, FM, OD 9:30
rock – Vol 2:00, Tone 2:00, Vintage, OD 3:15

44 Voodoo Lab Sparkle Drive   **1:11**
blues – Gain 10:00, Tone 12:00, Clean 10:30, Vol 1:45
rock – Gain 2:00, Tone 11:30, Clean 10:00, Vol 1:00

45 Jacques Tube Blower   **1:11**
blues – Low 3:00, Hi 1:00, Drive 10:00, Level 1:00
rock – Low 2:00, Hi 12:00, Drive 2:00, Level 11:00

46 HomeBrew Electronics Power Screamer   **1:11**
blues – Gain 9:30, Tone 2:30, Level 12:30, Diode – Heavy Comp
rock – Gain 3:15, Tone 2:30, Level 12:30, Diode – Tight

47 Boss OD-1   **1:11**
blues – Level 12:00, Over Drive 10:45
rock – Level 12:30, Over Drive 5:00 (max)

48 Frantone Brooklyn   **1:11**
blues – Drive 10:45, Tone 3:00, Vol 12:00
rock – Drive 3:00, Tone 1:30, Vol 10:15

49 Ibanez TS-808 Tube Screamer (c1980)   **1:11**
blues – Drive 10:15, Tone 11:00, Level 3:00
rock – Drive 3:00, Tone 12:00, Level 1:00
NOTES: single JRC4558D chip.

50   Ibanez TS9 Tube Screamer   **1:11**
blues – Drive 10:15, Tone 11:00, Level 3:00
rock – Drive 3:00, Tone 12:00, Level 1:00
NOTES: JRC2043 chip.

51   Ibanez TS10 Tube Screamer   **1:11**
blues – Drive 10:15, Tone 11:00, Level 3:00
rock – Drive 3:00, Tone 12:00, Level 1:00
NOTES: Taiwanese but with JRC4558D chip.

52   Visual Sound Route 66 (OD side only)   **1:11**
blues – Drive 10:45, Tone 11:00, Level 1:15
rock – Drive 3:00, Tone 12:00, Level 12:00

53   Roger Mayer Concorde+ (set as OD)   **1:11**
blues – Output 1:45, Drive 12:30, Tone 3:15
rock – Output 11:15, Drive 3:00, Tone 5:00 (max)

54   Dinosaural Tube Bender   **1:11**
blues – Drive 10:30, Tone 12:30, Output 2:00, Tone Shift 'Out'
rock – Drive 3:00, Tone 11:45, Output 12:30, Tone Shift 'In'

55   Boss SD-1   **1:11**
blues – Level 1:00, Tone 12:30, Drive 9:30
rock – Level 12:30, Tone 11:30, Drive 3:15

56   Fender Tremolux (Tweed 1960)   **0:26**
blues riff only – Tone 5.5, Inst Vol 12 (max)

TREMOLOS
(Strat middle pickup, through 1960 Tremolux)

57   Fender Tremolux tremolo (Tweed 1960)   **0:32**
Depth 7, Speed 9 (both out of 12)

58   Demeter Opto Tremulator   **0:32**
Depth 12:30, Speed 3:30

59   Nobels TR-X Tremolo   **0:32**
Level 3:15, Speed 10:30, Tone 12:00, Intensity 12:00,
Mode: soft square

60   Frantone Vibutron   **0:32**
Speed 11:00, Waveform Triangle, Depth 1:00

61   Boss PN-2 Tremolo/Pan   **0:32**
Rate 2:30, Depth 1:00, Mode: Trem/triangle

62   **Boss VB-2 Vibrato (as 'tremulant' vibrato)**   **0:32**
Rate 10:30, Depth 10:30, Rise Time: N/A, Mode: Latch

63   **Danelectro Tuna Melt Tremolo**   **0:32**
Speed 2:00, Soft, Depth 10:00

DELAYS
(first long-echo Strat, neck p'up, then slapback @ 0:54 on Strat bridge)

64   **Ibanez AD9**   **1:26**
long – Delay Time 5:00 (max), Repeats 12:00, Level 3:00
slap – Delay Time 10:15, Repeats 9:00, Level 1:30

65   **MXR Analog Delay**   **1:26**
long – Delay 2:45, Mix 11:45, Regen 11:00
slap – Delay 10:00, Mix 10:15, Regen 9:00

66   **Boss DM-2 Analog Delay**   **1:27**
long – Echo 5:00 (max), Rate 1:45, Intensity 11:45
slap – Echo 2:45, Rate 10:00, Intensity 10:30

67   **Boss DSD-2 Digital Sampler/Delay**   **1:26**
long – E.Level 11:00, F.Back 10:30, Delay Time 1:00, Mode 800ms
slap – E.Level 1:00, F.Back 8:30, Delay Time 12:30, Mode 200ms

68   **Boss DD-2 Digital Delay**   **1:26**
long – E.Level 11:00, F.Back 10:30, Delay Time 1:00, Mode 800ms
slap – E.Level 1:00, F.Back 8:30, Delay Time 12:30, Mode 200ms

69   **Ibanez AD-80**   **1:28**
long – Delay Time 5:00 (max), Blend 11:00, Repeat 10:00
slap – Delay Time 10:30, Blend 10:30, Repeat 8:00

70   **Danelectro Reel Echo**   **1:28**
long – Mix 11:15, Tube, LoFi 9:00, Warble Off, Repeats 1:15, Speed 450ms
slap – Mix 19:15, Tube, LoFi 12:00, Warble On, Repeats 8:00, Speed 190ms

DISTORTIONS
(rhythm panned 80 per cent left, Strat bridge pickup; lead panned
80 per cent right, Strat neck pickup; both DI'd through PAiA SIB)

71   **Ibanez SS20 Session Man**   **0:50**
rhythm – Distortion 10:00, Dist Tone 2:00, D.Time 2:30,
D.Level 2:00
lead – Distortion 2:00, Dist Tone 3:00, D.Time 5:00 (max),
D.Level 11:45

72   **Ibanez OD9 Overdrive**   **0:50**
rhythm – Dist 8:30, Tone 1:45, Level 3:00
lead – Dist 3:00, Tone 3:00, Level 2:00

73   **Marshall ShredMaster (original black)**   **0:51**
rhythm – Gain 1:00, Bass 1:30, Contour 1:30,
Treble 2:30, Vol 3:15
lead – Gain 5:00 (max), Bass 12:30, Contour 2:30,
Treble 3:00, Vol 3:00

74   **Boss DF-2 Super Distortion & Feedbacker**   **1:01**
rhythm – Level 3:00, Tone 12:00, Dist 10:30, Over Tone - Out
lead – Level 3:00, Tone 12:45, Dist 3:00, Over Tone 1:45
NOTES: the Over Tone, being electronic, drops out instantly
when the pedal is released, and can't be bent or vibratoed.

75   **Rat 2**   **0:50**
rhythm – Distortion 9:30, Filter 12:30, Volume 12:30
lead – Distortion 2:00, Filter 10:15, Volume 12:30

76   **Boss DS-1**   **0:50**
rhythm – Tone 12:00, Level 3:15, Dist 10:00
lead – Tone 12:30, Level 3:00, Dist 3:00

'UNI-VIBE'-STYLE EFFECTS
(first fast'n'dirty on Strat neck pickup with TS-808 after 'Vibe, set Drive
9:00, Tone 12:00, Level 1:30; then slow'n'clean on Strat middle pickup)

77   **Fulltone Deja-Vibe 2**   **0:54**
fast – Intensity 3:30 (approx 80 per cent), Chorus Mode,
Vintage Mode, Speed on treadle approx 75 per cent
slow – Intensity full, Chorus Mode, Modern Mode,
Speed approx 40 per cent

78   **Voodoo Lab Micro Vibe**   **0:53**
fast – Intensity 1:00, Speed 5:00 (max)
slow – Intensity 3:30, Speed 2:30

79   **Sweet Sound Mojo Vibe**   **0:54**
fast – Vol 3:00, Intensity 12:00, Speed 4:00, Chorus
slow – Vol 4:00, Intensity 3:00, Speed 12:30, Chorus
NOTES: internal mode dip switch set to Modern both times

80   **Electro-Harmonix Clone Theory**   **0:53**
fast – Chor/Vib max Chorus, Edge On, Rate 80 per cent,
Depth 70 per cent
slow – chor/Vib 80 per cent to Ch, Edge Off,
Rate 45 per cent, Depth 80

81	**Roger Mayer Voodoo-Vibe Jr**	0:56

fast – Sweep 2:00, Speed 3:00, Mix 5:00 (max Chorus), Intens 11:45
slow - Sweep 12:15, Speed 1:00, Mix 2:00, Intens 2:30

82	**Danelectro Rocky Road**	0:53

fast – Speed 3:15, Ramp Fast, Drive 7:30
slow – Speed 8:45, Ramp Fast, Drive 7:30

83	**Dunlop Uni-Vibe**	0:55

fast – Speed 4:45, Volume 5:00 (max), Intensity 10:00
slow – Speed 12:00, Volume 5:00, Intensity 2:00

PHASERS & FLANGERS
(Strat bridge pickup; TS-808 set Drive 2:00, Tone 11:00, Level 12:00 comes @ approx 0:32)

84	**Roland Phase II**	0:53

Rate 12:00, Resonance 10:30

85	**MXR Phase 45 (original box logo)**	0:58

Rate 12:00

86	**MXR Phase 90 (original script logo)**	0:57

Rate 12:00

87	**Ibanez DFL Digital Flanger**	0:53

Speed 3:00, Width 2:00, Mode M, Regen 1:00, D-Time 2:00

88	**Yamaha FL-01 Flanger**	1:19

Depth 10:00, Manual off, Speed 11:00, Feedback 10:15
NOTES: extra noises created by rotating Feedback control.

TRUE BYPASS TESTS
(Strat bridge pickup through TopHat set as usual)

89	**Straight-to-Amp (18′ cord to TopHat)**	0:23
90	**True Bypass through four pedals all Off**	0:23
91	**Buffered by Roger Mayer Voodoo-Axe then into four true bypass pedals**	0:23
92	**Buffered by Visual Sound True Tone stage in Route 66 then into four true bypass pedals**	0:23

INDEX &
ACKNOWLEDGMENTS

INDEX

ACKNOWLEDGMENTS

Thank you to...

Charlie Chandler for the loan of his toothsome pedalboard, and of other new and used pedals from his Guitar Experience shop in Hampton Wick, SW London, UK; Phil Harris for opening the safe to reveal his extensive pedal collection for our delectation and photography; Mike Fahey for loaning a juicy boxful of quirky and lesser seen units from the 1980s; Roger Mayer for talking so extensively, sharing pedals, providing top-notch technical commentary, and buying his round; Marcus Leadley, John Callaghan, Steve Bailey, Jenny Knight and Rick Batey of *Guitar Magazine* (UK) for their ever-cheerful reception and assistance in the face of my continued imposition and plundering of the photo files; Rick Lowe at Sounds Great in Stockport; Derek Peachey at Peach Guitars in Braintree; and Gibson Keddie at JHS in Leeds. Also to the other great makers who shared their knowledge here, including Dan Coggins of Lovetone & Dinosaural, Pete Cornish, Josh Fiden of Voodoo Lab, Mike Fuller of Fulltone, Mike Matthews of Electro-Harmonix, Mia Theodoratus of Frantone, Bob Weil of Visual Sound, and Zachary Vex of Z.Vex. And to Carl Gee for info and advice, to Tim Moore for supplying a lovely Boss DS-1 at the 11th hour, and to my brother-in-law Julian Harris for forgetting to claim back his Ibanez Bi-Mode Chorus for nearly 20 years (well, he's a keyboardist...). A special thanks to Paul Quinn, too, for his editorial guidance and attention to detail.

The literature

Compared to the recorded minutiae of the guitar world – which has reliably noted everything from the dates and sources pre-WWII Martin herringbone trim to the chemical composition of the plastic used to mold Maccaferri guitars – effects pedals are notoriously under-documented. The author, therefore, respectfully acknowledges the fine work of many other writers in the field, whose essays, reviews, books and articles prove an ongoing inspiration and revelation. Among them are Craig Anderton, Adrian Clark, R.G. Keen, Marcus Leadley, Jim Matthews, Ronald C. Neely II, Aron Nelson, Jack Orman, Mike Piera, Huw Price, Kevin O'Connor, James Stevens, and Art Thompson.

Ownership credits

Many of the pedals photographed for the book and recorded for the CD were loaned specifically for the project, and deserve to be recognized in some detail. The following is a list of people who provided significant numbers of effects for either purpose, with details of the makes and models provided and notations on whether these can be found in a photograph (p), a CD track (CD), or both.

Charlie Chandler (www.guitarexperience.co.uk)

Arion Stage Tuner (p), Arion Stereo Chorus (p), Blackstone 2SV3 MOSFET Overdrive (p&CD), Boss SD-1 Super Overdrive (p&CD), Dallas-Arbiter Fuzz Face (CD), DOD FX65 Stereo Chorus (p&CD), Marshall Guv'Nor (p), Roland Phase-II AP-2 (CD), Klon Centaur (p&CD), Electro-Harmonix Clone Theory (p&CD), Demeter Tremulator (p&CD), Demeter Opto Compulator (p&CD), Dunlop Uni-Vibe Stereo Chorus (CD), Ibanez Compressor (p&CD), Ibanez Analog Delay AD9 (p&CD), Pearl CH-02 Chorus (p&CD), Rat 2 (CD), Sweet Sound Mojo Vibe (p&CD), MXR Analog Delay (CD), MXR Dyna Comp (p&CD), MXR Phase 90 (p&CD), MXR Phase 45 (CD), T.C. Electronics Stereo Chorus+ Pitch Modulator & Flanger (p&CD), Voodoo Lab Proctavia (p&CD).

Mike Fahey
Boss Dynamic Filter FT-2 (p), Boss Tremolo/Pan PN-2 (p&CD), Boss Harmonist HR-2 (p), Boss Chorus CE-2 (p&CD), Boss Digital Sampler/Delay DSD-2 (p&CD), Boss Super Distortion & Feedbacker DF-2 (p&CD), Boss Digital Delay DD-2 (p&CD), Boss Vibrato VB-2 (p&CD), Boss Digital Dimension DC-3 (p&CD), Boss Dimension C DC-2 (p&CD), Boss Delay DM-2 (p&CD), Boss Over Drive OD-1 (p&CD), Ibanez Session Man II SS20 (p&CD), Ibanez Analog Delay AD-80 (p&CD), Ibanez Digital Flanger DFL (p&CD), Ibanez Overdrive OD-9 (p&CD), Ibanez Chorus CS-505 (p&CD), MXR Distortion+ (p), Marshall ShredMaster (p&CD), Yamaha Flanger FL-01 (p&CD), Cry Baby Wah-Wah (CD).

Phil Harris (www.harrishire.com) – all as photographs (p)
Boss CE-1 Chorus Ensemble, Dallas-Arbiter Fuzz Face (grey), Dallas-Arbiter Fuzz Face (c1968/69?), ProCo Rat, MXR Gate/Line Drive, Jen Fuzz, Dallas-Arbiter Tone Bender, Fender Blender, MXR Analog Delay, T.C. Electronics Sustainer+ Parametric EQ, Dallas-Arbiter Wah Face, Electro-Harmonix Volume Pedal, Electro-Harmonix Talking Pedal, Colorsound Tone Bender Jumbo, Colorsound Tone Bender Mark III, Colorsound Jumbo Tone Bender, Colorsound Sustain Module, Colorsound Flanger, Colorsound Fuzz Phazer, Colorsound Overdriver, Colorsound Supa Tone Bender, Colorsound Fuzz Wah Swell, Colorsound Supa Wah Fuzz Swell, Cry Baby (early Jen), Musitronics Mu-Tron III, Electro-Harmonix 10-Band Graphic EQ, Electro-Harmonix Crying Tone Wah, Electro-Harmonix Little Big Muff, Electro-Harmonix Full Double Tracking Effect, Electro-Harmonix Attack Decay, Electro-Harmonix Poly Phase, Electro-Harmonix Bad Stone, Electro-Harmonix Big Muff Pi, Electro-Harmonix Doctor Q, Electro-Harmonix Memory Man Deluxe, Electro-Harmonix Electric Mistress, Electro-Harmonix Small Stone, Ibanez Phase Tone II, Ibanez ST9 Super Tube Screamer, Ibanez TS-808 Tube Screamer, Ibanez FL9 Flanger, CBS-Arbiter Fuzz King, Electro-Harmonix LPB2, Jen KPS900 Phase Shifter, Jen Repeat Percussion, Lovetone Doppelganger, MXR Flanger, MXR Blue Box, MXR Phase 45, MXR Phase 100, MXR Micro Amp, MXR 6-Band Graphic EQ, Pearl Flanger, Roland Phase II, Marshall Supa-Wah, Marshall Supa Fuzz, Dallas Rangemaster Treble Booster, Univox Uni-Vibe, Vox Chorus, Vox Wah (chrome treadle), Vox Wah (early silver cast casing).

Rick Lowe & Sounds Great (www.soundsgreatmusic.com)
Jacques Fuse Blower (p&CD), Jacques Tube Blower (p&CD), Voodoo Lab Sparkle Drive (p&CD), Voodoo Lab Micro Vibe (p&CD), Xotic Effects Robotalk (p&CD), Z.Vex Fuzz Factory (p&CD), Z.Vex Seek Wah (p&CD), Z.Vex Super Duper 2-in-1 (p&CD), Z.Vex Wah Probe (p).

Derek Peachey & Peach Guitars (www.peachideas.com)
Fulltone Clyde Wah (p&CD), Fulltone Full-Drive 2 (p&CD), Fulltone Deja-Vibe 2 (p&CD), Pharaoh Sweet Cheetah II (p), Pharaoh Rodeo Drive (p).

About the author

Dave Hunter is an American musician and journalist who has worked in both Britain and the USA. He is a former editor of *The Guitar Magazine* (UK), has contributed to TV and radio documentaries, and has edited and contributed to books such as: *Acoustic Guitars – The Illustrated Encyclopedia*; *The Tube Amp Book – Deluxe Revised Edition*; *Guitar – A Complete Guide For The Player;* and *Recording Guitar & Bass.*